MANAGEMENT CLASSICS

THIRD EDITION

Edited by

Michael T. Matteson

Professor of Organizational Behavior and Management
University of Houston

John M. Ivancevich

Cullen Chair
and
Professor of Organizational Behavior and Management
University of Houston

1986
BUSINESS PUBLICATIONS, INC.
Plano, Texas   75075

© Business Publications, Inc., 1986

ISBN 0-256-03449-4
Library of Congress Catalog Card No. 85–71479

Printed in the United States of America

1 2 3 4 5 6 7 8 9 0 ML 3 2 1 0 9 8 7 6

MANAGEMENT CLASSICS

Preface

The practice of management is as old as humankind. Throughout time, people have joined with others to accomplish goals, first in families, later in tribes, and still later in more sophisticated political and organizational units. Ancient peoples transported entire nations across great distances; pyramids, temples, shrines, ships, and cities were constructed; systems of government, farming, and commerce were created; wars were waged against other tribes and nation-states. These elaborate social endeavors were undertaken through the use of management techniques and processes. Despite the use of management procedures by our forebears, virtually no attempts were made to accumulate and synthesize knowledge of management practice. What knowledge that did exist was passed along between tribal leaders or parents and offspring or was learned through experience.

The principal objective of the two previous editions of this book of readings was to provide the reader with what the editors believed were classics in the field of management—writings that have had a demonstrated and continuing impact on the development of management thought and practice. We attempted to accumulate and synthesize those classical writings by recognized contributors so that the knowledge of management functions and processes would be available in one volume to students, practitioners, and teachers.

This has remained the principal objective of this third edition, as well, and its attainment is facilitated by three major subgoals of the book. First, an anthology of management must *include the works of recognized, respected, and pioneer scholars in the field of management.* The list of contributors is a veritable Who's Who of management thought and practice. Second, the readings should *broaden the understanding of management* which the reader receives from studying textbooks in the field of management. A guide to using this book as a supplement to the most

v

widely accepted management books is presented in the Cross-Reference Table beginning on page xiv. Finally, the readings, many written years ago, need to *have relevance for contemporary managers and students* who spend much of their time working in, learning about, coping with, and shaping organizations.

The importance and diversity of management as a field of inquiry necessitates a book of readings such as this. The complexity and dynamic nature of management stems in part from the variety of disciplines from which it borrows principles, procedures, and models; economics, sociology, statistics, and mathematics are several of the contributing fields. Not surprisingly, this diversity of background produces different interpretations of organizations and employee dimensions with which managers must deal daily. The practicing manager is consequently faced with sorting out these differences and, hopefully, reaching some point where enlightened and successful practice can be initiated.

The difference in opinion, the general lack of preciseness of interpretation, and the pervasiveness of management certainly suggest that some form of accumulation of knowledge is critical; failure to accumulate and synthesize knowledge often causes loss of important information. This third edition of *Management Classics,* like its predecessors, attempts to prevent this loss of information.

Some, understandably, might ask why a book composed of "classics" needs to undergo periodic revision. There are a number of reasons. In every edition, we have been forced to make choices among many excellent articles. Not every article meeting the criteria of being a classic could be included in previous editions. In this edition we have included several articles which, were it not for space limitations, would have appeared in earlier editions.

Second, it has been almost ten years since the first edition of *Management Classics.* In the intervening time, the range of selections which could be considered "classic" has increased.

Finally, and perhaps most importantly, feedback from users of previous editions has played a significant role in shaping this edition. The ultimate test of any book is how useful it is. Using your feedback, we have revised *Management Classics* to make the current edition an even more effective tool.

The book is organized into six sections with editorial comments for each section. We have prepared these comments so that the section is clearly introduced and the reader understands the management process which will be covered. Additional comments introduce each reading selection and provide an introduction to that selection. Part One includes six articles which discuss traditional, behavioral, and systems approaches to management. Part Two contains five articles on the planning process in management. In Part Three, five articles focus on organizing processes. Controlling is the thrust of five articles in Part Four. Part Five contains eight articles which discuss directing processes, evenly divided between motivation and leadership topics. Finally, Part Six presents five articles which focus on decision making.

This edition of *Management Classics* could not have been compiled without the contribution of the writers of the articles to the field of management. We wish to sincerely thank each of these writers and their publishers for permission to publish the articles in this anthology. Finally, we wish to thank all the users of the two previous editions who gave us the benefit of their experience. We hope you find this edition continues and improves upon the effectiveness of the earlier volumes.

Michael T. Matteson
John M. Ivancevich

Contents

Contributors

Robert C. Albrook

Chester I. Barnard

Warren G. Bennis

C. West Churchman

Ernest Dale

Peter F. Drucker

Amitai Etzioni

Henri Fayol

Fred E. Fiedler

Mary Parker Follett

John W. Gardner

Frank B. Gilbreth

Lillian M. Gilbreth

Frederick Herzberg

George C. Homans

Fremont E. Kast

Steven Kerr

Harold Koontz

Rensis Likert

Charles E. Lindblom

David C. McClelland

Douglas M. McGregor

Norman R. F. Maier

Abraham H. Maslow

Henry Mintzberg

Cyril J. O'Donnell

C. Northcote Parkinson

Elias Porter

James E. Rosenzweig

Warren H. Schmidt

William G. Scott

Stanley E. Seashore

Herbert A. Simon

George A. Steiner

Robert Tannenbaum

Frederick W. Taylor

Max Weber

CROSS-REFERENCE TABLE

Selected Textbooks	Part One: Foundations For Understanding Management Theory and Practice	Parts in *Management Classics*, 3d edition				
		Part Two: Planning Processes in Management	Part Three: Organizing Processes in Management	Part Four: Controlling Processes in Management	Part Five: Directing Processes in Management	Part Six: Decision-Making Processes in Management
Anderson, Carl R. *Management* (Dubuque, Ia.: Wm. C. Brown, 1984).	Chs. 1, 2, 3, 4, 11	Chs. 12, 15, 16	Chs. 13, 14, 17, 21	Chs. 19, 20	Chs. 7, 18	Ch. 26
Bedian, Arthur G., and William F. Glueck. *Management* (Hinsdale, Ill.: Dryden, 1983).	Chs. 1, 2, 4	Chs. 7, 8	Chs. 10, 11, 12	Chs. 20, 21	Chs. 5, 6, 13, 14, 15	Chs. 9, 16
Certo, Samuel C. *Principles of Modern Management* (Dubuque, Ia.: Wm. C. Brown, 1986).	Chs. 1, 2, 3	Chs. 4, 6, 7	Chs. 8, 9, 10, 11	Chs. 16, 17, 18	Chs. 12, 13, 14, 15	Ch. 5
Donnelly, James H., James L. Gibson, and John M. Ivancevich. *Fundamentals of Management* (Plano, Tex.: Business Publications, 1984).	Chs. 1, 2, 3, 23, 24	Chs. 4, 5, 6, 21	Chs. 7, 8	Chs. 9, 22	Chs. 10, 11, 12, 13, 14	Chs. 15, 19, 20
Griffin, Ricky W. *Management* (Boston: Houghton-Mifflin, 1984).	Chs. 1, 2, 3	Chs. 4, 5, 6	Chs. 9, 10, 11, 20	Chs. 17, 18, 19	Chs. 13, 14, 15	Chs. 7, 8, 16
Haimann, Theo, William G. Scott, and Patrick E. Connor. *Management* (Boston: Houghton-Mifflin, 1985).	Chs. 1, 2, 3, 32	Chs. 5, 6, 7, 8	Chs. 9, 10, 11, 12, 13, 14, 15, 16, 17	Chs. 18, 26 27, 28, 29, 30	Chs. 20, 21, 22, 23	Chs. 4, 24

Source					
Hitt, Michael A., R. Dennis Middlement, and Robert L. Mathis. *Management* (St. Paul, Minn.: West Publishing, 1983).	Chs. 1, 2, 19, 20	Chs. 4, 5, 6, 9, 15	Chs. 7, 8	Chs. 16, 17, 18	Chs. 10, 11, 12	Chs. 3, 13
Ivancevich, John M., James H. Donnelly, and James L. Gibson. *Managing for Performance* (Plano, Tex.: Business Publications, 1986).	Chs. 1, 2, 20	Chs. 3, 4, 5	Chs. 7, 8, 9	Chs. 14, 15, 16	Chs. 10, 12, 13	Chs. 6, 11
Koontz, Harold, Cyril O'Donnell, and H. Wechrich. *Management* (New York: McGraw-Hill, 1984).	Chs. 1, 2, 3, 4	Chs. 5, 6, 7	Chs. 9, 10, 11, 12, 13, 14	Chs. 23, 24, 25, 26, 27	Chs. 19, 20, 21, 22	Ch. 8
Kreitner, Robert. *Management* (Boston: Houghton-Mifflin, 1986).	Chs. 1, 2, 3, 18	Chs. 4, 5, 6	Chs. 7, 8, 9, 10	Chs. 15, 16, 17	Chs. 11, 12, 13, 14	Ch. 6
Mescon, Michael H., Michael Albert, and Khedouri. *Management* (New York: Harper & Row, 1985).	Chs. 1, 2, 3, 4, 21	Chs. 8, 17	Chs. 9, 10, 20	Chs. 12, 18, 19	Chs. 11, 13, 14	Chs. 5, 6, 7
Schermerhorn, John R. *Management for Productivity* (New York: John Wiley & Sons, 1984).	Chs. 1, 2, 21	Chs. 4, 5	Chs. 6, 7, 8, 9	Chs. 14, 15, 16	Chs. 10, 12, 13	Chs. 3, 11

CROSS-REFERENCE TABLE (concluded)

Selected Textbooks	Parts in *Management Classics*, 3d edition					
	Part One: Foundations For Understanding Management Theory and Practice	*Part Two: Planning Processes in Management*	*Part Three: Organizing Processes in Management*	*Part Four: Controlling Processes in Management*	*Part Five: Directing Processes in Management*	*Part Six: Decision-Making Processes in Management*
Steers, Richard M., Gerado Ungson, and Richard T. Mowday. *Managing Effective Organizations* (1985).	Chs. 1, 2, 3, 20	Chs. 4, 15	Ch. 5	Chs. 7, 8, 14	Chs. 9, 10, 11	Chs. 6, 12
Stoner, James A. F. *Management* (Englewood Cliffs, N.J.: Prentice-Hall, 1982).	Chs. 1, 2, 3	Chs. 4, 5, 7	Chs. 9, 10, 11, 13	Chs. 21, 22, 23	Chs. 16, 17, 20	Chs. 6, 19
Szilagyi, Andrew D. *Management and Performance* (Glenview, Ill.: Scott, Foresman, 1983).	Chs. 1, 2, 3	Chs. 4, 5, 6	Chs. 8, 9, 10	Chs. 15, 16, 17, 18	Chs. 12, 13, 14	Chs. 7, 11
Williams, J. Clifton, Andrew DuBrin, and Henry Sisk, *Management and Organizations* (Cincinatti: South-Western, 1985).	Chs. 1, 2, 3	Chs. 4, 5, 6, 7, 8	Chs. 9, 10, 11, 12, 13	Chs. 18, 19, 20, 21	Chs. 4, 13, 16	

PART ONE

Foundations for Understanding
Management Theory and Practice

There is continued debate about whether management theory is or is not useful. First, it is difficult to isolate any particular set of principles or models (classical, behavioral, management science) in "pure" form from various modifications and efforts to translate those principles into practice. Second, particular principles of management are interpreted differently by various individuals, and the result is often confusion and misinterpretation. Principles are selectively defined and interpreted according to an individual's school of thought. Third, the major schools of thought espousing management principles house people with differing backgrounds, values, and managerial experience. These differences create some conflict among the disciples of management theory and principles which is manifested by their turning a deaf ear on ideas, propositions, and principles proposed by individuals outside their particular school of thought. The classicist ignores the behavioralist, and they both ignore the management scientist. This practice unfortunately delays our efforts to understand what managers do in organizations.

Each of the three major schools of thought contributes valuable knowledge about the functions and processes of management. Each has provided the following positive contributions to the field of management:

- Knowledge which can be used by practicing managers.
- The translation of knowledge so that it can be used by managers.
- Propositions and hypotheses which can be used scientifically to research managerial processes and functions.

1

- Adding to the already existing theories, models, and techniques which serve as the foundation for theorists, researchers, and managers.
- Terminology which has been used to understand what managers do.

These positive contributions should suggest that each of the schools needs to be thoroughly examined when attempting to comprehend the planning, organizing, controlling, directing, and decision-making processes of management.

The pioneers of management thought such as Fayol, Barnard, Urwick, Follet, and Mooney intended their ideas about the processes of management to be a cumulative body of knowledge. For example, Fayol argued that because of their widespread value and applicability, management concepts should be taught in universities. The goal of a cumulative body of knowledge known as management thought has not been achieved. Instead, what we find are various schools of management thought, each with a slightly different perspective or orientation. In this first section of *Management Classics,* we have purposely included the writings of pioneers such as Taylor, Follet, and Homans. In this and later sections, we will include articles that are associated with all three of the major schools of management thought: classical, behavioral, and management science. As you will see, these different schools or approaches are not mutually exclusive; rather in many ways they draw from and build upon one another.

1

What Is Scientific Management?

Frederick W. Taylor

In this excerpt from Congressional testimony, the "Father of Scientific Management" explains the true nature of scientific management and the mental revolution it involves. From this selection we see it is far more than a simple efficiency process or time saving device; rather it is a mental attitude which must permeate an organization.—Eds.

Scientific management is not any efficiency device, not a device of any kind for securing efficiency; nor is any bunch or group of efficiency devices. It is not a new system of figuring costs; it is not a new scheme of paying men; it is not a piecework system; it is not a bonus system; it is not a premium system; it is no scheme for paying men; it is not holding a stop watch on a man and writing things down about him; it is not time study; it is not motion study nor an analysis of the movements of men; it is not the printing and ruling and unloading of a ton or two of blanks on a set of men and saying, "Here's your system; go use it." It is not divided foremanship or functional foremanship; it is not any of the devices which the average man calls to mind when scientific management is spoken of. The average man thinks of one or more of these things when he hears the words "scientific management" mentioned, but scientific management is not any of these devices. I am not sneering at cost-keeping systems, at time study, at functional foremanship, nor at any new and improved scheme of paying men, nor at any efficiency devices, if they are really devices that make for efficiency. I believe in them; but what I am emphasizing is that these devices in whole or in part are not scientific manage-

SOURCE: Excerpt from testimony of Frederick W. Taylor at hearings before the Special Committee of the House of Representatives to Investigate Taylor and Other Systems of Shop Management, January 25, 1912, pp. 1387–89.

ment; they are useful adjuncts to scientific management, so are they also useful adjuncts of other systems of management.

Now, in its essence, scientific management involves a complete mental revolution on the part of the workingman engaged in any particular establishment or industry—a complete mental revolution on the part of these men as to their duties toward their work, toward their fellow men, and toward their employees. And it involves the equally complete mental revolution on the part of those on the management's side—the foreman, the superintendent, the owner of the business, the board of directors—a complete mental revolution on their part as to their duties toward their fellow workers in the management, toward their workmen, and toward all of their daily problems. And without this complete mental revolution on both sides scientific management does not exist.

That is the essence of scientific management, this great mental revolution. Now, later on, I want to show you more clearly what I mean by this great mental revolution. I know that it perhaps sounds to you like nothing but bluff—like buncombe—but I am going to try and make clear to you just what this great mental revolution involves, for it does involve an immense change in the minds and attitude of both sides, and the greater part of what I shall say today has relation to the bringing about of this great mental revolution. So that whether the details may be interesting or uninteresting, what I hope you will see is that this great change in attitude and viewpoint must produce results which are magnificent for both sides, just as fine for one as for the other. Now, perhaps I can make clear to you at once one of the very great changes in outlook which come to the workmen, on the one hand, and to those in the management on the other hand.

I think it is safe to say that in the past a great part of the thought and interest both of the men, on the side of the management, and of those on the side of the workmen in manufacturing establishments has been centered upon what may be called the proper division of the surplus resulting from their joint efforts, between the management on the one hand, and the workmen on the other hand. The management have been looking for as large a profit as possible for themselves, and the workmen have been looking for as large wages as possible for themselves, and that is what I mean by the division of the surplus. Now, this question of the division of the surplus is a very plain and simple one (for I am announcing no great fact in political economy or anything of that sort). Each article produced in the establishment has its definite selling price. Into the manufacture of this article have gone certain expenses, namely, the cost of materials, the expenses connected with selling it, and certain indirect expenses, such as the rent of the building, taxes, insurance, light and power, maintenance of machinery, interest on the plant, etc. Now, if we deduct these several expenses from the selling price, what is left over may be called the surplus. And out of this surplus comes the profit to the manufacturer on the one hand, and the wages of the workmen on the other hand. And it is largely upon the division of this surplus that the attention of the workmen and of the management has been centered in the past. Each side has had its eye upon this surplus, the working man wanting as large a share in the form of wages as he could get, and the management wanting as large a share in the form of profits as it could get; I think I am safe in saying that in the past it has been in the division of this surplus that the great labor troubles have come between employers and employees.

Frequently, when the management have found the selling price going down they have turned toward a cut in the wages—toward reducing the workman's share of the surplus—as their way of getting out whole, of preserving their profits intact. While the workman (and you can hardly blame him) rarely feels willing to relinquish a dollar of his wages, even in dull times, he wants to keep all that he has had in the past, and when busy times come again very naturally he wants to get more. Thus it is over this division of the surplus that most of the troubles have arisen; in the extreme cases this has been the cause of serious disagreements and strikes. Gradually the two sides have come to look upon one another as antagonists, and at times even as enemies—pulling apart and matching the strength of the one against the strength of the other.

The great revolution that takes place in the mental attitude of the two parties under scientific management is that both sides take their eyes off of the division of the surplus as the all-important matter, and together turn their attention toward increasing the size of the surplus until this surplus becomes so large that it is unnecessary to quarrel over how it shall be divided. They come to see that when they stop pulling against one another, and instead both turn and push shoulder to shoulder in the same direction, the size of the surplus created by their joint efforts is truly astounding. They both realize that when they substitute friendly cooperation and mutual helpfulness for antagonism and strife they are together able to make this surplus so enormously greater than it was in the past that there is ample room for a large increase in wages for the workmen and an equally great increase in profits for the manufacturer. This, gentlemen, is the beginning of the great mental revolution which constitutes the first step toward scientific management. It is along this line of complete change in the mental attitude of both sides; of the substitution of peace for war; the substitution of hearty brotherly cooperation for contention and strife; of both pulling hard in the same direction instead of pulling apart; of replacing suspicious watchfulness with mutual confidence; of becoming friends instead of enemies; it is along this line, I say, that scientific management must be developed.

The substitution of this new outlook—this new viewpoint—is of the very essence of scientific management, and scientific management exists nowhere until after this has become the central idea of both sides; until this new idea of cooperation and peace has been substituted for the old idea of discord and war.

This change in the mental attitude of both sides toward the "surplus" is only a part of the great mental revolution which occurs under scientific management. I will later point out other elements of this mental revolution. There is, however, one more change in viewpoint which is absolutely essential to the existence of scientific management. Both sides must recognize as essential the substitution of exact scientific investigation and knowledge for the old individual judgment or opinion, either of the workman or the boss, in all matters relating to the work done in the establishment. And this applies both as to the methods to be employed in doing the work and the time in which each job should be done.

Scientific management cannot be said to exist, then, in any establishment until after this change has taken place in the mental attitude of both the management and the men, both as to their duty to cooperate in producing the largest possible surplus and as to the necessity for substituting exact scientific knowledge for opinions or the old rule of thumb or individual knowledge.

These are the two absolutely essential elements of scientific management.

2

Management as a Profession

Mary Parker Follett

In this article, Mary Follett, whose philosophy was that any productive organization must give recognition to the human element, argues for the professionalism of management and for the need for managers to prepare themselves as seriously for the profession of management as for any other. Written sixty years ago, its contents are as timely today as if they were written yesterday.—Eds.

The word "profession" connotes for most people a foundation of *science* and a motive of *service*. That is, a profession is said to rest on the basis of a proved body of knowledge, and such knowledge is supposed to be used in the service of others rather than merely for one's own purposes. Let us tonight ask ourselves two questions: (1) How far does business management rest on scientific foundations? (2) What are the next steps to be taken in order that business management shall become more scientific?

PRESENT SIGNS OF A SCIENTIFIC BASIS FOR BUSINESS MANAGEMENT

We have many indications that scientific method is being more and more applied to business management. First, of course, is the development of so-called "scientific management" which, after its early stages, began to concern itself with the technique of management as well as with the technique of operating.

Secondly, there is the increasing tendency toward specialized, or what is being called functionalized, management. Functionalized man-

SOURCE: Reprinted from Chapter IV of *Business Management as a Profession,* edited by Henry C. Metcalf (A. W. Shaw Company, Chicago, 1927), pp. 73–87, by permission of McGraw-Hill Book Company.

agement has, indeed, not yet been carried far. In some cases the only sign we see of it, beyond the recognition that different departments require different kinds of knowledge, different kinds of ability, is the employing of experts for special problems. In other cases a further step is taken and a planning department is created; but the powers given to planning departments vary greatly from plant to plant—some take up only occasional problems as they are asked, some are only advisory bodies. Yet in most plants the functionalization of management is a process which in one way or another has gained a good deal of ground recently. That is, the fact is very generally accepted that different types of problems require different bodies of knowledge.

In the third place, arbitrary authority is diminishing, surely an indication that more value is being put on scientific method. The tendency today is to vest authority in the person who has most knowledge of the matter in question and most skill in applying that knowledge. Hiring, for instance, is now based on certain principles and special knowledge. The job of hiring is given to those who have that knowledge. It is not assumed by someone by virtue of a certain position.

Perhaps nowhere do we see more clearly the advance of business management toward becoming a profession than in our conception of the requirements of the administrative head. It would be interesting to take some firm and note how one duty after another has in recent years passed from the president to various experts, down to that most recent addition to many businesses, the economic adviser. One president, of whom I inquired what he thought exactly his job to be, said to me: "I can't define my job in terms of specific duties because I can't tell what special duty which I have today may be given at any moment to someone better able than I to handle it." One of the interesting things about that remark (there are several) is that he recognized that someone might handle some of his duties better than he could; and yet he is an exceedingly able man. He saw that some particular task might develop a special technique and that men might be trained as experts in that technique.

The stereotype of the successful businessman is indeed changing. The image of the masterful man carrying all before him by the sheer force of his personality has largely disappeared. One good result of this is that we now consider that executive leadership can in part (remember, I say only "in part") be learned. Sheldon calls executive leadership "an intangible capacity." I do not wholly agree. Someone else says it is "beyond human calculation." There are many things, we hope, which have not yet been calculated which are not beyond calculation. I think that one of the hopes for business management lies in the fact that executive leadership is capable of analysis and that men can be trained to occupy such positions. I do not, of course, mean every man; but not every man can become a doctor or an architect. I mean that for business management, exactly as for other professions, training is gaining in importance over mere personality. I know a man who told me ten or fifteen years ago that he relied on his personality in business dealings. He has not made a success of his business. It was once thought that the executive's work rested largely on "hunch," and his subordinates' on obeying—no science in either case. The administrative head who relies first on the magic shortcut of "hunch," and secondly on his adroitness or masterfulness in getting others to accept his "hunch," is, I believe, about to be superseded by a man of different type.

Can you not remember the picture we used to have of the man in the swivel chair? A trembling subordinate enters, states his problem; snap goes the decision from the chair. This man disappears only for another to enter. And so it goes. The massive brain in the swivel chair all day communicates to his followers his special knowledge. An excellent plan if—there seem to be too many if's in the way! And so we resort to the humbler method of scientific research, the method of all the professions.

But with this agreed to, there is another misconception in regard to the administrative head. Many writers speak as if he were only the glue to hold together all these departments and functions of our big modern plants. As the need of coordination is daily and hourly felt in these vast, complex organizations, it is said that the president must do the coordinating. True; but I think that coordination is very different from matching up the pieces of a picture puzzle, to change our metaphor. Later, I am going to say just what I think it is; but let me say now that those of us who think of the administrative head as more than a mere coordinator and those of us who think that administrative decisions should rest on more than "hunch" (although "hunch," too, is important) are thinking of scientific foundations for business management.

A significant indication of the different type of management required today is the fact that managers are somewhat less inclined to justify their behavior by a claim of abstract "rights." An employer used to say, "I have a right to treat my men so and so." Or, "My behavior in this matter is perfectly reasonable." Today there are many who are more inclined to say: "If I treat my men so and so, how will they behave? *Why* will they behave in that way?" It takes far more science to understand human beings—and their "rights"—than to proclaim loudly our own rights and reasonableness.

We have a very interesting indication of the new demand made upon management in the fact that the idea, which is everywhere gaining ground, that we may have greater conscious control of our lives is seen in the business world most significantly. For example, those fatalistic rhythms, business cycles, are now considered susceptible to study, not as mysteries wholly beyond the comprehension of man. Again, take unemployment. Consider the steel industry. There you have an imperishable commodity. Moreover, you can calculate pretty well the demand. And you have rather permanently located firms and mills. There seems no reason, therefore, why the steel industry should not eventually be stabilized. Every time we take a problem out of the unsolvable class and put it into the solvable, and work at it as such, we are helping to put business management on a scientific basis. Mr. John Maynard Keynes, in an address last summer, spoke of the three great epochs of history described by Dr. John R. Commons,[1] and stated his belief that we are on the threshold of the third of those epochs. The first of these was the era of scarcity, which came to an end in about the fifteenth century. Next came the era of abundance, the dominating idea of which was the doctrine of laissez faire. Finally, there has come the era of stabilization upon which we are now entering and in which the doctrine of laissez faire must be abandoned in favor of deliberate, conscious control of economic forces for the sake of the general social good.

Many people today think of business not as a game of chance, not as a speculative enterprise depending on rising and falling markets, but as largely controllable. The mysteriousness of business is in fact disappearing as knowledge in regard to business methods steadily increases.

This is seen in the increased sense of responsibility for failure. You know the old excuses if a business failed or was not getting on well: the hard terms of bankers, the unscrupulousness of competitors, the abominable behavior of trade unions. I think that today there is less inclination to take refuge in such excuses; that there is a tendency to seek the difficulty in the running of the business. There is greater frankness in facing difficulties and a keener zest in overcoming them. You know, perhaps, the story of little Mary who was naughty and was told by her mother to go into the next room and ask God to forgive her. When she came back her mother said, "Did you do what I told you to?" And received the reply, "Yes, I did; and God said, 'Mercy me, little Mary, I know heaps worse'n you.'" Many an employer takes this attitude, but their numbers are diminishing.

Moreover, many of the points disputed with trade unions, many points which both sides have thought to be legitimate fighting issues, are now considered problems which we should try to solve. To increase wages without increasing price is sometimes a solvable problem. Wherever thinking takes the place of fighting, we have a striking indication that management is coming to rest on scientific foundations. In international relations—but I have only to mention that term for you to see the analogy, for you to see the barbarous stage we are yet in, in international relations. Businessmen have the chance to lead the world in substituting thinking for fighting. And businessmen are thinking. One of the things I have been most struck with in the last four or five years has been the vitality of the thinking of businessmen. I said last winter to a professor of philosophy, "Do you realize that you philosophers have got to look to your laurels, that businessmen are doing some very valuable thinking and may get ahead of you?" And he acknowledged this fully and generously, which I thought was a significant concession.

Finally, management, not bankers nor stockholders, is now seen to be the fundamental element in industry. It is good management that draws credit, that draws workers, that draws customers. Moreover, whatever changes come, whether industry is owned by individual capitalists or by the state or by the workers, it will always have to be managed. Management is a permanent function of business.

There are many circumstances, let us note in concluding the first part of this talk, which are impelling us toward a truly scientific management: (1) efficient management has to take the place of that exploitation of our natural resources whose day is now nearly over; (2) keener competition; (3) scarcity of labor; (4) a broader conception of the ethics of human relations; (5) the growing idea of business as a public service which carries with it a sense of responsibility for its efficient conduct.

WHAT ARE THE NEXT STEPS TOWARD MAKING BUSINESS MANAGEMENT MORE SCIENTIFIC?

Recognizing that business management is every day coming more and more to rest on scientific foundations, what has it yet to do? First, the scientific standard must be applied to the whole of business management; it is now often applied to only one part. Business management includes: (1) on the technical side, as it is usually called, a knowledge of production and distribution, and (2) on the personnel side, a knowledge of how to deal fairly and fruitfully with one's fellows. While the first has been recognized as a matter capable of being taught, the latter has been often thought to be a gift which some men possess and some do not. That is, one part of business management rested on science; the other part, it was thought, never could. Oliver Sheldon says: "Broadly, management is concerned with two primary elements—things and men. The former element is susceptible to scientific treatment, the latter is not."[2] And again: "Where human beings are concerned, scientific principles may be so much waste paper."[3] If we believed that, we should not be here tonight in a Bureau of Personnel Administration. Let us take that statement—that human relations are not susceptible of scientific treatment—and ask what scientific treatment is. Science has been defined as "knowledge gained by systematic observation, experiment, and reasoning; knowledge coordinated, arranged, and systematized." Can we not accumulate in regard to human relations knowledge gained by systematic observation, experiment, and reasoning? Can we not coordinate, arrange, and systematize that knowledge? I think we can.

Sheldon says further: "There may be a science of costing, of transportation, of operation, but there can be no science of cooperation."[4] The reason we are here studying human relations in industry is that we believe there can be a science of cooperation. By this I mean that cooperation is not, and this I insist on, merely a matter of good intentions, of kindly feeling. It must be based on these, but you cannot have successful cooperation until you have worked out the methods of cooperation—by experiment after experiment, by a comparing of experiments, by a pooling of results. . . . It is my plea above everything else that we learn *how* to cooperate. Of course, one may have a special aptitude for dealing with men as others may have for dealing with machines, but there is as much to learn in the one case as in the other.

In all our study of personnel work, however, we should remember that we can never wholly separate the human and the mechanical problem. This would seem too obvious to mention if we did not so often see that separation made. Go back to that sentence of Sheldon's: "There may be a science of costing, of transportation, of operation, but there can be no science of cooperation." But take Sheldon's own illustration, that of transportation. The engineering part of transportation is not the larger part. Please note that I do not say it is a small part. It is a large part, and it is the dramatic part, and it is the part we have done well, and yet the chief part of transportation is the personal thing. Everyone knows that the main difficulty about transportation is that there have not always been sensible working arrangements between the men concerned. But you all see every day that the study of human relations in business and the study of technique of operating are bound up together. You know that the way the worker is treated affects output. You know that the routing of materials and the maintenance of machines is a matter partly of human relations. You know, I hope, that there is danger in "putting in" personnel work if it is superadded instead of being woven through the plant. You remember the man who wanted to know something about Chinese metaphysics and so looked up China in the encyclopedia and then metaphysics, and put them together. We shall not have much better success if we try merely to add personnel work. Even although there is, as I certainly believe there should be, a special personnel department run by a trained expert, yet it seems to me that every executive should make some study of personnel work a part of that broad foundation which is today increasingly felt to be necessary for the businessman.

If, then, one of the first things to be done to make business management more scientific is to apply scientific methods to those problems of management which involve human relations, another requirement is that we should make an analysis of managers' jobs somewhat corresponding to the analysis of workers' jobs in the Taylor system. We need to get away from tradition, prejudice, stereotypes, guesswork, and find the factual basis for managerial jobs. We know, for instance, what has been accomplished in elimination of waste by scientific methods of research and experiment applied to operating, to probable demand for commodities, and so on. I believe that this has to be carried further, and that managerial waste, administrative waste, should be given the same research and experiment. How this can be done, I shall take up later.

The next step business management should take is to organize the body of knowledge on which it should rest. We have defined science as an organized body of exact knowledge. That is, scientific method consists of two parts: (1) research, and (2) the organization of the knowledge obtained by research. The importance of research, of continued research, receives every year fuller and fuller appreciation from businessmen; but methods of organizing the results of such research have not kept pace with this appreciation. While business management is collecting more and more exact knowledge, while it is observing more keenly, experimenting more widely, it has not yet gone far in organizing this knowledge. We have drawn a good many conclusions, have thought out certain principles, but have not always seen the relation between these conclusions or these principles.

I have not time to speak here of more than one way of organizing in industrial plants our accumulating knowledge in regard to executive technique. There should be, I think, in every plant, an official, one of whose duties should be to classify and interpret managerial experience with the aid of the carefully kept records which should be required of every executive. From such classification and interpretation of experience—this experience which in essentials repeats itself so often from time to time, from department to department, from plant to plant—it would be possible to draw useful conclusions. The importance of this procedure becomes more obvious when we remember that having experience and profiting by experience are two different matters. Experience may leave us with mistaken notions, with prejudice or suspicion.

A serious drawback to a fuller understanding of and utilization of executive experience is that we have at present (1) no systematic follow-up of decisions, of new methods, of experiments in managing; and (2) no carefully worked out system of recording. Poorly kept records, or the absence of any systematic recording, are partly responsible for what seems in some plants like a stagnant management, and in all plants for certain leaks in management. For instance, the fact that we have no follow-up for executive decisions with a comparing of results—a procedure necessary before business management can be considered fully on a scientific basis—is partly a deficiency in recording. The fact that an executive, if he wishes to introduce a certain method (not in operating but in management itself), cannot find in any records whether that method has been tried before or anything like it, and what the results have been, is a serious deficiency in recording. If an executive is facing a certain problem, he should be able to find out: (1) whether other executives have had to meet similar problems, (2) how they met them, (3) what the results were. It seems to me very unfortunate that it is possible for one man to say to another, as I heard someone say at the suggestion of a new method, "I believe our department tried that a few years ago, but I've forgotten what we thought of it."

I have heard it said that the Harvard football team was put on its feet when Percy Haughton introduced the system of recording football experience. After that, if someone thought he had a brilliant idea that such and such a play could be tried on Yale, the first thing done was to examine the records; and it might be found that that play had been tried two years before and failed. It might even be discovered why it had failed. This system of recording—I believe it already existed at Yale—was Mr. Haughton's great contribution to Harvard football. Because of it, the team could not, at any rate, go on making the *same* mistakes.

The recording of executive experience, which will probably need a technique somewhat different from that used for the rest of business recording, should have, I think, our immediate attention. The system of both recording and reporting should be such that records and reports can be quickly mastered, and thus be practically useful to all, instead of buried underneath their own verbiage, length, and lack of systematization. And there should be required, from every executive, training in the technique of keeping records and making reports.

But we need more than records. We need a new journal, or a new department in some present journal; we need sifted bibliographies of reports; ways of getting information from other parts of the country, from other countries; above all, we need executive conferences with carefully worked out methods for comparing experience which has been scientifically recorded, analyzed, and organized. When many different plants are willing to share with one another the results of their experience, then we shall have business policies based on wider data than those of the present.

The Graduate School of Business Administration and the Bureau of Business Research of Harvard University are now collecting cases of business policy, thus opening the way for classifying and cross-indexing. Harvard has, of course, been able to get hold of a very small number of cases, but this seems to be a valuable and significant undertaking.

I have been interested also in what a certain recent committee, with representatives from various firms, deliberately stated as its object: "the comparison of experience." I should like to know how frank and full their exchange of experience was; but any attempt of this kind is interesting, indicating, as it does, the attitude on the part of those participating that they expect to gain more by working together than they will lose (the old idea) by allowing other firms to gain any intimate knowledge of their affairs.

Moreover, not only should we analyze and compare our experience, but we should deliberately experiment. We should make experiments, observe experiments, compare and discuss these with each other, and see what consensus we can come to in our conclusions. For this we should be wholly frank with one another. If we have the scientific attitude toward our work, we shall be willing to tell our failures. I heard of a man who made an ice machine which did not work, and the following conversation took place between him and a friend he met:

Friend: "I was sorry to hear your experiment was a failure!"

Man: "Who told you it was a failure?"

Friend: "Why, I heard your ice machine wouldn't work."

Man: "Oh, that was true enough, but it was a great success as an experiment. You can learn as much from your failures as from your successes."

From such experimenting and from the comparison of experience, I think certain standards would emerge. But we should remember that, as no Taylorite thinks there is anything final in "standardization," so we should not aim at a static standardization of managerial method, executive technique. We should make use of all available present experience, knowing that experience and our learning from it should be equally continuous matters.

If science gives us research and experimentation as its two chief methods, it at the same time shows us that nothing is too small to claim our attention. There is nothing unimportant in business procedure. For instance, I spoke above of record keeping. I know a firm where they tell me that they are not getting nearly so much advantage as they should from their records because they have not yet worked out a system of cross-indexing. Yet to some, cross-indexing may not seem to be of great importance. I know a man who says frequently about this detail or that, "Oh, that doesn't matter." Everything matters to the scientist. The following incident seems to me to have some significance. I told a man that I was working at the technique of the business interview, at which he seemed rather amused and said, "I guess most businessmen know how to conduct interviews." It was evident that he thought he did—but he is a man who has never risen above a small position. Later, I said the same thing to a clever man in a good position, a New York man, by the way. I said it a little hesitatingly, for I thought he too might consider it beneath his notice, but he was much interested and asked if he might see my paper when finished.

I have spoken of the classification of experience, the organizing of knowledge, as one of the necessary preliminaries to putting business management on a scientific basis. This organized body of knowledge tends at first to remain in the hands of a few. Measures should be taken to make it accessible to the whole managerial force. There should be opportunities for the training of executives through talks, suggested readings (including journals on management), through wisely led discussion groups and conferences, through managers' associations, foremen's associations, and the like. The organized knowledge of managerial methods which many of the higher officials possess should spread to the lower executives. In some cases, the higher official does not even think of this as part of his responsibility. He will say to a subordinate, "Here is what I want done; I don't care how you do it, that's up to you." Indeed, many an official has prided himself on this way of dealing with subordinates. But this is changing. It is part of the Taylor system that standards and methods for each worker's job are made accessible to the worker; also knowledge of the quality of work expected, which is shown him by specifications or drawings. Some such system should be developed for management. To develop it might be made part of that analysis of managerial jobs which I spoke of a few moments ago. Indeed, more and more of the higher executives are seeing now that managers' jobs as well as workers' jobs are capable of carrying with them accepted standards and methods.

Of course, it is recognized that many of these standards and methods need the sanction of custom rather than of authority, that they should be indicated rather than prescribed, also that much more elasticity should be allowed than in the detailed instructions of the Taylor system—but this is all part of that large subject, the method of training executives. Possibly in time, as business organization develops, we shall have an official for executives corresponding to the functional foreman who is sometimes known as the "methods instructor," an official whose duty it will be to see that certain managerial methods are understood and followed, as it is the duty of the functional foreman to see that certain operating methods are understood and followed. But I should not advocate this unless the executives were allowed fullest opportunity for contributing to such prescribed methods. The development of managerial technique has been thought by some to involve the risk of crushing originality, the danger of taking away initiative. I think that, rightly managed, it should give executives increased opportunity for the fruitful exercise of initiative and originality, for it is they themselves who must develop this technique even if helped by experts. The choice here presented is not that between originality and a mechanical system, but between a haphazard, hit-or-miss way of performing executive duties and a scientifically determined procedure.

Yet when business management has gained something of an accepted technique, there still remains, as part of the training of executives, the acquiring of skill in its application. Managerial skill cannot be painted on the outside of executives; it has to go deeper than that. Like manual workers, managerial workers have to acquire certain habits and attitudes. And just as in the case of manual workers, for the acquisition of these habits and attitudes three conditions must be given: (1) detailed information in regard to a new method; (2) the stimulus to adopt this method; and (3) the opportunity to practice it so that it may become a habit.

A businessman tells me that I should emphasize the last point particularly. He says that his firm has been weak just here; that they have done more preaching than giving opportunity for practice. He says: "We've given them a lecture on piano playing and then put them on the concert stage. This winter we are going to try to invent ways of giving real practice to foremen so that a set of habits can be formed." No subject is more important than the training of executives, but as it is a subject which would require an evening for the most superficial consideration, we cannot speak further of it tonight. Let me just say, however, as a hint of what I shall elaborate later, that if you wish to train yourself for higher executive positions, the first thing for you to decide is what you are training for. Ability to dominate or manipulate others? That ought to be easy enough, since most of the magazines advertise sure ways of developing something they call "personality." But I am convinced that the first essential of business success is the capacity for organized thinking.

In conclusion: What does all this imply in regard to the profession of business management? It means that men must prepare themselves as seriously for this profession as for any other. They must realize that they, as all professional men, are assuming grave responsibilities, that they are to take a creative part in one of the large functions of society, a part which, I believe, only trained and disciplined men can in the future hope to take with success.

NOTES AND REFERENCES

1. John Rogers Commons, 1862–1945. American economist, educator, and author. Also had considerable influence in labor legislation.—Editor
2. Oliver Sheldon, *Bulletin of Taylor Society,* Vol. 8, No. 6 (December, 1913), p. 211.
3. Oliver Sheldon, *The Philosophy of Management* (London: Sir Isaac Pitman & Sons, Ltd., 1923), p. 36.
4. *Ibid.,* p. 35.

3

The Management Theory Jungle

Harold Koontz

A true modern day classic, this selection is perhaps the most frequently reprinted article in the management literature. In it, Koontz classifies the major schools of management theory into six main groups which, he argues, have resulted in a "semantics jungle." The article describes the need to disentangle the resulting confusion and integrate management and other disciplines.—Eds.

Although students of management would readily agree that there have been problems of management since the dawn of organized life, most would also agree that systematic examination of management, with few exceptions, is the product of the present century and more especially of the past two decades. Moreover, until recent years almost all of those who have attempted to analyze the management process and look for some theoretical underpinnings to help improve research, teaching, and practice were alert and perceptive practitioners of the art who reflected on many years of experience. Thus, at least in looking at *general* management as an intellectually based art, the earliest meaningful writing came from such experienced practitioners as Fayol, Mooney, Alvin Brown, Sheldon, Barnard, and Urwick. Certainly not even the most academic worshipper of empirical research can overlook the empiricism involved in distilling fundamentals from decades of experience by such discerning practitioners as these. Admittedly done without questionnaires, controlled interviews, or mathematics, observations by such men can hardly be accurately regarded as a priori or "armchair."

SOURCE: Reprinted by pemission of the author and publisher from "The Management Theory Jungle," *The Academy of Management Journal,* December 1961, pp. 174–88.

The noteworthy absence of academic writing and research in the formative years of modern management theory is now more than atoned for by a deluge of research and writing from the academic halls. What is interesting and perhaps nothing more than a sign of the unsophisticated adolescence of management theory is how the current flood has brought with it a wave of great differences and apparent confusion. From the orderly analysis of management at the shop-room level by Frederick Taylor and the reflective distillation of experience from the general management point of view by Henri Fayol, we now see these and other early beginnings overgrown and entangled by a jungle of approaches and approachers to management theory.

There are the behavioralists, born of the Hawthorne experiments and the awakened interest in human relations during the 1930s and 1940s, who see management as a complex of interpersonal relationships and the basis of management theory the tentative tenets of the new and undeveloped science of psychology. There are also those who see management theory as simply a manifestation of the institutional and cultural aspects of sociology. Still others, observing that the central core of management is decision making, branch in all directions from this core to encompass everything in organization life. Then, there are mathematicians who think of management primarily as an exercise in logical relationships expressed in symbols and the omnipresent and ever revered model. But the entanglement of growth reaches its ultimate when the study of management is regarded as a study of one of a number of systems and subsystems, with an understandable tendency for the researcher to be dissatisfied until he has encompassed the entire physical and cultural universe as a management system.

With the recent discovery of an ages old problem area by social, physical, and biological scientists, and with the supersonic increase in interest by all types of enterprise managers, the apparent impenetrability of the present thicket which we call management theory is not difficult to comprehend. One can hardly be surprised that psychologists, sociologists, anthropologists, sociometricists, economists, mathematicians, physicists, biologists, political scientists, business administration scholars, and even practicing managers, should hop on this interesting, challenging, and profitable band wagon.

This welling of interest from every academic and practicing corner should not upset anyone concerned with seeing the frontiers of knowledge pushed back and the intellectual base of practice broadened. But what is rather upsetting to the practitioner and the observer, who sees great social potential from improved management, is that the variety of approaches to management theory has led to a kind of confused and destructive jungle warfare. Particularly among academic disciplines and their disciples, the primary interests of many would-be cult leaders seem to be to carve out a distinct (and hence "original") approach to management. And to defend this originality, and thereby gain a place in posterity (or at least to gain a publication which will justify academic status or promotion), it seems to have become too much the current style to downgrade, and sometimes misrepresent, what anyone else has said, or thought, or done.

In order to cut through this jungle and bring to light some of the issues and problems involved in the present management theory area so that the tremendous interest, intelligence, and research results may become more meaningful, it is my purpose here to classify the various "schools" of management theory, to identify briefly what I believe to be the major source of differences, and to offer some suggestions for disentangling the jungle. It is hoped that a movement for clarification can be started so at least we in the field will not be a group of blind men identifying the same elephant with our widely varying and sometimes viciously argumentative theses.

THE MAJOR "SCHOOLS" OF MANAGEMENT THEORY

In attempting to classify the major schools of management theory into six main groups, I am aware that I may overlook certain approaches and cannot deal with all the nuances of each approach. But it does seem that most of the approaches to management theory can be classified in one of these so-called schools.

The Management Process School

This approach to management theory perceives management as a process of getting things done through and with people operating in organized groups. It aims to analyze the process, to establish a conceptual framework for it, to identify principles underlying it, and to build up a theory of management from them. It regards management as a universal process, regardless of the type of enterprise, or the level in a given enterprise, although recognizing, obviously, that the environment of management differs widely between enterprises and levels. It looks upon management theory as a way of organizing experience so that practice can be improved through research, empirical testing of principles, and teaching of fundamentals involved in the management process.[1]

Often referred to, especially by its critics, as the "traditional" or "universalist" school, this school can be said to have been fathered by Henri Fayol, although many of his offspring did not know of their parent, since Fayol's work was eclipsed by the bright light of his contemporary, Frederick Taylor, and clouded by the lack of a widely available English translation until 1949. Other than Fayol, most of the early contributors to this school dealt only with the organization portion of the management process, largely because of their greater experience with this facet of management and the simple fact that planning and control, as well as the function of staffing, were given little attention by managers before 1940.

This school bases its approach to management theory on several fundamental beliefs:

(1) that managing is a process and can best be dissected intellectually by analyzing the functions of the manager;

(2) that long experience with management in a variety of enterprise situations can be grounds for distillation of certain fundamental truths or generalizations—usually referred to as principles—which have a clarifying and predictive value in the understanding and improvement of managing;

(3) that these fundamental truths can become focal points for useful research both to ascertain their validity and to improve their meaning and applicability in practice;

(4) that such truths can furnish elements, at least until disproved, and certainly until sharpened, of a useful theory of management;

(5) that managing is an art, but one like medicine or engineering, which can be improved by reliance on the light and understanding of principles;

(6) that principles in management, like principles in the biological and physical sciences, are nonetheless true even if a prescribed treatment or design by a practitioner in a given case situation chooses to ignore a principle and the costs involved, or attempts to do something else to offset the costs incurred (this is, of course, not new in medicine, engineering, or any other art, for art is the creative task of compromising fundamentals to attain a desired result); and

(7) that, while the totality of culture and of the physical and biological universe have varying effects on the manager's environment and subjects, as indeed they do in every other field of science and art, the theory of management does not need to encompass the field of all knowledge in order for it to serve as a scientific or theoretical foundation.

The basic approach of this school, then, is to look, first, to the functions of managers. As a second step in this approach, many of us have taken the functions of managers and further dissected them by distilling what we see as fundamental truths in the understandably complicated practice of management. I have found it useful to classify my analysis of these functions around the essentials involved in the following questions:

(1) What is the nature of the function?

(2) What is the purpose of the function?

(3) What explains the structure of the function?

(4) What explains the process of the function?

Perhaps there are other more useful approaches, but I have found that I can place everything pertaining to management (even some of the rather remote research and concepts) in this framework.

Also, purely to make the area of management theory intellectually manageable, those who subscribe to this school do not usually attempt to include in the theory the entire areas of sociology, economics, biology, psychology, physics, chemistry, or others. This is done not because these other areas of knowledge are unimportant and have no bearing on management, but merely because no real progress has ever been made in science or art without significant partitioning of knowledge. Yet, anyone would be foolish not to realize that a function which deals with people in their various activities of producing and marketing anything from money to religion and education is completely independent of the physical, biological, and cultural universe in which we live. And, are there not such relationships in other "compartments" of knowledge and theory?

The Empirical School

A second approach to management I refer to as the "empirical" school. In this, I include those scholars who identify management as a study of experience, sometimes with intent to draw generalizations but usually merely as a means of teaching experience and transferring it to the practitioner or student. Typical of this school are those who see management or "policy" as the study and analysis of cases and those with such approaches as Ernest Dale's "comparative approach."[2]

This approach seems to be based upon the premise that, if we study the experience of successful managers, or the mistakes made in management, or if we attempt to solve management problems, we will somehow understand and learn to apply the most effective kinds of management techniques. This approach, as often applied, assumes that, by finding out what worked or did not work in individual circumstances, the student or the practitioner will be able to do the same in comparable situations.

No one can deny the importance of studying experience through such study, or of analyzing the "how-it-was-done" of management. But management, unlike law, is not a science based on precedent, and situations in the future exactly comparable to the past are exceedingly unlikely to occur. Indeed, there is a positive danger of relying too much on past experience and on undistilled history of managerial problem solving for the simple reason that a technique or approach found "right" in the past may not fit a situation of the future.

Those advocating the empirical approach are likely to say that what they really do in analyzing cases or history is to draw from certain generalizations which can be applied as useful guides to thought or action in future case situations. As a matter of fact, Ernest Dale, after claiming to find "so little practical value" from the principles enunciated by the "universalists," curiously drew certain "generalizations" or "criteria" from his valuable study of a number of great practitioners of management.[3] There is some question as to whether Dale's "comparative" approach is not really the same as the "universalist" approach he decries, except with a different distiller of basic truths.

By the emphasis of the empirical school on study of experience, it does appear that the research and thought so engendered may assist in hastening the day for verification of principles. It is also possible that the proponents of this school may come up with a more useful framework of principles than that of the management process school. But, to the extent that the empirical school draws generalizations from its research, and it would seem to be a necessity to do so unless its members are satisfied to exchange meaningless and structureless experience, this approach tends to be and do the same as the management process school.

The Human Behavior School

This approach to the analysis of management is based on the central thesis that, since managing involves getting things done with and through people, the study of management must be centered on interpersonal relations. Variously called the "human relations," "leadership," or "behavioral sciences" approach, this school brings to bear "existing and newly developed theories, methods, and techniques of the relevant social sciences upon the study of inter- and intrapersonal phenomena, ranging fully from the personality dynamics of individuals at one extreme to the relations of cultures at the other."[4] In other words, this school concentrates on the "people" part of management and rests on the principle that, where people work together as groups in order to accomplish objectives, "people should understand people."

The scholars in this school have a heavy orientation to psychology and social psychology. Their primary focus is the individual as a sociopsychological being and what motivates him. The members of this school vary from those who see it as a portion of the manager's job, a tool to help him understand and get the best from people by meeting their needs and responding to their motivations, to those who see the psychological behavior of individuals and groups as the total of management.

In this school are those who emphasize human relations as an art that the manager should advantageously understand and practice. There are those who focus attention on the manager as a leader and sometimes equate management to leadership, thus, in effect, tending to treat all group activities as "managed" situations. There are those who see the study of group dynamics and interpersonal relationships as simply a study of socio-psychological relationships and seem, therefore, merely to be attaching the term "management" to the field of social psychology.

That management must deal with human behavior can hardly be denied. That the study of human interactions, whether in the environment of management or in unmanaged situations, is important and useful one could not dispute. And it would be a serious mistake to regard good leadership as unimportant to good managership. But whether the field of human behavior is the equivalent of the field of management is quite another thing. Perhaps it is like calling the study of the human body the field of cardiology.

The Social System School

Closely related to the human behavior school and often confused or intertwined with it is one which might be labeled the social system school. This includes those researchers who look upon management as a social system, that is, a system of cultural interrelationships. Sometimes, as in the case of March and Simon,[5] the system is limited to formal organizations, using the term "organization" as equivalent to enterprise, rather than the authority-activity concept used most often in management. In other cases, the approach is not to distinguish the formal organization, but rather to encompass any kind of system of human relationships.

Heavily sociological in flavor, this approach to management does essentially what any study of sociology does. It identifies the nature of the cultural relationships of various social groups and attempts to show these as a related, and usually an integrated, system.

Perhaps the spiritual father of this ardent and vocal school of management theorists is Chester Barnard.[6] In searching for an answer to fundamental explanations underlying the managing process, this thoughtful business executive developed a theory of cooperation grounded in the needs of the individual to solve, through cooperation, the biological, physical, and social limitations of himself and his environment. Barnard then carved from the total of cooperative systems so engendered one set of interrelationships which he defines as "formal organization." His formal organization concept, quite unlike that usually held by management practitioners, is any cooperative system in which there are persons able to communicate with each other and who are willing to contribute action toward a conscious common purpose.

The Barnard concept of cooperative systems pervades the work of many contributors to the social system school of management. For example, Herbert Simon at one time defined the subject of organization theory and the nature of human organizations as "systems of interdependent activity, encompassing at least several primary groups and usually characterized, at the level of consciousness of participants, by a high degree of rational direction of behavior toward ends that are objects of common knowledge."[7] Simon and others have subsequently seemed to have expanded this concept of social systems to include any cooperative and purposeful group interrelationship or behavior.

This school has made many noteworthy contributions to management. The recognition of organized enterprise as a social organism, subject to all the pressures and conflicts of the cultural environment, has been helpful to the management theorist and the practitioner alike. Among some of the more helpful aspects are the awareness of the institutional foundations of organization authority, the influence of informal organization, and such social factors as those Wight Bakke has called the "bonds of organization."[8] Likewise, many of Barnard's helpful insights, such as his economy of incentives and his theory of opportunism, have brought the power of sociological understanding into the realm of management practice.

Basic sociology, analysis of concepts of social behavior, and the study of group behavior in the framework of social systems do have great value in the field of management. But one may well ask the question whether this *is* management. Is the field of management coterminous with the field of sociology? Or is sociology an important underpinning like language, psychology, physiology, mathematics, and other fields of knowledge? Must management be defined in terms of the universe of knowledge?

The Decision Theory School

Another approach to management theory, undertaken by a growing and scholarly group, might be referred to as the decision theory school. This group concentrates on rational approach to decision—the selection from among possible alternatives of a course of action or of an idea. The approach of this school may be to deal with the decision itself, or with the persons or organizational group making the decision, or with an analysis of the decision process. Some limit themselves fairly much to the economic rationale of the decision, while others regard anything which happens in an enterprise the subject of their analysis, and still others expand decision theory to cover the psychological and sociological aspect and environment of decisions and decision makers.

The decision making school is apparently an outgrowth of the theory of consumer's choice with which economists have been concerned since the days of Jeremy Bentham early in the nineteenth century. It has arisen out of such economic problems and analyses as utility maximization, indifference curves, marginal utility, and economic behavior under risks and uncertainties. It is, therefore, no surprise that one finds most of the members of this school to be economic theorists. It is likewise no surprise to find the content of this school to be heavily oriented to model construction and mathematics.

The decision theory school has tended to expand its horizon considerably beyond the process of evaluating alternatives. That point has become for many only a springboard for examination of the entire sphere of human activity, including the nature of the organization structure, psychological and social reactions of individuals and groups, the development of basic information for decisions, an analysis of values and particularly value considerations with respect to goals, communications networks, and incentives. As one would expect, when the decision theorists study the small, but central, area of decision *making*, they are led by this keyhole look at management to consider the entire field of enterprise operation and its environment. The result is that decision theory becomes no longer a neat and narrow concentration on decision, but rather a broad view of the enterprise as a social system.

There are those who believe that, since management is characterized by its concentration on decisions, the future development of management theory will tend to use the decision as its central focus and the rest of management theory will be hung on this structural center. This may occur and certainly the study of the decision, the decision process, and the decision maker can be extended to cover the entire field of management as anyone might conceive it. Nevertheless, one wonders whether this focus cannot also be used to build around it the entire area of human knowledge. For, as most decision theorists recognize, the problem of choice is individual, as well as organizational, and most of what has been said that is pure decision theory can be applied to the existence and thinking of a Robinson Crusoe.

The Mathematical School

Although mathematical methods can be used by any school of management theory, and have been, I have chosen to group under a school those theorists who see management as a system of mathematical models and processes. Perhaps the most widely known group I arbitrarily so lump are the operations researchers or operations analysts, who have sometimes anointed themselves with the rather pretentious name of "management scientists." The abiding belief of this group is that, if management, or organization, or planning, or decision making is a logical process, it can be expressed in terms of mathematical symbols and relationships. The central approach of this school is the model, for it is through these devices that the problem is expressed in its basic relationships and in terms of selected goals or objectives.

There can be no doubt of the great usefulness of mathematical approaches to any field of inquiry. It forces upon the researcher the definition of a problem or problem area, it conveniently allows the insertion of symbols for unknown data, and its logical methodology, developed by years of scientific application and abstraction, furnishes a powerful tool for solving or simplifying complex phenomena.

But it is hard to see mathematics as a truly separate school of management theory, any more than it is a separate "school" in physics, chemistry, engineering, or medicine. I only deal with it here as such because there has appeared to have developed a kind of cult around mathematical analysts who have subsumed to themselves the area of management.

In pointing out that mathematics is a tool, rather than a school, it is not my intention to underestimate the impact of mathematics on the science and practice of management. By bringing to this immensely important and complex field the tools and techniques of the physical sciences, the mathematicians have already made an immense contribution to orderly thinking. They have forced on people in management the means and desirability of seeing many problems more clearly, they have pressed on scholars and practitioners the need for establishing goals and measures of effectiveness, they have been extremely helpful in getting the management area seen as a logical system of relationships, and they have caused people in management to review and occasionally reorganize information sources and systems so that mathematics can be given sensible quantitative meaning. But with all this meaningful contribution and the greater sharpness and sophistication of planning which is resulting, I cannot see that mathematics is management theory any more than it is astronomy.

THE MAJOR SOURCES OF MENTAL ENTANGLEMENT IN THE JUNGLE

In outlining the various schools, or approaches, of management theory, it becomes clear that these intellectual cults are not drawing greatly different inferences from the physical and cultural environment surrounding us. Why, then, have there been so many differences between them and why such a struggle, particularly among our academic brethren, to obtain a place in the sun by denying the approaches of others? Like the widely differing and often contentious denominations of the Christian religion, all have essentially the same goals and deal with essentially the same world.

While there are many sources of the mental entanglement in the management theory jungle, the major ones are the following:

The Semantics Jungle

As is so often true when intelligent men argue about basic problems, some of the trouble lies in the meaning of key words. The semantics problem is particularly severe in the field of management. There is even a difference in the meaning of the word "management." Most people would agree that it means getting things done through and with people, but is it people in formal organizations, or in all group activities? Is it governing, leading, or teaching?

Perhaps the greatest single semantics confusion lies in the word "organization." Most members of the management process school use it to define the activity-authority structure of an enterprise and certainly most practitioners believe that they are "organizing" when they establish a framework of activity groupings and authority relationships. In this case, organization represents the formal framework within an enterprise that furnishes the environment in which people perform. Yet a large number of "organization" theorists conceive of organization as the sum total of human relationships in any group activity; they thus seem to make it equivalent to *social* structure. And some use "organization" to mean "enterprise."

If the meaning of organization cannot be clarified and a standard use of the term adopted by management theorists, understanding and criticism should not be based on this difference. It hardly seems to me to be accurate for March and Simon, for example, to criticize the organization theories of the management process, or "universalist," school for not considering the management planning function as part of organizing, when they have chosen to treat it separately. Nor should those who choose to treat the training, selecting, guiding or leading of people under staffing and direction be criticized for a tendency to "view the employee as an inert instrument" or a "given rather than a variable."[9] Such accusations, proceeding from false premises, are clearly erroneous.

Other semantic entanglements might be mentioned. By some, decision making is regarded as a process of choosing from among alternatives; by others, the total managerial task and environment. Leadership is often made synonymous with managership and is analytically separated by others. Communications may mean everything from a written or oral report to a vast network of formal and informal relationships. Human relations to some implies a psychiatric manipulation of people, but to others the study and art of understanding people and interpersonal relationships.

Differences in Definition of Management as a Body of Knowledge

As was indicated in the discussion of semantics, "management" has far from a standard meaning, although most agree that it at least involves getting things done through and with people. But, does it mean the dealing with all human relationships? Is a street peddler a manager? Is a parent a manager? Is a leader of a disorganized mob a manager? Does the field of management equal the fields of sociology and social psychology combined? Is it the equivalent of the entire system of social relationships?

While I recognize that sharp lines cannot be drawn in management any more than they are in medicine or engineering, there surely can be a sharper distinction drawn than at present. With the plethora of management writing and experts, calling almost everything under the sun management, can one expect management theory to be regarded as very useful or scientific to the practitioner?

The A Priori Assumption

Confusion in management theory has also been heightened by the tendency for many newcomers in the field to cast aside significant observations and analyses of the past on the grounds that they are a priori in nature. This is an often-met accusation made by those who wish to cast aside the work of Fayol, Mooney, Brown, Urwick, Gulick, and others who are branded as "universalists." To make the assumption that the distilled experiences of men such as these represent a priori reasoning is to forget that experience in and with managing *is* empirical. While the conclusions that perceptive and experienced practitioners of the art of management draw are not infallible, they represent an experience which is certainly real and not "armchair." No one could deny, I feel sure, that the ultimate test of accuracy of management theory must be practice and management theory and science must be developed from reality.

The Misunderstanding of Principles

Those who feel that they gain caste or a clean slate for advancing a particular notion or approach often delight in casting away anything which smacks of management principles. Some have referred to them as platitudes, forgetting that a platitude is still a truism and a truth does not become worthless because it is familiar. (As Robert Frost has written, "Most of the changes we think we see in life are merely truths going in or out of favor.") Others cast away principles of Fayol and other practitioners, only to draw apparently different generalizations from their study of management; but many of the generalizations so discovered are often the same fundamental truths in different words that certain criticized "universalists" have discovered.

One of the favorite tricks of the managerial theory trade is to disprove a whole framework of principles by reference to one principle which the observer sees disregarded in practice. Thus, many critics of the universalists point to the well-known cases of dual subordination in organized enterprise, coming to the erroneous conclusion that there is no substance to the principle of unity of command. But this does not prove that there is no cost to the enterprise by designing around, or disregarding, the principle of unity of command; nor does it prove that there were not other advantages which offset the costs, as there often are in cases of establishing functional authorities in organization.

Perhaps the almost hackneyed standby for those who would disprove the validity of all principles by referring to a single one is the misunderstanding around the principle of span of management (or span of control). The usual source of authority quoted by those who criticize is Sir Ian Hamilton, who never intended to state a universal principle, but rather to make a personal observation in a book of reflections on his Army experience, and who did say, offhand, that he found it wise to limit his span to 3 to 6 subordinates. No modern universalist relies on this single observation, and, indeed, few can or will state an absolute or universal numerical ceiling. Since Sir Ian was not a management theorist and did not intend to be, let us hope that the ghost of his innocent remark may be laid to deserved rest!

What concerns those who feel that a recognition of fundamental truths, or generalizations, may help in the diagnosis and study of management, and who know from managerial experience that such truths or principles do serve an extremely valuable use, is the tendency for some researchers to prove the wrong things through either misstatement or misapplication of principles. A classic case of such misunderstanding and misapplication is in Chris Argyris' interesting book on *Personality and Organization*.[10] This author, who in this book and his other works has made many noteworthy contributions to management, concludes that "formal organization principles make demands on relatively healthy individuals that are incongruent with their needs," and that "frustration, conflict, failure, and short-time perspective are predicted as results of this basic incongruency."[11] This startling conclusion—the exact opposite of what "good" formal organization based on "sound" organization principles should cause, is explained when one notes that, of four "principles" Argyris quotes, one is not an organization principle at all but the economic principle of specialization and three other "principles" are quoted incorrectly.[12] With such a postulate, and with no attempt to recognize, correctly or incorrectly, any other organization and management principles, Argyris has simply proved that wrong principles badly applied will lead to frustration; and every management practitioner knows this to be true!

The Inability or Unwillingness of Management Theorists to Understand Each Other

What has been said above leads one to the conclusion that much of the management theory jungle is caused by the unwillingness or inability of the management theorists to understand each other. Doubting that it is inability, because one must assume that a person interested in management theory is able to comprehend, at least in concept and framework, the approaches of the various "schools," I can only come to the conclusion that the roadblock to understanding is unwillingness.

Perhaps this unwillingness comes from the professional "walls" developed by learned disciplines. Perhaps the unwillingness stems from a fear that someone or some new discovery will encroach on professional and academic status. Perhaps it is fear of professional or intellectual obsolescence. But whatever the cause, it seems that these walls will not be torn down until it is realized that they exist, until all cultists are willing to look at the approach and content of other schools, and until, through exchange and understanding of ideas some order may be brought from the present chaos.

DISENTANGLING THE MANAGEMENT THEORY JUNGLE

It is important that steps be taken to disentangle the management theory jungle. Perhaps, it is too soon and we must expect more years of wandering through a thicket of approaches, semantics, thrusts, and counter thrusts. But in any field as important to society where the many blunders of an unscientifically based managerial art can be so costly, I hope that this will not be long.

There do appear to be some things that can be done. Clearly, meeting what I see to be the major sources of the entanglement should remove much of it. The following considerations are important:

1. The need for definition of a body of knowledge. Certainly, if a field of knowledge is not to get bogged down in a quagmire of misunderstandings, the first need is for definition of the field. Not that it need be defined in sharp, detailed, and inflexible lines, but rather along lines which will give it fairly specific content. Because management is reality, life, practice, my suggestion would be that it be defined in the light of the able and discerning practitioner's frame of reference. A science unrelated to the art for which it is to serve is not likely to be a very productive one.

Although the study of managements in various enterprises, in various countries, and at various levels made by many persons, including myself, may neither be representative nor adequate, I have come to the conclusion that management is the art of getting things done through and with people in *formally organized groups,* the art of creating an environment in such an organized group where people can perform as individuals and yet cooperate toward attainment of group goals, the art of removing blocks to such performance, the art of optimizing efficiency in effectively reaching goals. If this kind of definition of the field is unsatisfactory, I suggest at least an agreement that the area should be defined to reflect the field of the practitioner and that further research and study of practice be done to this end.

In defining the field, too, it seems to me imperative to draw some limits for purposes of analysis and research. If we are to call the entire cultural, biological, and physical universe the field of management, we can no more make progress than could have been done if chemistry or geology had not carved out a fairly specific area and had, instead, studied all knowledge.

In defining the body of knowledge, too, care must be taken to distinguish between tools and content. Thus mathematics, operations research, accounting, economic theory, sociometry, and psychology, to mention a few, are significant *tools* of management but are not, in themselves, a part of the *content* of the field. This is not to mean that they are unimportant or that the practicing manager should not have them available to him, nor does it mean that they may not be the means of pushing back the frontiers of knowledge of management. But they should not be confused with the basic content of the field.

This is not to say that fruitful study should not continue on the underlying disciplines affecting management. Certainly knowledge of sociology, social systems, psychology, economics, political science, mathematics, and other areas, pointed toward contributing to the field of management, should be continued and encouraged. And significant findings in these and other fields of knowledge might well cast important light on, or change concepts in, the field of management. This has certainly happened in other sciences and in every other art based upon significant science.

2. Integration of management and other disciplines. If recognition of the proper content of the field were made, I believe that the present crossfire of misunderstanding might tend to disappear. Management would be regarded as a specific discipline and other disciplines would be looked upon as important bases of the field. Under these circumstances, the allied and underlying disciplines would be welcomed by the business and public administration schools, as well as by practitioners, as loyal and helpful associates. Integration of management and other disciplines would then not be difficult.

3. The clarification of management semantics. While I would expect the need for clarification and uniformity of management semantics would largely be satisfied by definition of the field as a body of knowledge, semantics problems might require more special attention. There are not too many places where semantics are important enough to cause difficulty. Here again, I would suggest the adoption of the semantics of the intelligent practitioners, unless words are used by them so inexactly as to require special clarification. At least, we should not complicate an already complex field by developing a scientific or academic jargon which would build a language barrier between the theorist and the practitioner.

Perhaps the most expeditious way out of this problem is to establish a commission representing academic societies immediately concerned and associations of practicing managers. This would not seem to be difficult to do. And even if it were, the results would be worth the efforts.

4. Willingness to distill and test fundamentals. Certainly, the test of maturity and usefulness of a science is the sharpness and validity of the principles underlying it. No science, now regarded as mature, started out with a complete statement of incontrovertibly valid principles. Even the oldest sciences, such as physics, keep revising their underlying laws and discovering new principles. Yet any science has proceeded, and more than that has been useful, for centuries on the basis of generalizations, some laws, some principles, and some hypotheses.

One of the understandable sources of inferiority of the social sciences is the recognition that they are inexact sciences. On the other hand, even the so-called exact sciences are subject to a great deal of inexactness, have principles which are not completely proved, and use art in the design of practical systems and components. The often-encountered defeatist attitude of the social sciences, of which management is one, overlooks the fact that management may be explained, practice may be improved, and the goals of research may be more meaningful if we encourage attempts at perceptive distillation of experience by stating principles (or generalizations) and placing them in a logical framework. As two scientists recently said on this subject:

The reason for this defeatist point of view regarding the social sciences may be traceable to a basic misunderstanding of the nature of scientific endeavor. What matters is not whether or to what extent inexactitudes in procedures and predictive capability can eventually be removed . . . : rather it is *objectivity*, i.e., the intersubjectivity of findings independent of any one person's intuitive judgment, which distinguishes science from intuitive guesswork however brilliant. . . . But once a new fact or a new idea has been conjectured, no matter how intuitive a foundation, it must be capable of objective test and confirmation by anyone. And it is this crucial standard of scientific objectivity rather than any purported criterion of exactitude to which the social sciences must conform.[13]

In approaching the clarification of management theory, then, we should not forget a few criteria:

1. The theory should deal with an area of knowledge and inquiry that is "manageable"; no great advances in knowledge were made so long as man contemplated the whole universe;
2. The theory should be *useful* in improving practice and the task and person of the practitioner should not be overlooked;
3. The theory should not be lost in semantics, especially useless jargon not understandable to the practitioner;
4. The theory should give direction and efficiency to research and teaching; and
5. The theory must recognize that it is a part of a larger universe of knowledge and theory.

NOTES AND REFERENCES

1. It is interesting that one of the scholars strongly oriented to human relations and behavioral approaches to management has recently noted that "theory can be viewed as a way of organizing experience" and that "once initial sense is made out of experienced environment, the way is cleared for an even more adequate organization of this experience." See Robert Dubin in "Psyche, Sensitivity, and Social Structure," critical comment in Robert Tannenbaum, I. R. Weschler, and Fred Massarik, *Leadership and Organization: A Behavioral Science Approach* (New York: McGraw-Hill Book Co., 1961), p. 401.
2. *The Great Organizers* (New York: McGraw-Hill Book Co., 1960), pp. 11–28.
3. *Ibid.*, pp. 11, 26–28, 62–68.
4. R. Tannenbaum, I. R. Weschler, and F. Massarik, *Leadership and Organization* (New York: McGraw-Hill Book Co., 1961), p. 9.
5. *Organizations* (New York: John Wiley & Sons, Inc., 1958).
6. *The Functions of the Executive* (Cambridge, Mass.: Harvard University Press, 1938).
7. "Comments on the Theory of Organizations," *American Political Science Review*, Vol. 46, No. 4 (December, 1952), p. 1130.

8. *Bonds of Organization* (New York: Harper & Brothers, 1950). These "bonds" or "devices" of organization are identified by Bakke as (1) the functional specifications system (a system of teamwork arising from job specifications and arrangements for association); (2) the status system (a vertical hierarchy of authority); (3) the communications system; (4) the reward and penalty system; and (5) the organization charter (ideas and means which give character and individuality to the organization, or enterprise).

9. J. G. March and H. A. Simon, *Organizations* (New York: John Wiley & Sons, Inc., 1958), pp. 29–33.

10. New York: Harper & Brothers, 1957.

11. *Ibid.*, p. 74.

12. *Ibid.*, pp. 58–66.

13. O. Helmer and N. Rescher, "On the Epistemology of the Inexact Sciences" (Santa Monica, California: The RAND Corporation, P-1513, 1958), pp. 4–5.

4

The Western Electric Researches

George C. Homans

Perhaps no single research study has had a greater impact on manage-ment theory and practice than that conducted at the Hawthorne Works of Western Electric. This article describes part of this multi-year project and the conclusions which flowed from it. No study of management is complete without a look at the "Hawthorne Research," credited by many as giving birth to the behavioral management thrust.—Eds.

Perhaps the most important program of research studied by the Commit-tee on Work in Industry of the National Research Council is that which has been carried on at the Hawthorne (Chicago) Works of the Western Electric Company. This program was described by H. A. Wright and M. L. Putnam of the Western Electric Company and by F. J. Roethlisberger, now Professor of Human Relations, Graduate School of Business Admin-istration, Harvard University, particularly at a meeting of the Commit-tee held on March 9, 1938. These men, together with Elton Mayo and G. A. Pennock, both members of the Committee, had been intimately associ-ated with the research.

A word about the Western Electric Company is a necessary introduc-tion to what follows. This company is engaged in manufacturing equip-ment for the telephone industry. Besides doing this part of its work, it has always shown concern for the welfare of its employees. In the matter of wages and hours, it has maintained a high standard. It has provided good physical conditions for its employees; and it has tried to make use of every established method of vocational guidance in the effort to suit the worker to his work. The efforts of the company have been rewarded in

SOURCE: Reprinted from *Fatigue of Workers* by George C. Homans (Reinhold, 1941), pp. 56–65, by permission from the author.

good industrial relations: there has been no strike or other severe symptom of discontent for over twenty years. In short, there is no reason to doubt that while these researches were being carried out, the morale of the company was high and that the employees, as a body, had confidence in the abilities and motives of the company management. These facts had an important bearing on the results achieved.

The program of research which will be described grew out of a study conducted at Hawthorne by the Western Electric Company in collaboration with the National Research Council, the aim of which was to determine the relation between intensity of illumination and efficiency of workers, measured in output. One of the experiments made was the following: Two groups of employees doing similar work under similar conditions were chosen, and records of output were kept for each group. The intensity of the light under which one group worked was varied, while that under which the other group worked was held constant. By this method the investigators hoped to isolate from the effect of other variables the effect of changes in the intensity of illumination on the rate of output.

In this hope they were disappointed. The experiment failed to show any simple relation between experimental changes in the intensity of illumination and observed changes in the rate of output. The investigators concluded that this result was obtained, not because such a relation did not exist, but because it was in fact impossible to isolate it from the other variables entering into any determination of productive efficiency. This kind of difficulty, of course, has been encountered in experimental work in many fields. Furthermore, the investigators were in agreement as to the character of some of these other variables. They were convinced that one of the major factors which prevented their securing a satisfactory result was psychological. The employees being tested were reacting to changes in light intensity in the way in which they assumed that they were expected to react. That is, when light intensity was increased they were expected to produce more; when it was decreased they were expected to produce less. A further experiment was devised to demonstrate this point. The light bulbs were changed, as they had been changed before, and the workers were allowed to assume that as a result there would be more light. They commented favorably on the increased illumination. As a matter of fact, the bulbs had been replaced with others of just the same power. Other experiments of the sort were made, and in each case the results could be explained as a "psychological" reaction rather than as a "physiological" one.

This discovery seemed to be important. It suggested that the relations between other physical conditions and the efficiency of workers might be obscured by similar psychological reactions. Nevertheless, the investigators were determined to continue in their course. They recognized the existence of the psychological factors, but they thought of them only as disturbing influences. They were not yet ready to turn their attention to the psychological factors themselves. Instead, they were concerned with devising a better way of eliminating them from the experiments, and the experiments they wanted to try by no means ended with illumination. For instance, there was the question of what was called "fatigue." Little information existed about the effect on efficiency of changes in the hours of work and the introduction of rest pauses. The investigators finally came to the conclusion that if a small group of workers were isolated in a separate room and asked to cooperate, the psychological reaction would in time disappear, and they would work exactly as they felt. That is, changes in their rate of output would be the direct result of changes in their physical conditions of work and nothing else.

The decision to organize such a group was in fact taken. A small number of workers was to be selected and placed in a separate room, where experiments were to be made with different kinds of working conditions in order to see if more exact information could be secured. Six questions were asked by those setting up the experiment. They were the following:

1. Do employees actually get tired out?
2. Are rest pauses desirable?
3. Is a shorter working day desirable?
4. What is the attitude of employees toward their work and toward the company?
5. What is the effect of changing the type of working equipment?
6. Why does production fall off in the afternoon?

It is obvious that several of these questions could be answered only indirectly by the proposed experiment, and several of them touched upon the "psychological" rather than the "physiological" factors involved. Nevertheless, all of them arose out of the bewilderment of men of experience faced with the problem of dealing with fellow human beings in a large industrial organization. In fact, one of the executives of the company saw the purpose of the experiment in even simpler and more general terms. He said that the experiment grew out of a desire on the part of the management to "know more about our workers." In this way began the experiment which is referred to as the Relay Assembly Test Room. With this experiment and the others that followed, members of the Department of Industrial Research of the Graduate School of Business Administration, Harvard University, came to be closely associated.

In April, 1927, six girls were selected from a large shop department of the Hawthorne Works. They were chosen as average workers, neither inexperienced nor expert, and their work consisted of the assembling of telephone relays. A coil, armature, contact springs, and insulators were put together on a fixture and secured in position by means of four machine screws. The operation at that time was being completed at the rate of about five relays in six minutes. This particular operation was chosen for the experiment because the relays were being assembled often enough so that even slight changes in output rate would show themselves at once on the output record. Five of the girls were to do the actual assembly work; the duty of the sixth was to keep the others supplied with parts.

The test room itself was an area divided from the main department by a wooden partition eight feet high. The girls sat in a row on one side of a long workbench. Their bench and assembly equipment was identical with that used in the regular department, except in one respect. At the right of each girl's place was a hole in the bench, and into this hole she dropped completed relays. It was the entrance to a chute, in which there was a flapper gate opened by the relay in its passage downward. The opening of the gate closed an electrical circuit which controlled a perforating device, and this in turn recorded the completion of the relay by punching a hole in a tape. The tape moved at the rate of one-quarter of an inch a minute and had space for a separate row of holes for each operator. When punched, it thus constituted a complete output record for each girl for each instant of the day. Such records were kept for five years.

In this experiment then, as in the earlier illumination experiments, great emphasis was laid on the rate of output. A word of caution is needed here. The Western Electric Company was not immediately interested in increasing output. The experiments were not designed for that purpose. On the other hand, output is easily measured; i.e., it yields precise quantitative data, and experience suggested that it was sensitive to at least some of the conditions under which the employees worked. Output was treated as an index. In short, the nature of the experimental conditions made the emphasis on output inevitable.

From their experience in the illumination experiments, the investigators were well aware that factors other than those experimentally varied might affect the output rate. Therefore arrangements were made that a number of other records should be kept. Unsuitable parts supplied by the firm were noted down, as were assemblies rejected for any reason upon inspection. In this way the type of defect could be known and related to the time of day at which it occurred. Records were kept of weather conditions in general and of temperature and humidity in the test room. Every six weeks each operator was given a medical examination by the company doctor. Every day she was asked to tell how many hours she had spent in bed the night before and, during a part of the experiment, what food she had eaten. Besides all these records, which concerned the physical condition of the operators, a log was kept in which were recorded the principal events in the test room hour by hour, including among the entries snatches of conversation between the workers. At first these entries related largely to the physical condition of the operators: how they felt as they worked. Later the ground they covered somewhat widened, and the log ultimately became one of the most important of the test room records. Finally, when the so-called Interviewing Program was instituted at Hawthorne, each of the operators was interviewed several times by an experienced interviewer.

The girls had no supervisor in the ordinary sense, such as they would have had in a regular shop department, but a "test room observer" was placed in the room, whose duty it was to maintain the records, arrange the work, and secure a cooperative spirit on the part of the girls. Later, when the complexity of his work increased, several assistants were assigned to help him.

When the arrangements had been made for the test room, the operators who had been chosen to take part were called in for an interview in the office of the superintendent of the Inspection Branch, who was in general charge of the experiment and of the researches which grew out of it. The superintendent described this interview as follows:

> The nature of the test was carefully explained to these girls and they readily consented to take part in it, although they were very shy at the first conference. An invitation to six shop girls to come up to a superintendent's office was naturally rather startling. They were assured that the object of the test was to determine the effect of certain changes in working conditions, such as rest periods, midmorning lunches, and shorter working hours. They were expressly cautioned to work at a comfortable pace, and under no circumstances to try to make a race out of the test.

This conference was only the first of many. Whenever any experimental change was planned, the girls were called in, the purpose of the change was explained to them, and their comments were requested. Certain suggested changes which did not meet with their approval were abandoned. They were repeatedly asked, as they were asked in the first interview, not to strain but to work "as they felt."

The experiment was now ready to begin. Put in its simplest terms, the idea of those directing the experiment was that if an output curve was studied for a long enough time under various changes in working conditions, it would be possible to determine which conditions were the most satisfactory. Accordingly, a number of so-called experimental periods were arranged. For two weeks before the operators were placed in the test room, a record was kept of the production of each one without her knowledge. In this way the investigators secured a measure of her productive ability while working in the regular department under the usual conditions. This constituted the first experimental period. And for five weeks after the girls entered the test room no change was made in working conditions. Hours remained what they had been before. The investigators felt that this period would be long enough to reveal any changes in output incidental merely to the transfer. This constituted the second experimental period.

The third period involved a change in the method of payment. In the regular department, the girls had been paid according to a scheme of group piecework, the group consisting of a hundred or more employees.

Under these circumstances, variations in an individual's total output would not be immediately reflected in her pay, since such variations tended to cancel one another in a large group. In the test room, the six operators were made a group by themselves. In this way each girl received an amount more nearly in proportion to her individual effort, and her interests became more closely centered on the experiment. Eight weeks later, the directly experimental changes began. An outline will reveal their general character: Period IV: two rest pauses, each five minutes in length, were established, one occurring in midmorning and the other in the early afternoon. Period V: these rest pauses were lengthened to ten minutes each. Period VI: six five-minute rests were established. Period VII: the company provided each member of the group with a light lunch in the midmorning and another in the midafternoon accompanied by rest pauses. This arrangement became standard for subsequent Periods VIII through XI. Period VIII: work stopped a half-hour earlier every day—at 4:30 P.M. Period IX: work stopped at 4 P.M. Period X: conditions returned to what they were in Period VII. Period XI: a five-day work week was established. Each of these experimental periods lasted several weeks.

Period XI ran through the summer of 1928, a year after the beginning of the experiment. Already the results were not what had been expected. The output curve, which had risen on the whole slowly and steadily throughout the year, was obviously reflecting something other than the responses of the group to the imposed experimental conditions. Even when the total weekly output had fallen off, as it could hardly fail to do in such a period as Period XI, when the group was working only five days a week, daily output continued to rise. Therefore, in accordance with a sound experimental procedure, as a control on what had been done, it was agreed with the consent of the operators that in experimental Period XII a return should be made to the original conditions of work, with no rest pauses, no special lunches, and a full-length working week. This period lasted for twelve weeks. Both daily and weekly output rose to a higher point than ever before: the working day and the working week were both longer. The hourly output rate declined somewhat but it did not approach the level of Period III, when similar conditions were in effect.

The conclusions reached after Period XII may be expressed in terms of another observation. Identical conditions of work were repeated in three different experimental periods: Periods VII, X, and XII. If the assumptions on which the study was based had been correct, that is to say, if the output rate were directly related to the physical conditions of work, the expectation would be that in these three experimental periods there would be some similarity in output. Such was not the case. The only apparent uniformity was that in each experimental period output was higher than in the preceding one. In the Relay Assembly Test Room, as in the previous illumination experiments, something was happening which could not be explained by the experimentally controlled conditions of work.

There is no need here to go into the later history of the test room experiment, which came to an end in 1933. It is enough to say that the output of the group continued to rise until it established itself on a high plateau from which there was no descent until the time of discouragement and deepening economic depression which preceded the end of the test. The rough conclusions reached at the end of experimental Period XII were confirmed and sharpened by later research. T. N. Whitehead, Associate Professor of Business in the Graduate School of Business Administration, Harvard University, has made a careful statistical analysis of the output records. He shows that the changes which took place in the output of the group have no simple correlation with the experimental changes in working conditions. Nor can they be correlated with changes in other physical conditions of which records were kept, such as temperature, humidity, hours of rest, and changes of relay type. Even when the girls themselves complained of mugginess or heat, these conditions were not apparently affecting their output. This statement, of course, does not mean that there is never any relation between output rate and these physical conditions. There is such a thing as heat prostration. It means only that, within the limits in which these conditions were varying in the test room, they apparently did not affect the rate of work.

The question remains: with what facts, if any, can the changes in the output rate of the operators in the test room be correlated? Here the statements of the girls themselves are of first importance. Each girl knew that she was producing more in the test room than she ever had in the regular department, and each said that the increase had come about without any conscious effort on her part. It seemed easier to produce at the faster rate in the test room than at the slower rate in the regular department. When questioned further, each girl stated her reasons in slightly different words, but there was uniformity in the answers in two respects. First, the girls liked to work in the test room; "it was fun." Secondly, the new supervisory relation or, as they put it, the absence of the old supervisory control, made it possible for them to work freely without anxiety.

For instance, there was the matter of conversation. In the regular department, conversation was in principle not allowed. In practice it was tolerated if it was carried on in a low tone and did not interfere with work. In the test room an effort was made in the beginning to discourage conversation, though it was soon abandoned. The observer in charge of the experiment was afraid of losing the cooperation of the girls if he insisted too strongly on this point. Talk became common and was often loud and general. Indeed the conversation of the operators came to occupy an important place in the log. T. N. Whitehead has pointed out that the girls in the test room were far more thoroughly supervised than they ever had been in the regular department. They were watched by an observer of their own, an interested management, and outside experts. The point is that the character and purpose of the supervision were different and were felt to be so.

The operators knew that they were taking part in what was considered an important and interesting experiment. They knew that their work was expected to produce results—they were not sure what results—which would lead to the improvement of the working conditions of their fellow employees. They knew that the eyes of the company were upon them. Whitehead has further pointed out that, although the experimental changes might turn out to have no physical significance, their social significance was always favorable. They showed that the management of the company was still interested, that the girls were still part of a valuable piece of research. In the regular department, the girls, like the other employees, were in the position of responding to changes the source and purpose of which were beyond their knowledge. In the test room, they had frequent interviews with the superintendent, a high officer of the company. The reasons for the contemplated experimental changes were explained to them. Their views were consulted and in some instances they were allowed to veto what had been proposed. Professor Mayo has argued that it is idle to speak of an experimental period like Period XII as being in any sense what it purported to be—a return to the original conditions of work. In the meantime, the entire industrial situation of the girls had been reconstructed.

Another factor in what occurred can only be spoken of as the social development of the group itself. When the girls went for the first time to be given a physical examination by the company doctor, someone suggested as a joke that ice cream and cake ought to be served. The company provided them at the next examination, and the custom was kept up for the duration of the experiment. When one of the girls had a birthday, each of the others would bring her a present, and she would respond by offering the group a box of chocolates. Often one of the girls would have some good reason for feeling tired. Then the others would "carry" her. That is, they would agree to work especially fast to make up for the low output expected from her. It is doubtful whether this "carrying" did have any effect, but the important point is the existence of the practice, not its effectiveness. The girls made friends in the test room and went together socially after hours. One of the interesting facts which has appeared from Whitehead's analysis of the output records is that there were times when variations in the output rates of two friends were correlated to a high degree. Their rates varied simultaneously and in the same direction—something, of course, which the girls were not aware of and could not have planned. Also, these correlations were destroyed by such apparently trivial events as a change in the order in which the girls sat at the workbench.

Finally, the group developed leadership and a common purpose. The leader, self-appointed, was an ambitious young Italian girl who entered the test room as a replacement after two of the original members had left. She saw in the experiment a chance for personal distinction and advancement. The common purpose was an increase in the output rate. The girls had been told in the beginning and repeatedly thereafter that they were to work without straining, without trying to make a race of the test, and all the evidence shows that they kept this rule. In fact, they felt that they were working under less pressure than in the regular department. Nevertheless, they knew that the output record was considered the most important of the records of the experiment and was always closely scrutinized. Before long they had committed themselves to a continuous increase in production. In the long run, of course, this ideal was an impossible one, and when the girls found out that it was, the realization was an important element of the change of tone which was noticeable in the second half of the experiment. But for a time they felt that they could achieve the impossible. In brief, the increase in the output rate of the girls in the Relay Assembly Test Room could not be related to any changes in their physical conditions of work, whether experimentally induced or not. It could, however, be related to what can only be spoken of as the development of an organized social group in a peculiar and effective relation with its supervisors.

Many of these conclusions were not worked out in detail until long after the investigators at Hawthorne had lost interest in the Relay Assembly Test Room, but the general meaning of the experiment was clear at least as early as Period XII. A continuous increase in productivity had taken place irrespective of changing physical conditions of work. In the words of a company report made in January, 1931, on all the research which had been done up to that date:

> Upon analysis, only one thing seemed to show a continuous relationship with this improved output. This was the mental attitude of the operators. From their conversations with each other and their comments to the test observers, it was not only clear that their attitudes were improving but it was evident that this area of employee reactions and feelings was a fruitful field for industrial research.

5

General Systems Theory: Applications for Organizations and Management

Fremont E. Kast
and
James E. Rosenzweig

World War II marked the beginning of the Systems Age, although it was not until many years after the war that systems science found its way into the management literature. This article discusses applying systems theory to the real world of organizations and concludes by looking at what steps need to be taken to make general systems theory a more useful model for both organizational analysis and application by practicing managers who must function on a day-to-day basis.—Eds.

Biological and social scientists generally have embraced systems concepts. Many organization and management theorists seem anxious to identify with this movement and to contribute to the development of an approach which purports to offer the ultimate—the unification of all science into one grand conceptual model. Who possibly could resist? General systems theory seems to provide a relief from the limitations of more mechanistic approaches and a rationale for rejecting "principles" based on relatively "closed-system" thinking. This theory provides the paradigm for organization and management theorists to "crank into their systems model" all of the diverse knowledge from relevant underlying disciplines. It has become almost mandatory to have the word "system" in the title of recent articles and books (many of us have compromised and placed it only in the subtitle).[1]

SOURCE: From *Academy of Management Journal*, December, 1972, pp. 447–65. Reprinted by permission.

44

But where did it all start? This question takes us back into history and brings to mind the long-standing philosophical arguments between mechanistic and organismic models of the nineteenth and early twentieth centuries. As Deutsch says:

> Both mechanistic and organismic models were based substantially on experiences and operations known before 1850. Since then, the experience of almost a century of scientific and technological progress has so far not been utilized for any significant new model for the study of organization and in particular of human thought [12, p. 389].

General systems theory even revives the specter of the "vitalists" and their views on "life force" and most certainly brings forth renewed questions of teleological or purposeful behavior of both living and nonliving systems. Phillips and others have suggested that the philosophical roots of general systems theory go back even further, at least to the German philosopher Hegel (1770–1831) [29, p. 56]. Thus, we should recognize that in the adoption of the systems approach for the study of organizations we are not dealing with newly discovered ideas—they have a rich genealogy.

Even in the field of organization and management theory, systems views are not new. Chester Barnard used a basic systems framework.

> A cooperative system is a complex of physical, biological, personal, and social components which are in a specific systematic relationship by reason of the cooperation of two or more persons for at least one definite end. Such a system is evidently a subordinate unit of larger systems from one point of view; and itself embraces subsidiary systems—physical, biological, etc.— from another point of view. One of the systems comprised within a cooperative system, the one which is implicit in the phrase "cooperation of two or more persons;" is called an "organization" [3, p. 65].

And Barnard was influenced by the "systems views" of Vilfredo Pareto and Talcott Parsons. Certainly this quote (dressed up a bit to give the term "system" more emphasis) could be the introduction to a 1972 book on organizations.

Miller points out that Alexander Bogdanov, the Russian philosopher, developed a theory of tektology or universal organization science in 1912 which foreshadowed general systems theory and used many of the same concepts as modern systems theorists [26, p. 249–250].

However, in spite of a long history of organismic and holistic thinking, the utilization of the systems approach did not become the accepted model for organization and management writers until relatively recently. It is difficult to specify the turning point exactly. The momentum of systems thinking was identified by Scott in 1961 when he described the relationship between general systems theory and organization theory.

> The distinctive qualities of modern organization theory are its conceptual-analytical base, its reliance on empirical research data, and above all, its integrating nature. These qualities are framed in a philosophy which accepts

the premise that the only meaningful way to study organization is to study it as a system . . . Modern organization theory and general system theory are similar in that they look at organization as an integrated whole [33, pp. 15–21].

Scott said explicitly what many in our field had been thinkng and/or implying—he helped us put into perspective the important writings of Herbert Simon, James March, Talcott Parsons, George Homans, E. Wight Bakke, Kenneth Boulding, and many others.

But how far have we really advanced over the past decade in applying general systems theory to organizations and their management? Is it still a "skeleton;' or have we been able to "put some meat on the bones"? The systems approach has been touted because of its potential usefulness in understanding the complexities of "live" organizations. Has this approach really helped us in this endeavor or has it compounded confusion with chaos? Herbert Simon describes the challenge for the systems approach:

> In both science and engineering, the study of "systems" is an increasingly popular activity. Its popularity is more a response to a pressing need for synthesizing and analyzing complexity than it is to any large development of a body of knowledge and technique for dealing with complexity. If this popularity is to be more than a fad, necessity will have to mother invention and provide substance to go with the name [35, p. 114].

In this article we will explore the issue of whether we are providing substance for the term *systems approach* as it relates to the study of organizations and their management. There are many interesting historical and philosophical questions concerning the relationship between the mechanistic and organistic approaches and their applicability to the various fields of science, as well as other interesting digressions into the evolution of systems approaches. However, we will resist those temptations and plunge directly into a discussion of the key concepts of general systems theory, the way in which these ideas have been used by organization theorists, the limitations in their application, and some suggestions for the future.

KEY CONCEPTS OF GENERAL SYSTEMS THEORY

The key concepts of general systems theory have been set forth by many writers [6, 7, 13, 17, 25, 28, 39] and have been used by many organization and management theorists [10, 14, 18, 19, 21, 22, 24, 32]. It is not our purpose here to elaborate on them in great detail because we anticipate that most readers will have been exposed to them in some depth. Figure 1 provides a very brief review of those characteristics of systems which seem to have wide acceptance. The review is far from complete. It is difficult to identify a "complete" list of characteristics derived from general systems theory; moreover, it is merely a first-order classification. There are many derived second- and third-order characteristics which

FIGURE 1 Key Concepts of General Systems Theory

Subsystems or Components: A system by definition is composed of interrelated parts or elements. This is true for all systems—mechanical, biological, and social. Every system has at least two elements, and these elements are interconnected.

Holism, Synergism, Organicism, and Gestalt: The whole is not just the sum of the parts; the system itself can be explained only as a totality. Holism is the opposite of elementarism, which views the total as the sum of its individual parts.

Open Systems View: Systems can be considered in two ways: (1) closed or (2) open. Open systems exchange information, energy, or material with their environments. Biological and social systems are inherently open systems; mechanical systems may be open or closed. The concepts of open and closed systems are difficult to defend in the absolute. We prefer to think of open-closed as a dimension; that is, systems are relatively open or relatively closed.

Input-Transformation-Output Model: The open system can be viewed as a transformation model. In a dynamic relationship with its environment, it receives various inputs, transforms these inputs in some way, and exports outputs.

System Boundaries: It follows that systems have boundaries which separate them from their environments. The concept of boundaries helps us understand the distinction between open and closed systems. The relatively closed system has rigid, impenetrable boundaries; whereas the open system has permeable boundaries between itself and a broader suprasystem. Boundaries are relatively easily defined in physical and biological systems, but are very difficult to delineate in social systems, such as organizations.

Negative Entropy: Closed, physical systems are subject to the force of entropy which increases until eventually the entire system fails. The tendency toward maximum entropy is a movement to disorder, complete lack of resource transformation, and death. In a closed system, the change in entropy must always be positive; however, in open biological or social systems, entropy can be arrested and may even be transformed into negative entropy—a process of more complete organization and ability to transform resources—because the system imports resources from its environment.

Steady State, Dynamic Equilibrium, and Homeostasis: The concept of steady state is closely related to that of negative entropy. A closed system eventually must attain an equilibrium state with maximum entropy—death or disorganization. However, an open system may attain a state where the system remains in dynamic equilibrium through the continuous inflow of materials, energy, and information.

Feedback: The concept of feedback is important in understanding how a system maintains a steady state. Information concerning the outputs or the process of the system is fed back as an input into the system, perhaps leading to changes in the transformation process and/or future outputs. Feedback can be both positive and negative, although the field of cybernetics is based on negative feedback. Negative feedback is informational input which indicates that the system is deviating from a prescribed course and should readjust to a new steady state.

Hierarchy: A basic concept in systems thinking is that of hierarchical relationships between systems. A system is composed of subsystems of a lower order and is also part of a suprasystem. Thus, there is a hierarchy of the components of the system.

Internal Elaboration: Closed systems move toward entropy and disorganization. In contrast, open systems appear to move in the direction of greater differentiation, elaboration, and a higher level of organization.

Multiple Goal-Seeking: Biological and social systems appear to have multiple goals or purposes. Social organizations seek multiple goals, if for no other reason than that they are composed of individuals and subunits with different values and objectives.

Equifinality of Open Systems: In mechanistic systems there is a direct cause and effect relationship between the initial conditions and the final state. Biological and social systems operate differently. Equifinality suggests that certain results may be achieved with different initial conditions and in different ways. This view suggests that social organizations can accomplish their objectives with diverse inputs and with varying internal activities (conversion processes).

could be considered. For example, James G. Miller sets forth *165* hypotheses, stemming from open systems theory, which might be applicable to two or more levels of systems [25]. He suggests that they are *general* systems theoretical hypotheses and qualifies them by suggesting that they are propositions applicable to general systems *behavior* theory and would thus exclude nonliving systems. He does not limit these propositions to individual organisms, but considers them appropriate for social systems as well. His hypotheses are related to such issues as structure, process, subsystems, information, growth, and integration. It is obviously impossible to discuss all of these hypotheses; we want only to indicate the extent to which many interesting propositions are being posed which might have relevance to many different types of systems. It will be a very long time (if ever) before most of these hypotheses are validated; however, we are surprised at how many of them can be agreed with intuitively, and we can see their possible verification in studies of social organizations.

We turn now to a closer look at how successful or unsuccessful we have been in utilizing these concepts in the development of "modern organization theory."

A BEGINNING: ENTHUSIASTIC BUT INCOMPLETE

We have embraced general systems theory but, really, how completely? We could review a vast literature in modern organization theory which has explicitly or implicitly adopted systems theory as a frame of reference, and we have investigated in detail a few representative examples of the literature in assessing the "state of the art" [18, 19, 21, 22, 31, 38]. It was found that most of these books professed to utilize general systems theory. Indeed, in the first few chapters, many of them did an excellent job of presenting basic systems concepts and showing their relationship to organizations; however, when they moved further into the discussion of more specific subject matter, they departed substantially from systems theory. The studies appear to use a "partial systems approach" and leave for the reader the problem of integrating the various ideas into a systemic whole. It also appears that many of the authors are unable, because of limitations of knowledge about subsystem relationships, to carry out the task of using general systems theory as a conceptual basis for organization theory.

Furthermore, it is evident that each author had many "good ideas" stemming from the existing body of knowledge or current research on organizations which did not fit neatly into a "systems model." For example, they might discuss leadership from a relatively closed-system point of view and not consider it in relation to organizational technology, structure, or other variables. Our review of the literature suggests that much remains to be done in applying general systems theory to organization theory and management practice.

SOME DILEMMAS IN APPLYING GST TO ORGANIZATIONS

Why have writers embracing general systems theory as a basis for studying organizations had so much difficulty in following through? Part of
this difficulty may stem from the newness of the paradigm and our inability to operationalize "all we think we know" about this approach. Or it
may be because we know too little about the systems under investigation.
Both of these possibilities will be covered later, but first we need to look
at some of the more specific conceptual problems.

Organizations as Organisms

One of the basic contributions of general systems theory was the rejection
of the traditional closed-system or mechanistic view of social organizations. But, did general systems theory free us from this constraint only to
impose another, less obvious one? General systems theory grew out of the
organismic views of von Bertalanffy and other biologists; thus, many of
the characteristics are relevant to the living organism. It is conceptually
easy to draw the analogy between living organisms and social organizations. "There is, after all, an intuitive similarity between the organization of the human body and the kinds of organizations men create. And
so, undaunted by the failures of the human-social analogy through time,
new theorists try afresh in each epoch" [2, p. 660]. General systems theory would have us accept this analogy between organism and social organization. Yet, we have a hard time swallowing it whole. Katz and Kahn
warn us of the danger:

> There has been no more pervasive, persistent, and futile fallacy handicap-
> ping the social sciences than the use of the physical model for the under-
> standing of social structures. The biological metaphor, with its crude compar-
> isons of the physical parts of the body to the parts of the social system, has
> been replaced by more subtle but equally misleading analogies between bio-
> logical and social functioning. This figurative type of thinking ignores the
> essential difference between the socially contrived nature of social systems
> and the physical structure of the machine or the human organism. So long as
> writers are committed to a theoretical framework based upon the physical
> model, they will miss the essential social-psychological facts of the highly
> variable, loosely articulated character of social systems [19, p. 31].

In spite of this warning, Katz and Kahn do embrace much of the general
systems theory concepts which are based on the biological metaphor. We
must be very cautious about trying to make this analogy too literal. We
agree with Silverman who says, "It may, therefore, be necessary to drop
the analogy between an organization and an organism: organizations
may be systems but not necessarily natural systems" [34, p. 31].

Distinction between Organization and an Organization

General systems theory emphasizes that systems are organized—they
are composed of interdependent components in some relationship. The

social organization would then follow logically as just another system. But, we are perhaps being caught in circular thinking. It is true that all systems (physical, biological, and social) are by definition organized, but are all systems organizations? Rapoport and Horvath distinguish "organization theory" and "the theory of organizations" as follows:

> We see organization theory as dealing with general and abstract organizational principles; it applies to any system exhibiting organized complexity. As such, organization theory is seen as an extension of mathematical physics or, even more generally, of mathematics designed to deal with organized systems. The theory of organizations, on the other hand, purports to be a social science. It puts real human organizations at the center of interest. It may study the social structure of organizations and so can be viewed as a branch of sociology; it can study the behavior of individuals or groups as members of organizations and can be viewed as a part of social psychology; it can study power relations and principles of control in organizations and so fits into political science [30, pp. 74-75].

Why make an issue of this distinction? It seems to us that there is a vital matter involved. All systems may be considered to be organized, and more advanced systems may display differentiation in the activities of component parts—such as the specialization of human organs. However, all systems *do not* have purposeful entities. Can the heart or lungs be considered as purposeful entities in themselves or are they only components of the larger purposeful system, the human body? By contrast, the social organization is composed of two or more purposeful elements. "An organization consists of elements that have and can exercise their own wills" [1, p. 669]. Organisms, the foundation stone of general systems theory, do not contain purposeful elements which exercise their own will. This distinction between the organism and the social organization is of importance. In much of general systems theory, the concern is primarily with the way in which the organism responds to environmentally generated inputs. Feedback concepts and the maintenance of a steady state are based on internal adaptations to environmental forces. (This is particularly true of cybernetic models.) But, what about those changes and adaptations which occur from *within* social organizations? Purposeful elements within the social organization may initiate activities and adaptations which are difficult to subsume under feedback and steady state concepts.

Opened and Closed Systems

Another dilemma stemming from general systems theory is the tendency to dichotomize all systems as opened or closed. We have been led to think of physical systems as closed, subject to the laws of entropy, and to think of biological systems as open to their environment and, possibly, becoming negentropic. But applying this strict polarization to social organizations creates many difficulties. In fact, most social organizations and their subsystems are "partially open" and "partially closed." Open and closed are a matter of degree. Unfortunately, there seems to be a widely held view (often more implicit than explicit) that *open-system thinking is good and closed-system thinking is bad*. We have not become sufficiently sophisticated to recognize that both are appropriate under certain conditions. For example, one of the most useful conceptualizations set forth by Thompson is that the social organization *must seek* to use closed-system concepts (particularly at the technical core) to reduce uncertainty and to create more effective performance at this level.

Still Subsystems Thinking

Even though we preach a general systems approach, we often practice subsystems thinking. Each of the academic disciplines and each of us personally have limited perspective of the system we are studying. While proclaiming a broad systems viewpoint, we often dismiss variables outside our interest or competence as being irrelevant, and we only open our system to those inputs which we can handle with our disciplinary bag of tools. We are hampered because each of the academic disciplines has taken a narrow "partial systems view" and find comfort in the relative certainty which this creates. Of course, this is not a problem unique to modern organization theory. Under the more traditional process approach to the study of management, we were able to do an admirable job of delineating and discussing planning, organizing, and controlling as separate activities. We were much less successful in discussing them as integrated and interrelated activities.

How Does Our Knowledge Fit?

One of the major problems in utilizing general systems theory is that we know (or think we know) more about certain relationships than we can fit into a general systems model. For example, we are beginning to understand the two-variable relationship between technology and structure. But, when we introduce another variable, say psychosocial relationships, our models become too complex. Consequently, in order to discuss all the things we know about organizations, we depart from a systems approach. Perhaps it is because we know a great deal more about the elements or subsystems of an organization than we do about the interrelationships and interactions between these subsystems. And, general systems theory forces us to consider those relationships about which we know the least— a true dilemma. So we continue to elaborate on those aspects of the organization which we know best—a partial systems view.

Failure to Delineate a Specific System

When the social sciences embraced general systems theory, the total system became the focus of attention and terminology tended toward vagueness. In the utilization of systems theory, we should be more precise in delineating the specific system under consideration. Failure to do this leads to much confusion. As Murray suggests:

> I am wary of the word "system" because social scientists use it very frequently without specifying which of several possible different denotations they have in mind; but more particularly because, today, "system" is a highly cathected term, loaded with prestige; hence, we are all strongly tempted to employ it even when we have nothing definite in mind and its only service is to indicate that we subscribe to the general premise respecting the interdependence of things—basic to organismic theory, holism, field theory, interactionism, transactionism, etc. . . . When definitions of the units of a system are lacking, the term stands for no more than an article of faith, and is misleading to boot, insofar as it suggests a condition of affairs that may not actually exist [27, pp. 50-51].

We need to be much more precise in delineating both the boundaries of the system under consideration and the level of our analysis. There is a tendency for current writers in organization theory to accept general systems theory and then to move indiscriminately across systems boundaries and between levels of systems without being very precise (and letting their readers in on what is occurring). James Miller suggests the need for clear delineation of levels in applying systems theory, "It is important to follow one procedural rule in systems theory in order to avoid confusion. Every discussion should begin with an identification of the level of reference, and the discourse should not change to another level without a specific statement that this is occurring" [25, p. 216]. Our field is replete with these confusions about systems levels. For example, when we use the term "organizational behavior" are we talking about the way the organization behaves as a system or are we talking about the behavior of the individual participants? By goals, do we mean the goals of the organization or the goals of the individuals within the organization? In using systems theory we must become more precise in our delineation of systems boundaries and systems levels if we are to prevent confusing conceptual ambiguity.

Recognition that Organizations Are "Contrived Systems"

We have a vague uneasiness that general systems theory truly does not recognize the "contrived" nature of social organizations. With its predominate emphasis on natural organisms, it may understate some characteristics which are vital for the social organization. Social organizations do not occur naturally in nature; they are contrived by man. They have structure; but it is the structure of events rather than of physical components, and it cannot be separated from the processes of the system. The fact that social organizations are contrived by human beings suggests that they can be established for an infinite variety of purposes and do not follow the same life-cycle patterns of birth, growth, maturity, and death as biological systems. As Katz and Kahn say:

> Social structures are essentially contrived systems. They are made of men and are imperfect systems. They can come apart at the seams overnight, but they can also outlast by centuries the biological organisms which originally created them. The cement which holds them together is essentially psychological rather than biological. Social systems are anchored in the attitudes, perceptions, beliefs, motivations, habits, and expectations of human beings [19, p. 33].

Recognizing that the social organization is contrived again cautions us against making an exact analogy between it and physical or biological systems.

Questions of Systems Effectiveness

General systems theory with its biological orientation would appear to have an evolutionary view of system effectiveness. That living system which best adapts to its environment prospers and survives. The primary measure of effectiveness is perpetuation of the organism's species. Teleological behavior is therefore directed toward survival. But, is survival the only criterion of effectiveness of the social system? It is probably an essential but not all-inclusive measure of effectiveness.

General systems theory emphasizes the organism's survival goal and does not fully relate to the question of the effectiveness of the system in its supra-system—the environment. Parsonian functional-structural views provide a contrast. "The *raison d'etre* of complex organizations, according to this analysis, is mainly to benefit the society in which they belong, and that society is, therefore, the appropriate frame of reference for the evaluation of organizational effectiveness" [41, p. 896].

But, this view seems to go to the opposite extreme from the survival view of general systems theory—the organization exists to serve the society. It seems to us that the truth lies somewhere between these two viewpoints. And it is likely that a systems viewpoint (modified from the species survival view of general systems theory) will be most appropriate. Yuchtman and Seashore suggest:

> The organization's success over a period of time in this competition for resources—i.e., its bargaining position in a given environment—is regarded as an expression of its overall effectiveness. Since the resources are of various kinds, and the competitive relationships are multiple, and since there is interchangeability among classes of resources, the assessment of organizational effectiveness must be in terms not of any single criterion but of an open-ended multidimensional set of criteria [41, p. 891].

This viewpoint suggests that questions of organizational effectiveness must be concerned with at least three levels of analysis. The level of the environment, the level of the social organization as a system, and the level of the subsystems (human participants) within the organization. Perhaps much of our confusion and ambiguity concerning organizational effectiveness stems from our failure to clearly delineate the level of our analysis and, even more important, our failure really to understand the relationships among these levels.

Our discussion of some of the problems associated with the application of general systems theory to the study of social organizations might suggest that we completely reject the appropriateness of this model. On the contrary, we see the systems approach as the new paradigm for the study of organizations; but, like all new concepts in the sciences, one which has to be applied, modified, and elaborated to make it as useful as possible.

SYSTEMS THEORY PROVIDES THE NEW PARADIGM

We hope the discussion of GST and organizations provides a realistic appraisal. We do not want to promote the value of the systems approach as a matter of faith; however, we do see systems theory as vital to the study of social organizations and as providing the major new paradigm for our field of study.

Thomas Kuhn provides an interesting interpretation of the nature of scientific revolution [20]. He suggests that major changes in all fields of science occur with the development of new conceptual schemes or "paradigms." These new paradigms do not just represent a step-by-step advancement in "normal" science (the science generally accepted and practiced) but, rather, a revolutionary change in the way the scientific field is perceived by the practitioners. Kuhn says:

> The historian of science may be tempted to exclaim that when paradigms change, the world itself changes with them. Led by a new paradigm, scientists adopt new instruments and look in new places. Even more important, during revolutions scientists see new and different things when looking with familiar instruments in places they have looked before. It is rather as if the professional community has been suddenly transported to another planet where familiar objects are seen in a different light and are joined by unfamiliar ones as well. . . . Paradigm changes do cause scientists to see the world of their research-engagement differently. Insofar as their only recourse to that world is through what they see and do, we may want to say that after a revolution scientists are responding to a different world [20, p110].

New paradigms frequently are rejected by the scientific community. (At first they may seem crude and limited—offering very little more than older paradigms.) They frequently lack the apparent sophistication of the older paradigms which they ultimately replace. They do not display the clarity and certainty of older paradigms which have been refined through years of research and writing. But, a new paradigm does provide for a "new start" and opens up new directions which were not possible under the old. "We must recognize how very limited in both scope and precision a paradigm can be at the time of its first appearance. Paradigms gain their status because they are more successful than their competitors in solving a few problems that the group of practitioners has come to recognize as acute. To be more successful is not, however, to be either completely successful with a single problem or notably successful with any large number" [20, p. 23].

Systems theory does provide a new paradigm for the study of social organizations and their management. At this stage it is obviously crude and lacking in precision. In some ways it may not be much better than older paradigms which have been accepted and used for a long time (such as the management process approach). As in other fields of scientific endeavor, the new paradigm must be applied, clarified, elaborated, and made more precise. But, it does provide a fundamentally different view of the reality of social organizations and can serve as the basis for major advancements in our field.

We see many exciting examples of the utilization of the new systems paradigm in the field of organization and management. Several of these have been referred to earlier [7, 13, 19, 21, 22, 24, 31, 38], and there have been many others. Burns and Stalker made substantial use of systems views in setting forth their concepts of mechanistic and organic managerial systems [8]. Their studies of the characteristics of these two organization types lack precise definition of the variables and relationships, but their colleagues have used the systems approach to look at the relationship of organizations to their environment and also among the technical, structural, and behavioral characteristics within the organization [24]. Chamberlain used a system view in studying enterprises and their environment, which is substantially different from traditional microeconomics [9]. The emerging field of "environmental sciences" and "environmental administration" has found the systems paradigm vital.

Thus, the systems theory paradigm is being used extensively in the investigation of relationships between subsystems within organizations and in studying the environmental interfaces. But, it still has not advanced sufficiently to meet the needs. One of the major problems is that the practical need to deal with comprehensive systems of relationships is overrunning our ability to fully understand and predict these relationships. *We vitally need the systems paradigm but we are not sufficiently sophisticated to use it appropriately.* This is the dilemma. Do our current failures to fully utilize the systems paradigm suggest that we reject it and return to the older, more traditional, and time-tested paradigms? Or do we work with systems theory to make it more precise, to understand the relationships among subsystems, and to gather the informational inputs which are necessary to make the systems approach really work? We think the latter course offers the best opportunity.

Thus, we prefer to accept current limitations of systems theory, while working to reduce them and to develop more complete and sophisticated approaches for its application. We agree with Rapoport who says:

The system approach to the study of man can be appreciated as an effort to restore meaning (in terms of intuitively grasped understanding of wholes) while adhering to the principles of *disciplined* generalizations and rigorous deduction. It is, in short, an attempt to make the study of man both scientific and meaningful [7, p. xxii].

We are sympathetic with the second part of Rapoport's comment, the need to apply the systems approach but to make disciplined generalizations and rigorous deductions. This is a vital necessity and yet a major current limitation. We do have some indication that progress (although very slow) is being made.

WHAT DO WE NEED NOW?

Everything is related to everything else—but how? General systems theory provides us with the macro paradigm for the study of social organizations. As Scott and others have pointed out, most sciences go through a macro-micro-macro cycle or sequence of emphasis [33]. Traditional bureaucratic theory provided the first major macro view of organizations. Administrative management theorists concentrated on the development of macro "principles of management" which were applicable to all organizations. When these macro views seemed incomplete (unable to explain important phenomena), attention turned to the micro level—more detailed analysis of components or parts of the organization, thus the interest in human relations, technology, or structural dimensions.

The systems approach returns us to the macro level with a new paradigm. General systems theory emphasizes a very high level of abstraction. Phillips classifies it as a third-order study [29] that attempts to develop macro concepts appropriate for all types of biological, physical, and social systems.

In our view, we are now ready to move down a level of abstraction to consider second-order systems studies or midrange concepts. These will be based on general systems theory but will be more concrete and will emphasize more specific characteristics and relationships in social organizations. They will operate within the broad paradigm of systems theory but at a less abstract level.

What should we call this new midrange level of analysis? Various authors have referred to it as a "contingency view," a study of "patterns of relationships," or a search for "configurations among subsystems." Lorsch and Lawrence reflect this view:

During the past few years there has been evident a new trend in the study of organizational phenomena. Underlying this new approach is the idea that the internal functioning of organizations must be consistent with the demands of the organization task, technology, or external environment, and the needs of its members if the organization is to be effective. Rather than searching for the panacea of the one best way to organize under all conditions, investigators have more and more tended to examine the functioning of organizations in relation to the needs of their particular members and the external pressures facing them. Basically, this approach seems to be leading to the development of a "contingency" theory of organization with the appropriate internal states and processes of the organization contingent upon external requirements and member needs [21, p. 1].

Numerous others have stressed a similar viewpoint. Thompson suggests that the essence of administration lies in understanding basic configurations which exist between the various subsystems and with the environment. "The basic function of administration appears to be co-alignment, not merely of people (in coalitions) but of institutionalized action—of technology and task environment into a viable domain, and of organizational design and structure appropriate to it [38, p. 157].

Bringing these ideas together we can provide a more precise definition of the contingency view:

> The contingency view of organizations and their management suggests that an organization is a system composed of subsystems and delineated by identifiable boundaries from its environmental suprasystem. The contingency view seeks to understand the interrelationships within and among subsystems as well as between the organization and its environment and to define patterns of relationships or configurations of variables. It emphasizes the multivariate nature of organizations and attempts to understand how organizations operate under varying conditions and in specific circumstances. Contingency views are ultimately directed toward suggesting organizational designs and managerial systems most appropriate for specific situations.

But, it is not enough to suggest that a "contingency view" based on systems concepts of organizations and their management is more appropriate than the simplistic "principles approach." If organization theory is to advance and make contributions to managerial practice, it must define more explicitly certain patterns of relationships between organizational variables. This is the major challenge facing our field.

Just how do we go about using systems theory to develop these midrange or contingency views? We see no alternative but to engage in intensive comparative investigation of many organizations following the advice of Blau:

> A theory of organization, whatever its specific nature, and regardless of how subtle the organizational processes it takes into account, has as its central aim to establish the constellations of characteristics that develop in organizations of various kinds. Comparative studies of many organizations are necessary, not alone to test the hypotheses implied by such a theory, but also to provide a basis for initial exploration and refinement of the theory by indicating the conditions on which relationships, originally assumed to hold universally are contingent. . . . Systematic research on many organizations that provides the data needed to determine the interrelationships between several organizational features is, however, extremely rare [5, p. 332].

FIGURE 2 Matrix of Patterns of Relationships between Organization Types and Systems Variables

Organizational Supra- and Subsystems	Continuum of Organization Types	
	Closed/Stable/ Mechanistic	Open/Adaptive/ Organic
Environmental relationships		
General nature	Placid	Turbulent
Predictability	Certain, determinate	Uncertain, indeterminate
Boundary relationships	Relatively closed; limited to few participants (sales, purchasing, etc.); fixed and well-defined	Relatively open; many participants have external relationships; varied and not clearly defined
Goals and values		
Organizational goals in general	Efficient performance, stability, maintenance	Effective problem-solving, innovation, growth
Goal set	Single, clear-cut	Multiple, determined by necessity to satisfy a set of constraints
Stability	Stable	Unstable
Technical		
Structural		
Psychosocial		
Managerial		

Various conceptual designs for the comparative study of organizations and their subsystems are emerging to help in the development of a contingency view. We do not want to impose our model as to what should be considered in looking for these patterns of relationships. However, the tentative matrix shown in Figure 2 suggests this approach. We have used as a starting point the two polar organization types which have been emphasized in the literature—closed/stable/mechanistic and open/adaptive/organic.

We will consider the environment suprasystem and organizational subsystems (goals and values, technical, structural, psychosocial, and managerial) plus various dimensions or characteristics of each of these systems. By way of illustration we have indicated several specific subcategories under the Environmental Suprasystem as well as the Goals and Values subsystem. This process would have to be completed and extended to all of the subsystems. The next step would be the development of appropriate descriptive language (based on research and conceptualization) for each relevant characteristic across the continuum of organization types. For example, on the "stability" dimension for Goals and Values we would have High, Medium, and Low at appropriate places on the continuum. If the entire matrix were filled in, it is likely that we would begin to see discernible patterns of relationships among subsystems.

We do not expect this matrix to provide *the* midrange model for everyone. It is highly doubtful that we will be able to follow through with the field work investigations necessary to fill in all the squares. Nevertheless, it does illustrate a possible approach for the translation of more abstract general systems theory into an appropriate midrange model which is relevant for organization theory and management practice. Frankly, we see this as a major long-term effort on the part of many researchers, investigating a wide variety of organizations. In spite of the difficulties involved in such research, the endeavor has practical significance. Sophistication in the study of organizations will come when we have a more complete understanding of organizations as total systems (configurations of subsystems) so that we can prescribe more appropriate organizational designs and managerial systems. Ultimately, organization theory should serve as the foundation for more effective management practice.

APPLICATION OF SYSTEMS CONCEPTS TO MANAGEMENT PRACTICE

The study of organizations is an applied science because the resulting knowledge is relevant to problem-solving in on-going institutions. Contributions to organization theory come from many sources. Deductive and inductive research in a variety of disciplines provide a theoretical base of propositions which are useful for understanding organizations and for managing them. Experience gained in management practice is also an important input to organization theory. In short, management is based on the body of knowledge generated by practical experience *and* eclectic scientific research concerning organizations. The body of knowledge developed through theory and research should be translatable into more effective organizational design and managerial practices.

Do systems concepts and contingency views provide a panacea for solving problems in organizations? The answer is an emphatic *no*; this approach does not provide "ten easy steps" to success in management. Such cookbook approaches, while seemingly applicable and easy to grasp, are usually shortsighted, narrow in perspective, and superficial—in short, unrealistic. Fundamental ideas, such as systems concepts and contingency views, are more difficult to comprehend. However, they facilitate more thorough understanding of complex situations and increase the likelihood of appropriate action.

It is important to recognize that many managers have used and will continue to use a systems approach and contingency views intuitively and implicitly. Without much knowledge of the underlying body of organization theory, they have an intuitive "sense of the situation," are flexible diagnosticians, and adjust their actions and decisions accordingly. Thus, systems concepts and contingency views are not new. However, if this approach to organization theory and management practice can be made more explicit, we can facilitate better management and more effective organizations.

Practicing managers in business firms, hospitals, and government agencies continue to function on a day-to-day basis. Therefore, they must use whatever theory is available, they cannot wait for the *ultimate* body of knowledge (there is none!). Practitioners should be included in the search for new knowledge because they control access to an essential ingredient—organizational data—and they are the ones who ultimately put the theory to the test. Mutual understanding among managers, teachers, and researchers will facilitate the development of a relevant body of knowledge.

Simultaneously with the refinement of the body of knowledge, a concerted effort should be directed toward applying what we do know. We need ways of making systems and contingency views more usable. Without oversimplification, we need some relevant guidelines for practicing managers.

The general tenor of the contingency view is somewhere between simplistic, specific principles and complex, vague notions. It is a mid-range concept which recognizes the complexity involved in managing modern organizations but uses patterns of relationships and/or configurations of subsystems in order to facilitate improved practice. The art of management depends on a reasonable success rate for actions in a probabilistic environment. Our hope is that systems concepts and contingency views, while continually being refined by scientists/researchers/theorists, will also be made more applicable.

NOTES

1. An entire article could be devoted to a discussion of ingenious ways in which the term "systems approach" has been used in the literature pertinent to organization theory and management practice.

REFERENCES

1. Ackoff, Russell L., "Towards a System of Systems Concepts," *Management Science* (July 1971).

2. Back, Kurt W., "Biological Models of Social Change," *American Sociological Review* (August 1971).

3. Barnard, Chester I., *The Functions of the Executive* (Cambridge, Mass.: Harvard University Press, 1938).

4. Berrien, F. Kenneth, *General and Social Systems* (New Brunswick, N.J.: Rutgers University Press, 1968).

5. Blau, Peter M., "The Comparative Study of Organizations," *Industrial and Labor Relations Review* (April 1965).

6. Boulding, Kenneth E., "General Systems Theory: The Skeleton of Science," *Management Science* (April 1956).

7. Buckley, Walter, ed., *Modern Systems Research for the Behavioral Scientist* (Chicago: Aldine Publishing Company, 1968).

8. Burns, Tom and G. M. Stalker, *The Management of Innovation* (London: Tavistock Publications, 1961).

9. Chamberlain, Neil W., *Enterprise and Environment: The Firm in Time and Place* (New York: McGraw-Hill Book Company, 1968).

10. Churchman, C. West, *The Systems Approach* (New York: Dell Publishing Company, Inc., 1968).

11. DeGreene, Kenyon, ed., *Systems Psychology* (New York: McGraw-Hill Book Company, 1970).

12. Deutsch, Karl W., "Toward a Cybernetic Model of Man and Society," in Walter Buckley, ed., *Modern Systems Research for the Behavioral Scientist* (Chicago: Aldine Publishing Company, 1968).

13. Easton, David, *A Systems Analysis of Political Life* (New York: John Wiley & Sons, Inc., 1965).

14. Emery, F. E. and E. L. Trist, "Socio-technical Systems," in C. West Churchman and Michele Verhulst, eds., *Management Sciences: Models and Techniques* (New York: Pergamon Press, 1960).

15. Emshoff, James R., *Analysis of Behavioral Systems* (New York: The Macmillan Company, 1971).

16. Gross, Bertram M., "The Coming General Systems Models of Social Systems," *Human Relations* (November 1967).

17. Hall, A. D. and R. E. Eagen, "Definition of System," *General Systems, Yearbook for the Society for the Advancement of General Systems Theory*, Vol 1 (1956).

18. Kast, Fremont E. and James E. Rosenzweig, *Organization and Management Theory: A Systems Approach* (New York: McGraw-Hill Book Company, 1970).

19. Katz, Daniel and Robert L. Kahn, *The Social Psychology of Organizations* (New York: John Wiley & Sons, Inc., 1966).

20. Kuhn, Thomas S., *The Structure of Scientific Revolutions* (Chicago: University of Chicago Press, 1962).

21. Litterer, Joseph A., *Organizations: Structure and Behavior*, Vol 1 (New York: John Wiley & Sons, Inc., 1969)

22. ——, *Organizations: Systems, Control and Adaptation*, Vol 2 (New York: John Wiley & Sons, Inc., 1969).

23. Lorsch, Jay W. and Paul R. Lawrence, *Studies in Organizational Design* (Homewood, Illinois: Irwin-Dorsey, 1970).

24. Miller, E. J. and A. K. Rice, *Systems of Organizations* (London: Tavistock Publications, 1967).

25. Miller, James G., "Living Systems: Basic Concepts," *Behavioral Science* (July 1965).

26. Miller, Robert F., "The New Science of Administration in the USSR," *Administrative Science Quarterly* (September 1971).

27. Murray, Henry A., "Preparation for the Scaffold of a Comprehensive System," in Sigmund Koch, ed., *Psychology: A Study of a Science,* Vol 3 (New York: McGraw-Hill Book Company, 1959).

28. Parsons, Talcott, *The Social System* (New York: The Free Press of Glencoe, 1951).

29. Phillips, D. C., "Systems Theory—A Discredited Philosophy," in Peter P. Schoderbek, *Management Systems* (New York: John Wiley & Sons, Inc., 1971).

30. Rapoport, Anatol and William J. Horvath, "Thoughts on Organization Theory," in Walter Buckley, ed., *Modern Systems Research for the Behavioral Scientist* (Chicago: Aldine Publishing Company, 1968).

31. Rice, A. K., *The Modern University* (London: Tavistock Publications, 1970).

32. Schein, Edgar, *Organizational Psychology,* rev. ed. (Englewood Cliffs, New Jersey: Prentice-Hall, Inc., 1970).

33. Scott, William G., "Organization Theory: An Overview and an Appraisal," *Academy of Management Journal* (April 1961).

34. Silverman, David, *The Theory of Organizations* (New York: Basic Books Inc., 1971).

35. Simon, Herbert A., "The Architecture of Complexity," in Joseph A. Litterer, *Organizations: Systems, Control and Adaptation,* Vol 2 (New York: John Wiley & Sons, Inc., 1969).

36. Springer, Michael, "Social Indicators, Reports, and Accounts: Toward the Management of Society," *The Annals of the American Academy of Political and Social Science* (March 1970).

37. Terreberry, Shirley, "The Evolution of Organizational Environments," *Administrative Science Quarterly* (March 1968).

38. Thompson, James D., *Organizations in Action* (New York: McGraw-Hill Book Company, 1967).

39. von Bertalanffy, Ludwig, *General System Theory* (New York: George Braziller, 1968).

40. ——, "The Theory of Open Systems in Physics and Biology," *Science* (January 13, 1950).

41. Yuchtman, Ephraim and Stanley E. Seashore, "A System Resource Approach to Organizational Effectiveness," *American Sociological Review* (December 1967).

6

The Manager's Job: Folklore and Fact

Henry Mintzberg

The most recent classic included in this collection, Mintzberg's article explores the popular notion that a manager's time is spent planning, organizing, controlling, and directing. He argues that instead, managerial time is spent in a variety of roles—most of which are a far cry from the usual perception of the job. Note that he argues for better training of managers by our business schools.—Eds.

If you ask a manager what he does, he will most likely tell you that he plans, organizes, coordinates, and controls. Then watch what he does. Don't be surprised if you can't relate what you see to these four words.

When he is called and told that one of his factories has just burned down, and he advises the caller to see whether temporary arrangements can be made to supply customers through a foreign subsidiary, is he planning, organizing, coordinating, or controlling? How about when he presents a gold watch to a retiring employee? Or when he attends a conference to meet people in the trade? Or on returning from that conference, when he tells one of his employees about an interesting product idea he picked up there?

The fact is that these four words, which have dominated management vocabulary since the French industrialist Henri Fayol first introduced them in 1916, tell us little about what managers actually do. At best, they indicate some vague objectives managers have when they work.

SOURCE: Reprinted by permission of the *Harvard Business Review*. "The Manager's Job: Folklore and Fact" by Henry Mintzberg (July-August 1975). Copyright © 1975 by the President and Fellows of Harvard College; all rights reserved.

The field of management, so devoted to progress and change, has for more than half a century not seriously addressed *the* basic question: What do managers do? Without a proper answer, how can we teach management? How can we design planning or information systems for managers? How can we improve the practice of management at all?

Our ignorance of the nature of managerial work shows up in various ways in the modern organization—in the boast by the successful manager that he never spent a single day in a management training program; in the turnover of corporate planners who never quite understood what it was the manager wanted; in the computer consoles gathering dust in the back room because the managers never used the fancy on-line MIS some analyst thought they needed. Perhaps most important, our ignorance shows up in the inability of our large public organizations to come to grips with some of their most serious policy problems.

Somehow, in the rush to automate production, to use management science in the functional areas of marketing and finance, and to apply the skills of the behavioral scientist to the problem of worker motivation, the manager—that person in charge of the organization or one of its subunits—has been forgotten.

My intention in this article is simple: to break the reader away from Fayol's words and introduce him to a more supportable, and what I believe to be a more useful, description of managerial work. This description derives from my review and synthesis of the available research on how various managers have spent their time.

In some studies, managers were observed intensively ("shadowed" is the term some of them used); in a number of others, they kept detailed diaries of their activities; in a few studies, their records were analyzed. All kinds of managers were studied—foremen, factory supervisors, staff managers, field sales managers, hospital administrators, presidents of companies and nations, and even street gang leaders. These "managers" worked in the United States, Canada, Sweden, and Great Britain. The insert [on the next page] is a brief review of the major studies that I found most useful in developing this description, including my own study of five American chief executive officers.

A synthesis of these findings paints an interesting picture, one as different from Fayol's classical view as a cubist abstract is from a Renaissance painting. In a sense, this picture will be obvious to anyone who has ever spent a day in a manager's office, either in front of the desk or behind it. Yet, at the same time, this picture may turn out to be revolutionary, in that it throws into doubt so much of the folklore that we have accepted about the manager's work.

I first discuss some of the folklore and contrast it with some of the discoveries of systematic research—the hard facts about how managers spend their time. Then I synthesize these research findings in a description of ten roles that seem to describe the essential content of all managers' jobs. In a concluding section, I discuss a number of implications of

Considering its central importance to every aspect of management, there has been surprisingly little research on the manager's work, and virtually no systematic building of knowledge from one group of studies to another. In seeking to describe managerial work, I conducted my own research and also scanned the literature widely to integrate the findings of studies from many diverse sources with my own. These studies focused on two very different aspects of managerial work. Some were concerned with the characteristics of the work—how long managers work, where, at what pace and with what interruptions, with whom they work, and through what media they communicate. Other studies were more concerned with the essential content of the work—what activities the managers actually carry out, and why. Thus, after a meeting, one researcher might note that the manager spent 45 minutes with three government officials in their Washington office, while another might record that he presented his company's stand on some proposed legislation in order to change a regulation. A few of the studies of managerial work are widely known, but most have remained buried as single journal articles or isolated books. Among the more important ones I cite (with full references in the footnotes) are the following:

□

Sune Carlson developed the diary method to study the work characteristics of nine Swedish managing directors. Each kept a detailed log of his activities. Carlson's results are reported in his book *Executive Behavior*. A number of British researchers, notably Rosemary Stewart, have subsequently used Carlson's method. In *Managers and Their Jobs*, she describes the study of 160 top and middle managers of British companies during four weeks, with particular attention to the differences in their work.

□

Leonard Sayles's book *Managerial Behavior* is another important reference. Using a method he refers to as "anthropological," Sayles studied the work content of middle- and lower-level managers in a large U.S. corporation. Sayles moved freely in the company, collecting whatever information struck him as important.

□

Perhaps the best-known source is *Presidential Power*, in which Richard Neustadt analyzes the power and managerial behavior of Presidents Roosevelt, Truman, and Eisenhower. Neustadt used secondary sources—documents and interviews with other parties—to generate his data.

□

Robert H. Guest, in *Personnel*, reports on a study of the foreman's working day. Fifty-six U.S. foremen were observed and each of their activities recorded during one eight-hour shift.

□

Richard C. Hodgson, Daniel J. Levinson, and Abraham Zaleznik studied a team of three top executives of a U.S. hospital. From that study they wrote *The Executive Role Constellation*. These researchers addressed in particular the way in which work and socio-emotional roles were divided among the three managers.

□

William F. Whyte, from his study of a street gang during the Depression, wrote *Street Corner Society*. His findings about the gang's leadership, which George C. Homans analyzed in *The Human Group*, suggest some interesting similarities of job content between street gang leaders and corporate managers.

□

My own study involved five American CEOs of middle- to large-size organizations—a consulting firm, a technology company, a hospital, a consumer goods company, and a school system. Using a method called "structural observation," during one intensive week of observation for each executive I recorded various aspects of every piece of mail and every verbal contact. My method was designed to capture data on both work characteristics and job content. In all, I analyzed 890 pieces of incoming and outgoing mail and 368 verbal contacts.

this synthesis for those trying to achieve more effective management, both in classrooms and in the business world.

SOME FOLKLORE AND FACTS ABOUT MANAGERIAL WORK

There are four myths about the manager's job that do not bear up under careful scrutiny of the facts.

1

Folklore: The manager is a reflective, systematic planner. The evidence on this issue is overwhelming, but not a shred of it supports this statement.

Fact: Study after study has shown that managers work at an unrelenting pace, that their activities are characterized by brevity, variety, and discontinuity, and that they are strongly oriented to action and dislike reflective activities. Consider this evidence:

Half the activities engaged in by the five chief executives of my study lasted less than nine minutes, and only 10% exceeded one hour.[1] A study of 56 U.S. foremen found that they averaged 583 activities per eight-hour shift, an average of 1 every 48 seconds.[2] The work pace for both chief executives and foremen was unrelenting. The chief executives met a steady stream of callers and mail from the moment they arrived in the morning until they left in the evening. Coffee breaks and lunches were inevitably work related, and ever-present subordinates seemed to usurp any free moment.

A diary study of 160 British middle and top managers found that they worked for a half hour or more without interruption only about once every two days.[3]

Of the verbal contacts of the chief executives in my study, 93% were arranged on an ad hoc basis. Only 1% of the executives' time was spent in open-ended observational tours. Only 1 out of 368 verbal contacts was unrelated to a specific issue and could be called general planning. Another researcher finds that "in *not one single case* did a manager report the obtaining of important external information from a general conversation or other undirected personal communication."[4]

No study has found important patterns in the way managers schedule their time. They seem to jump from issue to issue, continually responding to the needs of the moment.

Is this the planner that the classical view describes? Hardly. How, then, can we explain this behavior? The manager is simply responding to the pressures of his job. I found that my chief executives terminated many of their own activities, often leaving meetings before the end, and interrupted their desk work to call in subordinates. One president not only placed his desk so that he could look down a long hallway but also left his door open when he was alone—an invitation for subordinates to come in and interrupt him.

Clearly, these managers wanted to encourage the flow of current information. But more significantly, they seemed to be conditioned by their own work loads. They appreciated the opportunity cost of their own time, and they were continually aware of their ever-present obligations— mail to be answered, callers to attend to, and so on. It seems that no matter what he is doing, the manager is plagued by the possibilities of what he might do and what he must do.

When the manager must plan, he seems to do so implicitly in the context of daily actions, not in some abstract process reserved for two weeks in the organization's mountain retreat. The plans of the chief executives I studied seemed to exist only in their heads—as flexible, but often specific, intentions. The traditional literature notwithstanding, the job of managing does not breed reflective planners; the manager is a real-time responder to stimuli, an individual who is conditioned by his job to prefer live to delayed action.

2

Folklore: The effective manager has no regular duties to perform. Managers are constantly being told to spend more time planning and delegating, and less time seeing customers and engaging in negotiations. These are not, after all, the true tasks of the manager. To use the popular analogy, the good manager, like the good conductor, carefully orchestrates everything in advance, then sits back to enjoy the fruits of his labor, responding occasionally to an unforeseeable exception.

But here again the pleasant abstraction just does not seem to hold up. We had better take a closer look at those activities managers feel compelled to engage in before we arbitrarily define them away.

Fact: In addition to handling exceptions, managerial work involves performing a number of regular duties, including ritual and ceremony, negotiations, and processing of soft information that links the organization with its environment. Consider some evidence from the research studies:

A study of the work of the presidents of small companies found that they engaged in routine activities because their companies could not afford staff specialists and were so thin on operating personnel that a single absence often required the president to substitute.[5]

One study of field sales managers and another of chief executives suggest that it is a natural part of both jobs to see important customers, assuming the managers wish to keep those customers.[6]

Someone, only half in jest, once described the manager as that person who sees visitors so that everyone else can get his work done. In my study, I found that certain ceremonial duties—meeting visiting dignitaries, giving out gold watches, presiding at Christmas dinners—were an intrinsic part of the chief executive's job.

Studies of managers' information flow suggest that managers play a key role in securing "soft" external information (much of it available only to them because of their status) and in passing it along to their subordinates.

3

Folklore: The senior manager needs aggregated information, which a formal management information system best provides. Not too long ago, the words *total information system* were everywhere in the management literature. In keeping with the classical view of the manager as that individual perched on the apex of a regulated, hierarchical system, the literature's manager was to receive all his important information from a giant, comprehensive MIS.

But lately, as it has become increasingly evident that these giant MIS systems are not working—that managers are simply not using them—the enthusiasm has waned. A look at how managers actually process information makes the reason quite clear. Managers have five media at their command—documents, telephone calls, scheduled and unscheduled meetings, and observational tours.

Fact: Managers strongly favor the verbal media—namely, telephone calls and meetings. The evidence comes from every single study of managerial work. Consider the following:

In two British studies, managers spent an average of 66% and 80% of their time in verbal (oral) communication.[7] In my study of five American chief executives, the figure was 78%.

These five chief executives treated mail processing as a burden to be dispensed with. One came in Saturday morning to process 142 pieces of mail in just over three hours, to "get rid of all the stuff." This same manager looked at the first piece of "hard" mail he had received all week, a standard cost report, and put it aside with the comment, "I never look at this."

These same five chief executives responded immediately to 2 of the 40 routine reports they received during the five weeks of my study and to 4 items in the 104 periodicals. They skimmed most of these periodicals in seconds, almost ritualistically. In all, these chief executives of good-sized organizations initiated on their own—that is, not in response to something else—a grand total of 25 pieces of mail during the 25 days I observed them.

An analysis of the mail the executives received reveals an interesting picture—only 13% was of specific and immediate use. So now we have another piece in the puzzle: not much of the mail provides live, current information—the action of a competitor, the mood of a government legislator, or the rating of last night's television show. Yet this is the information that drove the managers, interrupting their meetings and rescheduling their workdays.

Consider another interesting finding. Managers seem to cherish "soft" information, especially gossip, hearsay, and speculation. Why? The reason is its timeliness; today's gossip may be tomorrow's fact. The manager who is not accessible for the telephone call imforming him that his biggest customer was seen golfing with his main competitor may read about a dramatic drop in sales in the next quarterly report. But then it's too late.

To assess the value of historical, aggregated, "hard" MIS information, consider two of the manager's prime uses for his information—to identify problems and opportunities[8] and to build his own mental models of the things around him (e.g., how his organization's budget system works, how his customers buy his product, how changes in the economy affect his organization, and so on). Every bit of evidence suggests that the manager identifies decision situations and builds models not with the aggregated abstractions an MIS provides, but with specific tidbits of data.

Consider the words of Richard Neustadt, who studied the information-collecting habits of Presidents Roosevelt, Truman, and Eisenhower:

> It is not information of a general sort that helps a President see personal stakes; not summaries, not surveys, not the *bland amalgams*. Rather . . . it is the odds and ends of *tangible detail* that pieced together in his mind illuminate the underside of issues put before him. To help himself he must reach out as widely as he can for every scrap of fact, opinion, gossip, bearing on his interests and relationships as President. He must become his own director of his own central intelligence.[9]

The manager's emphasis on the verbal media raises two important points:

First, verbal information is stored in the brains of people. Only when people write this information down can it be stored in the files of the organization—whether in metal cabinets or on magnetic tape—and managers apparently do not write down much of what they hear. Thus the strategic data bank of the organization is not in the memory of its computers but in the minds of its managers.

Second, the manager's extensive use of verbal media helps to explain why he is reluctant to delegate tasks. When we note that most of the manager's important information comes in verbal form and is stored in his head, we can well appreciate his reluctance. It is not as if he can hand a dossier over to someone; he must take the time to "dump memory"—to tell that someone all he knows about the subject. But this could take so long that the manager may find it easier to do the task himself. Thus the manager is damned by his own information system to a "dilemma of delegation"—to do too much himself or to delegate to his subordinates with inadequate briefing.

4

Folklore: Management is, or at least is quickly becoming, a science and a profession. By almost any definitions of science and profession, this statement is false. Brief observation of any manager will quickly lay to rest the notion that managers practice a science. A science involves the enaction of systematic, analytically determined procedures or programs. If we do not even know what procedures managers use, how can we prescribe them by scientific analysis? And how can we call management a profession if we cannot specify what managers are to learn? For after all, a profession involves "knowledge of some department of learning or science" *(Random House Dictionary).*[10]

Fact: The Managers' programs—to schedule time, process information, make decisions, and so on—remain locked deep inside their brains. Thus, to describe these programs, we rely on words like *judgment* and *intuition,* seldom stopping to realize that they are merely labels for our ignorance.

I was struck during my study by the fact that the executives I was observing—all very competent by any standard—are fundamentally indistinguishable from their counterparts of a hundred years ago (or a thousand years ago, for that matter). The information they need differs, but they seek it in the same way—by word of mouth. Their decisions concern modern technology, but the procedures they use to make them are the same as the procedures of the nineteenth-century manager. Even the computer, so important for the specialized work of the organization, has apparently had no influence on the work procedures of general managers. In fact, the manager is in a kind of loop, with increasingly heavy work pressures but no aid forthcoming from management science.

Considering the facts about managerial work, we can see that the manager's job is enormously complicated and difficult. The manager is overburdened with obligations; yet he cannot easily delegate his tasks. As a result, he is driven to overwork and is forced to do many tasks superficially. Brevity, fragmentation, and verbal communication characterize his work. Yet these are the very characteristics of managerial work that have impeded scientific attempts to improve it. As a result, the management scientist has concentrated his efforts on the specialized functions of the organization, where he could more easily analyze the procedures and quantify the relevant information.[11]

But the pressures of the manager's job are becoming worse. Where before he needed only to respond to owners and directors, now he finds that subordinates with democratic norms continually reduce his freedom to issue unexplained orders, and a growing number of outside influences (consumer groups, government agencies, and so on) expect his attention. And the manager has had nowhere to turn for help. The first step in providing the manager with some help is to find out what his job really is.

BACK TO A BASIC DESCRIPTION OF
MANAGERIAL WORK

Now let us try to put some of the pieces of this puzzle together. Earlier, I defined the manager as that person in charge of an organization or one of its subunits. Besides chief executive officers, this definition would include vice presidents, bishops, foremen, hockey coaches, and prime ministers. Can all of these people have anything in common? Indeed they can. For an important starting point, all are vested with formal authority over an organizational unit. From formal authority comes status, which leads to various interpersonal relations, and from these comes access to information. Information, in turn, enables the manager to make decisions and strategies for his unit.

The manager's job can be described in terms of various "roles," or organized sets of behaviors identified with a position. My description, shown in Exhibit 1, comprises ten roles. As we shall see, formal authority gives rise to the three interpersonal roles, which in turn give rise to the three informational roles; these two sets of roles enable the manager to play the four decisional roles.

Exhibit 1 The Manager's Roles

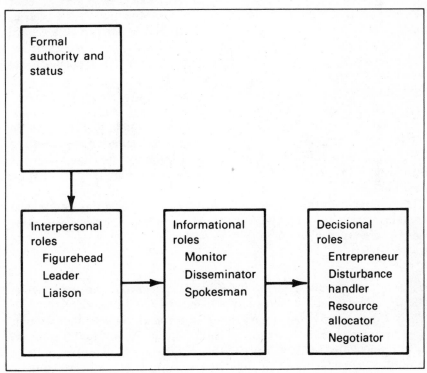

Interpersonal Roles

Three of the manager's roles arise directly from his formal authority and involve basic interpersonal relationships.

1

First is the *figurehead* role. By virtue of his position as head of an organizational unit, every manager must perform some duties of a ceremonial nature. The president greets the touring dignitaries, the foreman attends the wedding of a lathe operator, and the sales manager takes an important customer to lunch.

The chief executives of my study spent 12% of their contact time on ceremonial duties; 17% of their incoming mail dealt with acknowledgments and requests related to their status. For example, a letter to a company president requested free merchandise for a crippled schoolchild; diplomas were put on the desk of the school superintendent for his signature.

Duties that involve interpersonal roles may sometimes be routine, involving little serious communication and no important decision making. Nevertheless, they are important to the smooth functioning of an organization and cannot be ignored by the manager.

2

Because he is in charge of an organizational unit, the manager is responsible for the work of the people of that unit. His actions in this regard constitute the *leader* role. Some of these actions involve leadership directly—for example, in most organizations the manager is normally responsible for hiring and training his own staff.

In addition, there is the indirect exercise of the leader role. Every manager must motivate and encourage his employees, somehow reconciling their individual needs with the goals of the organization. In virtually every contact the manager has with his employees, subordinates seeking leadership clues probe his actions: "Does he approve?" "How would he like the report to turn out?" "Is he more interested in market share than high profits?"

The influence of the manager is most clearly seen in the leader role. Formal authority vests him with great potential power; leadership determines in large part how much of it he will realize.

3

The literature of management has always recognized the leader role, particularly those aspects of it related to motivation. In comparison, until recently it has hardly mentioned the *liaison* role, in which the manager makes contacts outside his vertical chain of command. This is remarkable in light of the finding of virtually every study of managerial work that managers spend as much time with peers and other people outside their units as they do with their own subordinates—and, surprisingly, very little time with their own superiors.

In Rosemary Stewart's diary study, the 160 British middle and top managers spent 47% of their time with peers, 41% of their time with people outside their unit, and only 12% of their time with their superiors. For Robert H. Guest's study of U.S. foremen, the figures were 44%, 46%, and 10%. The chief executives of my study averaged 44% of their contact time with people outside their organizations, 48% with subordinates, and 7% with directors and trustees.

The contacts the five CEOs made were with an incredibly wide range of people: subordinates; clients, business associates, and suppliers; and peers—managers of similar organizations, government and trade organization officials, fellow directors on outside boards, and independents with no relevant organizational affiliations. The chief executives' time with and mail from these groups is shown in Exhibit 2. Guest's study of fore-

Exhibit 2   The Chief Executives' Contacts

Note: The top figure indicates the proportion of total contact time spent with each group and the bottom figure, the proportion of mail from each group.

men shows, likewise, that their contacts were numerous and wide ranging, seldom involving fewer than 25 individuals, and often more than 50.

As we shall see shortly, the manager cultivates such contacts largely to find information. In effect, the liaison role is devoted to building up the manager's own external information system—informal, private, verbal, but, nevertheless, effective.

Informational Roles

By virtue of his interpersonal contacts, both with his subordinates and with his network of contacts, the manager emerges as the nerve center of his organizational unit. He may not know everything, but he typically knows more than any member of his staff.

Studies have shown this relationship to hold for all managers, from street gang leaders to U.S. presidents. In *The Human Group,* George C. Homans explains how, because they were at the center of the information flow in their own gangs and were also in close touch with other gang leaders, street gang leaders were better informed than any of their followers.[12] And Richard Neustadt describes the following account from his study of Franklin D. Roosevelt:

> The essence of Roosevelt's technique for information-gathering was competition. "He would call you in," one of his aides once told me, "and he'd ask you to get the story on some complicated business, and you'd come back after a couple of days of hard labor and present the juicy morsel you'd uncovered under a stone somewhere, and *then* you'd find out he knew all about it, along with something else you *didn't* know. Where he got this information from he wouldn't mention, usually, but after he had done this to you once or twice you got damn careful about *your* information."[13]

We can see where Roosevelt "got this information" when we consider the relationship between the interpersonal and informational roles. As leader, the manager has formal and easy access to every member of his staff. Hence, as noted earlier, he tends to know more about his own unit than anyone else does. In addition, his liaison contacts expose the manager to external information to which his subordinates often lack access. Many of these contacts are with other managers of equal status, who are themselves nerve centers in their own organization. In this way, the manager develops a powerful data base of information.

The processing of information is a key part of the manager's job. In my study, the chief executives spent 40% of their contact time on activities devoted exclusively to the transmission of information; 70% of their incoming mail was purely informational (as opposed to requests for action). The manager does not leave meetings or hang up the telephone in order to get back to work. In large part, communication *is* his work. Three roles describe these informational aspects of managerial work.

1

As *monitor,* the manager perpetually scans his environment for information, interrogates his liaison contacts and his subordinates, and receives unsolicited information, much of it as a result of the network of personal contacts he has developed. Remember that a good part of the information the manager collects in his monitor role arrives in verbal form, often as gossip, hearsay, and speculation. By virtue of his contacts, the manager has a natural advantage in collecting this soft information for his organization.

2

He must share and distribute much of this information. Information he gleans from outside personal contacts may be needed within his organization. In his *disseminator* role, the manager passes some of his privileged information directly to his subordinates, who would otherwise have no access to it. When his subordinates lack easy contact with one another, the manager will sometimes pass information from one to another.

3

In his *spokesman role,* the manager sends some of his information to people outside his unit—a president makes a speech to lobby for an organization cause, or a foreman suggests a product modification to a supplier. In addition, as part of his role as spokesman, every manager must inform and satisfy the influential people who control his organizational unit. For the foreman, this may simply involve keeping the plant manager informed about the flow of work through the shop.

The president of a large corporation, however, may spend a great amount of his time dealing with a host of influences. Directors and shareholders must be advised about financial performance; consumer groups must be assured that the organization is fulfilling its social responsibilities; and government officials must be satisfied that the organization is abiding by the law.

Decisional Roles

Information is not, of course, an end in itself; it is the basic input to decision making. One thing is clear in the study of managerial work: the manager plays the major role in his unit's decision-making system. As its formal authority, only he can commit the unit to important new courses of action; and as its nerve center, only he has full and current information to make the set of decisions that determines the unit's strategy. Four roles describe the manager as decision-maker.

1

As *entrepreneur,* the manager seeks to improve his unit, to adapt it to changing conditions in the environment. In his monitor role, the president is constantly on the lookout for new ideas. When a good one appears, he initiates a development project that he may supervise himself or delegate to an employee (perhaps with the stipulation that he must approve the final proposal).

There are two interesting features about these development projects at the chief executive level. First, these projects do not involve single decisions or even unified clusters of decisions. Rather, they emerge as a series of small decisions and actions sequenced over time. Apparently, the chief executive prolongs each project so that he can fit it bit by bit into his busy, disjointed schedule and so that he can gradually come to comprehend the issue, if it is a complex one.

Second, the chief executives I studied supervised as many as 50 of these projects at the same time. Some projects entailed new products or processes; others involved public relations campaigns, improvement of the cash position, reorganization of a weak department, resolution of a morale problem in a foreign division, integration of computer operations, various acquisitions at different stages of development, and so on.

The chief executive appears to maintain a kind of inventory of the development projects that he himself supervises—projects that are at various stages of development, some active and some in limbo. Like a juggler, he keeps a number of projects in the air; periodically, one comes down, is given a new burst of energy, and is sent back into orbit. At various intervals, he puts new projects on-stream and discards old ones.

2

While the entrepreneur role describes the manager as the voluntary initiator of change, the *disturbance handler* role depicts the manager involuntarily responding to pressures. Here change is beyond the manager's control. He must act because the pressures of the situation are too severe to be ignored: strike looms, a major customer has gone bankrupt, or a supplier reneges on his contract.

It has been fashionable, I noted earlier, to compare the manager to an orchestra conductor, just as Peter F. Drucker wrote in *The Practice of Management:*

> The manager has the task of creating a true whole that is larger than the sum of its parts, a productive entity that turns out more than the sum of the resources put into it. One analogy is the conductor of a symphony orchestra, through whose effort, vision and leadership individual instrumental parts that are so much noise by themselves become the living whole of music. But the conductor has the composer's score; he is only interpreter. The manager is both composer and conductor.[14]

Now consider the words of Leonard R. Sayles, who has carried out systematic research on the manager's job:

> [The manager] is like a symphony orchestra conductor, endeavoring to maintain a melodious performance in which the contributions of the various in-

struments are coordinated and sequenced, patterned and paced, while the orchestra members are having various personal difficulties, stage hands are moving music stands, alternating excessive heat and cold are creating audience and instrument problems, and the sponsor of the concert is insisting on irrational changes in the program.[15]

In effect, every manager must spend a good part of his time responding to high-pressure disturbances. No organization can be so well run, so standardized, that it has considered every contingency in the uncertain environment in advance. Disturbances arise not only because poor managers ignore situations until they reach crisis proportions, but also because good managers cannot possibly anticipate all the consequences of the actions they take.

3

The third decisional role is that of *resource allocator*. To the manager falls the responsibility of deciding who will get what in his organizational unit. Perhaps the most important resource the manager allocates is his own time. Access to the manager constitutes exposure to the unit's nerve center and decision-maker. The manager is also charged with designing his unit's structure, that pattern of formal relationships that determines how work is to be divided and coordinated.

Also, in his role as resource allocator, the manager authorizes the important decisions of his unit before they are implemented. By retaining this power, the manager can ensure that decisions are interrelated; all must pass through a single brain. To fragment this power is to encourage discontinuous decision making and a disjointed strategy.

There are a number of interesting features about the manager's authorizing others' decisions. First, despite the widespread use of capital budgeting procedures—a means of authorizing various capital expenditures at one time—executives in my study made a great many authorization decisions on an ad hoc basis. Apparently, many projects cannot wait or simply do not have the quantifiable costs and benefits that capital budgeting requires.

Second, I found that the chief executives faced incredibly complex choices. They had to consider the impact of each decision on other decisions and on the organization's strategy. They had to ensure that the decision would be acceptable to those who influence the organization, as well as ensure that resources would not be overextended. They had to understand the various costs and benefits as well as the feasibility of the proposal. They also had to consider questions of timing. All this was necessary for the simple approval of someone else's proposal. At the same time, however, delay could lose time, while quick approval could be ill considered and quick rejection might discourage the subordinate who had spent months developing a pet project.

One common solution to approving projects is to pick the man instead of the proposal. That is, the manager authorizes those projects presented to him by people whose judgment he trusts. But he cannot always use this simple dodge.

4

The final decisional role is that of *negotiator*. Studies of managerial work at all levels indicate that managers spend considerable time in negotiations: the president of the football team is called in to work out a contract with the holdout superstar; the corporation president leads his company's contingent to negotiate a new strike issue; the foreman argues a grievance problem to its conclusion with the shop steward. As Leonard Sayles puts it, negotiations are a "way of life" for the sophisticated manager.

These negotiations are duties of the manager's job; perhaps routine, they are not to be shirked. They are an integral part of his job, for only he has the authority to commit organizational resources in "real time," and only he has the nerve center information that important negotiations require.

The Integrated Job

It should be clear by now that the 10 roles I have been describing are not easily separable. In the terminology of the psychologist, they form a gestalt, an integrated whole. No role can be pulled out of the framework and the job be left intact. For example, a manager without liaison contacts lacks external information. As a result, he can neither disseminate the information his employees need nor make decisions that adequately reflect external conditions. (In fact, this is a problem for the new person in a managerial position, since he cannot make effective decisions until he has built up his network of contacts.)

Here lies a clue to the problems of team management.[16] Two or three people cannot share a single managerial position unless they can act as one entity. This means that they cannot divide up the ten roles unless they can very carefully reintegrate them. The real difficulty lies with the informational roles. Unless there can be full sharing of managerial information—and, as I pointed out earlier, it is primarily verbal—team management breaks down. A single managerial job cannot be arbitrarily split, for example, into internal and external roles, for information from both sources must be brought to bear on the same decisions.

To say that the ten roles form a gestalt is not to say that all managers give equal attention to each role. In fact, I found in my review of the various research studies that

. . . sales managers seem to spend relatively more of their time in the interpersonal roles, presumably a reflection of the extrovert nature of the marketing activity;

. . . production managers give relatively more attention to the decisional roles, presumably a reflection of their concern with efficient work flow;

. . . staff managers spend the most time in the informational roles, since they are experts who manage departments that advise other parts of the organization.

Nevertheless, in all cases the interpersonal, informational, and decisional roles remain inseparable.

TOWARD MORE EFFECTIVE MANAGEMENT

What are the messages for management in this description? I believe, first and foremost, that this description of managerial work should prove more important to managers than any prescription they might derive from it. That is to say, *the manager's effectiveness is significantly influenced by his insight into his own work.* His performance depends on how well he understands and responds to the pressures and dilemmas of the job. Thus managers who can be introspective about their work are likely to be effective at their jobs. The insert [on the next two pages] offers 14 groups of self-study questions for managers. Some may sound rhetorical; none is meant to be. Even though the questions cannot be answered simply, the manager should address them.

Let us take a look at three specific areas of concern. For the most part, the managerial logjams—the dilemma of delegation, the data base centralized in one brain, the problems of working with the management scientist—revolve around the verbal nature of the manager's information. There are great dangers in centralizing the organization's data bank in the minds of its managers. When they leave, they take their memory with them. And when subordinates are out of convenient verbal reach of the manager, they are at an information disadvantage.

1

The manager is challenged to find systematic ways to share his privileged information. A regular debriefing session with key subordinates, a weekly memory dump on the dictating machine, the maintaining of a diary of important information for limited circulation, or other similar methods may ease the logjam of work considerably. Time spent disseminating this information will be more than regained when decisions must be made. Of course, some will raise the question of confidentiality. But managers would do well to weigh the risks of exposing privileged information against having subordinates who can make effective decisions.

If there is a single theme that runs through this article, it is that the pressures of his job drive the manager to be superficial in his actions—to overload himself with work, encourage interruption, respond quickly to every stimulus, seek the tangible and avoid the abstract, make decisions in small increments, and do everything abruptly.

Self-Study Questions for Managers

1

Where do I get my information, and how? Can I make greater use of my contacts to get information? Can other people do some of my scanning for me? In what areas is my knowledge weakest, and how can I get others to provide me with the information I need? Do I have powerful enough mental models of those things I must understand within the organization and in its environment?

2

What information do I disseminate in my organization? How important is it that my subordinates get my information? Do I keep too much information to myself because dissemination of it is time-consuming or inconvenient? How can I get more information to others so they can make better decisions?

3

Do I balance information collecting with action taking? Do I tend to act before information is in? Or do I wait so long for all the information that opportunities pass me by and I become a bottleneck in my organization?

4

What pace of change am I asking my organization to tolerate? Is this change balanced so that our operations are neither excessively static nor overly disrupted? Have we sufficiently analyzed the impact of this change on the future of our organization?

5

Am I sufficiently well informed to pass judgment on the proposals that my subroutines make? Is it possible to leave final authorization for more of the proposals with subordinates? Do we have problems of coordination because subordinates in fact now make too many of these decisions independently?

6

What is my vision of direction for this organization? Are these plans primarily in my own mind in loose form? Should I make them explicit in order to guide the decisions of others in the organization better? Or do I need flexibility to change them at will?

7

How do my subordinates react to my managerial style? Am I sufficiently sensitive to the powerful influence my actions have on them? Do I fully understand their reactions to my actions? Do I find an appropriate balance between encouragement and pressure? Do I stifle their initiative?

8

What kind of external relationships do I maintain, and how? Do I spend too much of my time maintaining these relationships? Are there certain types of people whom I should get to know better?

9

Is there any system to my time scheduling, or am I just reacting to the pressures of the moment? Do I find the appropriate mix of activities, or do I tend to concentrate on one particular function or one type of problem just because I find it more interesting? Am I more efficient with particular kinds of work at special times of the day or week? Does my schedule reflect this? Can someone else (in addition to my secretary) take responsibility for much of my scheduling and do it more systematically?

10

Do I overwork? What effect does my work load have on my efficiency? Should I force myself to take breaks or to reduce the pace of my activity?

11

Am I too superficial in what I do? Can I really shift moods as quickly and frequently as my work patterns require? Should I attempt to decrease the amount of fragmentation and interruption in my work?

12

Do I orient myself too much toward current, tangible activities? Am I a slave to the action and excitement of my work, so that I am no longer able to concentrate on issues? Do key problems receive the attention they deserve? Should I spend more time reading and probing deeply into certain issues? Could I be more reflective? Should I be?

13

Do I use the different media appropriately? Do I know how to make the most of written communication? Do I rely excessively on face-to-face communication, thereby putting all but a few of my subordinates at an informational disadvantage? Do I schedule enough of my meetings on a regular basis? Do I spend time touring my organization to observe activity at first hand? Am I too detached from the heart of my organization's activities, seeing things only in an abstract way?

14

How do I blend my personal rights and duties? Do my obligations consume all my time? How can I free myself sufficiently from obligations to ensure that I am taking this organization where I want it to go? How can I turn my obligations to my advantage?

2

Here again, the manager is challenged to deal consciously with the pressures of superficiality by giving serious attention to the issues that require it, by stepping back from his tangible bits of information in order to see a broad picture, and by making use of analytical inputs. Although effective managers have to be adept at responding quickly to numerous and varying problems, the danger in managerial work is that they will respond to every issue equally (and that means abruptly) and that they will never work the tangible bits and pieces of informational input into a comprehensive picture of their world.

As I noted earlier, the manager uses these bits of information to build models of his world. But the manager can also avail himself of the models of the specialists. Economists describe the functioning of markets, operations researchers simulate financial flow processes, and behavioral scientists explain the needs and goals of people. The best of these models can be searched out and learned.

In dealing with complex issues, the senior manager has much to gain from a close relationship with the management scientists of his own organization. They have something important that he lacks—time to probe complex issues. An effective working relationship hinges on the resolution of what a colleague and I have called "the planning dilemma."[17] Managers have the information and the authority; analysts have the time and the technology. A successful working relationship between the two will be effected when the manager learns to share his information and the analyst learns to adapt to the manager's needs. For the analyst, adaptation means worrying less about the elegance of the method and more about its speed and flexibility.

It seems to me that analysts can help the top manager especially to schedule his time, feed in analytical information, monitor projects under his supervision, develop models to aid in making choices, design contingency plans for disturbances that can be anticipated, and conduct "quick-and-dirty" analysis for those that cannot. But there can be no cooperation if the analysts are out of the mainstream of the manager's information flow.

3

The manager is challenged to gain control of his own time by turning obligations to his advantage and by turning those things he wishes to do into obligations. The chief executives of my study initiated only 32% of their own contacts (and another 5% by mutual agreement). And yet to a considerable extent they seemed to control their time. There were two key factors that enabled them to do so.

First, the manager has to spend so much time discharging obligations that if he were to view them as just that, he would leave no mark on his organization. The unsuccessful manager blames failure on the obligations; the effective manager turns his obligations to his own advantage. A speech is a chance to lobby for a cause; a meeting is a chance to reorganize a weak department; a visit to an important customer is a chance to extract trade information.

Second, the manager frees some of his time to do those things that he—perhaps no one else—thinks important by turning them into obligations. Free time is made, not found, in the manager's job; it is forced into the schedule. Hoping to leave some time open for contemplation or general planning is tantamount to hoping that the pressures of the job will go away. The manager who wants to innovate initiates a project and obligates others to report back to him; the manager who needs certain environmental information establishes channels that will automatically keep him informed; the manager who has to tour facilities commits himself publicly.

The Educator's Job

Finally, a word about the training of managers. Our management schools have done an admirable job of training the organization's specialists— management scientists, marketing researchers, accountants, and organizational development specialists. But for the most part they have not trained managers.[18]

Management schools will begin the serious training of managers when skill training takes a serious place next to cognitive learning. Cognitive learning is detached and informational, like reading a book or listening to a lecture. No doubt much important cognitive material must be assimilated by the manager-to-be. But cognitive learning no more makes a manager than it does a swimmer. The latter will drown the first time he jumps into the water if his coach never takes him out of the lecture hall, gets him wet, and gives him feedback on his performance.

In other words, we are taught a skill through practice plus feedback, whether in a real or a simulated situation. Our management schools need to identify the skills managers use, select students who show potential in these skills, put the students into situations where these skills can be practiced, and then give them systematic feedback on their performance.

My description of managerial work suggests a number of important managerial skills—developing peer relationships, carrying out negotiations, motivating subordinates, resolving conflicts, establishing information networks and subsequently disseminating information, making decisions in conditions of extreme ambiguity, and allocating resources. Above all, the manager needs to be introspective about his work so that he may continue to learn on the job.

Many of the manager's skills can, in fact, be practiced, using techniques that range from role playing to videotaping real meetings. And our management schools can enhance the entrepreneurial skills by designing programs that encourage sensible risk taking and innovation.

No job is more vital to our society than that of the manager. It is the manager who determines whether our social institutions serve us well or whether they squander our talents and resources. It is time to strip away the folklore about managerial work, and time to study it realistically so that we can begin the difficult task of making significant improvements in its performance.

NOTES AND REFERENCES

1. All the data from my study can be found in Henry Mintzberg, *The Nature of Managerial Work* (New York: Harper & Row, 1973).

2. Robert H. Guest, "Of Time and the Foreman," *Personnel,* May 1956, p. 478.

3. Rosemary Stewart, *Managers and Their Jobs* (London: Macmillan, 1967); see also Sune Carlson, *Executive Behaviour* (Stockholm: Strömbergs, 1951), the first of the diary studies.

4. Francis J. Aguilar, *Scanning the Business Environment* (New York: Macmillan, 1967), p. 102.

5. Unpublished study by Irving Choran, reported in Mintzberg, *The Nature of Managerial Work.*

6. Robert T. Davis, *Performance and Development of Field Sales Managers* (Boston: Division of Research, Harvard Business School, 1957); George H. Copeman, *The Role of the Managing Director* (London: Business Publications, 1963).

7. Stewart, *Managers and Their Jobs;* Tom Burns, "The Directions of Activity and Communication in a Departmental Executive Group," *Human Relations* 7, no. 1 (1954): 73.

8. H. Edward Wrapp, "Good Managers Don't Make Policy Decisions," HBR September-October 1967, p. 91; Wrapp refers to this as spotting opportunities and relationships in the stream of operating problems and decisions; in his article Wrapp raises a number of excellent points related to this analysis.

9. Richard E. Neustadt, *Presidential Power* (New York: John Wiley, 1960), pp. 153–154; italics added.

10. For a more thorough, though rather different, discussion of this issue, see Kenneth R. Andrews, "Toward Professionalism in Business Management," HBR March-April 1969, p. 49.

11. C. Jackson Grayson, Jr., in "Management Science and Business Practice" HBR July-August 1973, p. 41, explains in similar terms why, as chairman of the Price Commission, he did not use those very techniques that he himself promoted in his earlier career as a management scientist.

12. George C. Homans, *The Human Group* (New York: Harcourt, Brace & World, 1950), based on the study by William F. Whyte entitled *Street Corner Society,* rev. ed. (Chicago: University of Chicago Press, 1955).

13. Neustadt, *Presidential Power,* p. 157.

14. Peter S. Drucker, *The Practice of Management* (New York: Harper & Row, 1954), pp. 341–342.

15. Leonard R. Sayles, *Managerial Behavior* (New York: McGraw-Hill, 1964), p. 162.

16. See Richard C. Hodgson, Daniel J. Levinson, and Abraham Zaleznik, *The Executive Role Constellation* (Boston: Division of Research, Harvard Business School, 1965), for a discussion of the sharing of roles.

17. James S. Hekimian and Henry Mintzberg, "The Planning Dilemma," *The Management Review,* May 1968, p. 4.

18. See J. Sterling Livingston, "Myth of the Well-Educated Manager," HBR January-February 1971, p. 79.

PART TWO

Planning Processes in Management

It has been said that poor managers work on yesterday's problems, good managers work on today's problems and the truly outstanding managers focus on tomorrow's problems. Focusing on tomorrow's problems clearly requires *planning*. Planning is an essential function of the management process and involves the application of thought, analysis, imagination, and judgment to future activities.

One of the themes of the classical school of management thought is that there is a distinct difference between planning and executing. Fayol and others argued that managers should plan and nonmanagers should execute. The behaviorists, on the other hand, would counter with the argument that managers and nonmanagers together should be active participants in both planning and executing. Both groups, however, would agree that the planning function includes those activities which result in a definition of goals and the determination of appropriate means to achieve these goals. Simply stated, planning is advance thinking as the basis for doing.

The planning process itself is frequently broken down into four distinct phases. The first phase involves establishing goals and fixing their priorities. This is a particularly important phase which involves the determination of future outcomes which if achieved will enable the organization to satisfy the demands and expectations of its relevant constituencies.

The second phase involves forecasting future events which can affect goal accomplishment. This applies particularly to *strategic planning* activities and is necessitated by the increased pace of environmental change which has been the norm in recent years. It is less a consideration in *functional* or *operational planning,* which focuses more on immediate objectives and problems.

Budgeting is an important part of planning in that proper consideration of the financial requirements in implementing plans is an obvious necessity. It does little good to plan for activities which the organization is unable to bring to fruition because of financial constraints. The final phase is policy statement and implementation. Policies are statements which reflect the basic objectives of the organization and which provide the guidelines for carrying out action throughout the organization.

Each of these four phases needs to be initiated and related to others to complete the planning process. An examination of these phases indicates that planning involves goal setting, establishing goal priorities, forecasting, integrating plans with budgets, and implementing programs. These properties suggest time, cost, and human constraints. which need to be weighted. Plans involve and affect people. Thus, planning is a major effort in organizations which must be successful if the organization is to survive.

7

Planning

Henri Fayol

Written well over 60 years ago by a true pioneer in discussing planning, this short essay is as current as if it were written yesterday. Fayol identifies the features of a good plan of action and outlines the method of drawing up a plan. Note also the emphasis Fayol places on the human element of planning.—Eds.

The maxim, "managing means looking ahead," gives some idea of the importance attached to planning in the business world and it is true that if foresight is not the whole of management at least it is an essential part of it. To foresee, in this context means both to assess the future and make provision for it; that is, foreseeing is itself action already. Planning is manifested on a variety of occasions and in a variety of ways, its chief manifestation, apparent sign and most effective instrument being the plan of action. The plan of action is, at one and the same time, the result envisaged, the line of action to be followed, the stages to go through, and methods to use. It is a kind of future picture wherein proximate events are outlined with some distinctness, whilst remote events appear progressively less distinct, and it entails the running of the business as foreseen and provided against over a definite period.

The plan of action rests: (1) On the firm's resources (buildings, tools, raw materials, personnel, productive capacity, sales outlets, public relations, etc.). (2) On the nature and importance of work in progress. (3) On future trends which depend partly on technical, commercial, financial and other conditions, all subject to change, whose importance and occurrence cannot be predetermined. The preparation of the plan of action is one of the most difficult and most important matters of every business

SOURCE: Reprinted by permission of Pitman Publishing Limited from Chapter V of *General and Industrial Management* by Henri Fayol (Sir Isaac Pitman and Sons, Ltd., 1949), pp. 43–52.

and brings into play all departments and all functions, especially the management function. It is, in effect, in order to carry out his managerial function that the manager takes the initiative for the plan of action, that he indicates its objective and scope, fixes the share of each department in the communal task, coordinates the parts and harmonizes the whole; that he decides, in fine, the line of conduct to be followed. In this line of conduct it is not only imperative that nothing should clash with principles and rules of good management, but also that the arrangement adopted should facilitate application of these principles and rules. Therefore, to the divers technical, commercial, financial and other abilities necessary on the part of a business head and his assistants, there must be added considerable managerial ability.

GENERAL FEATURES OF A GOOD PLAN OF ACTION

No one disputes the usefulness of a plan of action. Before taking action it is most necessary to know what is possible and what is wanted. It is known that absence of plan entails hesitation, false steps, untimely changes of direction, which are so many causes of weakness, if not of disaster, in business. The question of and necessity for a plan of action, then, does not arise and I think that I am voicing the general opinion in saying that a plan of action is indispensable. But there are plans and plans, there are simple ones, complex ones, concise ones, detailed ones, long- or short-term ones; there are those studied with meticulous attention, those treated lightly; there are good, bad, and indifferent ones. How are the good ones to be singled out from among the others? Experience is the only thing that finally determines the true value of a plan, i.e., on the services it can render to the firm, and even then the manner of its application must be taken into account. There is both instrument and player. Nevertheless, there are certain broad characteristics on which general agreement may be reached beforehand without waiting for the verdict of experience.

Unity of plan is an instance. Only one plan can be put into operation at a time; two different plans would mean duality, confusion, disorder. But a plan may be divided into several parts. In large concerns, there is found alongside the general plan a technical, commercial, and a financial one, or else an overall one with a specific one for each department. But all these plans are linked, welded, so as to make up one only, and every modification brought to bear on any one of them is given expression in the whole plan. The guiding action of the plan must be continuous. Now the limitations of human foresight necessarily set bounds to the duration of plans, so, in order to have no break in the guiding action, a second plan must follow immediately upon the first, a third upon the second, and so on. In large businesses the annual plan is more or less in current use. Other plans of shorter or longer term, always in close accord with the annual plan, operate simultaneously with this latter. The plan should be flexible enough to bend before such adjustments, as it is considered well to introduce, whether from pressure or circumstances or from any other reason. First as last, it is the law to which one bows. Another good point about a plan is to have as much accuracy as is compatible with the unknown factors bearing on the fate of the concern. Usually it is possible to mark out the line of proximate action fairly accurately, while a simple general indication does for remote activities, for before the moment for their execution has arrived sufficient enlightenment will have been forthcoming to settle the line of action more precisely. When the unknown factor occupies a relatively very large place there can be no preciseness in the plan, and then the concern takes on the name of venture.

Unity, continuity, flexibility, precision: such are the broad features of a good plan of action.

As for other specific points which it should have, and which turn on the nature, importance, and condition of the business for which the plan is drawn up, there could be no possibility of settling them beforehand save by comparison with other plans already recognized as effective in similar businesses. In each case, then, comparable elements and models must be sought in business practice, after the fashion of the architect with a building to construct. But the architect, better served than the manager, can call upon books, courses in architecture, whereas there are no books on plans of action, no lessons in foresight, for management theory has yet to be formulated.

There is no lack of good plans, they can be guessed at from the externals of a business but not seen at sufficiently close quarters to be known and judged. Nevertheless, it would be most useful for those whose concern is management to know how experienced managers go about drawing up their plans. By way of information or sample, I am going to set out the method which has long been followed in a great mining and metallurgical concern with which I am well acquainted.

Method of Drawing Up the Plan of Action
in a Large Mining and Metallurgical Firm

This company includes several separate establishments and employs about 10,000 personnel. The entire plan is made up of a series of separate plans called forecasts; and there are yearly forecasts, ten-yearly forecasts, monthly, weekly, daily forecasts, long-term forecasts, special forecasts, and all merge into a single program which operates as a guide for the whole concern.

(1) Yearly forecasts.   Each year, two months after the end of the budgetary period, a general report is drawn up of the work and results of this period. The report deals especially with production, sales, technical, commercial, financial position, personnel, economic consequences, etc. The report is accompanied by forecasts dealing with those same matters, the forecasts being a kind of anticipatory summary of the activities and results of the new budgetary period. The two months of the new plan

which have elapsed are not left without plan, because of provisional forecasts drawn up fifteen days before the end of the previous period. In a large mining and metallurgical firm not many activities are quite completed during the course of one year. Cooperative projects of a technical, commercial, and financial nature, which provide the business with its activities, need more time for their preparation and execution. From another aspect, account must be taken of the repercussions which proximate activities must have on ultimate ones and of the obligation to prepare far ahead sometimes for a requisite state of affairs.

Finally, thought must be given to constant modifications operating on the technical, commercial, financial, and social condition of the industrial world in general and of the business in particular, to avoid being overtaken by circumstances. These various circumstances come outside the framework of yearly forecasts and lead on to longer-term ones.

(2) **Ten-yearly forecasts.** Ten-yearly forecasts deal with the same matters as yearly ones. At the outset these two types of forecasts are identical, the yearly forecast merging into the first year of the ten-yearly one, but from the second year onwards notable divergences make their appearance. To maintain unity of plan each year the ten-yearly forecasts must be reconciled with annual ones so that at the end of some years the ten-yearly forecasts are generally so modified and transformed as to be no longer clear and need redrafting. In effect the custom of redrafting every five years has become established. It is the rule that ten-yearly forecasts always embrace a decade, and that they are revised every five years. Thus there is always a line of action marked out in advance for five years at least.

(3) **Special forecasts.** There are some activities whose full cycle exceeds one or even several ten-yearly periods; there are others which, occurring suddenly, must sensibly affect the conditions of the business. Both the one and the other are the object of special forecasts whose findings necessarily have a place in the yearly and ten-yearly forecasts. But it must never be lost sight of that there is one plan only.

These three sorts of forecasts, yearly, ten-yearly, and special, merged and harmonized, constitute the firm's general plan.

So, having been prepared with meticulous care by each regional management, with the help of departmental management, and then revised, modified, and completed by general management and then submitted for scrutiny and approval to the Board of Directors, these forecasts become the plan which, so long as no other has been put in its place, shall serve as guide, directive, and law for the whole staff.

Fifty years ago I began to use this system of forecasts, when I was engaged in managing a colliery, and it rendered me such good service that I had no hesitation in subsequently applying it to various industries whose running was entrusted to me. I look upon it as a precious managerial instrument and have no hesitation in recommending its use to those who have no better instrument available. It has necessarily some short-

TABLE 1. Yearly and Ten-Yearly Forecasts

CONTENTS

Technical Section

Mining rights. Premises. Plant.
Extraction. Manufacture. Output.
New workings. Improvements.
Maintenance of plant and buildings.
Production costs.

Commercial Section

Sales outlets.
Marketable goods.
Agencies. Contracts.
Customer importance. Credit standing.
Selling price.

Financial Section

Capital. Loans. Deposits.

Circulating assets $\begin{cases} \text{Supplies in hand.} \\ \text{Finished goods.} \\ \text{Debtors.} \\ \text{Liquid assets.} \end{cases}$

Available assets.
Reserves and sundry appropriations.

Creditors $\begin{cases} \text{Wages.} \\ \text{Suppliers.} \\ \text{Sundry.} \end{cases}$

Sinking funds. Dividends. Bankers.

Accounting

Balance sheet. Profit and Loss account.
Statistics.

Security

Accident precautions.
Works police. Claims. Health service.
Insurance.

Management

Plan of action.
Organization of personnel. Selection.
Command.
Coordination. Conferences.
Control.

comings, but its shortcomings are very slight compared with the advantages it offers. Let us glance at these advantages and shortcomings.

Advantages and Shortcomings of Forecasts

1. The study of resources, future possibilities, and means to be used for attaining the objective call for contributions from all departmental heads within the framework of their mandate: each one brings to this study the contribution of his experience together with recognition of the responsibility which will fall upon him in executing the plan.

Those are excellent conditions for ensuring that no resource shall be neglected and that future possibilities shall be prudently and courageously assessed and that means shall be appropriate to ends. Knowing what are its capabilities and its intentions, the concern goes boldly on, confidently tackles current problems and is prepared to align all its forces against accidents and surprises of all kinds which may occur.

2. Compiling the annual plan is always a delicate operation and especially lengthy and laborious when done for the first time, but each repetition brings some simplification and when the plan has become a habit the toil and difficulties are largely reduced. Conversely, the interest it offers increases. The attention demanded for executing the plan, the indispensable comparison between predicted and actual facts, the recognition of mistakes made and successes attained, the search for means of repeating the one and avoiding the other—all go to make the new plan a work of increasing interest and increasing usefulness.

Also, by doing this work the personnel increases in usefulness from year to year, and at the end is considerably superior to what it was in the beginning. In truth, this result is not due solely to the use of planning but everything goes together; a well-thought-out plan is rarely found apart from sound organizational, command, coordination, and control practices. This management element exerts an influence on all the rest.

3. Lack of sequence in activity and unwarranted changes of course are dangers constantly threatening businesses without a plan. The slightest contrary wind can turn from its course a boat which is unfitted to resist. When serious happenings occur, regrettable changes of course may be decided upon under the influence of profound but transitory disturbance. Only a program carefully pondered at an undisturbed time permits of maintaining a clear view of the future and of concentrating maximum possible intellectual ability and material resources upon the danger.

It is in difficult moments above all that a plan is necessary. The best of plans cannot anticipate all unexpected occurrences which may arise, but it does include a place for these events and prepare the weapons which may be needed at the moment of being surprised. The plan protects the business not only against undesirable changes of course which may be produced by grave events, but also against those arising simply from changes on the part of higher authority. Also, it protects against deviations, imperceptible at first, which end by deflecting it from its objective.

Conditions and Qualities Essential for Drawing Up a Good Plan of Action

To sum up: the plan of action facilitates the utilization of the firm's resources and the choice of best methods to use for attaining the objective. It suppresses or reduces hesitancy, false steps, unwarranted changes of course, and helps to improve personnel. It is a precious managerial instrument.

The question may be asked as to why such an instrument is not in general use and everywhere developed to the farthest extent. The reason is that its compilation demands of managerial personnel a certain number of qualities and conditions rarely to be found in combination. The compilation of a good plan demands for the personnel in charge:

1. The art of handling men.
2. Considerable energy.
3. A measure of moral courage.
4. Some continuity of tenure.
5. A given degree of competence in the specialized requirements of the business.
6. A certain general business experience.

(1) **The art of handling men.** In a large firm the majority of departmental managers take part in the compiling of the working arrangements. The execution of this task from time to time is in addition to ordinary everyday work and includes a certain responsibility and does not normally carry any special remuneration. So, to have in such conditions loyal and active cooperation from departmental heads an able manager of men is needed who fears neither trouble nor responsibility. The art of handling men is apparent from keenness of subordinates and confidence of superiors.

(2) **Energy.** Yearly and ten-yearly forecasts and special forecasts demand constant vigilance on the part of management.

(3) **Moral courage.** It is well known that the best-thought-out plan is never exactly carried out. Forecasts are not prophecies; their function is to minimize the unknown factor. Nevertheless, the public generally, and even shareholders best informed about the running of a business, are not kindly disposed toward a manager who has raised unfulfilled hopes, or allowed them to be raised. Whence the need for a certain prudence which has to be reconciled with the obligation of making every preparation and seeking out optimum possible results.

The timid are tempted to suppress the plan or else whittle it down to nothing in order not to expose themselves to criticism, but it is a bad policy even from the point of view of self-interest. Lack of plan, which compromises smooth running, also exposes the manager to infinitely graver charges than that of having to explain away imperfectly executed forecasts.

(4) Continuity of tenure. Some time goes by before a new manager is able to take sufficient cognizance of the course of affairs, its general setup and future possibilities, so as usefully to undertake the compiling of the plan. If, at such a moment, he feels that he will not have enough time to complete the work or only enough to start putting it into execution, or if, on the other hand, he is convinced that such work, condemned to bear no fruit, will only draw criticism upon him, is it to be thought that he will carry it out enthusiastically or even undertake it unless obliged? Human nature must be reckoned with. Without continuity of tenure on the part of management personnel there can be no good plan of action.

(5 and 6) Professional competence and general business knowledge. These are abilities just as necessary for drawing up a plan as for carrying it out.

Such are the conditions essential for compiling a good plan. They presuppose intelligent and experienced management. Lack of plan or a bad plan is a sign of managerial incompetence. To safeguard business against such incompetence:

1. A plan must be compulsory.
2. Good specimen plans must be made generally available. (Successful businesses could be asked to furnish such specimens. Experience and general discussion would single out the best.)
3. Planning (as a subject) must be introduced into education. Thus could general opinion be better informed and react upon management personnel, so that the latter's inefficiency would be less to be feared—a state of affairs which would in no wise detract from the importance of men of proven worth.

8

Planning Objectives

Cyril J. O'Donnell

The first step in planning is the identification and description of objectives. This article focuses on the important role played by objectives in the planning process. The author makes the very important point that organizations are not free to plan or select objectives in isolation; rather, planning requires careful consideration of all aspects of the organizational environment.—Eds.

So important is the need to select proper planning objectives that one would think that their nature and specification would be thoroughly understood and practiced with skill. But such is far from the case. Anyone who takes the trouble to examine enterprise "plans" will find that few of them qualify as true plans. Their chief fault lies in a misunderstanding of the planning process, and especially in vague statements of objective. This opens the door to vagaries of consistency, logic, and data, and invites pertinent questions concerning the need or the reason for "planning" in the first place.

The identification and description of objectives—the first step in planning—is absolutely essential to the success of any plan. One cannot specify how he will accomplish a vague and indeterminate purpose. It is not possible to develop a plan to enjoy oneself without identifying the parameters of enjoyment; neither can a firm develop a plan to improve its

SOURCE: © 1963 by the Regents of the University of California. Reprinted from *California Management Review*, Volume VI, Number 2, pp. 3–10, by permission of the Regents.

community relations, nor a bureau or agency make a plan to improve its image until it has described its purpose in such a way that ultimate success or failure can be determined with certitude.

Faulty specification and improper selection of a planning objective will vitiate the use of planning time and cost. The former will result in futility and bring the entire planning activity into disrepute. The latter will cause undesirable expenditures for a plan to accomplish unimportant or unrelated objectives, or objectives which are contrary to the social interest. Planning can be a most useful executive function, but it will not be if objectives are poorly or improperly selected.[1]

It is the purpose of this article to clarify the hierarchy of relationships between social purposes and enterprise goals and to inquire into the nature of the goal-setting process.

ENVIRONMENT

Enterprises are not free to plan in isolation. They must operate in a social environment of enormous scope, complexity, and change. Our planet, its peoples, and their institutions affect, in varying degree, the choice of objectives made by each enterprise. This environment may be viewed in terms of a scalar chain of authority, the degree of influence exercised over others, or the degree of freedom with which the enterprise can act. Internationally, there is a community of supposedly independent states which influence but do not control each other. Intranationally, the ultimate power rests in a political institution, democratic or authoritarian, which determines the degree of retained freedom of its peoples to act. There can be no doubt that the social purposes of the governing institution have top priority in the community. Ideally, if these are generally known and understood, all subordinate institutions should adopt, or will be constrained to adopt, purposes and objectives whose achievement will be consistent with them.

Organized societies, whether they be prehistoric villages, city-states, or nations, have certain purposes which they wish to achieve. Sometimes these are known and can be described. Archeologists suggest that the earliest organized group, simple though it probably was, had safety as its chief purpose. Cities are a social invention[2] whose prerequisites include a relatively dense population and availability of transportation facilities for bulk products. The original purpose of this organization is not known. It may have merely reflected a human preference for gregarious living; it certainly did provide an opportunity for extensive division of labor, and it had a power potential. The purposes of national states are equally uncertain. Despite the speculation on this subject by political historians, with their stress on natural boundaries, common language, etc., we really do not know why nations emerged. Perhaps success breeds power: The successful chief enjoyed the power which came by expanding his holding to a point where he was counterbalanced by other distant successes.

PURPOSE

We do have in our possession statements of purpose in the organization of the United States. This may be due to the great facility of our founding fathers in written expression happily combined with a world cultural stage highlighted by a relatively literate population, low cost of printing and distribution, and the discovery (much earlier) of the power of the written word. Whatever the explanations, statements of our national purposes are set forth in the Declaration of Independence and in the Constitution. Jefferson asserted that governments are instituted to secure to their peoples the rights of life, liberty, and the pursuit of happiness. The preamble of our Constitution states:

> We, the people of the United States, in order to form a more perfect union, establish justice, insure domestic tranquility, provide for the common defense, promote the general welfare, and secure the blessings of liberty to ourselves and our posterity, do ordain and establish this Constitution for the United States of America.

This is a formulation generally agreed upon at the time of its adoption and comes down to us as an inclusive statement. Undoubtedly there existed then, and there exist now, variant conceptions of our national purposes. Words mean different things to each person; priority issues must be faced; and there is no single authority with the power to determine exclusively, and require universal adherence to, a set of multiple purposes.

These uncertainties make it really difficult for a subordinate enterprise to adopt supportive or complementary purposes even if it would; they also permit wide latitude for conflicting, low priority, and even subversive purposes.

There are always various means by which the overall social purposes can be attained. In the United States the chief reliance is upon political and economic freedom, characterized by free enterprise, a system in which entrepreneurs are free to organize cooperative effort to produce goods and services whose (ultimate) consumption helps our people achieve certain aspects of the social purpose. Within limits, the what, who, how, when, and where are left to individuals to decide. It should be noted that not all enterprises are intended to provide entrepreneurial profit. Persons who develop many political, welfare, educational, religious, and specialized social groups, such as a trade association, may not have profit in mind, even potentially. They exchange their services for income which is begged or taxed from contributors, or which is obtained from the nonprofit sale of services.

While most enterprise is undertaken with freedom, there has been an expanding area of cooperative action in which freedom is limited. Even originally, the federal government obtained from the states exclusive rights to maintain defense, establish a supreme court, levy certain types of taxes, and conduct certain businesses, such as the post office. These functions, identified by Adam Smith as the legitimate activities of government, have not been subject to question. With the passage of time, additional restrictions and prohibitions on free enterprise have multiplied as complainants against certain aspects of free enterprise behavior have gained political power. These restrictive acts are familiar to students of economics, finance, agriculture, transportation, and trade. The power to tax business income at rates which many scholars think are confiscatory has an important effect in limiting the scope of free enterprise. It is intended that private enterprise, of whatever nature, will adopt purposes which square with regulations that are designed, we hope, to realize generally accepted social purposes. Enterprises which ignore this concept create enormous risks of losing all their resources. From a social viewpoint, this is as it should be if the regulations concerning government ownership and control are themselves consistent with social purposes.

Under the umbrella of social purposes, and contributory or complementary to them, every enterprise should face up to the problem of spelling out its own purposes. Failure to do this will result in an undertaking battered by coincidence of events and helpless because it is likely to have inconsistent and unrealistic plans or none at all. Further, to the extent that its purposes are vague, inconsistent, or unspecified, there will be no way of testing the degree to which its plans or behavior contribute toward the accomplishment of ends. On the other hand, clarity of purpose permits the identification of planning objectives, and planning, as we know, can greatly increase the probability of accomplishment, if properly executed. As L. Gulick has stated, "A clear statement of purpose universally understood is the outstanding guarantee of effective administration."[3]

NEW ENTERPRISES

In the United States each year several thousand enterprises are established. For what purpose? What is it that the entrepreneur, the prime mover, hopes to accomplish? Clearly it is to provide a product or service for exchange. He may have a variety of reasons in mind. Immediately, of course, he must see a need for the enterprise, and unless he is correct and unless the need to be served contributes to our social purposes, there is a high prospect of failure. But are we sure that the prime mover is really concerned about fulfilling others' needs? Certain men do wish to satisfy the need of the lowly for economic relief, health care, or religious service. Compassion and charity seem to be their driving power.

On the other hand many, and probably most, entrepreneurs see the fulfillment of others' needs merely as a means of satisfying personal desires for a way to make a living, achieve freedom, and perhaps acquire power. Nonprofit enterprises can and do provide very satisfactory standards of living for their employees; they can also provide freedom and power for the prime mover. Profit-making enterprises are the rule, however. Their variety is as diverse as the needs of men. It covers not merely what is generally called business: it includes hospitals, firms organized to raise money for charities, educational institutions, and even some sidelines of religious enterprise. In every case they have the potential for satisfying the income, freedom, and power needs of their founders.

It is chiefly the responsibility of the Board of Directors or its equivalent to establish and to review the enterprise's purposes. At this level, it is essential to consider whether the purposes are really complementary to the social purpose and not questionable. At the minimum, their responsibility is to avoid the risks of antisocial purposes, direct or indirect. Furthermore, there is a need to review purposes occasionally to make sure they conform to newly interpreted aspects of the social purpose. For instance, collusion is now forbidden in domestic trade but encouraged in foreign trade. Ambivalent as the social purpose is in this instance, directors must ensure that enterprise purpose will be achieved within the known or assumed confines of this legislation, and they should be alert to any modifications in the future.

Although it is perfectly clear that some enterprises are organized to achieve a short-run purpose and then be dissolved, this is unusual. Men tend to found enterprises for the indefinite long run and, if they use the corporate form, for perpetuity. Undoubtedly their hope is to realize purposes quickly, but they are more likely to be resigned to strive for them during their active years. Consequently the long-run purposes are likely to be spelled out with considerable vagueness and perhaps dissembled into terms considered inoffensive to their fellowman. Rather than admit to freedom and power as included in their long-run purpose, they may specify only a profit purpose. But even this purpose will normally be buried under a ponderous statement about fulfilling the needs of customers. In reality, the needs of customers are but the means to acquiring profit, freedom, and power. Hiding these long-run purposes for political reasons is incomprehensible if one understands our society and its component of human beings. Our society depends on people to strive for these real purposes, knowing full well that in the striving the needs of man will be served within the safeguards built into our social system.

The formulation of purposes is undertaken in a studied attempt to establish an image, ideal though it may be, of the enterprise as it will be when it reaches maturity. If this is not done, the firm is subject to the vagaries of chance. If it is, all plans for achievement can be directed toward a unifying concept.

Since an enterprise has ultimate purposes to achieve, usually much beyond the objectives of even long-range plans, experienced managers realize that general rather than specific descriptions are inevitable. The parameters of the image are spelled out on the assumption that it may take twenty, fifty, or a hundred years to mold the enterprise. To quantify purposes so far in the future is extremely hazardous. For instance, it would be much more sensible to establish one purpose as the earning of the competitive rate of return on investment rather than select an arbitrary figure. We do not know whether the specific figure will be reasonable in a distant future when the free enterprise system may be assaulted, capital scarce or plentiful, or inflation may bury the dollar under tons of paper. Specific figures should be used only at the stage where planning objectives are established.

MULTIPLE PURPOSES

These enterprises have multiple purposes. An educational enterprise may be thought of as having the purpose of educating students, but such a conception is inadequate because it does not develop the image sought. The image would become much more clear if it were stated that the purposes of the educational enterprise are to attract highly qualified graduate students to be trained in the liberal arts and sciences, to grant the Ph.D. degree to successful candidates, to attract only the most highly regarded faculty, to operate as a private school in the Spartan tradition, and be supported entirely by tuition fees and gifts of alumni and friends. Similarly, a business enterprise might spell out its multiple purposes to include earning a competitive rate of profit and return on investment, emphasizing research as a basis for a continuing flow of proprietary products, having public ownership, financing both by earnings plow-back and debt, distributing products internationally, pricing superior quality electronic products competitively, striving for stability and growth to a dominant position in the industry, and adhering as far as possible to the generally supported values of our society. Statements of purposes such as these would enable anyone to visualize the kind of enterprise the regents or directors would like to mold. They also establish several essential premises for the planning that must be done to accomplish each step on the way.

There are two sets of circumstances which could require the statement of purposes to be changed. The first is the technical matter of limiting the purposes so that change may be inevitable, due to changing circumstances. If one of the purposes is to retail or to manufacture kerosene oil lamps, any decision to manufacture or wholesale in the first case or to broaden the product line in the second would entail amendment to the enterprise charter. In some political circumstances this could easily spell trouble for incorporated enterprises.

There is another kind of circumstance which causes directors to modify statements of purpose. This includes changes in the law, elimination of free enterprise in the activity, radical technological innovations, changes in consumer living standards, reduction of the death rate, and higher literacy levels. Our society is highly dynamic, and therefore it is incumbent upon directors to review and modify purposes as seems wise. They are not absolved from this duty merely because the purposes are very distantly realizable. Purposes must be kept consistent with social change if the guided effort to achieve them is to be applied effectively and efficiently.

AN IMPORTANT FACTOR

One of the most important factors which influences the choice of purposes is the *environment* in which the enterprise will operate. All of its elements cannot be considered here, but they would include the nature of the economic order, affluence of the people in the society, national and international political stability, tax policies, competition, and state of the arts. One would not engage in the design and manufacture of fine furniture if he were intending to sell it to aborigines.

A second factor is *technical skill and knowledge*. People normally select an activity they know something about, particularly in product areas where technology is important. A truck driver is not likely to found a university or a corner grocer to establish a firm to produce power plants for space travel. There is, of course, the possibility of hiring the needed technical skill. This is often done, but the disparity between the technical knowledge of the founder and that required for operations is usually not as great as in the above examples. Even when it is, the difference normally occurs at the top level of management. It is also absolutely necessary that employees with technical ability be available. A movie queen might found a new university, but it would fail unless she could recruit a qualified staff.

Another element in the need for technical skill is the availability of satellite industries. Many firms have considered establishing a business in seemingly favorable places only to find that essential auxiliary industry—power, raw materials, refrigeration, finance, or transportation—is not available. Thus, the state of the art employed by the enterprise must be consonant with that of the environment.

A third factor in the choice of purpose concerns the *creativity* of founders or directors. The risks as well as the rewards for creative enterprise are well recognized. The firm that can command the services of really creative people is most likely to stress the purpose of gaining a recognized place at the forward fringe of the arts. It would concentrate on its potential for research, design, and development. Such a purpose is risky, not only because of the danger of creating unmarketable products, but especially because the services of creative employees may be lost. At the other extreme is the noncreative, tired imitator of existing firms. In between is the firm that chooses a purpose closely related to skill in innovation such as was reflected in the development of the supermarket, integrated functional operations, or new and unusual sites for an activity.

PRIMARY MOTIVATION

Finally, it should be remarked that some founders are primarily motivated by compassion for others. These men would be likely to establish a welfare purpose, among others, for this is their main interest. Tom Dooley and his enterprise for improving the health of Southeast Asians is a good example; the American hospital ship, *Hope,* is another.

There would be little need to design the purposes of enterprise if there were no intention of planning to achieve them. Without plans, the firm's history would have only an accidental relationship to purposes. Plans and their effective execution are an absolute requirement for the realization of enterprise purpose.

The objectives of long-range plans are quite different from enterprise purposes, especially in timing and specific detail. While the achievement of purpose may be thought of as a matter of decades or of continual striving, the accomplishment of long-range objectives is planned within a matter of a few years. There are, of course, a few firms—notably utilities[4]—that develop plans for building fixed assets whose life expectancy is 25 to 100 years, but most long-range planning is probably confined to a five-year span. This means, of course, that long-range objectives are not and cannot be identical to purposes. The latter perform a valuable function when used as planning premises. The objectives of the plan are merely pieces of the distant purposes, which, if achieved successfully in five-year series, eventually become equated with purposes.

In approaching the problem of defining long-range objectives, it is necessary to consider certain basic prerequisites and to select the enterprise image.

One obvious prerequisite to specifying long-range planning objectives is that their achievement must support the realization of enterprise purpose. It is as faulty to select an objective which makes no contribution to purpose as it is to select objectives which conflict with them. In both cases, effort is expended inefficiently or nonproductively. A positive contribution to purpose must be planned if it is to have more than a coincidental effect.

A second prerequisite concerns the practicality of achievement. This is no easy quality to attain. For most people, practicality and planning may seem to be contradictory concepts. They fail to see that the long-range objective sought is not a matter of guessing where the enterprise will be in five years but is a specific which proper planning and execution is most likely to make occur. As a practical matter, it can never occur unless the objective can be achieved. It is surely apparent that a five-year objective of a professional football team to obtain a monopoly in this type of entertainment is unreal. But an objective to reach the championship of the league in that time is practical.

In setting practical objectives managers must face up to the problem of whether to be conservative or expansive. For instance, should a firm set its five-year sales objective at a figure easily accomplished, or should it be optimistic and double the conservative figure? Much depends on what is occurring in the industry, what competitors are doing, [and] estimates of economic, political, and technological factors. Managers may feel that a conservative objective will avoid the risk of discouraging employees; or they may estimate that employees will work hard to exceed the low objective. Other managers may feel that high objectives act chiefly as a challenge, believing that great achievement results from striving for high goals. In the United States we seem to prefer the second approach.

There are many other elements to be considered in settling upon practical objectives. Innovation and creativity play very important parts. So do the state of the arts, the availability of investment funds, premises concerning family-owned firms, and the growth of resources that obey laws of nature rather than synthetic processes.

A third prerequisite concerns the logical relationships between long-range objectives and enterprise purpose. The objectives of the first plan to be made must be those on whose achievement the realization of the objectives of second and third generations of plans depends. This requirement is simply common sense, but the application in practical situations is not nearly so clear. For instance, in pursuing the purposes of the educational enterprise visualized above, should the objective of the first five-year plan be to raise a fund, hire a faculty, and/or recruit students? A business firm whose objective is to double its sales in five years cannot hope to do so entirely through internal expansion. It has such options as buying established firms, producing others' products under license, integrating vertically, or combining all types of approaches. Which step is first? If planners only knew!

BUILDING BLOCKS

Conceptualization of the enterprise image as it approaches maturity makes it possible to visualize in it the achieved objectives of successive long-range plans. These objectives may be viewed as building blocks in numbered order which, when appropriately arranged, become the integrated structure. The objectives of the earliest long-term plans provide the foundation blocks and succeeding plans yield the walls and roof of the mature structure.

Since each enterprise image is unique and surely changes with men, time, and circumstance, it follows that no generalization concerning the "right" objectives can be made and that the potentiality of achievement of the image itself is likely to be ephemeral. As a consequence, managers are forced to identify *de novo* the elements of the firm's ultimate image, determine the required order of their achievement, and establish a long-term plan to accomplish the objectives with top priority. Because the inherited and modified aspects of the image may require several generations of managers to realize, each manager should enjoy the satisfaction of having made a partial contribution and not be disappointed because the realization of the grand design is beyond his time and capability. Each generation of Americans should be happy in its contribution to

Jefferson's vision of our society's purpose rather than feel frustrated in the little progress it really makes.

It is of utmost importance that the selected objectives should be quantified. Vague statements such as improvement in sales, increased profit, or high morale are simply useless for planning purposes. There is a need to know "how much" in order to determine what resource commitment is necessary and whether the objective is achieved. One cannot know how to plan for an increase in sales, but one certainly does know how to plan for a 10 percent increase. With this target, the manager will ultimately know for certain the degree of success he achieved.

NO PROBLEM

For many objectives, quantification does not present a difficult physical problem. Such things as profits, sales, output, or quality are customarily stated in dollars or units or transactions. The only problem arises in persuading managers to select a quantified objective. This issue is psychological in nature. Some men shy away because they tend to stress the many unknowns in the picture. Others refuse because they do not wish their performance to be measured against specific objectives. Perhaps these fears can be overcome by education.

There will be some objectives which are difficult or impossible to quantify directly. Examples would include morale, developing and training managers, social responsibility, creativity, quality, and public image. Assuming that it is reasonable and desirable to select one or more of these objectives for planning purposes, it is advantageous to quantify them indirectly if possible. The objective should be analyzed to discover some quantifiable element which is closely related with the qualitative objective. For instance, since absenteeism closely correlates with low morale, the determination to cut absenteeism by 50 percent provides a substitute quantified objective for improvement in morale. Frequently a manager can find more than one correlative of the intended objective. The difficulty of this approach to indirect quantification is no excuse for avoiding these types of planning objectives. They should give impetus to the search because abandonment is a costly alternative. Unsought objectives cannot be realized beyond an occasional coincidence.

Important as it is to quantify, even by indirection, it is realistic to understand that such procedure is often frustrated by the press of continuing operations and by the difficulty of getting managerial agreement on a precise statement of objectives. While earnest attempts can, in time, reduce inchoate qualitative ends to more manageable proportions, it is fortunately true that the enterprise can still operate effectively when there is only agreement on broad objectives.

Short-range objectives support the hierarchy of long-range objectives, enterprise purposes, and social purposes. They are the one area where managers feel at home. It is difficult to project the distant future. So intangible are many elements and so rare is the talent to deal with them that most operating managers turn with relief to short-run specifications. They feel that here at last they can operate in a familiar environment.

Long-range plans, drawn to plot the accomplishment of objectives, are notably more vague for distant years than for the immediate future. This means that what is planned for accomplishment in the fifth year, if this is the length of the planning period, is more uncertain than what is planned for the fourth, third, second, and first year. Short-range objectives, typically to be realized in the first year of a long-range plan, are both comprehensive and specific. The approach to them should always be from the distant (fifth) year to the present and not vice versa. What is to be done in the immediate year must provide a foundation for the objectives of each successive year and this can only be guaranteed if short-range plans are part of the long-range plan.

The selection of short-range objectives proceeds from an evaluation of priorities relating to long-range objectives. Some things simply need to be done first either because they are a prerequisite to other objectives or because of lead time considerations. For instance, as a new firm is established to accomplish certain purposes, the raising of capital is a prime requisite when compared with any other objective. It must have capital for fixed and operating expenses and a plan is needed to secure it. Conceivably this may be the sole short-run objective. If so, the objectives visualized for the second year might be hiring managers for engineering, production, and sales; leasing space and equipment; and manning the organization. At the same time, if a three-year lead time is necessary, say for installing a piece of specialized equipment, then writing specifications and placing the order would also be an objective of the immediate year.

Thus, short-range objectives are identical with the objectives of the first year in a long-range plan. The problem becomes one of defining, clarifying, quantifying, and timing them. It is necessary to draw a plan for accomplishing each objective and combining these in a master plan for review in terms of logic, consistency, and practicality.

AFTER APPROVAL

Once the master plan is approved, the individual plans which are its elements are assigned to one or more subordinate managers for execution. Accomplishment of these several but separate objectives may be the duty of one manager or it may be the combined duty of several. The objective of raising funds to meet the requirements of operating activities may reasonably be assigned to the finance manager. But objectives relating to public relations, executive succession, or quality are clearly assignable to nearly every manager because each, willy-nilly, will make his individual contribution.

The logic of developing subsidiary plans is clear. The agreed objectives of the short-range plan are parcelled out to the chief executive's immediate subordinates. They, in turn, will assign elements of these objectives to their subordinates. This process of fractionation continues to the level of the front-line supervisor. Thus, every manager should have a group of assigned, quantified objectives to accomplish during the immediate year. For each of these he will develop specific plans.

Ideally, each manager may be viewed as executing several plans simultaneously, making consistent progress toward the realization of several objectives. It is difficult in practice to maintain this perspective for several reasons. The objectives themselves are quite diverse. For a sales manager they may range from rearranging sales territories, recruiting salesmen, manager development, service review and improvement, opening new markets, minimizing transportation and warehousing costs, and marketing research to securing new engineering or product design. It is difficult to apply simultaneous effort to these objectives. As a human being, the sales manager, for instance, will find he makes more progress by concentrating attention on each objective one after another. As he does so, planned accomplishment of all objectives is bound to suffer. Furthermore, every man tends to invest time in the objectives relating to his peculiar interests. This leads inevitably to neglected objectives.

Balance is difficult in the face of shifting priorities and changing costs—inevitable occurrences in any dynamic environment. For instance, market strategy may call for shifting to an alternative distribution plan, or advancing the predetermined shift by two years as a response to improperly evaluated competitive pressures. Executing this kind of decision may place second priority on an objective to complete a new product design. Similarly, a new research program, blithely adopted by naive managers, may have to be dropped entirely or modified drastically because its accumulating costs are gradually depriving other functions of their life-giving operating dollars, or even threatening the financial stability of the firm long before any substantial benefits can be converted to realized revenue.

Another difficulty in balancing objectives arises when unforeseen circumstances throw a plan out of phase. The loss of a key subordinate, a fire, bankruptcy of a vendor, a strike, and many similar occurrences have this effect. They may even jeopardize the planned action and force replanning.

Finally, managers give prime attention to those objectives in which their superiors show marked interest. A superior who is more interested in sales than in manager training will inquire into the former with regularity but perhaps never inquire into the latter. The reaction of subordinate managers is to attend particularly to the sales objective even though this means stealing time from the supervision of progress toward other objectives.

From these considerations it may be concluded that maintaining balanced progress toward accomplishing all objectives is almost insuperable. This need not be true. A sophisticated manager counters his own weaknesses and understands that all objectives are important, not only for their own sakes but especially because their proper accomplishment is a prerequisite to the success of the long-range plan. This type of manager understands his environment and himself, the responsibility resting upon his shoulders, and he will take intelligent action.

Planning objectives are seen in a hierarchical framework, logically based on social purposes. The discussion has been entirely in terms of logic and principle. Those readers who look for specific rules spelling out what objectives to select are bound to be disappointed. The basic point is that every manager must do his own thinking. He must, if he would be successful, be an educated man: He must know our history, understand his environment, know the principles of planning, and finally draw on his store of personal wisdom to select socially useful objectives.

NOTES AND REFERENCES

1. Although semantic problems are not too serious in this area, there are such terms as *purpose, goal,* and *target* which are often used synonymously. Perhaps greater clarity can be achieved by reserving *purpose* to describe the reason for the existence of an enterprise or any of its divisions and departments; *goal* and *target,* terms borrowed from games, to describe the aims of minor or informal plans such as a salesman's goal; and *objective* to describe the end for which a plan is designed.
2. After R. Linton, *The Tree of Culture* (New York: Vintage Books, Inc., 1958), p. 37.
3. *Administrative Reflections from World War II* (University, Alabama: University of Alabama Press, 1948), p. 77.
4. R. P. O'Brien "Electric Utility Planning" a paper presented to the Seminar on Long-Range Planning (University of California, Los Angeles: Research Division, Graduate School of Business Administration, September, 1962).

9

Long-Range Planning:
Challenge to
Management Science

Peter F. Drucker

In this article one of the most widely read contributors to the practice of management starts off by identifying what long-range planning is not. From there he defines the proper role of management science in the planning process, stressing that planning is a continuous, ongoing process. Drucker's perspective on planning is a little different from the usual and is well worth examining.—Eds.

I

It is easier to define long-range planning by what it is not rather than by what it is. Three things in particular, which it is commonly believed to be, it emphatically is not.

1. *First it is not "forecasting."* It is not masterminding the future, in other words. Any attempt to do so is foolish; human beings can neither predict nor control the future.

If anyone still suffers from the delusion that the ability to forecast beyond the shortest time span is given to us, let him look at the headlines in yesterday's paper, and then ask himself which of them he could possibly have predicted ten years ago.

SOURCE: Reprinted by permission of the author and publisher from "Long-Range Planning: Challenge to Management Science," *Management Science,* Vol. 5, No. 3, 1959, pp. 238-249.

- Could he have forecast that by today the Russians would have drawn even with us in the most advanced branches of physical sciences and of engineering?

- Could he have forecast that West Germany in complete ruins and chaos then would have become the most conservative country in the world and one of the most productive ones, let alone that it would become very stable politically?

- Could he have forecast that the Near East would become a central trouble spot, or would he have had to assume that the oil revenues there would take care of all problems?

This is the way the future always behaves. To try to mastermind it is therefore childish; we can only discredit what we are doing by attempting it. We must start out with the conclusion that forecasting is not respectable and not worthwhile beyond the shortest of periods. *Long-range planning is necessary precisely because we cannot forecast.*

But there is another, and even more compelling reason why forecasting is not long-range planning. Forecasting attempts to find the most probable course of events, or at best, a range of probabilities. But the entrepreneurial problem is the unique event that will change the possibilities, for the entrepreneurial universe is not a physical but a value universe. Indeed the central entrepreneurial contribution and the one which alone is rewarded with a profit, is to bring about the unique event, the *innovation* that changes the probabilities.

Let me give an example—a very elementary one which has nothing to do with innovation but which illustrates the importance of the improbable even for purely adaptive business behavior.

A large coffee distributor has for many years struggled with the problem of the location and capacity of its processing plants throughout the country. It had long been known that coffee prices were as important a factor in this, as location of market, volume, or transportation and delivery strategy. Now if we can forecast anything, it is single-commodity prices; and the price forecasts of the company economists have been remarkably accurate. Yet the decisions on plant location and capacity based on these forecasts have again and again proven costly blunders. Extreme pricing events, the probability of which at any one time was exceedingly low, had, even if they lasted only for a week at a time, impact on the economics of the system that were vastly greater than that of the accurately forecast "averages." Forecasting, in other words, obscured economic reality. What was needed (as the Theory of Games could have proven) was to look at the extreme possibilities, and to ask, "which of these can we not afford to disregard?"

The only thing atypical in this example is that it is so simple. Usually things are quite a bit more complex. But despite its (deceptive) simplicity it shows why forecasting is not an adequate basis even for purely adaptive behavior, let alone for the entrepreneurial decisions of long-range planning.

2. The next thing to be said about what long-range planning is not, is that it does not deal with future decisions. It deals with the *futurity of present decisions.*

Decisions exist only in the present. The question that faces the long-range planner is not what we should do tomorrow. It is what do we have to do today to be ready for an uncertain tomorrow. The question is not what will happen in the future. It is: what futurity do we have to factor into our present thinking and doing, what time spans do we have to consider, and how do we converge them to a simultaneous decision in the present?

Decision making is essentially a time machine which synchronizes into one present a great number of divergent time spans. This is, I think, something which we are only learning now. Our approach today still tends toward the making of plans for something we will decide to do in the future. This may be a very entertaining exercise, but it is a futile one.

Again, long-range planning is necessary because we can make decisions only in the present; the rest are pious intentions. And yet we cannot make decisions for the present alone; the most expedient, most opportunist decision—let alone the decision not to decide—may commit us on a long-range basis, if not permanently and irrevocably.

3. Finally, the most common misconception of all, *long-range planning is not an attempt to eliminate risk.* It is not even an attempt to minimize risk. Indeed any such attempt can only lead to irrational and unlimited risk and to certain disaster.

The central fact about economic activity is that, by definition, it commits present resources to future and therefore highly uncertain expectations. To take risk is therefore the essence of economic activity. Indeed one of the most rigorous theorems of economics (Boehm-Bawerk's Law) proves that existing means of production will yield greater economic performance only through greater uncertainty, that is, through greater risk.

But while it is futile to try to eliminate risk, and questionable to try to minimize it, it is essential that the risks taken be the *right risks.* The end result of successful long-range planning must be a capacity to take a greater risk; for this is the only way to improve *entrepreneurial* performance. To do this, however, we must know and understand the risks we take. We must be able to rationally choose among risk-taking courses of action rather than plunge into uncertainty on the basis of hunch, hearsay, or experience (no matter how meticulously quantified).

Now I think we can attempt to define what long-range planning is. It is the continuous process of making *present entrepreneurial (risk-taking) decisions* systematically and with the best possible knowledge of their futurity, organizing systematically *the efforts* needed to carry out these decisions, and measuring the results of these decisions against the expectations through *organized, systematic feedback.*

II

"This is all very well," many experienced businessmen might say (and do say). "But why make a production out of it? Isn't this what the entrepreneur has been doing all along, and doing quite successfully? Why then should it need all this elaborate mumbo jumbo? Why should it be an organized, perhaps even a separate activity? Why in other words, should we even talk about 'long-range planning,' let alone do it?"

It is perfectly true that there is nothing very new to entrepreneurial decisions. They have been made as long as we have had entrepreneurs. There is nothing new in here regarding the essentials of economic activity. It has always been the commitment of present resources to future expectations; and for the last three hundred years this has been done in contemplation of change. (This was not true earlier. Earlier economic activity was based on the assumption that there would be no change, which assumption was institutionally guarded and defended. Altogether up to the seventeenth century it was the purpose of all human institutions to prevent change. The business enterprise is a significant and rather amazing novelty in that it is the first human institution having the purpose of bringing about change.)

But there are several things which are new; and they have created the need for the organized, systematic, and above all, specific process that we call "long-range planning."[1]

1. The time span of entrepreneurial and managerial decisions has been lengthening so fast and so much as to make necessary systematic exploration of the uncertainty and risk of decisions.

In 1888 or thereabouts, an old and perhaps apocryphal story goes, the great Thomas Edison, already a world figure, went to one of the big banks in New York for a loan on something he was working on. He had plenty of collateral and he was a great man; so the vice-presidents all bowed and said "Certainly, Mr. Edison, how much do you need?" But one of them, out of idle curiosity asked, "Tell me, Mr. Edison, how long will it be before you have this new product?" Edison looked him in the eye and said, "Son, judging from past experience, it will be about eighteen months before I even know whether I'll have a product or not." Whereupon the vice-presidents collapsed in a body, and, despite the collateral, turned down the loan application. The man was obviously mad; eighteen months of uncertainty was surely not a risk a sane businessman would take!

Today practically every manager takes ten- or twenty-year risks without wincing. He takes them in product development, in research, in market development, in the development of a sales organization, and in almost anything. This lengthening of the time span of commitment is one of the most significant features of our age. It underlies our economic advances. But while quantitative in itself, it has changed the qualitative character of entrepreneurial decisions. It has, so to speak, converted time from being a dimension in which business decisions are being made into an essential element of the decisions themselves.

2. Another new feature is the speed and risk of innovation. To define what we mean by this term would go far beyond the scope of this paper.[2]

But we do not need to know more than that industrial research expenditures (that is, business expenditures aimed at innovating primarily peacetime products and processes) have increased in this country from less than $100 million in 1928 to $7 or 8 billion in 1958. Clearly, a technologically slow-moving, if not essentially stable economy has become one of violent technological flux, rapid obsolescence, and great uncertainty.

3. Then there is the growing complexity both of the business enterprise internally, and of the economy and society in which it exists. There is the growing specialization of work which creates increasing need for common vision, common understanding, and common language, without which top management decisions, however right, will never become effective action.

4. Finally—a subtle, but perhaps the most important point—the typical businessman's concept of the basis of entrepreneurial decision is, after all, a misconception.

Most businessmen still believe that these decisions are made by "top management." Indeed practically all text books lay down the dictum that "basic policy decisions" are the "prerogative of top management." At most, top management "delegates" certain decisions.

But this reflects yesterday's rather than today's reality, let alone that of tomorrow. It is perfectly true that top management must have the final say, the final responsibility. But the business enterprise of today is no longer an organization in which there are a handful of "bosses" at the top who make all the decisions while the "workers" carry out orders. It is primarily an organization[3] of professionals of highly specialized knowledge exercising autonomous, responsible judgment. And every one of them—whether manager or individual expert contributor—constantly makes truly entrepreneurial decisions, that is, decisions which affect the economic characteristics and risks of the entire enterprise. He makes them not by "delegation from above" but inevitably in the performance of his own job and work.

For this organization to be functioning, two things are needed: knowledge by the entire organization of what the direction, the goals, the expectations are; and knowledge by top management of what the decisions, commitments, and efforts of the people in the organization are. The needed focus—one might call it a *model of the relevants in internal and external environment*—only a "long-range plan" can provide.

One way to summarize what is new and different in the process of entrepreneurial decision making is in terms of information. The amount, diversity, and ambiguity of the information that is beating in on the decision maker have all been increasing so much that the built-in experience reaction that a good manager has cannot handle it. He breaks down; and his breakdown will take either of the two forms known to any experimental psychologist. One is withdrawal from reality, i.e., "I know what I know and I only go by it; the rest is quite irrelevant and I won't even look at it." Or there is a feeling that the universe has become completely irrational so that one decision is as good as the other, resulting in paralysis. We see both in executives who have to make decisions today. Neither is likely to result in rational or in successful decisions.

There is something else managers and management scientists might learn from the psychologists. Organization of information is often more important to the ability to perceive and act than analysis and understanding of the information. I recall one experience with the organization of research-planning in a pharmaceutical company. The attempt to analyze the research decisions—even to define alternatives of decisions—was a dismal failure. In the attempt, however, the decisions were classified to the point where the research people could know what kind of a decision was possible at what stage. They still did not know what factors should or should not be considered in a given decision, nor what its risks were. They could not explain why they made this decision rather than another one, nor spell out what they expected. But the mere organization of this information enabled them again to apply their experience and to "play hunches"—with measurable and very significant improvement in the performance of the entire research group.

"Long-range planning" is more than organization and analysis of information; it is a decision-making process. But even the information job cannot be done except as part of an organized planning effort—otherwise there is no way of determining which information is relevant.

III

What then are the requirements of long-range planning? We cannot satisfy all of them as yet with any degree of competence; but we can specify them.

Indeed, we can—and should—give two sets of specifications: One in terms of the characteristics of the process itself; another in terms of its major and specific new-knowledge content.

1. Risk-taking entrepreneurial decisions, no matter whether made rationally or by tea-leaf reading, always embody the same eight elements:

a. *Objectives.* This is, admittedly, an elusive term, perhaps even a metaphysical one. It may be as difficult for Management Science to define "objectives" as it is for biology to define "life." Yet, we will be as unable to do without "objectives" as the biologists are unable to do without "life." Any entrepreneurial decision, let alone the integrated decision system we call a "long-range plan," has objectives, consciously or not.

b. *Assumptions.* These are what is believed by the people who make and carry out decisions to be "real" in the internal and external universe of the business.

c. *Expectations.* The future events or results considered likely or attainable. These three elements can be said to *define the decision.*

d. *Alternative courses of action.* There never is—indeed, in a true uncertainty situation there never can be—"one right decision." There cannot even be "one best decision." There are always "wrong decisions," that is, decisions inadequate to the objectives, incompatible with the assumptions, or grossly improbable in the light of the expectations. But once these have been eliminated, there will still be alternatives left—each a different configuration of objectives, assumptions, and expectations, each with its own risks and its own ratio between risks and rewards, each with its own impact, its specific efforts, and its own results. Every decision is thus a value judgment—it is not the "facts that decide"; people have to choose between imperfect alternatives on the basis of uncertain knowledge and fragmentary understanding.

Two alternatives deserve special mention, if only because they have to be considered in almost every case. One is the alternative of no action (which is, of course, what postponing a decision often amounts to); the other is the very important choice between adaptive and innovating action—each having risks that differ greatly in character though not necessarily in magnitude.

e. The next element in the decision-making process is the *decision itself.*

f. But there is no such thing as one isolated decision; every decision is, of necessity, part of a *decision structure.*

Every financial man knows, for instance, that the original capital appropriation on a new investment implies a commitment to future and usually larger capital appropriations which, however, are almost never as much as mentioned in the proposal submitted. Few of them seem to realize, however, that this implies not only a positive commitment but also, by mortgaging future capital resources, limits future freedom of action. The structuring impact of a decision is even greater in respect to allocations of scarce manpower, such as research people.

g. A decision is only pious intention unless it leads to action. Every decision, therefore, has an *impact stage.*

This impact always follows Newton's Second Law, so to speak; it consists of action and reaction. It requires effort. But it also dislocates. There is, therefore, always the question: what effort is required, by whom, and where? What must people know, what must they do, and what must they achieve? But there is also the question—generally neglected—what does this decision do to other areas? Where does it shift the burden, the weaknesses, and the stress points; and what impact does it have on the outside; in the market, in the supply structure, in the community, and so on?

h. And, finally, there are *results*.

Each of these elements of the process deserves an entire book by itself. But I think I have said enough to show that both, the process itself and each element in it, are *rational*, no matter how irrational and arbitrary they may appear. Both the process and all its elements can therefore be defined, can be studied, and can be analyzed. And both can be improved through systematic and organized work. In particular, as in all rational processes, the entire process is improved and strengthened as we define, clarify, and analyze each of its constituent elements.

2. We can also, as said above, describe long-range planning in terms of its specific new-knowledge content. Among the areas where such new knowledge is particularly cogent, might be mentioned:

a. *The time dimensions of planning.* To say "long-range" or "short-range" planning implies that a given time span defines the planning; and this is actually how businesses look at it when they speak of a "five-year plan" or a "ten-year plan." But the essence of planning is to make present decisions with knowledge of their futurity. It is the futurity that determines the time span, and not vice versa.

Strictly speaking, "short range" and "long range" do not describe time spans but stages in every decision. "Short-range" is the stage before the decision has become fully effective, the stage during which it is only "costs" and not yet "results." The "short-range" of a decision to build a steel mill are the five years or so until the mill is in production. And the "long-range" of any decision is the period of expected performance needed to make the decision a successful one—the twenty or more years above break-even point operations in the case of the steel mill, for instance.

There are limitations on futurity. In business decisions the most precise mathematical statement is often that of my eighth grade teacher that parallels are two lines which do not meet this side of the school yard. Certainly, in the expectations and anticipations of a business the old rule of statistics usually applies that anything beyond twenty years equals infinity; and since expectations more than twenty years hence have normally a present value of zero, they should receive normally only a minimal allocation of present efforts and resources.

Yet it is also true that, if future results require a long gestation period, they will be obtained only if initiated early enough. Hence, long-range planning requires knowledge of futurity: what do we have to do today if we want to be some place in the future? What will not get done at all if we do not commit resources to it today?

If we know that it takes ninety-nine years to grow Douglas firs in the Northwest to pulping size, planting seedlings today is the only way we can provide for pulp supply in ninety-nine years. Someone may well develop some speeding-up hormone; but we cannot bank on it if we are in the paper industry. It is quite conceivable, may indeed be highly probable, that we will use trees primarily as a source of chemicals long before these trees grow to maturity. We may even get the bulk of paper supply thirty years hence from less precious, less highly structured sources of cellulose than a tree, which is the most advanced chemical factory in the plant kingdom. This simply means, however, that our forests may put us into the chemical industry some time within the next thirty years; and we had better learn now something about chemistry. If our paper plants depend on Douglas fir, our planning cannot confine itself to twenty years, but must consider ninety-nine years. For we must be able to say whether we have to plant trees today, or whether we can postpone this expensive job.

But on other decisions even five years would be absurdly long. If our business is buying up distress merchandise and selling it at auction, then next week's clearance sale is "long-range future"; and anything beyond is largely irrelevant to us.

It is the nature of the business and the nature of the decision which determine the time spans of planning.

Yet the time spans are not static or "given." The time decision itself is the first and a highly important risk-taking decision in the planning process. It largely determines the allocation of resources and efforts. It largely determines the risks taken (and one cannot repeat too often that to postpone a decision is in itself a risk-taking and often irrevocable decision). Indeed, the time decision largely determines the character and nature of the business.

b. *Decision structure and configuration.* The problem of the time dimension is closely tied in with that of decision structure.

Underlying the whole concept of long-range planning are two simple insights. We need an integrated decision structure for the business as a whole. There are really no isolated decisions on a product, or on markets, or on people. Each major risk-taking decision has impact throughout the whole; and no decision is isolated in time. Every decision is a move in a chess game, except that the rules of enterprise are by no means as clearly defined. There is no finite "board" and the pieces are neither as neatly distinguished nor as few in number. Every move opens some future opportunities for decision, and forecloses others. Every move, therefore, commits positively and negatively.

Let me illustrate these insights with a simple example, that of a major steel company today.

I posit that it is reasonably clear to any student of technology (not of steel technology but of technology in general) that steelmaking is on the threshold of major technological change. *What* they are perhaps the steelmaker knows, but *that* they are I think any study of the pattern, rhythm, and I would say morphology of technological development, might indicate. A logical—rather than metallurgical—analysis of the process would even indicate *where* the changes are likely to occur. At the same time, the steel company faces the need of building new capacity if it wants to keep its share of the market, assuming that steel consumption will continue to increase. A decision to build a plant today, when there is nothing but the old technology available, means in effect that for fifteen to twenty years the company cannot go into the new technology except at prohibitive cost. It is very unlikely, looking at the technological pattern, that these changes will be satisfied by minor modifications in existing facilities; they are likely to require new facilities to a large extent. By building today the company closes certain opportunities to itself, or at least it very greatly raises the future entrance price. At the same time, by making the decision to postpone building, it may foreclose other opportunities such as market position, perhaps irrevocably. Management therefore has to understand—without perhaps too much detail—the location of this decision in the continuing process of entrepreneurial decision.

At the same time, entrepreneurial decisions must be fundamentally expedient decisions. It is not only impossible to know all the contingent effects of a decision, even for the shortest time period ahead. The very attempt to know them would lead to complete paralysis.

But the determination of what should be considered and what should be ignored, is in itself a difficult and consequential decision. We need knowledge to make it—I might say that we need a theory of entrepreneurial inference.

c. *The characteristics of risks.* It is not only magnitude of risk that we need to be able to appraise in entrepreneurial decisions. It is above all the character of the risk. Is it, for instance, the kind of risk we can afford to take, or the kind of risk we cannot afford to take? Or is it that rare but singularly important risk, the risk we cannot afford not to take—sometimes regardless of the odds?

The best General Electric scientists, we are told, advised their management in 1945 that it would be at least forty years before nuclear energy could be used to produce electric power commercially. Yet General Electric—rightly—decided that it had to get into the atomic energy field. It could not afford not to take the risk as long as there was the remotest possibility that atomic energy would, after all, become a feasible source of electric power.

We know from experience that the risk we cannot afford not to take is like a "high-low" poker game. A middle hand will inevitably lose out. But we do not know why this is so. And the other, and much more common kinds of risk we do not really understand at all.

d. *Finally, there is the area of measurements.* I do not have to explain . . . why measurements are needed in management, and especially for the organized entrepreneurial decisions we call "long-range planning."

But it should be said that in human institutions, such as a business enterprise, measurements, strictly speaking, do not and cannot exist. It is the definition of a measurement that it be impersonal and objective, that is, extraneous to the event measured. A child's growth is not dependent on the yardstick or influenced by being recorded. But any measurement in a business enterprise determines action—both on the part of the measurer and the measured—and thereby directs, limits and causes behavior and performance of the enterprise. Measurement in the enterprise is always motivation, that is, moral force, as much as it is *ratio cognoscendi*.

In addition, in long-range planning we do not deal with observable events. We deal with future events, that is, with expectations. And expectations, being incapable of being observed, are never "facts" and cannot be measured.

Measurements, in long-range planning, thus present very real problems, especially conceptual ones. Yet precisely because what we measure and how we measure determines what will be considered relevant, and determines thereby not just what we see, but what we—and others—do, measurements are all-important in the planning process. Above all, unless we build expectations into the planning decision in such a way that we can very early realize whether they are actually fulfilled or not—including a fair understanding of what are significant deviations both in time and in scale—we cannot plan; and we have no feedback, no way of self-control in management.

We obviously also need for long-range planning *managerial* knowledge—the knowledge with respect to the operations of a business. We need such knowledge as that of the resources available, especially the human resources; their capacities and their limitations. We need to know how to "translate" from business needs, business results, and business decisions into functional capacity and specialized effort. There is, after all, no functional decision, there is not even functional data, just as there is no functional profit, no functional loss, no functional investment, no functional risk, no functional customer, no functional product, and no functional image of a company. There is only a unified company product, risk, investment, and so on, hence only company performance and company results. Yet at the same time the work obviously has to be done by people each of whom has to be specialized. Hence for a decision to be possible, we must be able to integrate divergent individual knowledges and capacities into one organization potential; and for a decision to be effective, we must be able to translate it into a diversity of individual and expert, yet focused efforts.

There are also big problems of knowledge in the entrepreneurial task that I have not mentioned—the problems of growth and change, for instance, or those of the moral values of a society and their meaning to business. But these are problems that exist for many areas and disciplines other than management.

And in this paper I have confined myself intentionally to knowledge that is specific to the process of long-range planning. Even so I have barely mentioned the main areas. But I think I have said enough to substantiate three conclusions:

1. Here are areas of genuine knowledge, not just areas in which we need data. What we need above all are basic theory and conceptual thinking.

2. The knowledge we need is new knowledge. It is not to be found in the traditional disciplines of business such as accounting or economics. It is also not available, by and large, in the physical or life sciences. From the existing disciplines we can get a great deal of help, of course, especially in tools and techniques. And we need all we can get. But the knowledge we need is distinct and specific. It pertains not to the physical, the biological, or the psychological universe, though it partakes of them all. It pertains to the specific institution, the enterprise, which is a social institution existing in contemplation of human values. What is "knowledge" in respect to this institution, let alone what is "scientific," must therefore always be determined by reference to the nature, function and purposes of this specific (and very peculiar) institution.

3. It is not within the decision of the entrepreneur whether he wants to make risk-taking decisions with long futurity; he makes them by definition. All that is within his power is to decide whether he wants to make them responsibly or irresponsibly, with a rational chance of effectiveness and success, or as blind gamble against all odds. And both because the process is essentially a rational process, and because the effectiveness of the entrepreneurial decisions depends on the understanding and voluntary efforts of others, the process will be the more responsible and the more likely to be effective, the more it is a rational, organized process based on knowledge.

IV

Long-range planning is risk-taking decision making. As such it is the responsibility of the policy maker, whether we call him entrepreneur or manager. To do the job rationally and systematically does not change this. Long-range planning does not "substitute facts for judgment," does not "substitute science for the manager." It does not even lessen the importance and role of managerial ability, courage, experience, intuition, or even hunch just as scientific biology and systematic medicine have not lessened the importance of these qualities in the individual physician. On the contrary, the systematic organization of the planning job and the supply of knowledge to it, should make more effective individual managerial qualities of personality and vision.

But at the same time long-range planning offers major opportunity and major challenge to Management Science and to the Management Scientist.[4] We need systematic study of the process itself and of every one of its elements. We need systematic work in a number of big areas of new knowledge—at least we need to know enough to organize our ignorance.

At the same time, long-range planning is the crucial area; it deals with the decisions which, in the last analysis, determine the character and the survival of the enterprise.

So far, it must be said, Management Science has not made much contribution to long-range planning. Sometimes one wonders whether those who call themselves "Management Scientists" are even aware of the risk-taking character of economic activity and of the resultant entrepreneurial job of long-range planning. Yet, in the long run, Management Science and Management Scientists may well, and justly, be judged by their ability to supply the knowledge and thinking needed to make long-range planning possible, simple, and effective.

NOTES AND REFERENCES

1. *Long-range planning* is not a term I like or would have picked myself. It is a misnomer—as are so many of our terms in economics and management, such as *capitalism, automation, operations research, industrial engineering,* or *depreciation.* But it is too late to do anything about the term; it has become common usage.

2. For a discussion see my book, *The Landmarks of Tomorrow* (New York: Harper and Brothers, 1958).

3. For a discussion of this "new organization," see again my *The Landmarks of Tomorrow,* mentioned above.

4. I would like to say here that I do not believe that the world is divided into "managers" and "management scientists." One man may well be both. Certainly, management scientists must understand the work and job of the manager, and vice versa. But conceptually and as a kind of work, the two are distinct.

10

Making Long-Range
Company Planning
Pay Off

George A. Steiner

This article makes a strong case for the importance of long-range planning to American companies. For those interested in prescriptions, the article outlines a series of "how to" steps designed to lead to effective plan development. Note particularly his first step—planning to plan.—Eds.

This article is devoted to a thumbnail sketch of two major aspects of long-range planning. First is the methodology or procedure for long-range planning. The second concerns the payoff to a company that does long-range planning.

I have chosen to dwell on these two points for several reasons. First, while long-range planning has grown rapidly in recent years and has paid off handsomely for many companies, there still are questions raised about its value. Second, while important progress has been made in the techniques of long-range planning, there are comparatively few detailed case studies and principles which are available for those who wish to initiate the process or improve their planning.

These two factors are related. I suspect, although solid proof is not available, that the major reason for the fact that more companies do not engage in long-range planning is that they do not know precisely how to go about it. Not wishing to admit this even to themselves, other reasons are given for the lack of long-range planning.[1]

SOURCE: © 1962 by the Regents of the University of California. Reprinted from *California Management Review*, Volume IV, Number 2, pp. 28–41, by permission of the Regents.

WHAT IS LONG-RANGE PLANNING?

Planning in general is the conscious determination of courses of action to achieve preconceived objectives. It is deciding in advance what is to be done, when it is to be done, by whom it is to be done, and how it is to be done. It can range from the detailed, specific and rigid to the broad, general and flexible design.

Long-range planning does this for extended periods of time. Long-range planning is a process for establishing long-range goals; working out strategies, programs, and policies to achieve these goals; and setting up the necessary machinery to insure that the company gets where it wants to go.

It is a process of choosing from among alternative courses of action and charting the use of time, resources, and effort to achieve the objective sought. The further into the future the plan stretches the less detailed are its specific parts. The subject matter of long-range plans should cover products, services, facilities, manpower, research and development, organization, marketing, financial matters, and various aspects of management itself.[2]

HOW LONG IS LONG-RANGE?

How long a time should a long-range plan cover? The answer to this question is much like the response of Abraham Lincoln when asked how long a man's legs ought to be. "Long enough to reach the ground," said the President.

Similarly, the length of a planning period will vary considerably from company to company and subject to subject. It is not fixed or rigid. The time span of a plan should cover the period encompassing important financial commitments and their payoff.

For example, depending upon subject matter, coverage should embrace product development time and period of major financial impact following development; resource development time (e.g., sources of supply, management talent, or labor skills); and time required to develop physical facilities plus payoff period for major capital investments. For most businesses such factors will establish a minimum long-range planning period of from 5 to 10 years.

FORMAL LONG-RANGE PLANNING IN INDUSTRY

All managers engage in long-range planning—if only to increase their own salaries. If they do not plan they are not doing their jobs. In the past, when top managers needed help in planning they often hired an assistant or created a vice-president for administration.

Large and complex organizations centuries ago had staff positions for planning. Long-range planning, therefore, is not new. What is new is charging someone with full-time responsibility for planning and giving him a staff to do the job. It is the growth of planning departments and staff specialists at the top levels of corporations and major divisions that is new.

Pressures on American companies to establish such formal organizations have been most strong during the past ten years. Among the major pressures are the following:

1. Business has become increasingly complex because of expanding enterprise size, decentralization of authority, diversification of product lines, mergers, and the growing sensitivity of internal operations to uncontrollable environmental forces.

2. Technological rates of change are increasing and placing a premium on those organizations which can foresee and adapt to them.

3. A variety of forces are squeezing profit margins.

4. End-use markets (domestic) are altering significantly and rapidly with geographic population shifts, changes in population composition, new social trends influencing market behavior of consumers, and growing competition for consumer savings.

5. End-use markets (abroad) are changing rapidly with new commercial alignments, and efforts to industrialize the underdeveloped countries of the world.

6. There has been a rapid development of tools for planning and a growing recognition of the need for skilled technical competence to apply them to long-range planning. This trend promises to accelerate. In mind are not alone the new powerful mathematical tools which have been adapted to business decision making (e.g., linear programming, game theory, probability theory, etc.); but the application of computers, simulation and systems concepts, and new developments in economics, psychology, and other social sciences.

7. Competitors are devoting more attention to long-range planning.[3]

Under such pressures more and more companies in the past ten years have been developing long-range planning programs and extending the field of inquiry further into the future. I believe, however, that effective long-range planning in industry is not as widespread as it ought to be.

Facts about the growth of formalized long-range planning are not plentiful nor reliable. *Nation's Business* concluded that about 20 percent of businesses had long-range planning in 1953 compared to about 50 percent in 1958.[4] The National Industrial Conference Board concluded in 1956 that of 189 manufacturing companies participating in its survey only one out of four had no formalized forward planning or failed to plan ahead beyond one year. About half of those having long-range plans said they included all the major elements of the enterprise in their planning. Only half said they placed much reliance on the plans.[5]

A survey made by *Management Methods* in 1958 revealed that among its respondents, only 18 percent had formal advanced plans while another 52 percent had informal advanced plans. No advanced plans were made in 30 percent of the companies covered. When asked whether respondents felt they were doing as much advanced planning as they should, 72 percent replied in the negative. Practically all planning in companies in this survey was for five years or less.

Professors Sord and Welsch found in a study published in the same year that two-thirds of the number surveyed had long-range plans, but the subject matter varied greatly. Two-thirds had long-range sales plans, but only about one-third had long-range research or expense plans. Only about half had long-range profit or cash plans. Practically all plans were for 5 years or less.[6]

These data, while not conclusive, are helpful. My own empirical observations, together with the data cited, lead me to conclude that, while formal long-range corporate planning has grown by leaps and bounds in the past ten years, the practice is heavily concentrated in larger enterprises, and it is centered there on a few major problem areas (capital expenditures, product development, and sales) for periods less than five years. The coverage, time span, and usage is not great enough in light of potential value.

HOW TO MAKE A LONG-RANGE PLAN

In developing long-range plans it is helpful to think in terms of a series of steps. But, since the planner must always think in terms of retracing his thinking, allowance must also be made for some overlapping of these steps.

The sequence of steps presented in the next few paragraphs illustrates one concrete framework upon which a company may plan. It is flexible and has been used successfully. This particular sequence has the virtue of focusing attention on product which is usually, although not always, the principal theme of a business long-range plan.

The specific methodology of planning may vary much from one company to another whether or not the steps presented here are followed. This arises because the process must be flexible to accommodate an unusually complex intermeshing of variables which are subject to constant change. In mind are such factors as the technical knowledge and wisdom of the planners, the particular needs of the enterprise, the organization for planning, availability of strategic facts, subject-matter of the plans, and uses to be made of the results.[7]

First: Plan to Plan

First is *planning to plan*. As the Cleveland Electric Illuminating Company has so well documented, company planning must be planned.[8] This may seem as redundant as Cole Porter's "Begin the Beguine." But planning does not just happen. It must be planned!

A suitable planning climate must be established, and the organization made planning conscious. Policy decisions must be made about who will do what in planning. And, step-by-step procedures must be worked out. In one major planning program of a large corporation in which I participated the first thing we did was to prepare a detailed letter covering the entire planning procedure for signature by the president. The letter was addressed to all parties involved. In this way everyone knew what was the plan to plan. The newer the plan the more important the thoroughness with which this step should be taken. But even where planning is well established the procedures should be carefully spelled out, as in, for example, the *Westinghouse Planning Guide*.[9]

On the other hand, care should be taken to avoid overdoing this step. It is easily possible to preplan too long, in too much detail and to spend too much time on clarification of procedures. There is too much feedback in going through the sequences of planning to warrant more than just enough detail in this step to get the process moving.

Basic assumptions must be made at various stages in the planning process. At the outset, however, some of the overall assumptions upon which planning rests should be set forth. In mind, for example, are premises which provide a framework for planning, such as the course of the cold war, population movements, or competitors' activities.

Purely methodological premises may also be established, such as— plans will be based upon constant rather than actual anticipated prices. But, whatever the premises determined, the point is that standards must be developed to guide the planning program. Otherwise, lack of coordination, unnecessary emphasis and study on less important subjects, excessive planning costs, and confusion in drawing conclusions are predictive consequences of poorly devised or neglected premises.

Second: Define Objectives

Second, *objectives of planning must be clearly specified*. The purpose of the plan, the objectives to be sought in the planning process, and the relation of planning goals to other goals and objectives in the enterprise must be clarified. Setting objectives provides the key to how planning will be done, the strategic factors to be emphasized in plan development, and methods by which planning will become the basis for action.

The objective of every business, of course, is to make a profit. Otherwise the business will not survive. But saying this is far from developing a set of goals which will best serve a company and its long-range planning program.

Be specific. Goals should be established as concretely as possible. What does this mean? Is the goal to be an aggregate absolute volume of profits? Is the goal to be expressed in terms of a percentage of sales? Is it to be in terms of percentage of investment? If it is return on investment, how is this to be calculated? Is it the E. I. du Pont de Nemours and Company or the Monsanto Chemical Company formula? Will a rising rate of return on investment be accepted even if sales do not increase?

Is sales growth in itself a goal? Is sales stability a goal? How are conflicts among goals to be resolved? Are there other objectives which need to be expressed as a guide to the planning program?

Defining corporate goals. There has recently been a growing interest in defining corporate goals, probably in part as an outgrowth of long-range planning needs. Often-stated economic-type objectives, besides those mentioned in preceding paragraphs, are: growth, expressed in terms of sales, assets, employees, profits, or product line; stability, usually expressed in terms of sales, manpower, and profits; flexibility, expressed in numerous ways, such as ability to innovate, speed of response to new environment, especially competition; diversity in preparedness to compete; sensitivity to technological and market changes; and acquisition of a given status of technical skill.

Very frequently, goals express ethical or moral considerations. These are generally described in terms such as leadership of the firm in the industry, integrity and honesty in dealing with others, maintenance of amicable community relations, and assumption of social responsibilities with respect to community problems.[10]

Must be realistic. Long-range company goals should be given the greatest thought and formulated as realistically as possible. The validity of goals for planning should be tested upon the basis of past experience of the company and its industry, and future prospects for both. Unrealistic goals are not very helpful.

Sometimes an immediate problem will serve as the focal point for planning. If, for example, rate of return on stockholders' investment for a company has been well below the industry average for the past five years the prime goal for the company planning may be to achieve the industry average or better.

Similarly, actual or anticipated trouble with a product may provide the basis for a concrete goal, e.g., "eliminate the product and substitute others," "undertake new research on the product to improve its salability," or "cut costs of the product by X percent of sales so that it will attract a new level of demand."

Realistic projections of company operations must be placed against any goals established for the future. The difference between the two sets of numbers will reveal the magnitude of the tasks that lie ahead for the corporation. If, for example, a sales objective of 1,000,000 units is established for five years in the future, and 1,500,000 for ten years ahead, and a realistic forecast shows 750,000 units in 1967 and 1,150,000 in 1972, the magnitude of the problem for the company is revealed.

Through this process long-range company goals should be established for sales, profits, capital requirements, new and old product requirements. Then, for each of these, the gap between aspirations and projections on present plans and trends must be measured or defined.

Third: Explore Possible Strategies

The third step is to *develop strategies to fill the major gaps*. The problem here is to bring to the foreground and examine the principal alternatives open to the company in filling the gaps and then to choose from among them those most acceptable. There obviously are many ways to do this.

In this step companies must come face to face with major questions of policy. If there is a sales gap, for example, to what extent will it be filled with old products, by further penetration of old markets, or entrance into new markets? If this is not enough, to what extent should the old product be importantly modified by research? Where can and should costs be reduced or increased? Should new products be introduced? If so, should they be developed by the present company or acquired through merger? Should all new acquisitions have an affinity with present product lines, or is this not necessary?

While the central focus of planning is naturally on products, the question of strategies is not exclusively concerned with products. Strategies may be developed, for example, for management training, management succession, organization, investments of surplus cash, dividend policy, or public relations.

The precise steps to be followed in developing strategies to answer the kinds of questions given above obviously vary from case to case. One illustrative approach is as follows.

To begin with, tentative alternative courses of action may be set forth for testing in the planning process. These may be suggested by managers at different levels. A planning group itself may, and probably will, think up alternative strategies. The planning process will apply several screenings to the suggestions, the sifting measures which will become more rigorous in successive planning stages.

It is also healthy and often indispensable to undertake an objective and honest appraisal of company strengths and weaknesses in relevant areas. For example, if a company is planning a diversification program, analysis is important in the following areas—management competence to digest proposed mergers; financial capability; marketing abilities for the new product; and, if stock is used to acquire a new company, the ability of the present management to continue control of the enterprise. Other areas of review might include basic research and engineering competence, advertising and promotion skills, labor relations, quality of management, capacity to control costs and production, and product and service acceptability.

Elemental, of course, is the build-up of information important in choosing between alternative courses of action. This is a critical stage in planning because it is frequently difficult to acquire reliable information about the most crucial strategic factors in decision making. It is most important at this stage to concentrate on the strategic data, or those which will have the most significance in choice conclusions.

The range of phenomena about which data should be collected is very wide. For a new product possibility, for example, the analysis may cover technological matters, ranging from projection of prospective scientific advances affecting the product to costs and timing of research, development, tests, and engineering for the product. There are many economic matters of interest, including market changes, possible demand at different pricing levels, estimated fixed and variable costs, break-even volume, prospective return on investment, and probabilities of profit amounts at different price-volume-cost ranges. Where applicable, there are also, of course, social, political, military, and internal administrative matters demanding attention.

The next step is to *select strategies from among alternative possibilities*. More or less simultaneously, four analytical processes merge at this point. The first is the application, where appropriate, of new mathematical techniques to get a quantitative optimization of objectives.

The second is a modification of quantitative conclusions by a broad range of qualitative factors which will have a determining impact on final choices. Included in the latter, for example, would be estimates of what competitors are likely to do under given circumstances.

Break-even calculations. Third, to the extent practicable, the financial impact of decisions should be measured individually and in their entirety. This should be done by the preparation of break-even calculations, cash flow analyses, and balance sheet and profit and loss statements. The detail of analysis should naturally be tailored to fit the need and importance of the data to the reliability of conclusions. Computer simulation, while not now used very extensively in this step, is a fourth process which promises to grow in importance.

The net results of this stage should be the development of strategies to fill the gaps apparent in step two. These broad plans of action should be either the best possible solutions to the problems or, at the very least, suitable ones. They should be tested for feasibility in terms of management, manpower, finances, competitor actions, technical expectations, and market acceptability. Broad magnitudes and timing should be established.

Resulting strategies can be broad or relatively narrow. One important aerospace company in the United States recently matched a frank appraisal of its strengths and weaknesses in various disciplines of knowledge used in the industry against prospective new product developments. It reasoned that it could not maintain strength in all the areas of knowledge which it now covered. The result was an increase in strength in some areas and an elimination of many other areas.

Some companies have decided to expand through merger even though the resulting product line is heterogeneous. Other companies feel it a better strategy to acquire new products through merger only when there is a close relationship with present product line. Some companies mix these two strategies. Certain companies have decided to lead their industry in research and development. Others are content to follow.

A manufacturer of ceramics ware recently decided to concentrate only on products requiring advanced scientific and engineering skills and to abandon mass production of dinnerware. One electronics producer recently decided, following an agonizing appraisal, to abandon his computer line.

A medium-sized California food processor worked out a completely new detailed strategy for timing of annual sales promotion and new product development. A large oil company recently completed a detailed strategy covering its foreign investment program. These are illustrations of results from this step.

Fourth: Subplan to Fit Strategy

The fourth step in long-range planning is to *develop derivative operational plans*. A planning process is not complete until subsidiary plans are made to put into effect the strategies developed in step three. This seems elementary but is not always followed in practice. Decisions made without methods to carry them out are ineffective. The following cover the most important functional areas where derivative plans must be made.

Research and development programs should be supported, timed, and controlled to achieve the new product or other requirements needed to reach goals. These other requirements may, for example, include improving old products, reducing production costs, hiring new scientific skills, or increasing basic research.

Production programs should reflect digestion of new equipment, scheduling, new quality controls and inspection methods, and associated activities.

Marketing and promotion plans would, of course, include new selling efforts, advertising programs, reorganization of sales territories, pricing, and perhaps packaging.

Organizational changes may be required as a result of the new program which in turn, of course, needs detailed planning before implementation. Included here might be new management training programs.

Financial plans would include preparations for new equity financing or borrowing, budgeting of capital, and detailed financial forecasts to support the feasibility of the operational plans.

Parallel planning. An important feature of long-range planning is parallel planning. It would be a waste of time and resources to insist that production await engineering before beginning its derivative plans, or that marketing await production, or that organization await all of them. It is true that what is decided in one functional area will have a determining impact on other areas. But planning in all areas must proceed in parallel to the fullest extent practicable to save time. This can be accomplished by good communications in planning and sharpening of abilities to guess correctly what is going on in other functional areas that will affect planning in another area.

Naturally, the nearer term plans should be sufficiently detailed to permit operations and control. For this purpose detailed budgets or other planning and control techniques should be prepared. The further away in time the less detail should be needed or justified in terms of cost.

Fifth: Integrate Plans

The fifth and final step is to *assure the integration of long-range and short-range plans and to introduce the necessary controls to be sure operations take place in conformance with plans.*

Sequential stages. Short-range plans must, of course, be prepared in light of longer-range goals. Meshing the two can be accomplished by developing sequential stages to meet long-range goals, as for example, promotion plans, the near-term aspects of which would be included in specific budgetary items. Where long-range plans are not specified in concrete terms, as for example, outlines to improve the quality of management, the connection is looser.

In such instances, short-range plans should reflect the longer-range goals and policies set to achieve them. In some companies the problem of meshing short-range and long-range plans is accomplished by developing five-year plans in which the first year is the current operating budget.

The control process designed to insure that operations take place in conformance with plans extends too far beyond the planning function discussed in this paper and will not be treated here. It is perhaps unnecessary to say that plans which are not executed are only exercises. They may be important as exercises but they are not plans in the sense the term is used here. Reciprocally, efficient control of operations is rather difficult without the goals and standards of performance which plans establish.

Organization for planning. Too large a field of inquiry for extended treatment here is the subject of business practices and principles in organizing for long-range planning. But, since it has a direct bearing upon the way planning steps such as the above are performed, a few observations are in order.

First of all, organization for planning is not a simple matter of working out procedural or data flows. It must face the fundamental question of who is going to do what about basic decision making in an organization.

Boards of directors have superior authority but there is great variation in the extent to which they choose to use this power. At E. I. du Pont de Nemours and Company, for example, the board has delegated great power to subcommittees of the board, principally the executive committee. Long-range planning at Du Pont centers in this group. In other companies the board has delegated its planning powers to the president. In some, the president in turn has delegated his powers in varying degrees to committees, departments, or individuals.

Top management support. Second, and closely associated with the above issue, long-range planning will be most useful and effective if the top executives of the company have confidence and faith in it. A long-range planning program is not likely to be of much value if the chief executives do not support it actively.

Third, rather widespread participation in the process should be encouraged, but not to the extent that timetables cannot be met, objectivity in analyzing facts is lost, or strategic decisions become known to too many people. Long-range plans are usually rather important to a great many people in an enterprise. Their participation in and execution of the plan will be enhanced if they can point to some contribution of theirs in it, or if they can find in it a goal worth striving for.

Effective planning requires decentralization. It is true that top management itself may define basic long-range planning strategies. But the execution of these programs requires effective coordination of many people. As Peter Drucker has pointed out, planning and doing are separate parts of the same job. They are not separate jobs. Planning proceeds best when both top management and operating people participate fully in it.

DOES PLANNING PAY OFF?

Determining payoff is a matter of relating the value of planning results to the costs of planning. Every planning program should be examined to determine the margin between value and cost. On the whole, payoff calculations are probably more easily determined for short-range than for long-range plans.

Long-range planning may not pay off for five, ten or more years. It is because of the difficulties in making cost-value calculations, together with the length of time needed to draw conclusions, that questions often arise about payoff for long-range planning.

"Extinct by Instinct"

Two extreme approaches seem to be taken by companies that either ignore or improperly face the question of payoff. One approach is to minimize costs by ignoring basic steps in planning. This method depends upon conclusions derived without encumbrances of carefully developed facts or lines of reasoning. For this approach the practitioner feels little need for a conscious and deliberate assessment of relevant considerations upon which judgments can be developed. In common parlance this is called "flying by the seat of your pants." I prefer to call it the road to becoming extinct by instinct.

"Paralysis by Analysis"

At the other extreme is overemphasis of value in relation to cost. With this approach there is recognition of the need for planning. An assignment is made to a dedicated hard-working soul with a reputation for thoroughness. Work is begun without much reference to the complexities of the task and before long a large number of people are involved at substantial cost.

Somewhere along the line, usually later than sooner, a voluminous report is prepared and promptly filed away "for future reference." Either the need for decision has long since passed or the report is too complex and bulky for busy people to read and digest. This I call the road to paralysis by analysis[11]

Cost-Value Equation

For planning to pay off, a happy balance between the two extremes must be struck. The precise payoff for any particular planning operation is difficult to determine. No one can do this without examining the cost-value equation for that program. But planning has paid off for companies that have considered this equation and achieved the balance required.

The Stanford Research Institute studied the question "Why Companies Grow." One major conclusion of the study was that: "In the cases of both high-growth and low-growth companies, those that now support planning programs have shown a superior growth rate in recent years."[12]

The Stanford study observed that most companies with formalized planning programs were enthusiastic about their value. Well might they be if, partly as a result of planning, their growth rates have been exceptional. For these companies planning has clearly paid off.

Ford's Experience

Ernest Breech, former Chairman of the Board of the Ford Motor Company, has observed: "We believe it is our business, and that of other large companies, to make trends, not to follow them. A confident aggressive spirit, backed up by intelligent planning and hard-hitting management, can be contagious."[13] For Ford, planning has paid off handsomely as the last ten years of that company's history will testify.

On the other hand the path to bankruptcy is strewn with corpses who failed to plan or planned poorly. A study by the Bureau of Business Research at the University of Pittsburgh concluded that among the ten companies chosen for intensive study every one was guilty of poor planning, and this shortcoming was the major cause of failure in the majority of cases.[14]

It is probably true that the only certainty about long-range planning is that the conclusions will prove to be in error. There is no such thing as 20/20 foresight. But, one great advantage of forward planning is that coming to grips with uncertainty by analysis and study should result in a reduction of the margin of doubt about the future. Despite the fog enshrouding the future many companies have planned ahead and hit goals surprisingly accurately.

FORWARD PLANNING

Ralph Cordiner, commenting on this point in his book *New Frontiers for Professional Managers,* has observed that one of the three principal new horizons ahead for managers lies in the area of long-range planning. As he put it, "In a time of radical worldwide change, when every day introduces new elements of uncertainty, forward planning may seem to be nearly impossible—an exercise in futility. Yet there never was a more urgent need for long-range planning on the part of every business, and indeed every other important element of our national life."[15]

The argument is often presented that for large companies the choices for investing funds are many and necessitate advance planning. But since a range of choice in investment of funds in a small single-product company does not exist, for it, advance planning is a waste of time.

This idea is most erroneous. Small companies have just as great a need for long-range planning as large ones. They may not have the cash to support technical specialists, but there are other means to acquire the needed expertise. Many small companies, through long-range planning, have opened the door to successful expansion, new products, and new markets by multiplying ranges of desirable choices.

In considering payoff for long-range planning, value is generally considered to lie in the areas of improved profit stability, growth, more efficient sales, capital expenditure, inventory, research and development, or cost reduction programs. Or long-range planning may prove its worth in better management replacement and improvement programs; or some other tangible and concrete activities of the enterprise.

ANCILLARY BENEFITS

It should also be pointed out that a number of important ancillary and intangible benefits have accrued to companies having formal long-range planning programs. A brief list of them would include the following points. The planning process constitutes an excellent channel of communication throughout the organization. It identifies problems ahead for a firm long before they become acute. It focuses attention on the principal determinants of the business. It provides an organized mechanism for testing value judgments.

It opens new horizons for profitable study. It prevents piecemeal solutions to problems. It is a good training ground for future managers, and it brings to those responsible for running the business a comprehensive, coordinated, and uniform picture of present and future business.

TABLE 1   Five Steps for Long-Range Planning

1—PLANNING TO PLAN

2—SPECIFYING OBJECTIVES OF ENTERPRISE
  • forecasting future prospects
  • measuring the gaps between aspirations and projections

3—DEVELOPING STRATEGIES
  • to fill in the major gaps

4—DEVELOPING DERIVATIVE OR DETAILED PLANS IN MAJOR FUNCTIONAL AREAS TO FIT THE STRATEGIES
  • research and development
  • production
  • marketing and promotion

5—INTEGRATION OF LONG-RANGE AND SHORT-RANGE PLANS
  • introducing necessary controls

CONCLUSIONS

Despite the phenomenal growth of formal long-range planning, and its important payoff to many companies, there are still too many companies that do not employ the process effectively. The reasons are often anchored in their lack of knowledge about how to do it, misunderstanding of its cost-value calculation, or both.

Five operational steps for long-range planning have been set forth and examined. They are recapitulated in graphic form [Table 1].

For long-range planning to pay off, a balance must be struck between minimizing cost by ignoring basic steps and principles of effective planning and incurring overly heavy cost by excessive analysis. While full benefits may not be derived for many years, efforts should be made to measure them and offset them against costs. This article has been devoted to the proposition that available knowledge about how to undertake long-range planning is quite sufficient, and full understanding of the cost-value equation is so pervasive, that all businesses, large and small, should have a more or less formal long-range planning program and reap rich rewards from it.

NOTES AND REFERENCES

(This article, translated into Italian, appeared abroad under the title "Il rendimento della Programmazione d'impresa a lungo termine" in a recent issue of the *Rivista Internazionale di Scienze Economiche e Commerciali,* a periodical published by the Universita Bocconi in Milan. G.A.S.)

  1. For example, other reasons given are: Our business is too cyclical. Our customers do not know their plans, so how can we know ours? Long-range plan-

ning is too vague. Not enough time exists for short-range planning, let alone long-range planning. We cannot afford specialists needed to do the job. It costs more than it is worth.

2. For other definitions, see George A. Steiner, "What Do We Know About Using Long-Range Plans?" *California Management Review,* Fall, 1959; Peter F. Drucker, "Long-Range Planning, Challenge to Management Science," *Management Science,* April, 1959; Bruce Payne and James H. Kennedy, "Making Long-Range Planning Work," *The Management Review,* February, 1959; and William H. Newman and Charles E. Summer, Jr., *The Process of Management* (Englewood Cliffs, N.J.: Prentice-Hall, Inc., 1961), pp. 430–436.

3. See Charles E. Summer, Jr., "The Future Role of the Corporate Planner," *California Management Review,* Winter, 1961.

4. "Planning Tomorrow's Profits," *Nation's Business,* August, 1958.

5. "Long-Range Planning Pays Off," *Business Record,* October, 1956.

6. Burnard H. Sord and Glenn A. Welsch, *Business Budgeting* (New York: Controllership Foundation, 1958).

7. For other operational planning sequences see David W. Ewing, *Long-Range Planning for Management* (New York: Harper & Brothers, 1958); William E. Hill, "Planning for Profits: A Four-Stage Method," *California Management Review,* Spring, 1959, which is a method much like that presented here; Bruce Payne and James H. Kennedy, "Making Long-Range Planning Work," *The Management Review,* February, 1959; *Westinghouse Planning Guide,* Westinghouse Electric Corporation, 1959; *Guide to Profit Improvement Program,* American Brake Shoe Company, 1959; and Arthur W. Lucas and William G. Livingston, "Long-Range Planning and the Capital Appropriations Program," in *Financial Planning for Greater Profits,* American Management Association Report No. 44, 1960. For a detailed analytical planning sequence see Preston P. Le Breton and Dale A. Henning, Planning Theory (Englewood Cliffs, N.J.: Prentice-Hall, Inc., 1961).

8. Ralph M. Besse, "Company Planning Must Be Planned!" *Dun's Review,* April, 1957.

9. See note 7.

10. See, for example, Stewart Thompson, *Management Creeds and Philosophies,* Research Study No. 32, American Management Association, New York, 1958; Richard Fells, *The Meaning of Modern Business,* Chapter 6, "Corporate Goals" (New York: Columbia University Press, 1960); Peter Drucker, *The Practice of Management,* Chapter 7, "The Objectives of a Business" (New York: Harper & Brothers, 1954); and George R. Terry, *Principles of Management,* Chapter 9, "Management Objectives and Ethics" (Homewood, Illinois: Richard D. Irwin, Inc., 1956).

11. From Charles R. Schwartz, "The Return-on-Investment Concept as a Tool for Decision Making" in *Improving the Caliber of Company Management,* General Management Series, No. 183, American Management Association, 1956, p. 46.

12. N. R. Maines, *Why Companies Grow* (Palo Alto, California: Stanford Research Institute, 1957), p. 4.

13. Ernest R. Breech, "Planning the Basic Strategy of a Large Business," *Planning the Future Strategy of Your Business,* ed. Edward C. Bursk and Dan H. Fenn (New York: McGraw-Hill Book Company, 1956), p. 17.

14. A. M. Woodruff and T. G. Alexander, *Success and Failure in Small Manufacturing* (Pittsburgh: University of Pittsburgh Press, 1958), pp. 48 and 100.

15. Ralph Cordiner, *New Frontiers for Professional Managers* (New York: McGraw-Hill Book Company, 1956), p. 82.

11

How to Prevent
Organizational Dry Rot

John W. Gardner

Organizational renewal is the concern of this essay. The key is to make provisions for it in the planning process. In short, an organization must incorporate renewal in its plans or it runs the real risk of rotting away from within. Do not be mislead by the lighter tone of this article; what it has to say is important food for thought.—Eds.

Like people and plants, organizations have a life cycle. They have a green and supple youth, a time of flourishing strength, and a gnarled old age. We have all seen organizations that are still going through the diseases of childhood, and others so far gone in the rigidities of age that they ought to be pensioned off and sent to Florida to live out their days.

But organizations differ from people and plants in that their cycle isn't even approximately predictable. An organization may go from youth to old age in two or three decades, or it may last for centuries. More important, it may go through a period of stagnation and then revive. In short, decline is not inevitable. Organizations need not stagnate. They often do, to be sure, but that is because the arts of organizational renewal are not yet widely understood. Organizations can renew themselves continuously. That fact has far-reaching implications for our future.

We know at least some of the rules for organizational renewal. And those rules are relevant for all kinds of organizations—U.S. Steel, Yale University, the U.S. Navy, a government agency, or your local bank.

The first rule is that the organization must have an effective program for the recruitment and development of talent. People are the ultimate source of renewal. The shortage of able, highly trained, highly motivated

---

men will be a permanent feature of our kind of society; and every organization that wants its share of the short supply is going to have to get out and fight for it. The organization must have the kind of recruitment policy that will bring in a steady flow of able and highly motivated individuals. And it cannot afford to let those men go to seed, or get sidetracked or boxed in. There must be positive, constructive programs of career development. In this respect, local, state, and federal government agencies are particularly deficient, and have been so for many years. Their provisions for the recruitment and development of talent are seriously behind the times.

The second rule for the organization capable of continuous renewal is that it must be a hospitable environment for the individual. Organizations that have killed the spark of individuality in their members will have greatly diminished their capacity for change. Individuals who have been made to feel like cogs in the machine will behave like cogs in the machine. They will not produce ideas for change. On the contrary, they will resist such ideas when produced by others.

The third rule is that the organization must have built-in provisions for self-criticism. It must have an atmosphere in which uncomfortable questions can be asked. I would lay it down as a basic principle of human organization that the individuals who hold the reins of power in any enterprise cannot trust themselves to be adequately self-critical. For those in power the danger of self-deception is very great, the danger of failing to see the problems or refusing to see them is ever-present. And the only protection is to create an atmosphere in which anyone can speak up. The most enlightened top executives are well aware of this. Of course, I don't need to tell those readers who are below the loftiest level of management that even with enlightened executives a certain amount of prudence is useful. The Turks have a proverb that says, "The man who tells the truth should have one foot in the stirrup."

But it depends on the individual executive. Some welcome criticism, others don't. Louis Armstrong once said, "There are some people that if they don't know, you can't tell 'em."

The fourth requirement for the organization that seeks continuous renewal is fluidity of internal structure. Obviously, no complex modern organization can exist without the structural arrangements of divisions, branches, departments, and so forth. I'm not one of those who imagine that the modern world can get away from specialization. Specialization and division of labor are at the heart of modern organization. In this connection I always recall a Marx Brothers movie in which Groucho played a shyster lawyer. When a client commented on the dozens of flies buzzing around his broken-down office, Groucho said, ""We have a working agreement with them. They don't practice law and we don't climb the walls."

But jurisdictional boundaries tend to get set in concrete. Pretty soon, no solution to a problem is seriously considered if there is any danger that it will threaten jurisdictional lines. But those lines aren't sacred. They were established in some past time to achieve certain objectives. Perhaps the objectives are still valid, perhaps not. *Most organizations have a structure that was designed to solve problems that no longer exist.*

The fifth rule is that the organization must have an adequate system of internal communication. If I may make a rather reckless generalization, I'd say that renewal is a little like creativity in this respect—that it depends on the existence of a large number of diverse elements in a situation that permits an infinite variety of combinations and recombinations. The enormous potentialities of the human brain are in part explainable in terms of such possibilities for combination and recombination. And such recombination is facilitated by easy communication, impeded by poor communication.

The sixth rule: The organization must have some means of combating the process by which men become prisoners of their procedures. The rule book grows fatter as the ideas grow fewer. Thus almost every well-established organization is a coral reef of procedures that were laid down to achieve some long-forgotten objective.

It is in our nature to develop an affection for customary ways of doing things. Some years ago a wholesale firm noted that some of its small shopkeeper customers were losing money because of antiquated merchandising methods. The firm decided that it would be good business to assist the shopkeepers in bringing their methods up-to-date, but soon discovered that many had no desire to modernize. They loved the old, money-losing ways.

Sometimes the organization procedures men devise to advance their purposes serve in the long run to block those purposes. This was apparent in an experience a friend of mine had in Germany in the last days of World War II. He was in Aachen, which had only recently been occupied by the American forces, when he received a message instructing him to proceed to London immediately. He went directly to U.S. Army headquarters, and showed the message to a sergeant in the Adjutant's office.

The sergeant said that the only plane for London within the next few days was leaving from the nearest airfield in thirty minutes. He added that the airfield was twenty-five minutes away.

It was discouraging news. My friend knew that he could not proceed to London without written orders, and that was a process that took from an hour to a couple of days in a well-established and smoothly functioning headquarters. The present headquarters had been opened the day before, and was in a totally unorganized state.

My friend explained his dilemma to the sergeant and handed over his papers. The sergeant scratched his head and left the room. Four minutes later he returned and said, "Here are your orders, sir."

My friend said he had never been in such an efficient headquarters. The sergeant looked at him with a twinkle in his eye and said, "Sir, it's just lucky for you we weren't organized!"

The seventh rule: The organization capable of continuous renewal will have found some means of combating the vested interests that grow up in every human institution. We commonly associate the term "vested interests" with people of wealth and power, but in an organization vested interests exist at every level. The lowest employees have their vested interests, every foreman has his, and every department head has his. Every change threatens someone's privileges, someone's authority, someone's status. What wise managers try to do, of course, is to sell the idea that in the long run everyone's overriding vested interest is in the continuing vitality of the organization itself. If that fails, everyone loses. But it's a hard message to get across.

Nowhere can the operation of vested interests be more clearly seen than in the functioning of university departments. There are exceptions, of course: some departments rise above their vested interests. But the average department holds like grim death to its piece of intellectual terrain. It teaches its neophytes a jealous devotion to the boundaries of the field. It assesses the significance of intellectual questions by the extent to which they can be answered without going outside the sacred territory. Such vested interests effectively block most efforts to reform undergraduate instruction.

The eighth rule is that the organization capable of continuous renewal is interested in what it is going to become and not what it has been. When I moved to New London, Connecticut, in 1938 I was astonished at the attitude of New Londoners toward their city's future. Having grown up in California, I was accustomed to cities and towns that looked ahead habitually (often with an almost absurd optimism). I was not prepared for a city that, so far as I could discover, had no view of its future, though it had a clear view of its past.

The need to look to the future is the reason so many corporations today have research and development programs. But an organization cannot guarantee its future by ritualistic spending on research. Its research-and-development progam must be an outgrowth of a philosophy of innovation that guides the company in everything it does. The research program, which is a way of looking forward, cannot thrive if the rest of the organization has the habit of looking backward.

The ninth rule is obvious but difficult. An organization runs on motivation, on conviction, on morale. Men have to believe that it really makes a difference whether they do well or badly. They have to care. They have to believe that their efforts as individuals will mean something for the whole organization, and will be recognized by the whole organization.

Change is always risky, usually uncomfortable, often painful. It isn't accomplished by apathetic men and women. It requires high motivation to break through the rigidities of the aging organization.

So much for the rules.

One of the ominous facts about growth and decay is that the present success of an organization does not necessarily constitute grounds for optimism. In 1909 it would have been unwise to judge the future of the Central Leather Company by the fact that it ranked seventh in the nation in total assets. It would have been a disastrous long-term investment. A better bet would have been the relatively small Ford Motor Company which had been founded only six years earlier and was about to launch its Model T. As a company it wasn't huge or powerful, but to borrow a phrase from C. P. Snow, it had the future in its bones. (Not many of 1909's top twenty companies did—only four of them are in the top twenty today.)

Businessmen are fond of saying that, unlike other executives, they have a clear measure of present performance—the profit-and-loss statement. But the profits of today *may* be traceable to wise decisions made a good many years earlier. And current company officers may be making bad decisions that will spell disaster ten years from now.

I have collected many examples of organizations that experienced crises as a result of their failure to renew themselves. In the great majority, certainly nine out of ten, the trouble was not difficult to diagnose and there was ample warning of the coming catastrophe. In the case of a manufacturing concern that narrowly averted bankruptcy recently, the conditions that led to trouble were diagnosed by an outside consultant two years before the crisis came. In the case of another well-known organization, a published article outlined every essential difficulty that later led to disaster.

But if warning signals are plentiful, why doesn't the ailing organization take heed? The answer is clear: most ailing organizations have developed a functional blindness to their own defects. They are not suffering because they can't *solve* their problems but because they won't see their problems. They can look straight at their faults and rationalize them as virtues or necessities.

I was discussing these matters with a corporation president recently, and he said, "How do I know that *I* am not one of the blind ones? What do I do to find out? And if I am, what do I do about it?"

There are several ways to proceed. One way is to bring in an outside consultant who is not subject to the conditions that create functional blindness inside the organization.

A more direct approach, but one that is surrounded by subtle difficulties, is for the organization to encourage its internal critics. Every organization, no matter how far deteriorated, has a few stubbornly honest individuals who are not blinded by their own self-interest and have never quite accepted the rationalizations and self-deceptions shared by others in the organization. If they are encouraged to speak up they probably will. The head of a government agency said to me recently, "The shrewdest critics of this organization are right under this roof. But it would take a major change of atmosphere to get them to talk."

A somewhat more complicated solution is to bring new blood into at least a few of the key positions in the organization. If the top level of the organization is salted with vigorous individuals too new to be familiar with all the established ways of doing and thinking, they can be a source of fresh insights for the whole organization.

Still another means of getting fresh insights is rotation of personnel between parts of the organization. Not only is the individual broadened by the experience, but he brings a fresh point of view to his new post. After a few years of working together, men are likely to get so used to one another that the stimulus of intellectual conflict drops almost to zero. A fresh combination of individuals enlivens the atmosphere.

In the last analysis, however, everything depends on the wisdom of those who shape the organization's policy. Most policy makers today understand that they must sponsor creative research. But not many of them understand that the spirit of creativity and innovation so necessary in the research program is just as essential to the rest of the organization.

The future of this nation depends on its capacity for self-renewal. And that in turn depends on the vitality of the organizations and individuals that make it up. Americans have always been exceptionally gifted at organizational innovation. In fact, some observers say that this is the true American inventiveness. Thanks to that inventiveness we now stand on the threshold of new solutions to some of the problems that have destroyed the vitality of human institutions since the beginning of time. We have already made progress in discovering how we may keep our institutions vital and creative. We could do even better if we put our minds to it.

PART THREE

Organizing Processes in Management

Whenever goals and tasks require the efforts of two or more people the need for organizing arises. For example, when an object is too heavy for one person to lift, the efforts of others must be used. If more than one person is involved in the lifting, the effort must be coordinated. Organizing refers to the process of achieving coordinated effort. The organizing function in management is the means by which managers seek to achieve a coordinated effort through the design of a structure of task and authority relationships.

The organizing function is often discussed in terms of dividing tasks, departmentalizing tasks, and delegating authority. The principles of specialization, departmentalization, span of control, and unity of command provide the basic elements of discussing the organizing function. These principles are not ironclad laws or facts but guidelines which serve to aid the manager faced with organizing decisions.

The principles included in the discussion of the organizing function have existed for years. For example, Adam Smith over 200 years ago in his *Wealth of Nations* identified the specialization principle. He noted that ten men, each doing particular tasks in the manufacturing of pins, could produce 4,800 pins a day. He proposed, however, that if each man were working individually, doing all the tasks necessary to create one pin, the ten workmen combined would be fortunate to make as many as 200 pins per day. The drawing of the wire, cutting, pounding of the heads for the pins, sharpening of points, soldering, and packaging were activities that were specialized in the pin industry. Thus, principles and interest in them have improved managerial attempts at organizing work so that effectiveness is increased.

The articles in this section illustrate that individuals from various backgrounds interpret the basic organizing principles differently and in fact consider different principles. Classical organization theory, for example, a body of literature which emerged during the early part of the 20th century, focused on defining principles of organizing such as the frequently cited division of labor, the principle of centralization, and the scalar chain. Bureaucratic organization theory, on the other hand, was oriented toward the establishment of organizational rules and regulations designed to assure predictablilty of the behavior of employees. Other approaches to organizing emphasize still other variables, such as Likerts' System 4 which places primary attention on trying to create effective work groups which have high performance goals. Regardless of the approach or variables emphasized, all organizing efforts share a common goal of channelling individual and group behavior into patterns which contribute to effective organizational performance.

12

Classifying the Elements of Work

Frank B. Gilbreth and Lillian M. Gilbreth

In this article two famous industrial engineers suggest a "one best way" approach to organizing work. They suggest that their classification system is applicable to all kinds of work and will significantly increase worker efficiency. This article and the system it describes give an excellent example of the "scientific management" approach, to which the Gilbieths made major contributions.—Eds.

This paper presents a complete method of visualizing a classification of all the subdivisions and the true motion-study elements of The One Best Way to Do Work.

NEED FOR SUCH A CLASSIFICATION

Such a classification is vitally necessary, in order that fundamental super-standards shall be made by the scientific method of selecting and measuring the best units, for synthesis into methods of least waste.

This classification furnishes the basis of a definite mnemonic classification for filing all motion-study and time-study data for the work of the industrial engineer, the machine designer, and the behavior psychologist—that their various pieces of information, usually obtained through entirely different channels and methods of attack, may be automatically brought together, to the same filing folders, under the same filing subdivisions.

So far as we are able to learn, there are no other classifications or bases for filing that accomplish this purpose, and we have found that such

SOURCE: Reprinted by permission of the publisher from "Classifying the Elements of Work," *Management and Administration,* Vol. 8, No. 2 (August 1924), pp. 151–54.

a classification is absolutely necessary for our work of finding The One Best Way to Do Work, standardizing the trades, and making and enforcing standing orders for best management.

It is hoped that teachers of industrial engineering in our colleges will learn that *one* demonstration of building up The One Best Way to Do Work from the ultimate elements, in any kind of activity, will do more to teach a student the principles of motion study and most efficient methods of management than dozens of lessons dealing with generalities.

The coming generation should be taught a definite filing system for data of scientific management, laid out under a complete classification of all work; should be taught the method of selecting the right units to measure and the methods of measuring these units; and should be furnished with the devices for making the cost of measuring cheap, and with a method for synthesizing the resulting information. This would result in a general progress in world efficiency and an increase in quality of living that would mark an epoch in the history of industry and civilization.

USE OF FUNDAMENTAL ELEMENTS

The literature of scientific management abounds with examples of units of work improperly called "elements," which are in no sense elements. A classification for finding The One Best Way to Do Work must deal with *true elements,* not merely with subdivisions that are arbitrarily called "elements."

There has recently appeared a well-written biography of a great engineer[1] in which subdivisions of operations, requiring in many instances more than 30 seconds to perform, have been erroneously described as "elements." That error will again mislead many people. These so-called elements should be taken for what they really are, namely, subdivisions and not elements, and not confused with true elements, or fundamental units which cannot be further subdivided.

SCOPE OF THE CLASSIFICATION

This classification for finding The One Best Way to Do Work is applicable to all kinds of work. It was used by one of the authors while serving as ranking officer in the field under the training committee of the General Staff, standardizing the methods of The One Best Way to Do Work for teaching the five million men and officers in the World War. It has also been used in analyzing the work of the surgeon, nurse, hospital management, large department stores, selling, a great many kinds of manufacturing, accounting, office work in general, and many other kinds of work.

TRUE ELEMENTS OF WORK

The classification of all work of any and all organizations for the purpose of finding The One Best Way to Do Work may be visualized as follows:

I. A complete organization, which consists of

II. Processes, such as
  (a) Financing
  (b) Advertising
  (c) Marketing
  (d) Distributing
  (e) Selling
  (f) Accounting
  (g) Purchasing
  (h) Manufacturing
  (i) Planning
  (j) Teaching
  (k) Charting
  (l) Maintaining
  (m) Filing

  These processes consist of

III. Operations, which consist of

IV. Cycles of motions, which consist of

V. Subdivisions, or events, or therbligs[2] of a cycle of motions which consist of
  (a) Search
  (b) Find
  (c) Select
  (d) Grasp
  (e) Transport loaded
  (f) Position
  (g) Assemble
  (h) Use
  (i) Disassemble
  (j) Inspect
  (k) Pre-position for next operation
  (l) Release load
  (m) Transport empty
  (n) Rest for overcoming fatigue
  (o) Other periods of unavoidable delay
  (p) Avoidable delay
  (q) Plan

VI. Variables of motions
  (a) Variables of the worker
    1. Anatomy
    2. Brawn
    3. Contentment
    4. Creed
    5. Earning power

6. Experience
7. Fatigue
8. Habits
9. Health
10. Mode of living
11. Nutrition
12. Size
13. Skill
14. Temperament
15. Training

(b) Variables of the surroundings, equipment, and tools
1. Appliances
2. Clothes
3. Colors
4. Entertainment, music, reading, etc.
5. Heating, cooling, ventilating
6. Lighting
7. Quality of material
8. Reward and punishment
9. Size of unit moved
10. Special fatigue-eliminating devices
11. Surroundings
12. Tools
13. Union rules

(c) Variables of the motion
1. Acceleration
2. Automaticity
3. Combination with other motions and sequences
4. Cost
5. Direction
6. Effectiveness
7. Foot-pounds of work accomplished
8. Inertia and momentum overcome
9. Length
10. Necessity
11. Path
12. "Play for position"
13. Speed

Under I, a complete organization, are included all kinds of organizations, including financial, industrial, commercial, professional, educational, and social.

Under II, processes, it should be noted that processes are divided in the same way from a motion-study analyst's standpoint, regardless in which department or in which function they are found.

Under III, operations, the operations include mechanical as well as physiological, and mental as well as manual.

The reasons for these inclusions are:

1. From the motion-study standpoint there are not always clear dividing lines between the *operations of devices* and the *mental and manual operations of the human being,* for they are often mutually interchangeable, sometimes in part and sometimes as a whole.[3]

2. Records of many and probably all mental operations can now be obtained by the chronocyclegraph and micromotion photographic methods, and each year such photographic records can more and more be deciphered and used to practical advantage. Enough can already be read and used to serve our present needs. Careful examination of all our old micromotion and chronocyclegraph films taken under conditions of actual practice show that they are literally full of examples of such records of mental processes.

Under IV, cycles of motions are arbitrary subdivisions of operations. They have distinct and natural boundaries of beginning and ending. Usually and preferably there are certain sequences of therbligs that are especially suitable for standardization and transference to other kinds of work, and serve every purpose of finding The One Best Way to Do Work.

Under V, therbligs, we would emphasize that we do not place "motions" as the next subdivision under "cycle of motions" because "motions" have neither distinct and definite boundaries nor beginnings and endings. For example: It is difficult to determine correctly how many "motions" are required to take a fountain pen from the pocket and prepare to write with it. It will be found difficult to agree on just how many "motions" are made and as to where are located the boundaries of the "motions" of so simple a cycle as this, or of any other similarly common cycle of motions.

However, the 17 subdivisions, or events, or therbligs, as they are variously called, seem to be all that are necessary from which to synthesize all of the *cycles of motions* of all the *operations* of all the *processes* of all the *organizations* of every kind whatever. The science of motion study consists, therefore, of finding The One Best Sequence of therbligs for each kind of work and the science of management consists of deriving, installing, and enforcing the conditions that will permit the work to be done repeatedly in The One Best Way. It is conceivable that sometime in the future an eighteenth and possibly more therbligs will be found, and we seem near to their discovery at the present time. The discovery of additional therbligs pertaining to the phenomena of skill and automaticity seems inevitable.[4]

Under VI, variables of motions, provision is made for filing all information regarding any kind of motion made by either hand, device, or machine. It provides for all information regarding the structures in which work is performed. It provides for filing all data regarding human behavior— supernormal, normal, and subnormal. It supplies the basis of filing all data of the educator, psychologist, psychiatrist, and the expert in personnel, placement, and promotion problems.

This classification can be carried on and subdivided indefinitely. It furnishes an efficient and quickly usable plan for synthesizing the components of The One Best Way to Do Work in such shape that they can be cumulatively improved.

However, our present information regarding the 17 therbligs is sufficient to revolutionize all kinds of work, and if the industries of the various nations would eliminate the obviously unnecessary therbligs and standardize the kinds, sequences, and combinations of the remaining efficient therbligs, the resulting savings each year would be sufficient to pay the outstanding debts of most nations.

HISTORY OF THIS CLASSIFICATION

For many years we have used these therbligs as divisions for dissecting cycles of motions of a great many different kinds of work, but it was not until we began to use photography in motion study in 1892 that we made our greatest progress. It was not until 1912, when we used our first micromotion processes intensively, that we were able to make such great advances as projecting the motions of experts faster and slower, as well as at the speed of experts' demonstration. We were then also able to project and examine therbligs backwards, or in the reversed directions. This enabled us to get a new fund of information that resulted in many suggestions from seeing, measuring, and comparing the therbligs performed in the reversed sequence and opposite directions. This was used to great advantage in finding the methods of least waste and especially in the process of taking machines apart and putting them together again in front of a motion picture camera, and then running the film backwards, showing the films of assembling as dissembling and vice versa.

EXAMPLES OF PROFITABLE USE

Running films of superexperts backwards, to see what we could get for automatically suggesting inventions, or as "thought detonators" when seeing the operation done thus, presented peculiarities and combinations of therbligs never seen before. This was, of course, supplemented by examining one picture, or frame, at a time which, with motion study experts, will always be the most efficient method for getting facts from the films. Great progress was made, for example, in *pre-positioning for next operation* (therblig *k*) parts and tools so that *grasp* (therblig *d*) was performed with quite the same motions and actions and performed within a time equal to that of *release load* (therblig *l*).

As an example of the importance of recognizing the therblig as the fundamental element, the result of that particular study in 1912 was that our organization enabled a client to have his machine assemblers put together 66 machines per day with less fatigue than they had previously accumulated while assembling 18 machines per day. Because this method was synthesized from fundamentally correct units, the same methods are still in use today in this same factory.[5]

This increase in output should not be considered as an exceptional case. On the contrary, it is quite typical. In fact we have a great many illustrations that we could give where the savings were much greater. For example: One large motion-study laboratory, as a result of this method of attack, synthesized and demonstrated new methods which averaged an output of five times as much product per man. This method used in assembling carburetors enabled messenger boys to do the work in one-tenth the time required by skilled mechanics.[6] It has been used on work of assembling pumps with still greater results.[7]

THERBLIG SEQUENCES

It was early recognized that certain similar operations have similar sequences of therbligs. For example: The operations of feeding pieces into a drill press or into a punch press, time tickets into a time stamp, and paper into a printing press, have practically the same sequence of therbligs. A typical sequence of therbligs for one complete cycle of handling one piece on a drill press is *search, find, select, grasp, transport loaded, position, assemble, use, disassemble, inspect, transport loaded, pre-position for next operation, release load* and *transport empty*. This cycle of motions can and should be done with the following therbligs: *grasp, transport loaded, position, assemble, use, release load* and *transport empty*, which are half the number of therbligs of the usual method.

While the former is the usual sequence of therbligs on a drill press, it is by no means the best one. There is The One Best Sequence of therbligs on each machine and each kind of work, and it should always be found, standardized, taught, and maintained.

ANOTHER WORK CLASSIFICATION

Now let us look at another method of subdividing and classifying all work. There is another and better known type of division and classification for visualizing all activity which was early recognized. The importance of considering this simple classification can be seen in the unfairness and trouble that have been caused by giving the same piece rate for large lots as for small. This classification divides all work, both large and small, into three parts, as follows:

1. Get ready.
2. Do it, or make it.
3. Clean up.

Now, applying this division to one piece on the drill press, we have:

1. *Get ready,* or pick up the piece and put it under the drill. This consists of all therbligs that come before *use* (therblig *h*).
2. *Drill it* (do it or make it). This consists of only one therblig, namely *use* (therblig *h*).
3. *Clean up,* or take the piece out from under the drill and inspect it and lay it down. This consists of all therbligs that come after *use* (therblig *h*).

THE IMPORTANCE OF USE

It should be recognized that the therblig *use* is the difficult one to learn in mastering a trade. It is the most productive and, therefore, the most important therblig of all.

All other therbligs of all kinds of work are desirable and necessary only so far as they facilitate, prepare for, or assist in increasing *use*. Any therbligs that do not foster *use* should be under suspicion as being unnecessary. *Use* is the highest paid therblig, because it usually requires the most skill. The more of the therbligs of "get ready" and "clean up" that are performed by less skilled and consequently lower priced workers the better for all workers, for they all will be employed a larger portion of the day at the highest priced work at which they are each individually capable. This is true not only in the consideration of the therbligs but also in the trades in general. For example: The bricklayer, the plumber, the steamfitter, the office executive, and many others, each have their specially assigned helpers, but they still habitually do much pay-reducing work for which in the long run they suffer a loss due to less personal activity. It will help to analyze and classify all work if it is recognized that the hod carrier bears the same relation to the bricklayer, and the secretary to the executive, as do the therbligs that compose "get ready" bear to the therblig *use;* and the laborer's work of "clean up" after the work of the bricklayer, is quite the same as the therbligs that compose "clean up" after therblig *use.*

Further investigations of a typical sequence of therbligs, such as on the drill press or other examples cited, from the standpoint of the classification of the therbligs show that *grasp* (therblig *d*) of "get ready" is used before *use* (therblig *h*) and that *release load* (therblig *l*) done after *use* may be quite the same except that it is performed in motions that are the reverse of those of *grasp.*

PAIRED THERBLIGS

There are a number of such paired therbligs which are almost always separated by the therblig *use.* For example [see Table 1].

TABLE 1

Paired Therblig Usually Performed before Use		Paired Therblig Usually Performed after Use
d. Grasp . . . . Use	. . . .	l. Release load
e. Transport loaded. . . . . Use	. . . .	m. Transport empty
f. Position . . . . Use	. . . .	k. Pre-position for next operation
g. Assemble. . . . . Use	. . . .	i. Disassemble
q. Plan . . . . Use	. . . .	j. Inspect

TABLE 2 Unpaired Therbligs

Order No. 4	Order No. 5
a. Search. . . . . .Use	n. Rest for overcoming fatigue
b. Find . . . . .Use	o. Other forms of unavoidable delay
c. Select. . . . . .Use	p. Avoidable delay

It was the absence of a therblig on the other side of *use* to pair with *inspect,* together with the fact that *plan* is actually found in the photographic records regardless of how much planning may be done prior to the beginning of an operation, that caused us to add to the list of therbligs, *plan* (therblig *q*). The therblig *plan* may occur in any place in the sequence of therbligs, but we have put it last in the list before cited because it was added last, and also to distinguish it from the "planning" that should be done before any "performing" of the operation is begun.

There are two more kinds of divisions, or orders, making a total of five orders of therbligs, namely, one consisting of *search, find* and *select* (therbligs *a, b,* and *c*) which usually come before *use,* and *rest for overcoming fatigue, other forms of unavoidable delay* and *avoidable delay* (therbligs *n, o,* and *p*) which usually come after *use.* Thus we have two orders of unpaired therbligs separated by *use,* as . . . [shown in Table 2].

In analyzing an operation of any kind a simultaneous motion cycle chart is prepared. The therbligs of motion are applied to this chart in studying it for present methods and determining the altered sequence which should be adopted to establish The One Best Way to Do Work.

NOTES AND REFERENCES

1. See *Frederick W. Taylor* by F. B. Copley.
2. This word was coined for the purpose of having a short word which will save the motions necessary to write such long descriptions as "The 17 categories into which the motion-study elementary subdivisions of a cycle of motions fall."

3. In 1910 and the years following, we collected and specially devised in our own laboratory, many devices for supplying, mechanically, the therbligs of cycles of motions that the crippled soldiers could not perform, due to their injuries. Such collections should be made by all museums and colleges that intend to teach motion study.

4. See Society of Industrial Engineers Bulletin, November 1923, pp. 6–7. "A Fourth Dimension for Recording Skill," by Frank B. Gilbreth and L. M. Gilbreth. The lateness in starting or finishing of a therblig performed by any one anatomical member as compared with the time of beginning or finishing of a therblig performed by another anatomical member is a most important unit for measuring skill and automaticity.

5. See *Management Engineering,* February 1923, p. 87. "Ten Years of Scientific Management," by John G. Aldrich, M. E., and also his discussion of paper 1378 on page 1131, vol. 34, 1912, American Society of Mechanical Engineers Transactions.

6. See Proceedings of the Institution of Automobile Engineers (English), "The Fundamentals of Cost Reduction," by H. Kerr Thomas, Member of the Council.

7. See Society of Industrial Engineers Transactions, vol. 2, 1920, "The One Best Way to Do Work," by Frank B. Gilbreth and L. M. Gilbreth.

13

Organization Theory:
An Overview and an Appraisal

William G. Scott

Organizing the organization is what organization theory is all about. In this article William Scott identifies three theories of organization which have had considerable impact on management thought and practice: classical, neoclassical, and modern. The article makes a cogent argument for unification of elements of all three theories.—Eds.

Man is intent on drawing himself into a web of collectivized patterns. "Modern man has learned to accommodate himself to a world increasingly organized. The trend toward ever more explicit and consciously drawn relationships is profound and sweeping; it is marked by depth no less than by extension."[1] This comment by Seidenberg nicely summarizes the pervasive influence of organization in many forms of human activity.

Some of the reasons for intense organizational activity are found in the fundamental transitions which revolutionized our society, changing it from a rural culture, to a culture based on technology, industry, and the city. From these changes, a way of life emerged characterized by the *proximity* and *dependency* of people on each other. Proximity and dependency, as conditions of social life, harbor the threats of human conflict, capricious antisocial behavior, instability of human relationships, and uncertainty about the nature of the social structure with its concomitant roles.

Of course, these threats to social integrity are present to some degree in all societies, ranging from the primitive to the modern. But, these

SOURCE: Reprinted by permission of the author and publisher from "Organization Theory: An Overview and an Appraisal," *The Academy of Management Journal,* April 1961, pp. 7–26.

threats become dangerous when the harmonious functioning of a society rests on the maintenance of a highly intricate, delicately balanced form of human collaboration. The civilization we have created depends on the preservation of a precarious balance. Hence, disrupting forces impinging on this shaky form of collaboration must be eliminated or minimized.

Traditionally, organization is viewed as a vehicle for accomplishing goals and objectives. While this approach is useful, it tends to obscure the inner workings and internal purposes of organization itself. Another fruitful way of treating organization is as a mechanism having the ultimate purpose of offsetting those forces which undermine human collaboration. In this sense, organization tends to minimize conflict, and to lessen the significance of individual behavior which deviates from values that the organization has established as worthwhile. Further, organization increases stability in human relationships by reducing uncertainty regarding the nature of the system's structure and the human roles which are inherent to it. Corollary to this point, organization enhances the predictability of human action, because it limits the number of behavioral alternatives available to an individual. As Presthus points out:

> Organization is defined as a system of structural interpersonal relations. . . . individuals are differentiated in terms of authority, status, and role with the result that personal interaction is prescribed. . . . Anticipated reactions tend to occur, while ambiguity and spontaneity are decreased.[2]

In addition to all of this, organization has built-in safeguards. Besides prescribing acceptable forms of behavior for those who elect to submit to it, organization is also able to counterbalance the influence of human action which transcends its established patterns.[3]

Few segments of society have engaged in organizing more intensively than business.[4] The reason is clear. Business depends on what organization offers. Business needs a system of relationships among functions; it needs stability, continuity, and predictability in its internal activities and external contacts. Business also appears to need harmonious relationships among the people and processes which make it up. Put another way, a business organization has to be free, relatively, from destructive tendencies which may be caused by divergent interests.

As a foundation for meeting these needs rests administrative science. A major element of this science is organization theory, which provides the grounds for management activities in a number of significant areas of business endeavor. Organization theory, however, is not a homogeneous science based on generally accepted principles. Various theories of organization have been, and are being evolved. For example, something called "modern organization theory" has recently emerged, raising the wrath of some traditionalists, but also capturing the imagination of a rather elite avant-garde.

The thesis of this paper is that modern organization theory, when stripped of its irrelevancies, redundancies, and "speech defects," is a logical and vital evolution in management thought. In order for this thesis to be supported, the reader must endure a review and appraisal of more traditional forms of organization theory which may seem elementary to him.

In any event, three theories of organization are having considerable influence on management thought and practice. They are arbitrarily labeled in this paper as the classical, the neoclassical, and the modern. Each of these is fairly distinct; but they are not unrelated. Also, these theories are ongoing, being actively supported by several schools of management thought.

THE CLASSICAL DOCTRINE

For lack of a better method of identification, it will be said that the classical doctrine deals almost exclusively with the *anatomy of formal organization*. This doctrine can be traced back to Frederick W. Taylor's interest in functional foremanship and planning staffs. But most students of management thought would agree that in the United States, the first systematic approach to organization, and the first comprehensive attempt to find organizational universals, is dated 1931 when Mooney and Reiley published *Onward Industry*.[5] Subsequently, numerous books, following the classical vein, have appeared. Two of the more recent are Brech's *Organization*[6] and Allen's *Management and Organization*.[7]

Classical organization theory is built around four key pillars. They are the division of labor, the scalar and functional processes, structure, and span of control. Given these major elements just about all of classical organization theory can be derived.

1. *The division of labor* is without doubt the cornerstone among the four elements.[8] From it the other elements flow as corollaries. For example, *scalar* and *functional* growth requires specialization and departmentalization of functions. Organization *structure* is naturally dependent upon the direction which specialization of activities travels in company development. Finally, *span of control* problems result from the number of specialized functions under the jurisdiction of a manager.

2. *The scalar and functional processes* deal with the vertical and horizontal growth of the organization, respectively.[9] The scalar process refers to the growth of the chain of command, the delegation of authority and responsibility, unity of command, and the obligation to report.

The division of the organization into specialized parts and the regrouping of the parts into compatible units are matters pertaining to the functional process. This process focuses on the horizontal evolution of the line and staff in a formal organization.

3. *Structure* is the logical relationships of functions in an organization, arranged to accomplish the objectives of the company efficiently. Structure implies system and pattern. Classical organization theory usu-

ally works with two basic structures, the line and the staff. However, such activities as committee and liaison functions fall quite readily into the purview of structural considerations. Again, structure is the vehicle for introducing logical and consistent relationships among the diverse functions which comprise the organization.[10]

4. *The span of control* concept relates to the number of subordinates a manager can effectively supervise. Graicunas has been credited with first elaborating the point that there are numerical limitations to the subordinates one man can control.[11] In a recent statement on the subject, Brech points out, "span" refers to ". . . the number of persons, themselves carrying managerial and supervisory responsibilities, for whom the senior manager retains his overembracing responsibility of direction and planning, coordination, motivation, and control."[12] Regardless of interpretation, span of control has significance, in part, for the shape of the organization which evolves through growth. Wide span yields a flat structure; short span results in a tall structure. Further, the span concept directs attention to the complexity of human and functional interrelationships in an organization.

It would not be fair to say that the classical school is unaware of the day-to-day administrative problems of the organization. Paramount among these problems are those stemming from human interactions. But the interplay of individual personality, informal groups, intraorganizational conflict, and the decision-making processes in the formal structure appears largely to be neglected by classical organization theory. Additionally, the classical theory overlooks the contributions of the behavioral sciences by failing to incorporate them in its doctrine in any systematic way. In summary, classical organization theory has relevant insights into the nature of organization, but the value of this theory is limited by its narrow concentration on the formal anatomy of organization.

NEOCLASSICAL THEORY OF ORGANIZATION

The neoclassical theory of organization embarked on the task of compensating for some of the deficiencies in classical doctrine. The neoclassical school is commonly identified with the human relations movement. Generally, the neoclassical approach takes the postulates of the classical school, regarding the pillars of organization as givens. But these postulates are regarded as modified by people, acting independently or within the context of the informal organization.

One of the main contributions of the neoclassical school is the introduction of behavioral sciences in an integrated fashion into the theory of organization. Through the use of these sciences, the human relationists demonstrate how the pillars of the classical doctrine are affected by the impact of human actions. Further, the neoclassical approach includes a systematic treatment of the informal organization, showing its influence on the formal structure.

Thus, the neoclassical approach to organization theory gives evidence of accepting classical doctrine, but superimposing on it modifications resulting from individual behavior, and the influence of the informal group. The inspiration of the neoclassical school was the Hawthorne studies.[13] Current examples of the neoclassical approach are found in human relations books like Gardner and Moore, *Human Relations in Industry*,[14] and Davis, *Human Relations in Business*.[15] To a more limited extent, work in industrial sociology also reflects a neoclassical point of view.[16]

It would be useful to look briefly at some of the contributions made to organization theory by the neoclassicists. First to be considered are modifications of the pillars of classical doctrine; second is the informal organization.

Examples of the Neoclassical Approach to the Pillars of Formal Organization Theory

1. The *division of labor* has been a long-standing subject of comment in the field of human relations. Very early in the history of industrial psychology, a study was made of industrial fatigue and monotony caused by the specialization of the work.[17] Later, attention shifted to the isolation of the worker, and his feeling of anonymity resulting from insignificant jobs which contributed negligibly to the final product.[18]

Also, specialization influences the work of management. As an organization expands, the need concomitantly arises for managerial motivation and coordination of the activities of others. Both motivation and coordination in turn relate to executive leadership. Thus, in part, stemming from the growth of industrial specialization, the neoclassical school has developed a large body of theory relating to motivation, coordination, and leadership. Much of this theory is derived from the social sciences.

2. Two aspects of the *scalar and functional* processes which have been treated with some degree of intensity by the neoclassical school are the delegation of authority and responsibility, and gaps in or overlapping of functional jurisdictions. The classical theory assumes something of perfection in the delegation and functionalization processes. The neoclassical school points out that human problems are caused by imperfections in the way these processes are handled.

For example, too much or insufficient delegation may render an executive incapable of action. The failure to delegate authority and responsibility equally may result in frustration for the delegatee. Overlapping of authorities often causes clashes in personality. Gaps in authority cause failures in getting jobs done, with one party blaming the other for shortcomings in performance.[19]

The neoclassical school says that the scalar and functional processes are theoretically valid, but tend to deteriorate in practice. The ways in which they break down are described, and some of the human causes are pointed out. In addition the neoclassicists make recommendations, suggesting various "human tools" which will facilitate the operation of these processes.

3. *Structure* provides endless avenues of analysis for the neoclassical theory of organization. The theme is that human behavior disrupts the best laid organizational plans, and thwarts the cleanness of the logical relationships founded in the structure. The neoclassical critique of structure centers on frictions which appear internally among people performing different functions.

Line and staff relations is a problem area, much discussed, in this respect. Many companies seem to have difficulty keeping the line and staff working together harmoniously. Both Dalton[20] and Juran[21] have engaged in research to discover the causes of friction, and to suggest remedies.

Of course, line-staff relations represent only one of the many problems of structural frictions described by the neoclassicists. As often as not, the neoclassicists will offer prescriptions for the elimination of conflict in structure. Among the more important harmony-rendering formulae are participation, junior boards, bottom-up management, joint committees, recognition of human dignity, and "better" communication.

4. An executive's *span of control* is a function of human determinants, and the reduction of span to a precise, universally applicable ratio is silly, according to the neoclassicists. Some of the determinants of span are individual differences in managerial abilities, the type of people and functions supervised, and the extent of communication effectiveness.

Coupled with the span of control question are the human implications of the type of structure which emerges. That is, is a tall structure with a short span or a flat structure with a wide span more conducive to good human relations and high morale? The answer is situational. Short span results in tight supervision; wide span requires a good deal of delegation with looser controls. Because of individual and organizational differences, sometimes one is better than the other. There is a tendency to favor the looser form of organization, however, for the reason that tall structures breed autocratic leadership, which is often pointed out as a cause of low morale.[22]

The Neoclassical View of the Informal Organization

Nothing more than the barest mention of the informal organization is given even in the most recent classical treatises on organization theory.[23] Systematic discussion of this form of organization has been left to the neoclassicists. The informal organization refers to people in group associations at work, but these associations are not specified in the "blueprint" of the formal organization. The informal organization means natural groupings of people in the work situation.

In a general way, the informal organization appears in response to the social need—the need of people to associate with others. However, for analytical purposes, this explanation is not particularly satisfying. Research has produced the following, more specific determinants underlying the appearance of informal organizations.

1. The *location* determinant simply states that in order to form into groups of any lasting nature, people have to have frequent face-to-face contact. Thus, the geography of physical location in a plant or office is an important factor in predicting who will be in what group.[24]

2. *Occupation* is a key factor determining the rise and composition of informal groups. There is a tendency for people performing similar jobs to group together.[25]

3. *Interests* are another determinant for informal group formation. Even though people might be in the same location, performing similar jobs, differences of interest among them explain why several small, instead of one large, informal organizations emerge.

4. *Special issues* often result in the formation of informal groups, but this determinant is set apart from the three previously mentioned. In this case, people who do not necessarily have similar interests, occupations, or locations may join together for a common cause. Once the issue is resolved, then the tendency is to revert to the more '"natural" group forms.[26] Thus, special issues give rise to a rather impermanent informal association; groups based on the other three determinants tend to be more lasting.

When informal organizations come into being they assume certain characteristics. Since understanding these characteristics is important for management practice, they are noted below:

1. Informal organizations act as agencies of *social control*. They generate a culture based on certain norms of conduct which, in turn, demands conformity from group members. These standards may be at odds with the values set by the formal organization. So an individual may very well find himself in a situation of conflicting demands.

2. The form of human interrelationships in the informal organization requires *techniques of analysis* different from those used to plot the relationships of people in a formal organization. The method used for determining the structure of the informal group is called sociometric analysis. Sociometry reveals the complex structure of interpersonal relations which is based on premises fundamentally unlike the logic of the formal organization.

3. Informal organizations have *status and communication* systems peculiar to themselves, not necessarily derived from the formal systems. For example, the grapevine is the subject of much neoclassical study.

4. Survival of the informal organization requires stable continuing relationships among the people in them. Thus, it has been observed that the informal organization *resists change*.[27] Considerable attention is given by the neoclassicists to overcoming informal resistance to change.

5. The last aspect of analysis which appears to be central to the neoclassical view of the informal organization is the study of the *informal leader*. Discussion revolves around who the informal leader is, how he assumes this role, what characteristics are peculiar to him, and how he can help the manager accomplish his objectives in the formal organization.[28]

This brief sketch of some of the major facets of informal organization theory has neglected, so far, one important topic treated by the neoclassical school. It is the way in which the formal and informal organizations interact.

A conventional way of looking at the interaction of the two is the "live and let live" point of view. Management should recognize that the informal organization exists, nothing can destroy it, and so the executive might just as well work with it. Working with the informal organization involves not threatening its existence unnecessarily, listening to opinions expressed for the group by the leader, allowing group participation in decision-making situations, and controlling the grapevine by prompt release of accurate information.[29]

While this approach is management centered, it is not unreasonable to expect that informal group standards and norms could make themselves felt on formal organizational policy. An honestly conceived effort by managers to establish a working relationship with the informal organization could result in an association where both formal and informal views would be reciprocally modified. The danger which at all costs should be avoided is that "working with the informal organization" does not degenerate into a shallow disguise for human manipulation.

Some neoclassical writing in organization theory, especially that coming from the management-oriented segment of this school, gives the impression that the formal and informal organizations are distinct, and at times, quite irreconcilable factors in a company. The interaction which takes place between the two is something akin to the interaction between the company and a labor union, or a government agency, or another company.

The concept of the social system is another approach to the interactional climate. While this concept can be properly classified as neoclassical, it borders on the modern theories of organization. The phrase "social system" means that an organization is a complex of mutually interdependent, but variable, factors.

These factors include individuals and their attitudes and motives, jobs, the physical work setting, the formal organization, and the informal organizations. These factors, and many others, are woven into an overall pattern of interdependency. From this point of view, the formal and informal organizations lose their distinctiveness, but find real meaning, in terms of human behavior, in the operation of the system as a whole. Thus, the study of organization turns away from descriptions of its component parts, and is refocused on the system of interrelationships among the parts.

One of the major contributions of the Hawthorne studies was the integration of Pareto's idea of the social system into a meaningful method of analysis for the study of behavior in human organizations.[30] This concept is still vitally important. But unfortunately some work in the field of human relations undertaken by the neoclassicists has overlooked, or perhaps discounted, the significance of this consideration.[31]

The fundamental insight regarding the social system, developed and applied to the industrial scene by the Hawthorne researchers, did not find much extension in subsequent work in the neoclassical vein. Indeed, the neoclassical school after the Hawthorne studies generally seemed content to engage in descriptive generalizations, or particularized empirical research studies which did not have much meaning outside their own context.

The neoclassical school of organization theory has been called bankrupt. Criticisms range from, "human relations is a tool for cynical puppeteering of people," to "human relations is nothing more than a trifling body of empirical and descriptive information." There is a good deal of truth in both criticisms, but another appraisal of the neoclassical school of organization theory is offered here. The neoclassical approach has provided valuable contributions to lore of organization. But, like the classical theory, the neoclassical doctrine suffers from incompleteness, a shortsighted perspective, and lack of integration among the many facets of human behavior studied by it. Modern organization theory has made a move to cover the shortcomings of the current body of theoretical knowledge.

MODERN ORGANIZATION THEORY

The distinctive qualities of modern organization theory are its conceptual-analytical base, its reliance on empirical research data and, above all, its integrating nature. These qualities are framed in a philosophy which accepts the premise that the only meaningful way to study organization is to study it as a system. As Henderson put it, the study of a system must rely on a method of analysis, ". . . involving the simultaneous variations of mutually dependent variables."[32] Human systems, of course, contain a huge number of dependent variables which defy the most complex simultaneous equations to solve.

Nevertheless, system analysis has its own peculiar point of view which aims to study organization in the way Henderson suggests. It treats organization as a system of mutually dependent variables. As a result, modern organization theory, which accepts system analysis, shifts the conceptual level of organization study above the classical and neoclassical theories. Modern organization theory asks a range of interrelated questions which are not seriously considered by the two other theories.

Key among these questions are: (1) What are the strategic parts of the system? (2) What is the nature of their mutual dependency? (3) What are the main processes in the system which link the parts together, and facilitate their adjustment to each other? (4) What are the goals sought by systems?[33]

Modern organization theory is in no way a unified body of thought. Each writer and researcher has his special emphasis when he considers the system. Perhaps the most evident unifying thread in the study of systems is the effort to look at the organization in its totality. Representative books in this field are March and Simon, *Organizations,*[34] and Haire's anthology, *Modern Organization Theory.*[35]

Instead of attempting a review of different writers' contributions to modern organization theory, it will be more useful to discuss the various ingredients involved in system analysis. They are the parts, the interactions, the processes, and the goals of systems.

The Parts of the System and Their Interdependency

The first basic part of the system is the *individual,* and the personality structure he brings to the organization. Elementary to an individual's personality are motives and attitudes which condition the range of expectancies he hopes to satisfy by participating in the system.

The second part of the system is the formal arrangement of functions, usually called the *formal organization.* The formal organization is the interrelated pattern of jobs which make up the structure of a system. Certain writers, like Argyris, see a fundamental conflict resulting from the demands made by the system, and the structure of the mature, normal personality. In any event, the individual has expectancies regarding the job he is to perform; and, conversely, the job makes demands on, or has expectancies relating to, the performance of the individual. Considerable attention has been given by writers in modern organization theory to incongruencies resulting from the interaction of organizational and individual demands.[36]

The third part in the organization system is the *informal organization.* Enough has been said already about the nature of this organization. But it must be noted that an interactional pattern exists between the individual and the informal group. This interactional arrangement can be conveniently discussed as the mutual modification of expectancies. The informal organization has demands which it makes on members in terms of anticipated forms of behavior, and the individual has expectancies of satisfaction he hopes to derive from association with people on the job. Both these sets of expectancies interact, resulting in the individual modifying his behavior to accord with the demands of the group, and the group, perhaps, modifying what it expects from an individual because of the impact of his personality on group norms.[37]

Much of what has been said about the various expectancy systems in an organization can also be treated using status and role concepts. Part of modern organization theory rests on research findings in social-psychology relative to reciprocal patterns of behavior stemming from role demands generated by both the formal and informal organizations, and role perceptions peculiar to the individual. Bakke's *fusion process* is largely concerned with the modification of role expectancies. The fusion process is a force, according to Bakke, which acts to weld divergent elements together for the preservation of organizational integrity.[38]

The fifth part of system analysis is the *physical setting* in which the job is performed. Although this element of the system may be implicit in what has been said already about the formal organization and its functions, it is well to separate it. In the physical surroundings of work, interactions are present in complex man-machine systems. The human "engineer" cannot approach the problems posed by such interrelationships in a purely technical, engineering fashion. As Haire says, these problems lie in the domain of the social theorist.[39] Attention must be centered on responses demanded from a logically ordered production function, often with the view of minimizing the error in the system. From this standpoint, work cannot be effectively organized unless the psychological, social, and physiological characteristics of people participating in the work environment are considered. Machines and processes should be designed to fit certain generally observed psychological and physiological properties of men, rather than hiring men to fit machines.

In summary, the parts of the system which appear to be of strategic importance are the individual, the formal structure, the informal organization, status and role patterns, and the physical environment of work. Again, these parts are woven into a configuration called the organizational system. The processes which link the parts are taken up next.

The Linking Processes

One can say, with a good deal of glibness, that all the parts mentioned above are interrelated. Although this observation is quite correct, it does not mean too much in terms of system theory unless some attempt is made to analyze the processes by which the interaction is achieved. Role theory is devoted to certain types of interactional processes. In addition, modern organization theorists point to three other linking activities which appear to be universal to human systems of organized behavior. These processes are communication, balance, and decision making.

1. Communication is mentioned often in neoclassical theory, but the emphasis is on description of forms of communication activity, i.e., formal-informal, vertical-horizontal, line-staff. Communication, as a mech-

anism which links the segments of the system together, is overlooked by way of much considered analysis.

One aspect of modern organization theory is study of the communication network in the system. Communication is viewed as the method by which action is evoked from the parts of the system. Communication acts not only as stimuli resulting in action, but also as a control and coordination mechanism linking the decision centers in the system into a synchronized pattern. Deutsch points out that organizations are composed of parts which communicate with each other, receive messages from the outside world, and store information. Taken together, these communication functions of the parts comprise a configuration representing the total system.[40] More is to be said about communication later in the discussion of the cybernetic model.

2. The concept of *balance* as a linking process involves a series of some rather complex ideas. Balance refers to an equilibrating mechanism whereby the various parts of the system are maintained in a harmoniously structured relationship to each other.

The necessity for the balance concept logically flows from the nature of systems themselves. It is impossible to conceive of an ordered relationship among the parts of a system without also introducing the idea of a stabilizing or an adapting mechanism.

Balance appears in two varieties—quasi-automatic and innovative. Both forms of balance act to insure system integrity in the face of changing conditions, either internal or external to the system. The first form of balance, quasi-automatic, refers to what some think are "homeostatic" properties of systems. That is, systems seem to exhibit built-in propensities to maintain steady states.

If human organizations are open, self-maintaining systems, then control and regulatory processes are necessary. The issue hinges on the degree to which stabilizing processes in systems, when adapting to change, are automatic. March and Simon have an interesting answer to this problem, which in part is based on the type of change and the adjustment necessary to adapt to the change. Systems have programs of action which are put into effect when a change is perceived. If the change is relatively minor, and if the change comes within the purview of established programs of action, then it might be fairly confidently predicted that the adaptation made by the system will be quasiautomatic.[41]

The role of innovative, creative balancing efforts now needs to be examined. The need for innovation arises when adaptation to a change is outside the scope of existing programs designed for the purpose of keeping the system in balance. New programs have to be evolved in order for the system to maintain internal harmony.

New programs are created by trial and error search for feasible action alternatives to cope with a given change. But innovation is subject to the limitations and possibilities inherent in the quantity and variety of information present in a system at a particular time. New combinations of alternatives for innovative purposes depend on:

(a) the possible range of output of the system, or the capacity of the system to supply information.

(b) the range of available information in the memory of the system.

(c) the operating rules (program) governing the analysis and flow of information within the system.

(d) the ability of the system to "forget" previously learned solutions to change problems.[42] A system with too good a memory might narrow its behavioral choices to such an extent as to stifle innovation. In simpler language, old learned programs might be used to adapt to change, when newly innovated programs are necessary.[43]

Much of what has been said about communication and balance brings to mind a cybernetic model in which both these processes have vital roles. Cybernetics has to do with feedback and control in all kinds of systems. Its purpose is to maintain system stability in the face of change. Cybernetics cannot be studied without considering communication networks, information flow, and some kind of balancing process aimed at preserving the integrity of the system.

Cybernetics directs attention to key questions regarding the system. These questions are: How are communication centers connected, and how are they maintained? Corollary to this question: what is the structure of the feedback system? Next, what information is stored in the organization, and at what points? And as a corollary: how accessible is this information to decision-making centers? Third, how conscious is the organization of the operation of its own parts? That is, to what extent do the policy centers receive control information with sufficient frequency and relevancy to create a real awareness of the operation of the segments of the system? Finally, what are the learning (innovating) capabilities of the system?[44]

Answers to the questions posed by cybernetics are crucial to understanding both the balancing and communication processes in systems.[45] Although cybernetics has been applied largely to technical-engineering problems of automation, the model of feedback, control, and regulation in all systems has a good deal of generality. Cybernetics is a fruitful area which can be used to synthesize the processes of communication and balance.

3. A wide spectrum of topics dealing with types of decisions in human systems makes up the core of analysis of another important process in organizations. Decision analysis is one of the major contributions of March and Simon in their book *Organizations*. The two major classes of

decisions they discuss are decisions to produce and decisions to participate in the system[46]

Decisions to produce are largely a result of an interaction between
individual attitudes and the demands of organization. Motivation analysis becomes central to studying the nature and results of the interaction.
Individual decisions to participate in the organization reflect on such
issues as the relationship between organizational rewards versus the
demands made by the organization. Participation decisions also focus
attention on the reasons why individuals remain in or leave organizations.

March and Simon treat decisions as internal variables in an organization which depend on jobs, individual expectations and motivations,
and organizational structure. Marschak[47] looks on the decision process as
an independent variable upon which the survival of the organization is
based. In this case, the organization is viewed as having, inherent to its
structure, the ability to maximize survival requisites through its established decision processes.

The Goals of Organization

Organization has three goals which may be either intermeshed or independent ends in themselves. They are growth, stability, and interaction.
The last goal refers to organizations which exist primarily to provide a
medium for association of its members with others. Interestingly enough
these goals seem to apply to different forms of organization at varying
levels of complexity, ranging from simple clockwork mechanisms to social systems.

These similarities in organizational purposes have been observed by
a number of people, and a field of thought and research called general
system theory has developed, dedicated to the task of discovering organizational universals. The dream of general system theory is to create a
science of organizational universals, or if you will, a universal science
using common organizational elements found in all systems as a starting
point.

Modern organization theory is on the periphery of general system
theory. Both general system theory and modern organization theory
study:

(1) the parts (individuals) in aggregates, and the movement of individuals into and out of the system.
(2) the interaction of individuals with the environment found in the
system.
(3) the interactions among individuals in the system.
(4) general growth and stability problems of systems.[48]

Modern organization theory and general system theory are similar in
that they look at organization as an integrated whole. They differ, how-

ever, in terms of their generality. General system theory is concerned with every level of system, whereas modern organizational theory focuses primarily on human organization.

The question might be asked, what can the science of administration gain by the study of system levels other than human? Before attempting an answer, note should be made of what these other levels are. Boulding presents a convenient method of classification:

(1) The static structure—a level of framework, the anatomy of a system; for example, the structure of the universe.

(2) The simple dynamic system—the level of clockworks, predetermined necessary motions.

(3) The cybernetic system—the level of the thermostat, the system moves to maintain a given equilibrium through a process of self-regulation.

(4) The open system—level of self-maintaining systems, moves toward and includes living organisms.

(5) The genetic-societal system—level of cell society, characterized by a division of labor among cells.

(6) Animal systems—level of mobility, evidence of goal-directed behavior.

(7) Human systems—level of symbol interpretation and idea communication.

(8) Social system—level of human organization.

(9) Transcendental systems—level of ultimates and absolutes which exhibit systematic structure but are unknowable in essence.[49]

This approach to the study of systems by finding universals common at all levels of organization offers intriguing possibilities for administrative organization theory. A good deal of light could be thrown on social systems if structurally analogous elements could be found in the simpler types of systems. For example, cybernetic systems have characteristics which seem to be similar to feedback, regulation, and control phenomena in human organizations. Thus, certain facets of cybernetic models could be generalized to human organization. Considerable danger, however, lies in poorly founded analogies. Superficial similarities between simpler system forms and social systems are apparent everywhere. Instinctually based ant societies, for example, do not yield particularly instructive lessons for understanding rationally conceived human organizations. Thus, care should be taken that analogies used to bridge system levels are not mere devices for literary enrichment. For analogies to have usefulness and validity, they must exhibit inherent structural similarities or implicitly identical operational principles.[50]

Modern organization theory leads, as it has been shown, almost inevitably into a discussion of general system theory. A science of organizational universals has some strong advocates, particularly among biologists.[51] Organization theorists in administrative science cannot afford to overlook the contributions of general system theory. Indeed, modern organization concepts could offer a great deal to those working with general system theory. But the ideas dealt with in the general theory are exceedingly elusive.

Speaking of the concept of equilibrium as a unifying element in all systems, Easton says, "It (equilibrium) leaves the impression that we have a useful general theory when in fact, lacking measurability, it is a mere pretence for knowledge."[52] The inability to quantify and measure universal organization elements undermines the success of pragmatic tests to which general system theory might be put.

Organization Theory: Quo Vadis?

Most sciences have a vision of the universe to which they are applied, and administrative science is not an exception. This universe is composed of parts. One purpose of science is to synthesize the parts into an organized conception of its field of study. As a science matures, its theorems about the configuration of its universe change. The direction of change in three sciences, physics, economics, and sociology, are noted briefly for comparison with the development of an administrative view of human organization.

The first comprehensive and empirically verifiable outlook of the physical universe was presented by Newton in his *Principia*. Classical physics, founded on Newton's work, constitutes a grand scheme in which a wide range of physical phenomena could be organized and predicted. Newtonian physics may rightfully be regarded as "macro" in nature, because its system of organization was concerned largely with gross events of which the movement of celestial bodies, waves, energy forms, and strain are examples. For years classical physics was supreme, being applied continuously to smaller and smaller classes of phenomena in the physical universe. Physicists at one time adopted the view that everything in their realm could be discovered by simply subdividing problems. Physics thus moved into the "micro" order.

But in the nineteenth century a revolution took place motivated largely because events were being noted which could not be explained adequately by the conceptual framework supplied by the classical school. The consequences of this revolution are brilliantly described by Eddington:

> From the point of view of philosophy of science the conception associated with entropy must I think be ranked as the great contribution of the nineteenth century to scientific thought. It marked a reaction from the view that everything to which science need pay attention is discovered by microscopic dissection of objects. It provided an alternative standpoint in which the centre of interest is shifted from the entities reached by the customary analysis

(atoms, electric potentials, etc.) to qualities possessed by the system as a whole, which cannot be split up and located—a little bit here, and a little bit there. . . .

We often think that when we have completed our study of *one* we know all about *two,* because "two" is "one and one." We forget that we have still to make a study of "and." Secondary physics is the study of "and"—that is to say, of organization.[53]

Although modern physics often deals in minute quantities and oscillations, the conception of the physicist is on the "macro" scale. He is concerned with the "and," or the organization of the world in which the events occur. These developments did not invalidate classical physics as to its usefulness for explaining a certain range of phenomena. But classical physics is no longer the undisputed law of the universe. It is a special case.

Early economic theory, and Adam Smith's *Wealth of Nations* comes to mind, examined economic problems in the macro order. The *Wealth of Nations* is mainly concerned with matters of national income and welfare. Later, the economics of the firm, micro-economics, dominated the theoretical scene in this science. And, finally, with Keynes' *The General Theory of Employment, Interest and Money,* a systematic approach to the economic universe was re-introduced on the macro level.

The first era of the developing science of sociology was occupied by the great social "system builders." Comte, the so-called father of sociology, had a macro view of society in that his chief works are devoted to social reorganization. Comte was concerned with the interrelationships among social, political, religious, and educational institutions. As sociology progressed, the science of society compressed. Emphasis shifted from the macro approach of the pioneers to detailed, empirical study of small social units. The compression of sociological analysis was accompanied by study of social pathology or disorganization.

In general, physics, economics, and sociology appear to have two things in common. First, they offered a macro point of view as their initial systematic comprehension of their area of study. Second, as the science developed, attention fragmented into analysis of the parts of the organization, rather than attending to the system as a whole. This is the micro phase.

In physics and economics, discontent was evidenced by some scientists at the continual atomization of the universe. The reaction to the micro approach was a new theory or theories dealing with the total system, on the macro level again. This third phase of scientific development seems to be more evident in physics and economics than in sociology.

The reason for the "macro-micro-macro" order of scientific progress lies, perhaps, in the hypothesis that usually the things which strike man first are of great magnitude. The scientist attempts to discover order in the vastness. But after macro laws or models of systems are postulated, variations appear which demand analysis, not so much in terms of the entire system, but more in terms of the specific parts which make it up. Then, intense study of microcosm may result in new general laws, replacing the old models of organization. Or, the old and the new models may stand together, each explaining a different class of phenomenon. Or, the old and the new concepts of organization may be welded to produce a single creative synthesis.

Now, what does all this have to do with the problem of organization in administrative science? Organization concepts seem to have gone through the same order of development in this field as in the three just mentioned. It is evident that the classical theory of organization, particularly as in the work of Mooney and Reiley, is concerned with principles common to all organizations. It is a macro-organizational view. The classical approach to organization, however, dealt with the gross anatomical parts and processes of the formal organization. Like classical physics, the classical theory of organization is a special case. Neither is especially well equipped to account for variation from its established framework.

Many variations in the classical administrative model result from human behavior. The only way these variations could be understood was by a microscopic examination of particularized, situational aspects of human behavior. The mission of the neoclassical school thus is "micro-analysis."

It was observed earlier, that somewhere along the line the concept of the social system, which is the key to understanding the Hawthorne studies, faded into the background. Maybe the idea is so obvious that it was lost to the view of researchers and writers in human relations. In any event, the press of research in the microcosmic universes of the informal organization, morale and productivity, leadership, participation, and the like forced the notion of the social system into limbo. Now, with the advent of modern organization theory, the social system has been resurrected.

Modern organization theory appears to be concerned with Eddington's "and." This school claims that its operational hypothesis is based on a macro point of view; that is, the study of organization as a whole. This nobility of purpose should not obscure, however, certain difficulties faced by this field as it is presently constituted. Modern organization theory raises two questions which should be explored further. First, would it not be more accurate to speak of modern organization theories? Second, just how much of modern organization theory is modern?

The first question can be answered with a quick affirmative. Aside from the notion of the system, there are few, if any, other ideas of a unifying nature. Except for several important exceptions,[54] modern organization theorists tend to pursue their pet points of view,[55] suggesting they are part of system theory, but not troubling to show by what mystical means they arrive at this conclusion.

The irony of it all is that a field dealing with systems has, indeed, little system. Modern organization theory needs a framework, and it needs an integration of issues into a common conception of organization. Admittedly, this is a large order. But it is curious not to find serious analytical treatment of subjects like cybernetics or general system theory in Haire's *Modern Organization Theory* which claims to be a representative example of work in this field. Beer has ample evidence in his book *Cybernetics and Management* that cybernetics, if imaginatively approached, provides a valuable conceptual base for the study of systems.

The second question suggests an ambiguous answer. Modern organization theory is in part a product of the past; system analysis is not a new idea. Further, modern organization theory relies for supporting data on microcosmic research studies, generally drawn from the journals of the last ten years. The newness of modern organization theory, perhaps, is its effort to synthesize recent research contributions of many fields into a system theory characterized by a reoriented conception of organization.

One might ask, but what is the modern theorist reorienting? A clue is found the almost snobbish disdain assumed by some authors of the neoclassical human relations school, and particularly, the classical school. Reevaluation of the classical school of organization is overdue. However, this does not mean that its contributions to organization theory are irrelevant and should be overlooked in the rush to get on the "behavioral science bandwagon."

Haire announces that the papers appearing in *Modern Organization Theory* constitute, "the ragged leading edge of a wave of theoretical development."[56] Ragged, yes; but leading, no! The papers appearing in this book do not represent a theoretical breakthrough in the concept of organization. Haire's collection is an interesting potpourri with several contributions of considerable significance. But readers should beware that they will not find vastly new insights into organizational behavior in this book, if they have kept up with the literature of the social sciences, and have dabbled to some extent in the esoterica of biological theories of growth, information theory, and mathematical model building. For those who have not maintained the pace, *Modern Organization Theory* serves the admirable purpose of bringing them up to date on a rather diversified number of subjects.

Some work in modern organization theory is pioneering, making its appraisal difficult and future uncertain. While the direction of this endeavor is unclear, one thing is patently true. Human behavior in organizations, and indeed, organization itself, cannot be adequately understood within the ground rules of classical and neoclassical doctrines. Appreciation of human organization requires a *creative* synthesis of massive amounts of empirical data, a high order of deductive reasoning, imaginative research studies, and a taste for individual and social values. Accomplishment of all these objectives, and the inclusion of them into a framework of the concept of the system, appears to be the goal of modern organization theory. The vitality of administrative science rests on the advances modern theorists make along this line.

Modern organization theory, 1960 style, is an amorphous aggregation of synthesizers and restaters, with a few extending leadership on the frontier. For the sake of these few, it is well to admonish that pouring old wine into new bottles may make the spirits cloudy. Unfortunately, modern organization theory has almost succeeded in achieving the status of a fad. Popularization and exploitation contributed to the disrepute into which human relations has fallen. It would be a great waste if modern organization theory yields to the same fate, particularly since both modern organization theory and human relations draw from the same promising source of inspiration—system analysis.

Modern organization theory needs tools of analysis and a conceptual framework uniquely its own, but it must also allow for the incorporation of relevant contributions of many fields. It may be that the framework will come from general system theory. New areas of research such as decision theory, information theory, and cybernetics also offer reasonable expectations of analytical and conceptual tools. Modern organization theory represents a frontier of research which has great significance for management. The potential is great, because it offers the opportunity for uniting what is valuable in classical theory with the social and natural sciences into a systematic and integrated conception of human organization.

NOTES AND REFERENCES

1. Roderick Seidenberg, *Post Historic Man* (Boston: Beacon Press, 1951), p. 1.

2. Robert V. Presthus, "Toward a Theory of Organizational Behavior," *Administrative Science Quarterly,* June, 1958, p. 50.

3. Regulation and predictability of human behavior are matters of degree varying with different organizations on something of a continuum. At one extreme are bureaucratic type organizations with tight bonds of regulation. At the other extreme are voluntary associations, and informal organizations with relatively loose bonds of regulation.

    This point has an interesting sidelight. A bureaucracy with tight controls and a high degree of predictability of human action appears to be unable to distinguish between destructive and creative deviations from established values. Thus the only thing which is safeguarded is the status quo.

4. The monolithic institutions of the military and government are other cases of organizational preoccupation.

5. James D. Mooney and Alan C. Reiley, *Onward Industry* (New York: Harper and Brothers, 1931). Later published by James D. Mooney under the title *Principles of Organization.*

6. E. F. L. Brech, *Organization* (London: Longmans, Green and Company, 1957).

7. Louis A. Allen, *Management and Organization* (New York: McGraw-Hill Book Company, 1958).

8. Usually the division of labor is treated under a topical heading of departmen-

tation; see for example: Harold Koontz and Cyril O'Donnell, *Principles of Management* (New York: McGraw-Hill Book Company, 1959), Ch. 7.

9. These processes are discussed at length in Ralph Currier Davis, *The Fundamentals of Top Management* (New York: Harper and Brothers, 1951), Ch. 7.

10. For a discussion of structure see William H. Newman, *Administrative Action* (Englewood Cliffs, N.J.: Prentice-Hall, Inc., 1951), Ch. 16.

11. V. A. Graicunas, "Relationships in Organization," *Papers on the Science of Administration* (New York: Columbia University, 1937).

12. Brech, op. cit., p. 78 (see note 6).

13. See: F. J. Roethlisberger and William J. Dickson, *Management and the Worker* (Cambridge, Mass.: Harvard University Press, 1939).

14. Burleigh B. Gardner and David G. Moore, *Human Relations in Industry* (Homewood, Ill.: Richard D. Irwin, 1955).

15. Keith Davis, *Human Relations in Business* (New York: McGraw-Hill Book Company, 1957).

16. For example, see Delbert C. Miller and William H. Form, *Industrial Sociology* (New York: Harper and Brothers, 1951).

17. See Hugo Munsterberg, *Psychology and Industrial Efficiency* (Boston: Houghton Mifflin Company, 1913).

18. Probably the classic work is Elton Mayo, *The Human Problems of an Industrial Civilization* (Cambridge, Mass.: Harvard University, 1946, first printed 1933).

19. For further discussion of the human relations implications of the scalar and functional processes see Keith Davis, op. cit., pp. 60–66 (see note 15).

20. Melville Dalton, "Conflicts between Staff and Line Managerial Officers," *American Sociological Review,* June, 1950, pp. 342–351.

21. J. M. Juran, "Improving the Relationship between Staff and Line," *Personnel,* May, 1956, pp. 515–524.

22. Gardner and Moore, op. cit., pp. 237–243 (see note 14).

23. For example: Brech, op. cit., pp. 27–29 (see note 6); and Allen, op. cit., pp. 61–62 (see note 7).

24. See Leon Festinger, Stanley Schachter, and Kurt Back, *Social Pressures in Informal Groups* (New York: Harper and Brothers, 1950), pp. 153–163.

25. For example see W. Fred Cottrell, *The Railroader* (Palo Alto, Calif.: Stanford University Press, 1940), Ch. 3.

26. Except in cases where the existence of an organization is necessary for the continued maintenance of employee interest. Under these conditions the previously informal association may emerge as a formal group, such as a union.

27. Probably the classic study of resistance to change is Lester Coch and John R. P. French, Jr., "Overcoming Resistance to Change," *Human Factors in Management,* ed. Schuyler Dean Hoslett (New York: Harper and Brothers, 1951), pp. 242–268.

28. For example see Robert Saltonstall, *Human Relations in Administration* (New York: McGraw-Hill Book Company, 1959), pp. 330–331; and Keith Davis, op. cit., pp. 99–101 (see note 15).

29. For an example of this approach see John T. Doutt, "Management Must Manage the Informal Group, Too," *Advanced Management,* May, 1959, pp. 26–28.

30. See Roethlisberger and Dickson, op. cit., Ch. 24 (see note 13).

31. A check of management human relations texts, the organization and human relations chapters of principles of management texts, and texts on conventional organization theory for management courses reveals little or no treatment of the concept of the social system.

32. Lawrence J. Henderson, *Pareto's General Sociology* (Cambridge, Mass.: Harvard University Press, 1935), p. 13.

33. There is another question which cannot be treated in the scope of this paper. It asks, What research tools should be used for the study of the system?

34. James G. March and Herbert A. Simon, *Organizations* (New York: John Wiley and Sons, 1958).

35. Mason Haire, ed., *Modern Organization Theory* (New York: John Wiley and Sons, 1959).

36. See Chris Argyris, *Personality and Organization* (New York: Harper and Brothers, 1957), esp. Ch. 2, 3, 7.

37. For a larger treatment of this subject see George C. Homans, *The Human Group* (New York: Harcourt, Brace and Company, 1950), Ch. 5.

38. E. Wight Bakke, "Concept of the Social Organization," *Modern Organization Theory,* ed. Mason Haire (New York: John Wiley and Sons, 1959), pp. 60–61.

39. Mason Haire, "Psychology and the Study of Business: Joint Behavioral Sciences," *Social Science Research on Business: Product and Potential* (New York: Columbia University Press, 1959), pp. 53–59.

40. Karl W. Deutsch, "On Communication Models in the Social Sciences," *Public Opinion Quarterly,* 16 (1952), pp. 356–380.

41. March and Simon, op. cit., pp. 139–140 (see note 34).

42. Mervyn L. Cadwallader, "The Cybernetic Analysis of Change in Complex Social Organization," *The American Journal of Sociology,* September, 1959, p. 156.

43. It is conceivable for innovative behavior to be programmed into the system.

44. These are questions adapted from Deutsch, op. cit., pp. 368–370 (see note 40).

45. Answers to these questions would require a comprehensive volume. One of the best approaches currently available is Stafford Beer, *Cybernetics and Management* (New York: John Wiley and Sons, 1959).

46. March and Simon, op. cit., Ch. 3 and 4 (see note 34).

47. Jacob Marschak, "Efficient and Viable Organizational Forms," *Modern Organization Theory,* ed. Mason Haire (New York: John Wiley and Sons, 1959), pp. 307–320.

48. Kenneth E. Boulding, "General System Theory—The Skeleton of a Science," *Management Science,* April, 1956, pp. 200–202.

49. Ibid., pp. 202–205.

50. Seidenberg, op. cit., p. 136 (see note 1). The fruitful use of the type of analo-

gies spoken of by Seidenberg is evident in the application of thermodynamic principles, particularly the entropy concept, to communication theory. See Claude E. Shannon and Warren Weaver, *The Mathematical Theory of Communication* (Urbana: University of Illinois Press, 1949). Further, the existence of a complete analogy between the operational behavior of thermodynamic systems, electrical communications systems, and biological systems has been noted by Y. S. Touloukian, *The Concept of Entropy in Communication, Living Organisms, and Thermodynamics,* Research Bulletin 130, Purdue Engineering Experiment Station.

51. For example see Ludwig von Bertalanffy, *Problem of Life* (London: Watts and Company, 1952).

52. David Easton, "Limits of the Equilibrium Model in Social Research," *Profits and Problems of Homeostatic Models in the Behavioral Sciences,* Publication 1, Chicago Behavioral Sciences, 1953, p. 39.

53. Sir Arthur Eddington, *The Nature of the Physical World* (Ann Arbor: University of Michigan Press, 1958), pp. 103–104.

54. For example, E. Wight Bakke, op. cit., pp. 18–75 (see note 38).

55. There is a large selection including decision theory, individual-organization interaction, motivation, vitality, stability, growth, and graph theory, to mention a few.

56. Mason Haire, "General Issues," *Modern Organization Theory,* ed. Mason Haire (New York: John Wiley and Sons, 1959), p. 2.

14

The Coming Death of Bureaucracy

Warren G. Bennis

Warren Bennis sounds the death knell of the bureaucratically organized structure. He argues that rapid and unexpected change, growth, complexity of modern technology and changes in managerial behavior are major threats to bureaucracies. Note Bennis' description of how future organizations will look and how inconsistent their needs will be with present day bureaucracies.—Eds.

Not far from the new Government Center in downtown Boston, a foreign visitor walked up to a sailor and asked why American ships were built to last only a short time. According to the tourist, "The sailor answered without hesitation that the art of navigation is making such rapid progress that the finest ship would become obsolete if it lasted beyond a few years. In these words which fell accidentally from an uneducated man, I began to recognize the general and systematic idea upon which your great people direct all their concerns."

The foreign visitor was that shrewd observer of American morals and manners, Alexis de Tocqueville, and the year was 1835. He would not recognize Scollay Square today. But he had caught the central theme of our country: its preoccupation, its *obsession* with change. One thing is, however, new since de Tocqueville's time: the *acceleration* of newness, the changing scale and scope of change itself. As Dr. Robert Oppenheimer said, ". . . the world alters as we walk in it, so that the years of man's life measure not some small growth or rearrangement or moderation of what was learned in childhood, but a great upheaval."

How will these accelerating changes in our society influence human organizations?

SOURCE: Reprinted by permission from *THINK Magazine,* published by IBM, copyright 1966 by International Business Machines Corporation.

A short while ago, I predicted that we would, in the next 25 to 50 years, participate in the end of bureaucracy as we know it and in the rise of new social systems better suited to the 20th-century demands of industrialization. This forecast was based on the evolutionary principle that every age develops an organizational form appropriate to its genius, and that the prevailing form, known by sociologists as bureaucracy and by most businessmen as "damn bureaucracy," was out of joint with contemporary realities. I realize now that my distant prophecy is already a distinct reality so that prediction is already foreshadowed by practice.

I should like to make clear that by bureaucracy I mean a chain of command structured on the lines of a pyramid—the typical structure which coordinates the business of almost every human organization we know of: industrial, governmental, of universities and research and development laboratories, military, religious, voluntary. I do *not* have in mind those fantasies so often dreamed up to describe complex organizations. These fantasies can be summarized in two grotesque stereotypes. The first I call "Organization as Inkblot"—an actor steals around an uncharted wasteland, growing more restive and paranoid by the hour, while he awaits orders that never come. The other specter is "Organization as Big Daddy"—the actors are square people plugged into square holes by some omniscient and omnipotent genius who can cradle in his arms the entire destiny of man by way of computer and TV. Whatever the first image owes to Kafka, the second owes to George Orwell's *Nineteen Eighty-Four*.

Bureaucracy, as I refer to it here, is a useful social invention that was perfected during the industrial revolution to organize and direct the activities of a business firm. Most students of organizations would say that its anatomy consists of the following components:

- A well-defined chain of command.
- A system of procedures and rules for dealing with all contingencies relating to work activities.
- A division of labor based on specialization.
- Promotion and selection based on technical competence.
- Impersonality in human relations.

It is the pyramid arrangement we see on most organizational charts.

The bureaucratic "machine model" was developed as a reaction against the personal subjugation, nepotism and cruelty, and the capricious and subjective judgments which passed for managerial practices during the early days of the industrial revolution. Bureaucracy emerged out of the organizations' need for order and precision and the workers' demands for impartial treatment. It was an organization ideally suited to the values and demands of the Victorian era. And just as bureaucracy emerged as a creative response to a radically new age, so today new organizational shapes are surfacing before our eyes.

First I shall try to show why the conditions of our modern industrialized world will bring about the death of bureaucracy. In the second part of this article I will suggest a rough model of the organization of the future.

FOUR THREATS

There are at least four relevant threats to bureaucracy:

(1) Rapid and unexpected change.

(2) Growth in size where the volume of an organization's traditional activities is not enough to sustain growth. (A number of factors are included here, among them: bureaucratic overhead; tighter controls and impersonality due to bureaucratic sprawls; outmoded rules and organizational structures.)

(3) Complexity of modern technology where integration between activities and persons of very diverse, highly specialized competence is required.

(4) A basically psychological threat springing from a change in managerial behavior.

It might be useful to examine the extent to which these conditions exist *right now*:

1. *Rapid and unexpected change.* Bureaucracy's strength is its capacity to efficiently manage the routine and predictable in human affairs. It is almost enough to cite the knowledge and population explosion to raise doubts about its contemporary viability. More revealing, however, are the statistics which demonstrate these overworked phrases:

- Our productivity output per man hour may now be doubling almost every 20 years rather than every 40 years, as it did before World War II.
- The Federal Government alone spent $16 billion in research and development activities in 1965; it will spend $35 billion by 1980.
- The time lag between a technical discovery and recognition of its commercial uses was: 30 years before World War I, 16 years between the Wars, and only 9 years since World War II.
- In 1946, only 42 cities in the world had populations of more than one million. Today there are 90. In 1930, there were 40 people for each square mile of the earth's land surface. Today there are 63. By 2000, it is expected, the figure will have soared to 142.

Bureaucracy, with its nicely defined chain of command, its rules and its rigidities, is ill-adapted to the rapid change the environment now demands.

2. *Growth in size.* While, in theory, there may be no natural limit to the height of a bureaucratic pyramid, in practice the element of complexity is almost invariably introduced with great size. International operation, to cite one significant new element, is the rule rather than exception

for most of our biggest corporations. Firms like Standard Oil Company (New Jersey) with over 100 foreign affiliates, Mobil Oil Corporation, The National Cash Register Company, Singer Company, Burroughs Corporation and Colgate-Palmolive Company derive more than half their income or earnings from foreign sales. Many others—such as Eastman Kodak Company, Chas. Pfizer & Company, Inc., Caterpillar Tractor Company, International Harvester Company, Corn Products Company and Minnesota Mining & Manufacturing Company—make from 30 to 50 percent of their sales abroad. General Motors Corporation sales are not only nine times those of Volkswagen, they are also bigger than the Gross National Product of the Netherlands and well over the GNP of a hundred other countries. If we have seen the sun set on the British Empire we may never see it set on the empires of General Motors, ITT, Shell and Unilever.

LABOR BOOM

3. *Increasing diversity. Today's activities require persons of very diverse, highly specialized competence.*

Numerous dramatic examples can be drawn from studies of labor markets and job mobility. At some point during the past decade, the U.S. became the first nation in the world ever to employ more people in service occupations than in the production of tangible goods. Examples of this trend:

- In the field of education, the *increase* in employment between 1950 and 1960 was greater than the total number employed in the steel, copper and aluminum industries.
- In the field of health, the *increase* in employment between 1950 and 1960 was greater than the total number employed in automobile manufacturing in either year.
- In financial firms, the *increase* in employment between 1950 and 1960 was greater than total employment in mining in 1960.

These changes, plus many more that are harder to demonstrate statistically, break down the old, industrial trend toward more and more people doing either simple or undifferentiated chores.

Hurried growth, rapid change and increase in specialization—pit these three factors against the five components of the pyramid structure described [earlier], and we should expect the pyramid of bureaucracy to begin crumbling.

4. *Change in managerial behavior.* There is, I believe, a subtle but perceptible change in the philosophy underlying management behavior. Its magnitude, nature and antecedents, however, are shadowy because of the difficulty of assigning numbers. (Whatever else statistics do for us, they most certainly provide a welcome illusion of certainty.) Nevertheless, real change seems under way because of:

a. A new concept of *man,* based on increased knowledge of his complex and shifting needs, which replaces an oversimplified, innocent, push-button idea of man.

b. A new concept of *power,* based on collaboration and reason, which replaces a model of power based on coercion and threat.

c. A new concept of *organizational values,* based on humanistic-democratic ideals, which replaces the depersonalized mechanistic value system of bureaucracy.

The primary cause of this shift in management philosophy stems not from the bookshelf but from the manager himself. Many of the behavioral scientists, like Douglas McGregor or Rensis Likert, have clarified and articulated—even legitimized—what managers have only half registered to themselves. I am convinced, for example, that the popularity of McGregor's book, *The Human Side of Enterprise,* was based on his rare empathy for a vast audience of managers who are wistful for an alternative to the mechanistic concept of authority, i.e., that he outlined a vivid utopia of more authentic human relationships than most organizational practices today allow. Furthermore, I suspect that the desire for relationships in business has little to do with a profit motive per se, though it is often rationalized as doing so. The real push for these changes stems from the need, not only to humanize the organization, but to use it as a crucible of personal growth and the development of self-realization.[1]

The core problems confronting any organization fall, I believe, into five major categories. First, let us consider the problems, then let us see how our 20th-century conditions of constant change have made the bureaucratic approach to these problems obsolete.

1. *Integration.* The problem is how to integrate individual needs and management goals. In other words, it is the inescapable conflict between individual needs (like "spending time with the family") and organizational demands (like meeting deadlines).

Under 20th-century conditions of constant change there has been an emergence of human sciences and a deeper understanding of man's complexity. Today, integration encompasses the entire range of issues concerned with incentives, rewards and motivations of the individual, and how the organization succeeds or fails in adjusting to these issues. In our society, where personal attachments play an important role, the individual is appreciated, and there is genuine concern for his well-being, not just in a veterinary-hygiene sense, but as a moral, integrated personality.

PARADOXICAL TWINS

The problem of integration, like most human problems, has a venerable past. The modern version goes back at least 160 years and was precipitated by an historical paradox: the twin births of modern individualism and modern industrialism. The former brought about a deep concern for and a passionate interest in the individual and his personal rights. The latter brought about increased mechanization of organized activity. Competition between the two has intensified as each decade promises more freedom and hope for man and more stunning achievements for technology. I believe that our society *has* opted for more humanistic and democratic values, however unfulfilled they may be in practice. It will "buy" these values even at loss in efficiency because it feels it can now afford the loss.

2. *Social influence*. This problem is essentially one of power and how power is distributed. It is a complex issue and alive with controversy, partly because of an ethical component and partly because studies of leadership and power distribution can be interpreted in many ways, and almost always in ways which coincide with one's biases (including a cultural leaning toward democracy).

The problem of power has to be seriously reconsidered because of dramatic situational changes which make the possibility of one-man rule not necessarily "bad" but impractical. I refer to changes in top management's role.

Peter Drucker, over twelve years ago, listed 41 major responsibilities of the chief executive and declared that "90 percent of the trouble we are having with the chief executive's job is rooted in our superstition of the one-man chief." Many factors make one-man control obsolete, among them: the broadening product base of industry; impact of new technology; the scope of international operation; the separation of management from ownership; the rise of trade unions and general education. The real power of the "chief" has been eroding in most organizations even though both he and the organization cling to the older concept.

3. *Collaboration*. This is the problem of managing and resolving conflicts. Bureaucratically, it grows out of the very same social process of conflict and stereotyping that has divided nations and communities. As organizations become more complex, they fragment and divide, building tribal patterns and symbolic codes which often work to exclude others (secrets and jargon, for example) and on occasion to exploit differences for inward (and always fragile) harmony.

Recent research is shedding new light on the problem of conflict. Psychologist Robert R. Blake in his stunning experiments has shown how simple it is to induce conflict, how difficult to arrest it. Take two groups of people who have never before been together, and give them a task which will be judged by an impartial jury. In less than an hour, each group devolves into a tightly-knit band with all the symptoms of an "in group." They regard their product as a "masterwork" and the other group's as "commonplace" at best. "Other" becomes "enemy." "We are good, they are bad; we are right, they are wrong."

RABBIE'S REDS AND GREENS

Jaap Rabbie, conducting experiments on intergroup conflict at the University of Utrecht, has been amazed by the ease with which conflict and stereotype develop. He brings into an experimental room two groups and distributes green name tags and pens to one group, red pens and tags to the other. The two groups do not compete; they do not even interact. They are only in sight of each other while they silently complete a questionnaire. Only 10 minutes are needed to activate defensiveness and fear, reflected in the hostile and irrational perceptions of both "reds" and "greens."

4. *Adaptation*. This problem is caused by our turbulent environment. The pyramid structure of bureaucracy, where power is concentrated at the top, seems the perfect way to "run a railroad." And for the routine tasks of the 19th and early 20th centuries, bureaucracy was (in some respects it still is) a suitable social arrangement. However, rather than a placid and predictable environment, what predominates today is a dynamic and uncertain one where there is a deepening interdependence among economic, scientific, educational, social and political factors in the society.

5. *Revitalization*. This is the problem of growth and decay. As Alfred North Whitehead has said: "The art of free society consists first in the maintenance of the symbolic code, and secondly, in the fearlessness of revision. . . . Those societies which cannot combine reverence to their symbols with freedom of revision must ultimately decay. . . ."

Growth and decay emerge as the penultimate conditions of contemporary society. Organizations, as well as societies, must be concerned with those social structures that engender buoyancy, resilience and a "fearlessness of revision."

I introduce the term "revitalization" to embrace all the social mechanisms that stagnate and regenerate, as well as the process of this cycle. The elements of revitalization are:

1. An ability to learn from experience and to codify, store and retrieve the relevant knowledge.
2. An ability to "learn how to learn," that is, to develop methods for improving the learning process.
3. An ability to acquire and use feedback mechanisms on performance, in short, to be self-analytical.
4. An ability to direct one's own destiny.

These qualities have a good deal in common with what John Gardner calls "self-renewal." For the organization, it means conscious attention to its own evolution. Without a planned methodology and explicit direction, the enterprise will not realize its potential.

Integration, distribution of power, collaboration, adaptation and *revitalization*—these are the major human problems of the next 25 years. How organizations cope with and manage these tasks will undoubtedly determine the viability of the enterprise.

Against this background I should like to set forth some of the conditions that will dictate organizational life in the next two or three decades.

1. *The environment*. Rapid technological change and diversification will lead to more and more partnerships between government and business. It will be a truly mixed economy. Because of the immensity and expense of the projects there will be fewer identical units competing in the same markets and organizations will become more interdependent.

The four main features of this environment are:

- Interdependence rather than competition.
- Turbulence and uncertainty rather than readiness and certainty.
- Large-scale rather than small-scale enterprises.
- Complex and multinational rather than simple national enterprises.

"NICE"—AND NECESSARY

2. *Population characteristics*. The most distinctive characteristic of our society is education. It will become even more so. Within 15 years, two-thirds of our population living in metropolitan areas will have attended college. Adult education is growing even faster, probably because of the rate of professional obsolescence. The Killian report showed that the average engineer required further education only 10 years after getting his degree. It will be almost routine for the experienced physician, engineer and executive to go back to school for advanced training every two or three years. All of this education is not just "nice." It is necessary.

One other characteristic of the population which will aid our understanding of organizations of the future is increasing job mobility. The ease of transportation, coupled with the needs of a dynamic environment, change drastically the idea of "owning" a job—or "having roots." Already 20 percent of our population change their mailing address at least once a year.

3. *Work values*. The increased level of education and mobility will change the values we place on work. People will be more intellectually committed to their jobs and will probably require more involvement, participation and autonomy.

Also, people will be more "other-oriented," taking cues for their norms and values from their immediate environment rather than tradition.

4. *Tasks and goals*. The tasks of the organization will be more technical, complicated and unprogrammed. They will rely on intellect instead of muscle. And they will be too complicated for one person to comprehend, to say nothing of control. Essentially, they will call for the collaboration of specialists in a project or a team form of organization.

There will be a complication of goals. Business will increasingly concern itself with its adaptive or innovative-creative capacity. In addition, supragoals will have to be articulated, goals which shape and provide the foundation for the goal structure. For example, one might be a system for detecting new and changing goals; another could be a system for deciding priorities among goals.

Finally, there will be more conflict and contradiction among diverse standards for organizational effectiveness. This is because professionals tend to identify more with the goals of their profession than with those of their immediate employer. University professors can be used as a case in point. Their inside work may be a conflict between teaching and research, while more of their income is derived from outside sources, such as foundations and consultant work. They tend not to be good "company men" because they divide their loyalty between their professional values and organizational goals.

KEY WORD: "TEMPORARY"

5. *Organization.* The social structure of organizations of the future will have some unique characteristics. The key word will be "temporary." There will be adaptive, rapidly changing *temporary* systems. These will be task forces organized around problems-to-be-solved by groups of relative strangers with diverse professional skills. The groups will be arranged on an organic rather than mechanical model; they will evolve in response to a problem rather than to programmed role expectations. The executive thus becomes a coordinator or "linking pin" between various task forces. He must be a man who can speak the polyglot jargon of research, with skills to relay information and to mediate between groups. People will be evaluated not vertically according to rank and status, but flexibly and functionally according to skill and professional training. Organizational charts will consist of project groups rather than stratified functional groups. (This trend is already visible in the aerospace and construction industries, as well as many professional and consulting firms.)

Adaptive, problem-solving, temporary systems of diverse specialists, linked together by coordinating and task-evaluating executive specialists in an organic flux—this is the organization form that will gradually replace bureaucracy as we know it. As no catchy phrase comes to mind, I call this an organic-adaptive structure. Organizational arrangements of this sort may not only reduce the intergroup conflicts mentioned earlier; it may also induce honest-to-goodness creative collaboration.

6. *Motivation.* The organic-adaptive structure should increase motivation and thereby effectiveness, because it enhances satisfactions intrinsic to the task. There is a harmony between the educated individual's need for tasks that are meaningful, satisfactory and creative and a flexible organizational structure.

There will also be, however, reduced commitment to work groups, for these groups will be, as I have already mentioned, transient structures. I would predict that in the organic-adaptive system, people will learn to develop quick and intense relationships on the job, and learn to bear the loss of more enduring work relationships. Because of the added ambiguity of roles, time will have to be spent on continual rediscovery of the appropriate organizational mix.

I think that the future I describe is not necessarily a "happy" one. Coping with rapid change, living in temporary work systems, developing meaningful relations and then breaking them—all augur social strains and psychological tensions. Teaching how to live with ambiguity, to identify with the adaptive process, to make a virtue out of contingency, and to be self-directing—these will be the tasks of education, the goals of maturity, and the achievement of the successful individual.

NO DELIGHTFUL MARRIAGES

In these new organizations of the future, participants will be called upon to use their minds more than at any other time in history. Fantasy, imagination and creativity will be legitimate in ways that today seem strange. Social structures will no longer be instruments of psychic repression but will increasingly promote play and freedom on behalf of curiosity and thought.

One final word: While I forecast the structure and value coordinates for organizations of the future and contend that they are inevitable, this should not bar any of us from giving the inevitable a little push. The French moralist may be right in saying that there are no delightful marriages, just good ones; it is possible that if managers and scientists continue to get their heads together in organizational revitalization, they *might* develop delightful organizations—just possibly.

I started with a quote from de Tocqueville and I think it would be fitting to end with one: "I am tempted to believe that what we call necessary institutions are often no more than institutions to which we have grown accustomed. In matters of social constitution, the field of possibilities is much more extensive than men living in their various societies are ready to imagine."

NOTES AND REFERENCES

1. Let me propose an hypothesis to explain this tendency. It rests on the assumption that man has a basic need for transcendental experiences, somewhat like the psychological rewards which William James claimed religion provided— "an assurance of safety and a temper of peace, and, in relation to others, a preponderance of loving affections." Can it be that as religion has become secularized, less transcendental, men search for substitutes such as close interpersonal relationships, psychoanalysis—even the release provided by drugs such as LSD?

15

Parkinson's Law

C. Northcote Parkinson

*One of the most famous articles on management, "Parkinson's Law," fo-
cuses on a specific aspect of organizing, namely staff size and demonstrates
how work expands to fill the time available for its completion. Many would
argue that the Law of Multiplication of Subordinates and the Law of
Multiplication of Work are validated constantly in oganizations throughout the world.—Eds.*

It is a commonplace observation that work expands so as to fill the time
available for its completion. Thus, an elderly lady of leisure can spend an
entire day in writing and despatching a postcard to her niece at Bognor
Regis. An hour will be spent in finding the postcard, another in hunting
for spectacles, half-an-hour in a search for the address, an hour and a
quarter in composition, and twenty minutes in deciding whether or not to
take an umbrella when going to the pillar-box in the next street. The
total effort which would occupy a busy man for three minutes all told may
in this fashion leave another person prostrate after a day of doubt, anxiety and toil.

Granted that work (and especially paper work) is thus elastic in its
demands of time, it is manifest that there need be little or no relationship
between the work to be done and the size of the staff to which it may be
assigned. Before the discovery of a new scientific law—herewith presented to the public for the first time, and to be called Parkinson's Law—
there has, however, been insufficient recognition of the implication of this
fact in the field of public administration. Politicians and taxpayers have
assumed (with occasional phases of doubt) that a rising total in the num-

SOURCE: From *Parkinson's Law* by C. Northcote Parkinson, published by Houghton
Mifflin Company. Copyright © 1957 by C. Northcote Parkinson. Reprinted by permission.

ber of civil servants must reflect a growing volume of work to be done. Cynics, in questioning this belief, have imagined that the multiplication of officials must have left some of them idle or all of them able to work for shorter hours. But this is a matter in which faith and doubt seem equally misplaced. The fact is that the number of the officials and the quantity of the work to be done are not related to each other at all. The rise in the total of those employed is governed by Parkinson's Law, and would be much the same whether the volume of the work were to increase, diminish or even disappear. The importance of Parkinson's Law lies in the fact that it is a law of growth based upon an analysis of the factors by which the growth is controlled.

The validity of this recently discovered law must rely mainly on statistical proofs, which will follow. Of more interest to the general reader is the explanation of the factors that underlie the general tendency to which this law gives definition. Omitting technicalities (which are numerous) we may distinguish, at the outset, two motive forces. They can be represented for the present purpose by two almost axiomatic statements, thus:

Factor I.   An official wants to multiply subordinates, not rivals; and
Factor II.   Officials make work for each other. We must now examine these motive forces in turn.

THE LAW OF MULTIPLICATION OF SUBORDINATES

To comprehend Factor I, we must picture a civil servant called A who finds himself overworked. Whether this overwork is real or imaginary is immaterial; but we should observe, in passing, that A's sensation (or illusion) might easily result from his own decreasing energy—a normal symptom of middle-age. For this real or imagined overwork there are, broadly speaking, three possible remedies:

1. He may resign.
2. He may ask to halve the work with a colleague called B.
3. He may demand the assistance of two subordinates to be called C and D.

There is probably no instance in civil service history of A choosing any but the third alternative. By resignation he would lose his pension rights. By having B appointed, on his own level in the hierarchy, he would merely bring in a rival for promotion to W's vacancy when W (at long last) retires. So A would rather have C and D, junior men, below him. They will add to his consequence; and, by dividing the work into two categories, as between C and D, he will have the merit of being the only man who comprehends them both.

It is essential to realize, at this point, that C and D are, as it were, inseparable. To appoint C alone would have been impossible. Why? Because C, if by himself, would divide the work with A and so assume almost the equal status which has been refused in the first instance to B: a status the more emphasized if C is A's only possible successor. Subordinates must thus number two or more, each being kept in order by fear of the other's promotion. When C complains in turn of being overworked (as he certainly will), A will, with the concurrence of C, advise the appointment of two assistants to help C. But he can then avert internal friction only by advising the appointment of two more assistants to help D, whose position is much the same. With this recruitment of E, F, G and H, the promotion of A is now practically certain.

THE LAW OF MULTIPLICATION OF WORK

Seven officials are now doing what one did before. This is where Factor II comes into operation. For these seven make so much work for each other that all are fully occupied and A is actually working harder than ever. An incoming document may well come before each of them in turn. Official E decides that it falls within the province of F, who places a draft reply before C, who amends it drastically before consulting D, who asks G to deal with it. But G goes on leave at this point, handing the file over to H, who drafts a minute, which is signed by D and returned to C, who revises his draft accordingly and lays the new version before A.

What does A do? He would have every excuse for signing the thing unread, for he has many other matters on his mind. Knowing now that he is to succeed W next year, he has to decide whether C or D should succeed to his own office. He had to agree to G going on leave, although not yet strictly entitled to it. He is worried whether H should not have gone instead, for reasons of health. He has looked pale recently—partly but not solely because of his domestic troubles. Then there is the business of F's special increment of salary for the period of the conference, and E's application for transfer to the Ministry of Pensions. A has heard that D is in love with a married typist and that G and F are no longer on speaking terms—no one seems to know why. So A might be tempted to sign C's draft and have done with it.

But A is a conscientious man. Beset as he is with problems created by his colleagues for themselves and for him—created by the mere fact of these officials' existence—he is not the man to shirk his duty. He reads through the draft with care, deletes the fussy paragraphs added by C and H and restores the thing back to the form preferred in the first instance by the able (if quarrelsome) F. He corrects the English—none of these young men can write grammatically—and finally produces the same reply he would have written if officials C to H had never been born. Far more people have taken far longer to produce the same result. No one has been idle. All have done their best. And it is late in the evening before A finally quits his office and begins the return journey to Ealing. The last of the office lights are being turned off in the gathering dusk which marks the end of another day's administrative toil. Among the last to leave, A reflects, with bowed shoulders and a wry smile, that late hours, like grey hairs, are among the penalties of success.

THE SCIENTIFIC PROOFS

From this description of the factors at work the student of political science will recognize that administrators are more or less bound to multiply. Nothing has yet been said, however, about the period of time likely to elapse between the date of A's appointment and the date from which we can calculate the pensionable service of H. Vast masses of statistical evidence have been collected and it is from a study of this data that Parkinson's Law has been deduced. Space will not allow of detailed analysis, but research began in the British Navy Estimates. These were chosen because the Admiralty's responsibilities are more easily measurable than those of (say) the Board of Trade.

The accompanying table is derived from Admiralty statistics for 1914 and 1928. The criticism voiced at the time centered on the comparison between the sharp fall in numbers of those available for fighting and the sharp rise in those available only for administration, the creation, it was said, of "a magnificent Navy on land." But that comparison is not to the present purpose. What we have to note is that the 2,000 Admiralty officials of 1914 had become the 3,569 of 1928; and that this growth was unrelated to any possible increase in their work. The Navy during that period had diminished, in point of fact, by a third in men and two-thirds in ships. Nor, from 1922 onwards, was its strength even expected to increase, for its total of ships (unlike its total of officials) was limited by the Washington Naval Agreement of that year. Yet in these circumstances we had a 78.45 percent increase in Admiralty officials over a period of fourteen years, an average increase of 5.6 percent a year on the earlier total. In fact, as we shall see, the rate of increase was not as regular as that. All we have to consider, at this stage, is the percentage rise over a given period.

	1914	1928	Percentage Increase or Decrease
Capital ships in commission	62	20	−67.74
Officers and men in Royal Navy	146,000	100,000	−31.50
Dockyard workers	57,000	62,439	+ 9.54
Dockyard officials and clerks	3,249	4,558	+40.28
Admiralty officials	2,000	3,569	+78.45

Can this rise in the total number of civil servants be accounted for except on the assumption that such a total must always rise by a law governing its growth? It might be urged, at this point, that the period under discussion was one of rapid development in naval technique. The use of the flying machine was no longer confined to the eccentric. Submarines were tolerated if not approved. Engineer officers were beginning to be regarded as almost human. In so revolutionary an age we might expect the storekeepers would have more elaborate inventories to compile. We might not wonder to see more draughtsmen on the payroll, more designers, more technicians and scientists. But these, the dockyard officials, increased only by 40 percent in number, while the men of Whitehall increased by nearly 80 percent. For every new foreman or electrical engineer at Portsmouth there had to be two or more clerks at Charing Cross. From this we might be tempted to conclude, provisionally, that the rate of increase in administrative staff is likely to be double that of the technical staff at a time when the actually useful strength (in this case, of seamen) is being reduced by 31.5 percent. It has been proved, however, statistically, that this last percentage is irrelevant. *The Officials would have multiplied at the same rate had there been no actual seamen at all.*

It would be interesting to follow the further progress by which the 8,118 Admiralty staff of 1935 came to number 33,788 by 1954. But the staff of the Colonial Office affords a better field of study during a period of Imperial decline. The relevant statistics are set down below. Before showing what the rate of increase is, we must observe that the extent of this department's responsibilities was far from constant during these twenty years. The colonial territories were not much altered in area or population between 1935 and 1939. They were considerably diminished by 1943, certain areas being in enemy hands. They were increased again in 1947, but have since then shrunk steadily from year to year as successive colonies achieve self-government.

Colonial Office Officials

1935	1939	1943	1947	1954
372	450	817	1,135	1,661

It would be rational, prior to the discovery of Parkinson's Law, to suppose that these changes in the scope of Empire would be reflected in the size of its central administration. But a glance at the figures shows that the staff totals represent automatic stages in an inevitable increase. And this increase, while related to that observed in other departments, has nothing to do with the size—or even the existence—of the Empire. What are the percentages of increase? We must ignore, for this purpose, the rapid increase in staff which accompanied the diminution of responsibility during World War II. We should note rather the peacetime rates of increase over 5.24 percent between 1935 and 1939, and 6.55 percent between 1947 and 1954. This gives an average increase of 5.89 percent each year, a percentage markedly similar to that already found in the Admiralty staff increase between 1914 and 1928.

Further and detailed statistical analysis of departmental staffs would be inappropriate in such an article as this. It is hoped, however, to reach a tentative conclusion regarding the time likely to elapse between a given official's first appointment and the later appointment of his two or more assistants. Dealing with the problem of pure staff accumulation, all the researches so far completed point to average increase of about 5¾ percent per year. This fact established, it now becomes possible to state Parkinson's Law in mathematical form, thus:

In any public administrative department not actually at war the staff increase may be expected to follow this formula:

$$x = \frac{2k^m + p}{n}$$

where k is the number of staff seeking promotion through the appointment of subordinates; p represents the difference between the ages of appointment and retirement; m is the number of man-hours devoted to answering minutes within the department; and n is the number of effective units being administered. Then x will be the number of new staff required each year.

Mathematicians will, of course, realize that to find the percentage increase they must multiply x by 100 and divide by the total of the previous year, thus:

$$\frac{100(2k^m + p)}{yn}\%$$

where y represents the total original staff. And this figure will invariably prove to be between 5.17 percent and 6.56 percent, irrespective of any variation in the amount of work (if any) to be done.

The discovery of this formula and of the general principles upon which it is based has, of course, no emotive value. No attempt has been made to inquire whether departments ought to grow in size. Those who hold that this growth is essential to gain full employment are fully entitled to their opinion. Those who doubt the stability of an economy based upon reading each other's minutes are equally entitled to theirs. Parkinson's Law is a purely scientific discovery, inapplicable except in theory to the politics of the day. It is not the business of the botanist to eradicate the weeds. Enough for him if he can tell us just how fast they grow.

16

The Parable of the Spindle

Elias H. Porter

This "parable" cleverly highlights how individuals with different back-grounds and operating under different assumptions can, by traveling dif-ferent routes, arrive at the same conclusion regarding a problem of orga-nizing work flow. The article recommends that organizing problems be analyzed by use of a systems framework.—Eds.

More and more we hear the word "systems" used in discussions of busi-ness problems. Research people are studying systems, experts are looking at organizations as systems, and a growing number of departments and companies have the word "systems" in their names.

Just what *is* a system in the business sense? What does it do? What good is it to management? To answer these questions I shall first use a parable from the restaurant industry. What, you may ask, can executives in manufacturing, retailing, or service systems learn from restaurant systems? I readily admit that if you envisage only menus, customers, waitresses, and cooks in a restaurant, you will find no transferable knowledge. But if you see (as I hope you will) inputs, rate variations, displays, feedback loops, memory devices, queuing, omissions, errors, chunking, approximating, channeling, and filtering in a restaurant sys-tem—then you should indeed find some practical value in my parable.

The implications of the parable will be discussed specifically in the second part of the article, after we have reduced it to a paradigm.

SOURCE: Elias Porter, "The Parable of the Spindle," *Harvard Business Review* (May-June 1962), pp. 58–66.

THE PARABLE

Once upon a time the president of a large chain of short-order restaurants attended a lecture on "Human Relations in Business and Industry." He attended the lecture in the hope he would learn something useful. His years of experience had led him to believe that if human relations problems ever plagued any business, then they certainly plagued the restaurant business.

The speaker discussed the many pressures which create human relations problems. He spoke of psychological pressures, sociological pressures, conflicts in values, conflicts in power structure, and so on. The president did not understand all that was said, but he did go home with one idea. If there were so many different sources of pressure, maybe it was expecting too much of his managers to think they would see them all, let alone cope with them all. The thought occurred to him that maybe he should bring in a team of consultants from several different academic disciplines and have each contribute his part to the solution of the human relations problems.

And so it came to pass that the president of the restaurant chain and his top-management staff met one morning with a sociologist, a psychologist, and an anthropologist. The president outlined the problem to the men of science and spoke of his hope that they might come up with an interdisciplinary answer to the human relations problems. The personnel manager presented exit-interview findings which he interpreted as indicating that most people quit their restaurant jobs because of too much sense of pressure caused by the inefficiencies and ill tempers of coworkers.

This was the mission which the scientists were assigned: find out why the waitresses break down in tears; find out why the cooks walk off the job; find out why the managers get so upset that they summarily fire employees on the spot. Find out the cause of the problems, and find out what to do about them.

Later, in one of the plush conference rooms, the scientists sat down to plan their attack. It soon became clear that they might just as well be three blind men, and the problem might just as well be the proverbial elephant. Their training and experience had taught them to look at events in different ways. And so they decided that inasmuch as they couldn't speak each others' languages, they might as well pursue their tasks separately. Each went to a different city and began his observations in his own way.

The Sociologist

First to return was the sociologist. In his report to top management he said:

"I think I have discovered something that is pretty fundamental. In one sense it is so obvious that it has probably been completely overlooked before. It is during the *rush hours* that your human relations problems arise. That is when the waitresses break out in tears. That is when the cooks grow temperamental and walk off the job. That is when your managers lose their tempers and dismiss employees summarily."

After elaborating on this theme and showing several charts with sloping lines and bar graphs to back up his assertions, he came to his diagnosis of the situation. "In brief, gentlemen," he stated, "you have a sociological problem on your hands." He walked to the blackboard and began to write. As he wrote, he spoke:

"You have a stress pattern during the rush hours. There is stress between the customer and the waitress. . . .

"There is stress between the waitress and the cook. . . .

"And up here is the manager. There is stress between the waitress and the manager. . . .

"And between the manager and the cook. . . .

"And the manager is buffeted by complaints from the customer.

"We can see one thing which, sociologically speaking, doesn't seem right. The manager has the highest status in the restaurant. The cook has the next highest status. The waitresses, however, are always 'local hire' and have the lowest status. Of course, they have higher status than bus boys and dish washers but certainly lower status than the cook, and yet they give orders to the cook.

"It doesn't seem right for a lower status person to give orders to a higher status person. We've got to find a way to break up the face-to-face relationship between the waitresses and the cook. We've got to fix it so that they don't have to talk with one another. Now my idea is to put a 'spindle' on the order counter. The 'spindle,' as I choose to call it, is a wheel on a shaft. The wheel has clips on it so the girls can simply put their orders on the wheel rather than calling out orders to the cook."

When the sociologist left the meeting, the president and his staff talked of what had been said. It made some sense. However, they decided to wait to hear from the other scientists before taking any action.

The Psychologist

Next to return from his studies was the psychologist. He reported to top management:

"I think I have discovered something that is pretty fundamental. In one sense it is so obvious that it has probably been completely overlooked before. It is during the *rush hours* that your human relations problems arise. That is when the waitresses break out in tears. That is when the cooks grow temperamental and walk off the job. That is when your managers lose their tempers and dismiss employees summarily."

Then the psychologist sketched on the blackboard the identical pattern of stress between customer, waitress, cook, and management. But his interpretation was somewhat different:

"Psychologically speaking," he said, "we can see that the manager is the father figure, the cook is the son, and the waitress is the daughter. Now we know that in our culture you can't have daughters giving orders to the sons. It louses up their ego structure.

"What we've got to do is to find a way to break up the face-to-face relationship between them. Now one idea I've thought up is to put what I call a 'spindle' on the order counter. It's kind of a wheel on a shaft with little clips on it so that the waitresses can put their orders on it rather than calling out orders to the cook."

What the psychologist said made sense, too, in a way. Some of the staff favored the status-conflict interpretation while others thought the sex-conflict interpretation to be the right one; the president kept his own counsel.

The Anthropologist

The next scientist to report was the anthropologist. He reported to top management:

"I think I have discovered something that is pretty fundamental. In one sense it is so obvious that it has probably been completely overlooked before. It is during the *rush hours* that your human relations problems arise. That is when the waitresses break out in tears. That is when the cooks grow temperamental and walk off the job. That is when your managers lose their tempers and dismiss employees summarily."

After elaborating for a few moments he came to his diagnosis of the situation. "In brief, gentlemen," he stated, "you have an anthropological problem on your hands." He walked to the blackboard and began to sketch. Once again there appeared the stress pattern between customer, waitress, cook, and management:

"We anthropologists know that man behaves according to his value systems. Now, the manager holds as a central value the continued growth and development of the restaurant organization. The cooks tend to share this central value system, for as the organization prospers, so do they. But the waitresses are a different story. The only reason most of them are working is to help supplement the family income. They couldn't care less whether the organization thrives or not as long as it's a decent place to work. Now, you can't have a noncentral value system giving orders to a central value system.

"What we've got to do is to find some way of breaking up the face-to-face contact between the waitresses and the cook. One way that has occurred to me is to place on the order counter an adaptation of the old-fashioned spindle.

By having a wheel at the top of the shaft and putting clips every few inches apart, the waitresses can put their orders on the wheel and not have to call out orders to the cook. Here is a model of what I mean."

Triumph of the Spindle

When the anthropologist had left, there was much discussion of which scientist was right. The president finally spoke. "Gentlemen, it's clear that these men don't agree on the reason for conflict, but all have come up with the same basic idea about the spindle. Let's take a chance and try it out."

And it came to pass that the spindle was introduced throughout the chain of restaurants. It did more to reduce the human relations problems in the restaurant industry than any other innovation of which the restaurant people knew. Soon it was copied. Like wildfire the spindle spread from coast to coast and from border to border.

So much for the parable. Let us now proceed to the paradigm.

THE PARADIGM

Each of the three scientists had seen a different problem: status conflict, sex rivalry, and value conflict. Maybe it was none of these but simply a problem in the division of work between men and machines and how they are related one to the other: a problem of system design. Let us explore this possibility by observing the functions which the spindle fulfills.

Functions Served

First of all, the spindle acts as a memory device for the cook. He no longer needs to remember all the orders given him by the waitresses. This makes his job easier and less "stressful"—especially during the rush hours.

Secondly, the spindle acts as a buffering device. It buffers the cook against a sudden, overwhelming load of orders. Ten waitresses can place their orders on the spindle almost simultaneously. The cook takes them off the spindle according to his work rate—not the input rate. This makes his job easier, more within reach of human capacity—especially during the rush hours.

Thirdly, the spindle acts as a queuing device—in two ways. It holds the orders in a proper waiting line until the cook can get to them. When dependent on his memory only, the cook can get orders mixed up. It also does all the "standing in line" for the waitresses. They need never again stand in line to pass an order to the cook. This makes their jobs easier—especially during the rush hours.

Fourthly, the spindle permits a visual display of all the orders waiting to be filled. The cook can often see that several of the orders call for the same item. He can prepare four hamburgers in about the same time as he can prepare one. By reason of having "random access" to all the orders in the system at that point he is able to organize his work around several orders simultaneously with greater efficiency. This makes his job easier—especially during the rush hours.

To appreciate the fifth function which the spindle serves, we must go back to the procedures used before the advent of the spindle. In looking at these procedures we are going to examine them in "general system behavior theory" terms:

On the menu certain "information" exists in the physical form of printed words. The customer "transforms" this information into the physical form of spoken words. The information is once again transformed by the waitress. Now it exists in the physical form of written notes made by the waitress. Once again the information is transformed as the waitress converts her notes into spoken words directed to the cook. The cook transforms the information from the physical form of spoken words to the physical form of prepared food. We have an "information flow" which looks like this:

$$\text{Menu} \xrightarrow{\text{Printed Words}} \text{Customer} \xrightarrow{\text{Spoken Words}}$$

$$\text{Waitress} \xrightarrow{\text{Written Notes}}$$

$$\xrightarrow{\text{Spoken Words}} \text{Cook} \xrightarrow{\text{Prepared Food}}$$

Now every so often it happened that an error was made, and the customer didn't get what he ordered. Of course you and I would have been the first to admit that we had made an error, but not all cooks and waitresses have this admirable character trait. This is rather understandable since the waitress was trying to do things correctly and rapidly (she wanted all the tips she could get!), and when she was suddenly confronted with the fact that an error had been made, her first reaction was that the cook had goofed. The cook, on the other hand, was trying to do his best. He knew in his own heart that he had prepared just what she had told him to prepare. "It's the waitress' fault," was his thought.

So what did the cook and waitress learn? Did they learn to prevent a recurrence of the error? Indeed not! The waitress learned that the cook was a stupid so-and-so, and the cook learned that the waitress was a scatterbrained so-and-so. This kind of emotionalized learning situation and strainer-of-interpersonal-relations any organization can do without—especially during the rush hours.

Changes Effected

Consider now how the spindle changes all this. The waitress prepares the order slip and the cook works directly from it. If the waitress records the order incorrectly, it is obvious to her upon examining the order slip. Similarly, if the cook misreads the slip, an examination of the order slip makes it obvious to him. The fifth function of the spindle, then, is to provide "feedback" to both waitress and cook regarding errors. The spindle markedly alters the emotional relationship and redirects the learning process.

As errors are examined under conditions of feedback, new responses are engendered. The cook and waitress may find the present order slip to be hard to read, and they may request the manager to try out a different style of order slip. Now they are working together to solve the system's problems rather than working against each other and disregarding the system's problems. Maybe they find that abbreviations cause some random errors. For example, it might be that HB (Hamburger) and BB (Beefburger) get mixed up just a little too often, so the cook and waitress get together with the manager and change the name of Beefburger to Caravan Special on the menu because the new symbol (CS) will transmit itself through the system with much less ambiguity—especially during the rush hours.

HANDLING OVERLOAD

Had I been asked a few years ago to advise on human relations problems in the restaurant industry as a professional psychologist, my approach would have been limited to what I now call a "component" approach. My thinking would have been directed at the components in the system—in this case, the people involved. I would have explored such answers as incentive schemes, human relations training, selection procedures, and possibly some time-and-motion studies. My efforts would have been limited to attempts to *change the components to fit in with the system as designed no matter how poor the design might be.*

But now I would first concern myself with the "information" which must be "processed" by the system. My concern would be centered on the functions which would have to be performed by the system and how they might best be performed. I would concern myself especially with how the system is designed to handle conditions of information overload.

It is significant that in our parable the three scientists each discovered that the human relations problems arose mostly during the rush hours, in the period of "information overload." How a system responds to conditions of overload depends on how the system is designed. Let us look at how various design features permit the handling of conditions of overload in a number of different kinds of systems.

Increase in Channels

One of the most common adjustments that a system makes to an excess input load is to increase the number of "channels" for handling the information. Restaurants put more waitresses and cooks on the job to handle rush-hour loads. The Post Office hires extra help before Christmas. The telephone system has recently introduced automatic-switching equipment to handle heavy communication loads; when the load gets to a certain point, additional lines are automatically "cut in" to handle the additional calls. Even our fire departments increase "channels." If there is not enough equipment at the scene, more is called in. Department stores put on additional clerks to handle holiday crowds. Military commanders augment crews in anticipation of overload conditions. Extra communication lines may be called up. More troops are deployed.

Almost everywhere we look we see that systems are very commonly designed to increase or decrease the number of channels according to the load.

Waiting Lines

But there comes a time when just increasing the number of channels is not enough. Then we see another common adjustment process, that of "queuing" or forming a waiting line. There are few readers who have not had the experience of waiting in a restaurant to be seated. Other examples are common. Raw materials are stored awaiting production processes. Orders wait in queue until filled. Manufactured goods are stored on docks awaiting shipment. The stock market ticker tape falls behind.

We have already seen how the spindle makes it unnecessary for the waitresses to queue to give orders. And we are all familiar with the modern custom in most restaurants of having a hostess take our names and the size of our party. What happens when the hostess takes our names down on paper? For one, we do not have to go through the exasperating business of jostling to hold our position in line. Also, the "holding of proper position" is done by machine; that is, it is done by the list rather than by our elbows.

Use of Filtering

The hostess' list also illustrates the way in which a system can make still a third type of adjustment, that of "filtering." Because she jots down the size of the group, she can now selectively pull groups out of the queue according to the size of the table last vacated. Some readers will recall that many restaurants used to have all tables or booths of the same size and that everyone was seated in turn according to how long he had waited. It used to be infuriating for a party of four to see a single person being seated at a table for four while they continued to wait. The modern notion of accommodations of varying sizes, combined with the means for filtering, makes the use of floor space much more efficient and the waiting less lengthy. We can see filtering in other systems as well:

- The Post Office handles registered mail before it handles other mail, delivers special delivery letters before other letters.

- In the case of our other most important communication system, the telephone system, there is no way for dial equipment to recognize an important call from an unimportant call; it cannot tell whether a doctor is dialing or the baby is playing. However, where long distance calls must go through operators, there is a chance for filtering. For instance, in trying to place a call to a disaster area the operator may accept only those calls which are of an emergency nature.
- Military systems assign priorities to messages so as to assure differential handling.
- Orders may be sent to production facilities in bunches that make up a full workday rather than in a first-in-first-out pattern. Special orders may be marked for priority attention.

Variations of Omission

A system can be so designed as to permit "omissions," a simple rejection or nonacceptance of an input. The long distance operator may refuse to accept a call as a means of preventing the lines from becoming overloaded. The dial system gives a busy signal and rejects the call. A manufacturing organization may reject an order it cannot fill within a certain time. A company may discontinue manufacture of one line temporarily in order to catch up on a more profitable line that is back ordered.

As another example of how the design determines what adjustments the system can make, consider the way the short-order restaurant system design utilizes the omission process:

> If waiting lines get too long, customers will turn away. That is not good for business, so restaurants often practice another kind of omission. On the menu you may find the words, "No substitutions." Instead of rejecting customers, the restaurants restrict the range of inputs they will accept in the way of orders. Thus time is saved in preparing the food, which in turn cuts down the waiting time in the queue.

The goal of most restaurants is to process as many customers per unit time as is possible. With a fixed profit margin per meal served, the more meals served, the more profit. But when people are in the queue, they are not spending money. One solution to this is the installation of a bar. This permits the customers to spend while waiting. It is a solution enjoyed by many customers as well as by management.

Chunking & Approximating

Another big timesaver in the restaurant system is the use of a fifth adjustment process, that of "chunking." Big chunks of information can be passed by predetermined arrangements. You may find a menu so printed that it asks you to order by number. The order may be presented to the cook as "4D" (No. 4 Dinner), for example. The cook already knows what makes up the dinner and does not need to be told each item with each order. Preplanning permits chunking, and chunking frees communication channels.

Somewhat akin to the chunking process is a sixth adjustment process, "approximating." To illustrate:

- A business forecaster may not be able to make an exact count of future sales, but he may predict confidently that the sales will be small, moderate, or large.
- An overburdened Post Office crew may do an initial sorting of mail as "local" or "out of town."
- An airborne radar crew may report a "large formation" headed toward the coast.
- An intelligence agency may get a report of "heightened" air activity in a given area.
- An investment house may predict "increased" activity in a certain line of stocks.
- Stock market reports state that industrials are "up" and utilities are "down."

Approximating thus means making a gross discrimination of the input rather than making a fine discrimination.

Trading Errors

A rather unusual adjustment process that a system can adopt to cope with overload is to accept an increase in the number of errors made. It is almost as if systems said to themselves, "It's better to make mistakes than not to deal with the input." For example, the sorting of mail is not checked during rush periods. Mail which is missent must be returned, but in a rush that risk is worth the cost; more mail gets sent where it is supposed to go even though there are more errors. Thus, quality control is given up for the sake of speed. On the other hand, some systems are so designed as to be insensitive to errors. The telephone system will permit you to dial as many wrong numbers as you are capable of dialing.

It is interesting to see in the restaurant system design a deliberate making of errors of one sort in order to prevent the making of errors of another sort during rush hours:

Picture yourself and a couple of friends dropping into a restaurant during the middle of an afternoon. You are the only customers there. The waitress takes your order. You ask for a hamburger with "everything on it." The next person asks for a hamburger but wants only lettuce and a slice of tomato on it. The third person asks for a hamburger but specifies relish and mayonnaise. The work load is low. There is time to individualize orders.

But during rush hours it would be too easy to make errors. Then the cook prepares only the meat and bun. The waitress goes to a table where there are bowls with lettuce leaves and tomato slices and little paper cups of relish and mayonnaise. On each plate she places a lettuce leaf, a tomato slice, a cup of relish, and a cup of mayonnaise. In most instances she will have brought something that the customer did not order, and in this sense she would have made an "error"; but she would have avoided the error of not bringing the customer something he *did* want.

Other examples of the same type are common. For instance, a sales department sends out brochures to everyone who inquires about a product so as not to miss someone who is really interested. Again, the Strategic Air Command, as a central policy, uses this deliberate making of one type of "error" to avoid a possible error of more severe consequences. The commander may order the force launched under "positive control." It is better to have launched in error than to be caught on the ground and destroyed.

CONCLUSION

And so we see that there is a new frame of reference, a new point of view coming into use in approaching the problems of organizations. This new frame of reference looks at organizations as systems which (1) process information, transforming the information from one form into another, and (2) are or are not designed to cope with the conditions of overload that may be imposed on them. This new frame of reference is expressed as an interest in how the structure or design of an organization dynamically influences the operating characteristics and the capacities of the system to handle various conditions of information overload.

At the University of Michigan there are some 50 scientists whose primary interests lie in looking for similarities and differences in system behavior at all levels. They examine single cells, whole organs, individuals, groups, and societies for the manners in which these systems cope with their environments in common and in unique ways. They search the work of other scientists for clues to system behavior at one level that is followed at higher or lower orders of organization. As for the application of this "system frame of reference," one finds such organizations as System Development Corporation, the RAND Corporation, and the MITRE Corporation using it in approaching the complex problems of advanced military systems. Here is just a sampling of specific developments that bear close watching:

- Because it is possible to view organizations as systems which process data in a continuous sequence of "information transformations" and which may make numerous types of adjustments at the points of transformation, a wholly new concept of training has arisen. In the past, training in business and industry as well as in the military was largely limited to training a man or men to do a given task in a certain way. Now training can be provided that teaches a man or men to adopt adjustment processes suited to the design of the system and the condition of overload. In other words, training for flexibility rather than rigidity is now possible. It should not be long before internal competition is replaced by internal cooperation as the main means of enhancing production.

- Because it is possible to view a business or industry as an information processing system, it is possible to simulate the information flow on digital computers and, by controlling the adjustment processes at each point where the data are transformed, to learn what effects and costs would be involved in change. The manager will then be able to test his policies realistically on the computer before committing himself in action. A computer program called SIMPAC (Simulation Package) has already been developed at System Development Corporation for this purpose.

- A digital computer program capable of "learning" has been developed. By analyzing how data can be sensed, compared with other data, and stored in the computer's "memory," scientists have been able to "teach" a prototype computer program to recognize letters of the alphabet, cartoon characters, and spoken words. One can look forward to the day when, opening a bank account, he will be asked to sign his name in a variety of situations—e.g., standing, sitting, bending over, and maybe even after a couple of martinis. The computer will learn to recognize his signature from these samples, and at the clearinghouse, after that, his account will be automatically debited and the payee's account automatically credited.

Ludwig von Bertalanffy, the father of general system theory, predicted that general system theory would unify the sciences thus making it possible for a scientist trained in one area to talk in common terms with another scientist trained in another area.[1] It also seems certain that business and industry will soon profit from the application of the theory of how systems behave.

NOTES AND REFERENCES

1. "General System Theory," *General Systems* (Ann Arbor: Society for General Systems Research, 1956), Volume 1, pp. 1–10.

PART FOUR

Controlling Processes in Management

For many students of management, the control processes are both the least understood and least appreciated managerial functions. Simply stated, control processes are those activities involved in setting standards, measuring performance against these standards, and correcting or adjusting for deviations from the standards. An important implication of this definition is that *plans* have been made and work has been *organized*—very important management activities which the two previous sections of this book addressed. Control, then, is what is necessary to insure that plans and organization are executed in a manner consistent with achieving the desired results.

That proper control is crucial to the success of any enterprise has long been recognized. One of the first large-scale examples of the use of control processes dates back to the fifteenth century. At that time Venice was a flourishing power, and to insure its naval supremacy, the Arsenal of Venice was developed into the largest industrial plant in the world. It covered a sixty-acre site and employed as many as two thousand workers. The Arsenal had three primary functions: ship and equipment building, storage of manufactured equipment until needed, and assembly and refitting of reserve ships. To insure that Arsenal objectives were being met, a variety of control processes were introduced. Accounting controls were developed to monitor the flow of materials and products and, most importantly, of men and their time. Inventory controls were established to keep records of what shipments left the Arsenal, what they contained, and to whom they were sent. Cost controls resulted in more efficient procedures for materials handling, thus eliminating waste and inefficiency. Finally, a merit-rating plan was used to evaluate each master employee according to how well he was meeting his duties and contributing to the overall objective of the Arsenal.

In terms of their objectives, modern day control processes do not differ from those in use at the Arsenal of Venice almost five hundred years ago. The purpose of control was then and is now to insure that the movement toward planned objectives is taking place in an effective and efficient manner. The functions designed to accomplish these objectives can be broken down into several types on the basis of the focus of their control activity. *Preliminary control* focuses on the problem of preventing deviations in the quality and quantity of resources used by the organization; *concurrent control* monitors ongoing operations to ensure that specific objectives are pursued; *feedback control* focuses on end-results and derives its name from the fact that historical results guide future actions.

Proper control processes are essential for organizational effectiveness and efficiency. The articles in this section examine this topic from a number of different and important perspectives.

17

The Theory of Authority

Chester I. Barnard

An extremely critical part of controlling is the use of authority. This article is a truly classical statement on the role and scope of authority in organizations. In it, Barnard considers the source of authority, the subjective and objective nature of authority and the conditions under which an employee will accept a communication as authoritative. Note particularly his concept of a "zone of indifference," as important an idea as when it was postulated half a century ago.—Eds.

In this article we consider a subject which in one aspect relates to the "willingness of individuals to contribute to organizations, . . ." and in a second aspect is the most general phase of the element "communication."

THE SOURCE OF AUTHORITY

If it is true that all complex organizations consist of aggregations of unit organizations and have grown only from unit organizations, we may reasonably postulate that, whatever the nature of authority, it is inherent in the simple organization unit; and that a correct theory of authority must be consistent with what is essentially true of these unit organizations. We shall, therefore, regard the observations which we can make of the actual conditions as at first a source for discovering what is essential in elementary and simple organizations.

SOURCE: Reprinted by permission of the publishers from *The Functions of the Executive* by Chester I. Barnard. Cambridge, Massachusetts: Harvard University Press. Copyright © 1938 by the President and Fellows of Harvard College; © 1966 by Grace F. Noers Barnard.

I

Now a most significant fact of general observation relative to authority is the extent to which it is ineffective in specific instances. It is so ineffective that the violation of authority is accepted as a matter of course and its implications are not considered. It is true that we are sometimes appalled at the extent of major criminal activities; but we pass over very lightly the universal violations, particularly of sumptuary laws, which are as "valid" as any others. Even clauses of constitutions and statutes carrying them "into effect," such as the Eighteenth Amendment, are violated in wholesale degrees.

Violation of law is not, however, peculiar to our own country. I observed recently in a totalitarian state under a dictator, where personal liberty is supposed to be at a minimum and arbitrary authority at a maximum, many violations of positive law or edict, some of them open and on a wide scale; and I was reliably informed of others.

Nor is this condition peculiar to the authority of the state. It is likewise true of the authority of churches. The Ten Commandments and the prescriptions and prohibitions of religious authority are repeatedly violated by those who profess to acknowledge their formal authority.

These observations do not mean that all citizens are lawless and defy authority; nor that all Christians are godless or their conduct unaffected by the tenets of their faith. It is obvious that to a large extent citizens are governed; and that the conduct of Christians is substantially qualified by the prescriptions of their churches. What is implied is merely that which specific laws will be obeyed or disobeyed by the individual citizen are decided by him under the specific conditions pertinent. This is what we mean when we refer to individual responsibility. It implies that which prescriptions of the church will be disobeyed by the individual are determined by him at a given time and place. This is what we mean by moral responsibility.

It may be thought that ineffectiveness of authority in specific cases is chiefly exemplified in matters of state and church, but not in those of smaller organizations which are more closely knit or more concretely managed. But this is not true. It is surprising how much that in theory is authoritative, in the best of organizations in practice lacks authority— or, in plain language, how generally orders are disobeyed. For many years the writer has been interested to observe this fact, not only in organizations with which he was directly connected, but in many others. In all of them, armies, navies, universities, penal institutions, hospitals, relief organizations, corporations, the same conditions prevail—dead laws, regulations, rules, which no one dares bury but which are not obeyed; obvious disobedience carefully disregarded; vital practices and major institutions for which there is no authority, like the Democratic and Republican parties, not known to the Constitution.

II

We may leave the secondary stages of this analysis for later consideration. What we derive from it is an approximate definition of authority for our purpose: Authority is the character of a communication (order) in a formal organization by virtue of which it is accepted by a contributor to or "member" of the organization as governing the action he contributes; that is, as governing or determining what he does or is not to do so far as the organization is concerned. According to this definition, authority involves two aspects: first, the subjective, the personal, the *accepting* of a communication as authoritative, the aspects of which I shall present in this section; and, second, the objective aspect—the character in the communication by virtue of which it is accepted—which I present in the second section, "The System of Coordination."

If a directive communication is accepted by one to whom it is addressed, its authority for him is confirmed or established. It is admitted as the basis of action. Disobedience of such a communication is a denial of its authority for him. Therefore, under this definition the decision as to whether an order has authority or not lies with the persons to whom it is addressed, and does not reside in "persons of authority" or those who issue these orders.

This is so contrary to the view widely held by informed persons of many ranks and professions, and so contradictory to legalistic conceptions, and will seem to many so opposed to common experience, that it will be well at the outset to quote two opinions of persons in a position to merit respectful attention. It is not the intention to "argue from authorities"; but before attacking the subject it is desirable at least to recognize that prevalent notions are not universally held. Says Roberto Michels in the monograph "Authority" in the *Encyclopaedia of the Social Sciences*,[1] "Whether authority is of personal or institutional origin it is created and maintained by public opinion, which in its turn is conditioned by sentiment, affection, reverence or fatalism. Even when authority rests on mere physical coercion it is *accepted*[2] by those ruled, although the acceptance may be due to a fear of force."

Again, Major General James G. Harbord, of long and distinguished military experience, and since his retirement from the Army a notable business executive, says on page 259 of his *The American Army in France*:[3]

> A democratic President had forgotten that the greatest of all democracies is an Army. Discipline and morale influence the inarticulate vote that is instantly taken by masses of men when the order comes to move forward— a variant of the crowd psychology that inclines it to follow a leader, but the Army does not move forward until the motion has "carried." "Unanimous consent" only follows cooperation between the *individual* men in the ranks.

These opinions are to the effect that even though physical force is involved, and even under the extreme condition of battle, when the regime is nearly absolute, authority nevertheless rests upon the acceptance or consent of individuals. Evidently such conceptions, if justified, deeply affect an appropriate understanding of organization and especially of the character of the executive functions.

Our definition of authority, like General Harbord's democracy in an army, no doubt will appear to many whose eyes are fixed only on enduring organizations to be a platform of chaos. And so it is—exactly so in the preponderance of attempted organizations. They fail because they can maintain no authority, that is, they cannot secure sufficient contributions of personal efforts to be effective or cannot induce them on terms that are efficient. In the last analysis the authority fails because the individuals in sufficient numbers regard the burden involved in accepting necessary orders as changing the balance of advantage against their interest, and they withdraw or withhold the indispensable contributions.

III

We must not rest our definition, however, on general opinion. The necessity of the assent of the individual to establish authority *for him* is inescapable. A person can and will accept a communication as authoritative only when four conditions simultaneously obtain: *(a)* he can and does understand the communication; *(b) at the time of his decision* he believes that it is not inconsistent with the purpose of the organization; *(c) at the time of his decision,* he believes it to be compatible with his personal interest as a whole; and *(d)* he is able mentally and physically to comply with it.

(a) A communication that cannot be understood *can* have no authority. An order issued, for example, in a language not intelligible to the recipient is no order at all—no one would so regard it. Now, many orders are exceedingly difficult to understand. They are often necessarily stated in general terms, and the persons who issued them could not themselves apply them under many conditions. Until interpreted they have no meaning. The recipient either must disregard them or merely do anything in the hope that that is compliance.

Hence, a considerable part of administrative work consists in the interpretation and reinterpretation of orders in their application to concrete circumstances that were not or could not be taken into account initially.

(b) A communication believed by the recipient to be incompatible with the purpose of the organization, as he understands it, could not be accepted. Action would be frustrated by cross purposes. The most common practical example is that involved in conflicts of orders. They are not rare. An intelligent person will deny the authority of that one which contradicts the purpose of the effort as *he* understands it. In extreme cases many

individuals would be virtually paralyzed by conflicting orders. They would be literally unable to comply—for example, an employee of a water system ordered to blow up an essential pump, or soldiers ordered to shoot their own comrades. I suppose all experienced executives know that when it is necessary to issue orders that will appear to the recipients to be contrary to the main purpose, especially as exemplified in prior habitual practice, it is usually necessary and always advisable, if practicable, to explain or demonstrate why the appearance of conflict is an illusion. Otherwise the orders are likely not to be executed, or to be executed inadequately.

(c) If a communication is believed to involve a burden that destroys the net advantage of connection with the organization, there no longer would remain a net inducement to the individual to contribute to it. The existence of a net inducement is the only reason for accepting *any* order as having authority. Hence, if such an order is received it must be disobeyed (evaded in the more usual cases) as utterly inconsistent with personal motives that are the basis of accepting any orders at all. Cases of voluntary resignation from all sorts of organizations are common for this sole reason. Malingering and intentional lack of dependability are the more usual methods.

(d) If a person is unable to comply with an order, obviously it must be disobeyed, or, better, disregarded. To order a man who cannot swim to swim a river is a sufficient case. Such extreme cases are not frequent; but they occur. The more usual case is to order a man to do things only a little beyond his capacity; but a little impossible is still impossible.

IV

Naturally the reader will ask: How is it possible to secure such important and enduring cooperation as we observe if in principle and in fact the determination of authority lies with the subordinate individual? It is possible because the decisions of individuals occur under the following conditions: *(a)* orders that are deliberately issued in enduring organizations usually comply with the four conditions mentioned above; *(b)* there exists a "zone of indifference" in each individual within which orders are acceptable without conscious questioning of their authority; *(c)* the interests of the persons who contribute to an organization as a group result in the exercise of an influence on the subject, or on the attitude of the individual, that maintains a certain stability of this zone of indifference.

(a) There is no principle of executive conduct better established in good organizations than that orders will not be issued that cannot or will not be obeyed. Executives and most persons of experience who have thought about it know that to do so destroys authority, discipline, and morale.[4] For reasons to be stated shortly, this principle cannot ordinarily be formally admitted, or at least cannot be professed. When it appears necessary to issue orders which are initially or apparently unacceptable,

either careful preliminary education, or persuasive efforts, or the prior offering of effective inducements will be made, so that the issue will not be raised, the denial of authority will not occur, and orders will be obeyed. It is generally recognized that those who least understand this fact— newly appointed minor or "first line" executives—are often guilty of "disorganizing" their groups for this reason, as do experienced executives who lose self-control or become unbalanced by a delusion of power or for some other reason. Inexperienced persons take literally the current notions of authority and are then said "not to know how to use authority" or "to abuse authority." Their superiors often profess the same beliefs about authority in the abstract, but their successful practice is easily observed to be inconsistent with their professions.

(b) The phrase "zone of indifference" may be explained as follows: If all the orders for actions reasonably practicable be arranged in the order of their acceptability to the person affected, it may be conceived that there are a number which are clearly unacceptable, that is, which certainly will not be obeyed; there is another group somewhat more or less on the neutral line, that is, either barely acceptable or barely unacceptable; and a third group unquestionably acceptable. This last group lies within the "zone of indifference." The person affected will accept orders lying within this zone and is relatively indifferent as to what the order is so far as the question of authority is concerned. Such an order lies within the range that in a general way was anticipated at the time of undertaking the connection with the organization. For example, if a soldier enlists, whether voluntarily or not, in an army in which the men are ordinarily moved about within a certain broad region, it is a matter of indifference whether the order be to go to A or B, C or D, and so on; and goings to A, B, C, D, etc., are in the zone of indifference.

The zone of indifference will be wider or narrower depending upon the degree to which the inducements exceed the burdens and sacrifices which determine the individual's adhesion to the organization. It follows that the range of orders that will be accepted will be very limited among those who are barely induced to contribute to the system.

(c) Since the efficiency of organization is affected by the degree to which individuals assent to orders, denying the authority of an organization communication is a threat to the interests of all individuals who derive a net advantage from their connection with the organization, unless the orders are unacceptable to them also. Accordingly, at any given time there is among most of the contributors an active personal interest in the maintenance of the authority of all orders which to them are within the zone of indifference. The maintenance of this interest is largely a function of informal organization. Its expression goes under the names of "public opinion," "organization opinion," "feeling in the ranks," "group attitude," etc. Thus the common sense of the community informally arrived at affects the attitude of individuals, and makes them, as individuals, loath to question authority that is within or near the zone of indifference. The formal statement of this common sense is the fiction that authority comes down from above, from the general to the particular. This fiction merely establishes a presumption among individuals in favor of the acceptability of orders from superiors, enabling them to avoid making issues of such orders without incurring a sense of personal subserviency or a loss of personal or individual status with their fellows.

Thus the contributors are willing to maintain the authority of communications because, where care is taken to see that only acceptable communications in general are issued, most of them fall within the zone of personal indifference; and because communal sense influences the motives of most contributors most of the time. The practical instrument of this sense is the fiction of superior authority, which makes it possible normally to treat a personal question impersonally.

The fiction[5] of superior authority is necessary for two main reasons:

(1) It is the process by which the individual delegates upward, or to the organization, responsibility for what is an organization decision—an action which is depersonalized by the fact of its coordinate character. This means that if an instruction is disregarded, an executive's risk of being wrong must be accepted, a risk that the individual cannot and usually will not take unless in fact his position is at least as good as that of another with respect to correct appraisal of the relevant situation. Most persons are disposed to grant authority because they dislike the personal responsibility which they otherwise accept, especially when they are not in a good position to accept it. The practical difficulties in the operation of organization seldom lie in the excessive desire of individuals to assume responsibility for the organization action of themselves or others, but rather lie in the reluctance to take responsibility for their own actions in organization.

(2) The fiction gives impersonal notice that what is at stake is the good of the organization. If objective authority is flouted for arbitrary or merely temperamental reasons, if, in other words, there is deliberate attempt to twist an organization requirement to personal advantage, rather than properly to safeguard a substantial personal interest, then there is a deliberate attack on the organization itself. To remain outside an organization is not necessarily to be more than not friendly or not interested. To fail in an obligation intentionally is an act of hostility. This no organization can permit; and it must respond with punitive action if it can, even to the point of incarcerating or executing the culprit. This is rather generally the case where a person has agreed in advance in general what he will do. Leaving an organization in the lurch is not often tolerable.

The correctness of what has been said above will perhaps appear most probable from a consideration of the difference between executive action in emergency and that under "normal" conditions. In times of war the disciplinary atmosphere of an army is intensified—it is rather obvious to all that its success and the safety of its members are dependent upon it. In other organizations, abruptness of command is not only tolerated in times of emergency, but expected, and the lack of it often would actually be demoralizing. It is the sense of the justification which lies in the obvious situation which regulates the exercise of the veto by the final authority which lies at the bottom. This is a commonplace of executive experience, though it is not a commonplace of conversation about it.[6]

NOTES AND REFERENCES

1. New York: Macmillan.

2. Italics mine.

3. Boston: Little, Brown and Co., 1936.

4. Barring relatively few individual cases, when the attitude of the individual indicates in advance likelihood of disobedience (either before or after connection with the organization), the connection is terminated or refused before the formal question arises.

   It seems advisable to add a caution here against interpreting the exposition in terms of "democracy," whether in governmental, religious, or industrial organizations. The dogmatic assertion that "democracy" or "democratic methods" are (or are not) in accordance with the principles here discussed is not tenable. As will be more evident after the consideration of objective authority, the issues involved are much too complex and subtle to be taken into account in *any* formal scheme. Under many conditions in the political, religious, and industrial fields democratic processes create artificial questions of more or less logical character, in place of the real questions, which are matters of feeling and appropriateness and of informal organization. By oversimplification of issues this may destroy objective authority. No doubt in many situations formal democratic processes may be an important element in the maintenance of authority, i.e., of organization cohesion, but may in other situations be disruptive and probably never could be, in themselves, sufficient. On the other hand the solidarity of some cooperative systems (General Harbord's army, for example) under many conditions may be unexcelled, though requiring formally autocratic processes.

   Moreover, it should never be forgotten that authority in the aggregate arises from *all* the contributors to a cooperative system, and that the weighting to be attributed to the attitude of individuals varies. It is often forgotten that in industrial (or political) organizations measures which are acceptable at the bottom may be quite unacceptable to the substantial proportion of contributors who are executives, and who will no more perform their essential functions than will others, if the conditions are, to them, impossible. The point to be emphasized is that the maintenance of the contributions necessary to the endurance of an organization requires the authority of *all* essential contributors.

5. The word "fiction" is used because from the standpoint of logical construction it merely explains overt acts. Either as a superior officer or as a subordinate, however, I know nothing that I actually regard as more "real" than "authority."

6. It will be of interest to quote a statement which has appeared since these lines were written, in a pamphlet entitled "Business—Well on the Firing Line" (No. 9 in the series "What Helps Business Helps You," in *Nation's Business*). It reads in part: "Laws don't create Teamplay. It is not called into play by law. For every written rule there are a thousand unwritten rules by which the course of business is guided, which govern the millions of daily transactions of which business consists. These rules are not applied from the top down, by arbitrary authority. They grow out of actual practice—from the bottom up. They are based upon mutual understanding and compromise, the desire to achieve common ends and further the common good. They are observed *voluntarily*, because they have the backing of experience and common sense."

18

The Ideal Bureaucracy

Max Weber

*To Max Weber control is an essential element in the efficient functioning of
any enterprise and the best control is that which is attained in a bureaucratic form of organizational arrangement. If you are one of those people
who associate bureaucracy with inefficiency and red tape this article
should convince you that that is not Weber's definition of an ideal bureaucracy at all. Rather, he sees it as the best known means of carrying out
imperative control of human beings.—Eds.*

The purest type of exercise of legal authority is that which employs a
bureaucratic administrative staff. Only the supreme chief of the organization occupies his position of authority by virtue of appropriation, of
election, or of having been designated for the succession. But even his
authority consists in a sphere of legal "competence." The whole administrative staff under the supreme authority then consists, in the purest
type, of individual officials who are appointed and function according to
the following criteria:

1. They are personally free and subject to authority only with respect to their impersonal official obligations.
2. They are organized in a clearly defined hierarchy of offices.
3. Each office has a clearly defined sphere of competence in the legal
   sense.
4. The office is filled by a free contractual relationship. Thus, in
   principle, there is free selection.

SOURCE: Reprinted with permission of Macmillan Publishing Company, Inc., from *The
Theory of Social and Economic Organizations* by Max Weber, translated by Talcott Parsons
and A. M. Henderson. Copyright © 1947, 1975 by Talcott Parsons.

5. Candidates are selected on the basis of technical qualifications. In the most rational case, this is tested by examination or guaranteed by diplomas certifying technical training, or both. They are appointed, not elected.

6. They are remunerated by fixed salaries in money, for the most part with a right to pensions. Only under certain circumstances does the employing authority, especially in private organizations, have a right to terminate the appointment, but the official is always free to resign. The salary scale is primarily graded according to rank in the hierarchy; but in addition to this criterion, the responsibility of the position and the requirements of the incumbent's social status may be taken into account.

7. The office is treated as the sole, or at least the primary, occupation of the incumbent.

8. It constitutes a career. There is a system of "promotion" according to seniority or to achievement, or both. Promotion is dependent on the judgment of superiors.

9. The official works entirely separated from ownership of the means of administration and without appropriation of his position.

10. He is subject to strict and systematic discipline and control in the conduct of the office.

This type of organization is in principle applicable with equal facility to a wide variety of different fields. It may be applied in profit-making business or in charitable organizations, or in any number of other types of private enterprises serving ideal or material ends. It is equally applicable to political and to religious organizations. With varying degrees of approximation to a pure type, its historical existence can be demonstrated in all these fields.

1. For example, this type of bureaucracy is found in private clinics as well as in endowed hospitals or the hospitals maintained by religious orders. Bureaucratic organization has played a major role in the Catholic Church. It is well illustrated by the administrative role of the priesthood in the modern church, which has expropriated almost all the old church benefices which were in former days to a large extent subject to private appropriation. It is also illustrated by the conception of the universal Episcopate, which is thought of as formally constituting a universal legal competence in religious matters. Similarly, the doctrine of papal infallibility is thought of as in fact involving a universal competence, but only one which functions ex cathedra in the sphere of the office, thus implying the typical distinction between the sphere of office and that of the private affairs of the incumbent. The same phenomena are found in the large-scale capitalistic enterprise; and the larger it is, the greater their role.

And this is not less true of political parties, which will be discussed separately. Finally, the modern army is essentially a bureaucratic organization administered by that peculiar type of military functionary, the "officer."

2. Bureaucratic authority is carried out in its purest form where it is most clearly dominated by the principle of appointment. There is no such thing as a hierarchy of elected officials in the same sense as there is a hierarchical organization of appointed officials. In the first place, election makes it impossible to attain a stringency of discipline even approaching that in the appointed type; for it is open to a subordinate official to compete for elective honors on the same terms as his superiors, and his prospects are not dependent on the superior's judgment.

3. Appointment by free contract, which makes free selection possible, is essential to modern bureaucracy. Where there is a hierarchical organization with impersonal spheres of competence but occupied by unfree officials—like slaves or dependents, who, however, function in a formally bureaucratic manner—the term "patrimonial bureaucracy" will be used.

4. The role of technical qualifications in bureaucratic organizations is continually increasing. Even an official in a party or a trade union organization is in need of specialized knowledge, though it is usually of an empirical character, developed by experience rather than by formal training. In the modern state, the only "offices" for which no technical qualifications are required are those of ministers and presidents. This only goes to prove that they are "officials" only in a formal sense and not substantively, as is true of the managing director or president of a large business corporation. Thus at the top of a bureaucratic organization, there is necessarily an element which is at least not purely bureaucratic. The category of bureaucracy is one applying only to the exercise of control by means of a particular kind of administrative staff.

5. The bureaucratic official normally receives a fixed salary. By contrast, sources of income which are privately appropriated will be called "benefices." Bureaucratic salaries are also normally paid in money. Though this is not essential to the concept of bureaucracy, it is the arrangement which best fits the pure type. Payments in kind are apt to have the character of benefices, and the receipt of a benefice normally implies the appropriation of opportunities for earnings and of positions. There are, however, gradual transitions in this field with many intermediate types. Appropriation by virtue of leasing or sale of offices or the pledge of income from office are phenomena foreign to the pure type of bureaucracy.

6. "Offices" which do not constitute the incumbent's principal occupation, in particular "honorary" offices, belong in other categories. The typical "bureaucratic" official occupies the office as his principal occupation.

7. With respect to the separation of the official from ownership of the means of administration, the situation is essentially the same in the field

of public administration and in private bureaucratic organizations, such as the large-scale capitalistic enterprise.

8. Collegial bodies are rapidly decreasing in importance in favor of types of organization which are in fact, and for the most part formally as well, subject to the authority of a single head. For example, the collegial "governments" in Prussia have long since given way to the monocratic "district president." The decisive factor in this development has been the need for rapid, clear decisions, free of the necessity of compromise between different opinions and also free of shifting majorities.

9. The modern army officer is a type of appointed official who is clearly marked off by certain class distinctions. In this respect such officers differ radically from elected military leaders, from charismatic condottieri, from the type of officers who recruit and lead mercenary armies as a capitalistic enterprise, and, finally, from the incumbents of commissions which have been purchased. There may be gradual transitions between these types. The patrimonial "retainer," who is separated from the means of carrying out his function and the proprietor of a mercenary army for capitalistic purposes have, along with the private capitalistic entrepreneur, been pioneers in the organization of the modern type of bureaucracy.

THE MONOCRATIC TYPE OF
BUREAUCRATIC ADMINISTRATION

Experience tends universally to show that the purely bureaucratic type of administrative organization—that is, the monocratic variety of bureaucracy—is, from a purely technical point of view, capable of attaining the highest degree of efficiency and is in this sense formally the most rational known means of carrying out imperative control over human beings. It is superior to any other form in precision, in stability, in the stringency of its discipline, and in its reliability. It thus makes possible a particularly high degree of calculability of results for the heads of the organization and for those acting in relation to it. It is finally superior both in intensive efficiency and in the scope of its operations and is formally capable of application to all kinds of administrative tasks.

The development of the modern form of the organization of corporate groups in all fields is nothing less than identical with the development and continual spread of bureaucratic administration. This is true of church and state, of armies, political parties, economic enterprises, organizations to promote all kinds of causes, private associations, clubs, and many others. Its development is, to take the most striking case, the most crucial phenomenon of the modern Western state. However many forms there may be which do not appear to fit this pattern—such as collegial representative bodies, parliamentary committees, soviets, honorary officers, lay judges, and what not—and however much people may complain about the "evils of bureaucracy," it would be sheer illusion to think for a moment that continuous administrative work could be carried out in any field except by means of officials working in offices. The whole pattern of everyday life is cut to fit this framework. For bureaucratic administration is, other things being equal, always, from a formal, technical point of view, the most rational type. For the needs of mass administration today, it is completely indispensable. The choice is only that between bureaucracy and dilettantism in the field of administration.

The primary source of the superiority of bureaucratic administration lies in the role of technical knowledge which, through the development of modern technology and business methods in the production of goods, has become completely indispensable. In this respect, it makes no difference whether the economic system is organized on a capitalistic or a socialistic basis. Indeed, if in the latter case a comparable level of technical efficiency were to be achieved, it would mean a tremendous increase in the importance of specialized bureaucracy.

When those subject to bureaucratic control seek to escape the influence of the existing bureaucratic apparatus, this is normally possible only by creating an organization of their own which is equally subject to the process of bureaucratization. Similarly the existing bureaucratic apparatus is driven to continue functioning by the most powerful interests which are material and objective, but also ideal in character. Without it, a society like our own—with a separation of officials, employees, and workers from ownership of the means of administration, dependent on discipline and on technical training—could no longer function. The only exception would be those groups, such as the peasantry, who are still in possession of their own means of subsistence. Even in case of revolution by force or of occupation by an enemy, the bureaucratic machinery will normally continue to function just as it had for the previous legal government.

The question is always who controls the existing bureaucratic machinery. And such control is possible only to a very limited degree for persons who are not technical specialists. Generally speaking, in the long run the trained permanent official is more likely to get his way than his nominal superior, the Cabinet minister, who is not a specialist.

Though by no means alone, the capitalistic system has undeniably played a major role in the development of bureaucracy. Indeed, without it capitalistic production could not continue, and any rational type of socialism would have simply to take it over and increase its importance. Its development, largely under capitalistic auspices, has created an urgent need for stable, strict, intensive, and calculable administration. It is this need which gives bureaucracy a crucial role in our society as the central element in any kind of large-scale administration. Only by reversion in every field—political, religious, economic, and so forth—to small-scale organization would it be possible to any considerable extent to escape its influence. On the one hand, capitalism in its modern stages of development strongly tends to foster the development of bureaucracy, although both capitalism and bureaucracy have arisen from many different historical sources. Conversely, capitalism is the most rational economic basis for bureaucratic administration and enables it to develop in the most rational form, especially because, from a fiscal point of view, it supplies the necessary money resources.

Along with these fiscal conditions of efficient bureaucratic administration, there are certain extremely important conditions in the field of communication and transportation. The precision of its functioning requires the services of the railway, the telegraph, and the telephone and becomes increasingly dependent on them. A socialistic form of organization would not alter this fact. It would be a question whether in a socialistic system it would be possible to provide conditions for carrying out as stringent bureaucratic organization as has been possible in a capitalistic order. For socialism would, in fact, require a still higher degree of formal bureaucratization than capitalism. If this should prove not to be possible, it would demonstrate the existence of another of those fundamental elements of irrationality in social systems—a conflict between formal and substantive rationality of the sort which sociology so often encounters.

Bureaucratic administration means fundamentally the exercise of control on the basis of knowledge. This is the feature of it which makes it specifically rational. This consists on the one hand in technical knowledge which, by itself, is sufficient to ensure it a position of extraordinary power. But in addition to this, bureaucratic organizations, or the holders of power who make use of them, have the tendency to increase their power still further by the knowledge growing out of experience in the service; for they acquire through the conduct of office a special knowledge of facts and have available a store of documentary material peculiar to themselves. While not peculiar to bureaucratic organizations, the concept of "official secrets" is certainly typical of them. It stands in relation to technical knowledge in somewhat the same position as commercial secrets do to technological training. It is a product of the striving for power.

Bureaucracy is superior in knowledge, including both technical knowledge and knowledge of the concrete fact within its own sphere of interest, which is usually confined to the interests of a private business—a capitalistic enterprise. The capitalistic entrepreneur is, in our society, the only type who has been able to maintain at least relative immunity from subjection to the control of rational bureaucratic knowledge. All the rest of the population have tended to be organized in large-scale corporate groups which are inevitably subject to bureaucratic control. This is as inevitable as the dominance of precision machinery in the mass production of goods.

The following are the principal more general social consequences of bureaucratic control:

1. The tendency to "leveling" in the interest of the broadest possible basis of recruitment in terms of technical competence.

2. The tendency to plutocracy growing out of the interest in the greatest possible length of technical training. Today this often lasts up to the age of thirty.

3. The dominance of a spirit of formalistic impersonality, without hatred or passion, and hence without affection or enthusiasm. The dominant norms are concepts of straightforward duty without regard for personal considerations. Everyone is subject to formal equality of treatment—that is, everyone in the same empirical situation. This is the spirit in which the ideal official conducts his office.

The development of bureaucracy greatly favors the leveling of social classes, and this can be shown historically to be the normal tendency. Conversely, every process of social leveling creates a favorable situation for the development of bureaucracy; for it tends to eliminate class privileges, which include the appropriation of means of administration and the appropriation of authority as well as the occupation of offices on an honorary basis or as an avocation by virtue of wealth. This combination everywhere inevitably foreshadows the development of mass democracy.

The "spirit" of rational bureaucracy normally has the following general characteristics:

1. Formalism, which is promoted by all the interests which are concerned with the security of their own personal situation, whatever this may consist in. Otherwise the door would be open to arbitrariness, and hence formalism is the line of least resistance.

2. There is another tendency, which is apparently in contradiction to the above—a contradiction which is in part genuine. It is the tendency of officials to treat their official function from what is substantively a utilitarian point of view in the interest of the welfare of those under their authority. But this utilitarian tendency is generally expressed in the enactment of corresponding regulatory measures which themselves have a formal character and tend to be treated in a formalistic spirit. This tendency to substantive rationality is supported by all those subject to authority who are not included in the class mentioned above as interested in the security of advantages already controlled. The problems which open up at this point belong in the theory of "democracy."

19

Leaders' Control and
Members' Compliance

Amitai Etzioni

*Etzioni suggests that organizations can be categorized in terms of how
their leaders exercise control through the use of coercive, remunerative, or
normative power. This classification may be developed further by examining how organizational members respond to these control attempts. He
suggests three categories of response: involvement, commitment, and alienation. It is the discussion of the relationship between types of control
and responses to them that makes this article such a significant one.—Eds.*

A CLASSIFICATION OF POWER

Power is an actor's ability to induce or influence another actor to carry
out his directives or any other norms he supports.[1] Goldhamer and Shils
state that "a person may be said to have power to the extent that he
influences the behavior of others in accordance with his own intentions."[2]
Of course, "his own intentions" might be to influence a person to follow
others' "intentions" or those of a collectivity. In organizations, enforcing
the collectivity norms is likely to be a condition determining the power-
holder's access to the means of power.

   Power positions are positions whose incumbents regularly have access to means of power. Statements about power positions imply a particular group (or groups) who are subject to this power. For instance, to state
that prison guards have a power position implies the subordination of

---

   SOURCE: Reprinted with permission of Macmillan Publishing Company, Inc., from *A
Comparative Analysis of Complex Organizations* by Amitai Etzioni. Copyright © 1961 by
Free Press of Glencoe, Inc.

inmates. In the following analysis we focus on power relations in organizations between those higher and those lower in rank. We refer to those in power positions, who are higher in rank, as *elites* or as organizational *representatives*. We refer to those in subject positions, who are lower in rank, as *lower participants*.

Power differs according to the means employed to make the subjects comply. These means may be physical, material, or symbolic.[3]

Coercive power rests on the application, or the threat of application, of physical sanctions such as infliction of pain, deformity, or death; generation of frustration through restriction of movement; or controlling through force the satisfaction of needs such as those for food, sex, comfort, and the like.

Remunerative power is based on control over material resources and rewards through allocation of salaries and wages, commissions and contributions, "fringe benefits," services, and commodities.

Normative power rests on the allocation and manipulation of symbolic rewards and deprivations through employment of leaders, manipulation of mass media, allocation of esteem and prestige symbols, administration of ritual, and influence over the distribution of "acceptance" and "positive response." (A more eloquent name for this power would be persuasive, or manipulative, or suggestive power. But all these terms have negative value connotations which we wish to avoid.)

There are two kinds of normative power. One is based on the manipulation of esteem, prestige, and ritualistic symbols (such as a flag or a benediction); the other, on allocation and manipulation of acceptance and positive response.[4] Although both powers are found both in vertical and in horizontal relationships, the first is more frequent in vertical relations, between actors who have different ranks, whereas the second is more common in horizontal relations, among actors equal in rank—in particular, in the power of an "informal" or primary group over its members. Lacking better terms, we refer to the first kind as *pure normative power* and to the second as *social power*.[5] Social power could be treated as a distinct kind of power. But since powers are here classed according to the means of control employed, and since both social and pure normative power rest on the same set of means—manipulation of symbolic rewards—we treat these two powers as belonging to the same category.

From the viewpoint of the organization, pure normative power is more useful, since it can be exercised directly down the hierarchy. Social power becomes organizational power only when the organization can influence the group's powers, as when a teacher uses the class climate to control a deviant child or a union steward agitates the members to use their informal power to bring a deviant into line.

Organizations can be ordered according to their power structure, taking into account which power is predominant, how strongly it is stressed compared with other organizations in which the same power is predominant, and which power constitutes the secondary source of control. . . .

NEUTRALIZATION OF POWER

Most organizations employ all three kinds of power, but the degree to which they rely on each differs from organization to organization. Most organizations tend to emphasize only one means of power, relying less on the other two.[6] Evidence to this effect is presented below in the analysis of the compliance structures of various organizations. The major reason for power specialization seems to be that when two kinds of power are emphasized at the same time, over the same subject group, they tend to neutralize each other.

Applying force, for instance, usually creates such a high degree of alienation that it becomes impossible to apply normative power successfully. This is one of the reasons that rehabilitation is rarely achieved in traditional prisons, that custodial measures are considered as blocking therapy in mental hospitals, and that teachers in progressive schools tend to oppose corporal punishment.

Similarly, the application of remunerative powers makes appeal to "idealistic" (pure normative) motives less fruitful. In a study of the motives which lead to purchase of war bonds, Merton pointed out that in one particularly effective drive (the campaign of Kate Smith), all "secular" topics were omitted and the appeal was centered on patriotic, "sacred" themes. Merton asked a sample of 978 people: "Do you think that it is a good idea to give things to people who buy bonds?"

> Fifty per cent were definitely opposed in principle to premiums, bonuses, and other such inducements, and many of the remainder thought it a good idea only for "other people" who might not buy otherwise.[7]
>
> By omitting this [secular] argument, the authors of her scripts were able to avoid the strain and incompatibility between the two main lines of motivation: unselfish, sacrificing love of country and economic motives of sound investment.[8]

It is possible to make an argument for the opposite position. It might be claimed that the larger the number of personal needs whose satisfaction the organization controls, the more power it has over the participants. For example, labor unions that cater to and have control over the social as well as the economic needs of their members have more power over those members than do unions that focus only on economic needs. There may be some tension between the two modes of control, some ambivalence and uneasy feeling among members about the combinations, but undoubtedly the total control is larger. Similarly, it is obvious that the church has more power over the priest than over the average parishioner. The parishioner is exposed to normative power, whereas the priest is controlled by both normative and remunerative powers.

The issue is complicated by the fact that the *amount* of each kind of power applied must be taken into account. If a labor union with social powers has economic power which is much greater than that of another union, this fact may explain why the first union has greater power in sum, despite some "waste" due to neutralization. A further complication follows from the fact that neutralization may also occur through application of the "wrong" power in terms of the cultural definition of what is appropriate to the particular organization and activity. For example, application of economic power in religious organizations may be less effective than in industries, not because two kinds of power are mixed, but because it is considered illegitimate to use economic pressures to attain religious goals. Finally, some organizations manage to apply two kinds of power abundantly and without much waste through neutralization, because they segregate the application of one power from that of the other. The examination below of combat armies and labor unions supplies an illustration of this point.

We have discussed some of the factors related to the tendency of organizations to specialize their power application. In conclusion, it seems that although there can be little doubt that such a tendency exists, its scope and a satisfactory explanation for it have yet to be established.

THREE KINDS OF INVOLVEMENT: A COMPARATIVE DIMENSION

Involvement, Commitment, and Alienation

Organizations must continually recruit means if they are to realize their goals. One of the most important of these means is the positive orientation of the participants to the organizational power. *Involvement*[9] refers to the cathectic-evaluative orientation of an actor to an object, characterized in terms of intensity and direction.

The intensity of involvement ranges from high to low. The direction is either positive or negative. We refer to positive involvement as *commitment*[10] and to negative involvement as *alienation*.[11] (The advantage of having a third term, *involvement,* is that it enables us to refer to the continuum in a neutral way.[12]) Actors can accordingly be placed on an involvement continuum which ranges from a highly intense negative zone through mild negative and mild positive zones to a highly positive zone.[13]

Three Kinds of Involvement

We have found it helpful to name three zones of the involvement continuum, as follows: *alienative,* for the high alienation zone; *moral,* for the high commitment zone; and *calculative,* for the two mild zones. This classification of involvement can be applied to the orientations of actors in all social units and to all kinds of objects. Hence the definitions and illustrations presented below are not limited to organizations but are applicable to orientations in general.

Alienative involvement. Alienative involvement designates an intense negative orientation; it is predominant in relations among hostile foreigners. Similar orientations exist among merchants in "adventure" capitalism, where trade is built on isolated acts of exchange, each side trying to maximize immediate profit.[14] Such an orientation seems to dominate the approach of prostitutes to transient clients.[15] Some slaves seem to have held similar attitudes to their masters and to their work. Inmates in prisons, prisoners of war, people in concentration camps, enlisted men in basic training, all tend to be alienated from their respective organizations.[16]

Calculative involvement. Calculative involvement designates either a negative or a positive orientation of low intensity. Calculative orientations are predominant in relationships of merchants who have continuous business contacts. Attitudes of (and toward) permanent customers are often predominantly calculative, as are relationships among entrepreneurs in modern (rational) capitalism. Inmates in prisons who have established contact with prison authorities, such as "rats" and "peddlers," often have predominantly calculative attitudes toward those in power.[17]

Moral involvement.[18] Moral involvement designates a positive orientation of high intensity. The involvement of the parishioner in his church, the devoted member in his party, and the loyal follower in his leader are all "moral."

There are two kinds of moral involvement, pure and social. They differ in the same way pure normative power differs from social power. Both are intensive modes of commitment, but they differ in their foci of orientation and in the structural conditions under which they develop. Pure moral commitments are based on internalization of norms and identification with authority (like Riesman's inner-directed "mode of conformity"); social commitment rests on sensitivity to pressures of primary groups and their members (Riesman's "other-directed"). Pure moral involvement tends to develop in vertical relationships, such as those between teachers and students, priests and parishioners, leaders and followers. Social involvement tends to develop in horizontal relationships like those in various types of primary groups. Both pure moral and social orientations might be found in the same relationships, but, as a rule, one orientation predominates.

Actors are means to each other in alienative and in calculative relations; but they are ends to each other in "social" relationships. In pure moral relationships the means-orientation tends to predominate; hence, for example, the willingness of devoted members of totalitarian parties or religious orders to use each other. But unlike the means-orientation of calculative relationships, the means-orientation here is expected to be geared to needs of the collectivity in serving its goals, and not to those of an individual.

NOTES AND REFERENCES

1. T. Parsons, *The Social System* (New York: Free Press of Glencoe, Inc., 1951), p. 121.

2. H. Goldhamer and E. A. Shils, "Types of Power and Status," *American Journal of Sociology*, 45 (1939), p. 171.

3. We suggest that this typology is exhaustive, although the only way we can demonstrate this is by pointing out that every type of power we have encountered so far can be classified as belonging to one of the categories or to a combination of them.

4. T. Parsons, *The Social System* (New York: Free Press of Glencoe, Inc., 1951), p. 108.

5. This distinction draws on the difference between social and normative integration, referred to by T. Parsons, R. F. Bales, and E. A. Shils, *Working Papers in the Theory of Action* (New York: Free Press of Glencoe, Inc., 1953), p. 182, as the distinction between the "integrative" and the "latent pattern maintenance" phases. . . . Shils distinguishes between social and ideological primary groups (private communication). J. S. Coleman, "Multidimensional Scale Analysis," *American Journal of Sociology*, 63 (1957), p. 255, has pointed to the difference between group-oriented and idea-oriented attachments.

6. In more technical language, one can say that the three continua of power constitute a three-dimensional property space. If we collapse each dimension into high, medium, and low segments, there are 27 possible combinations or cells. Our hypothesis reads that most organizations fall into cells which are high on one dimension and low or medium on the others; this excludes 18 cells (not counting three types of dual structures discussed below).

7. R. K. Merton, *Mass Persuasion: The Social Psychology of a War Bond Drive* (New York: Harper & Row, 1946), p. 47.

8. Ibid., p. 45.

9. *Involvement* has been used in a similar manner by Nancy C. Morse, *Satisfactions in the White-Collar Job* (Survey Research Center, University of Michigan, 1953), pp. 76–96. The term is used in a somewhat different way by students of voting, who refer by it to the psychological investment in the outcome of an election rather than in the party, which would be parallel to Morse's usage and ours. See, for example, A. Campbell, G. Gurin, and W. E. Miller, *The Voter Decides* (New York: Harper & Row, 1954), pp. 33–40.

10. Mishler defined *commitment* in a similar though more psychological way: "An individual is committed to an organization to the extent that central tensions are integrated through organizationally relevant instrumental acts." Cited by C. Argyris, *Personality and Organization* (New York: Harper & Row, 1957), p. 202.

11. We draw deliberately on the associations this term has acquired from its usage by Marx and others. For a good analysis of the idea of alienation in Marxism, and of its more recent development, see D. Bell, "The 'Rediscovery' of Alienation," *Journal of Philosophy*, 56 (1959), pp. 933–952; and D. Bell, *The End of Ideology* (New York: Free Press of Glencoe, Inc., 1960), pp. 335–

368. See also D. G. Dean, "Alienation and Political Apathy," *Social Forces,* 38 (1960), pp. 185–189.

12. An example of empirical indicators which can be used to translate the involvement continuum into directly observable terms is offered by E. A. Shils and M. Janowits, "Cohesion and Disintegration in the Wehrmacht in World War II," *Public Opinion Quarterly,* 12, No. 2 (1948), pp. 282–283. They classify "modes of social disintegration" in the armed forces as follows: desertion, active surrender, passive surrender, routine resistance, "last-ditch" resistance. In the terms used here, these measures indicate varying degrees of involvement, from highest alienation (desertion) to highest commitment (last-ditch resistance).

Nettler (1958) has developed a 17-item unidimensional scale which measures alienation from society. It seems that a similar scale could be constructed for measuring alienation from or commitment to organizational power without undue difficulties. A. Kornhauser, H. L. Sheppard, and A. J. Mayer, *When Labor Votes* (New York: University Books, 1956), pp. 147–148, have developed a 6-item scale, measuring the orientation of union members to their organization, which supplies another illustration of the wide use and measurability of these concepts, which are central to our analysis.

13. Several sociologists have pointed out that the relationship between intensity and direction of involvement is a curvilinear one: the more positive or negative the orientation, the more intensely it is held. L. Guttman, "The Cornell Technique for Scale and Intensity Analysis," *Education and Psychology Measurement,* 7 (4197), pp. 247–279.

14. H. H. Gerth and C. W. Mills, *From Max Weber: Essays in Sociology* (New York: Oxford University Press, 1946), p. 67.

15. K. Davis, "The Sociology of Prostitution," *American Sociological Review,* 2 (1937), pp. 748–-749.

16. For a description of this orientation in prisons see D. Clemmer, *The Prison Community* (New York: Holt, Rinehart & Winston, 1958), p. 152ff. Attitudes toward the police, particularly on the part of members of the lower class, are often strictly alienative. See, for example, E. Banfield, *The Moral Basis of a Backward Society* (New York: Free Press of Glencoe, Inc., 1958).

17. G. M. Sykes, *The Society of Captives* (Princeton: Princeton University Press, 1958), pp. 87–95.

18. The term *moral* is used here . . . to refer to an orientation of the actor; it does not involve a value-position of the observer. See T. Parsons et al., *Toward a General Theory of Action* (Cambridge, Mass.: Harvard University Press, 1952), pp. 170ff.

20

Criteria of Organizational Effectiveness

Stanley E. Seashore

Organizations have a variety of goals. Some of these will be more impor-
tant than others; some will be partially in conflict with others. Further-
more, over time, the priorities of objectives may change. It is this fact of
organizational life which is addressed in this article. Successfully control-
ling for organizational performance must take into account the multiple,
conflicting, and changing goals of the organization. This fact makes the
control process more difficult argues the author, but nonetheless very im-
portant.—Eds.

Summary: Most organizations have many goals, not one. These goals are
of unlike importance and their relative importance changes. Problems
arise because these goals are sometimes competing (i.e., have trade-off
value), and sometimes incompatible (negatively correlated). A strategy of
optimal realization of goals cannot be determined unless there exists
some conception of the dimensions of performance, their relative importance, and their relationships with one another. These relationships may
be ones of causation, of simple correlation, of interaction; they may be
linear and compensatory or nonlinear and noncompensatory. A framework is proposed for conceptualizing organizational performance, with
distinctions among several different classes of performance dimensions
and with consideration for several types of relationships among them.

MULTIPLE, CONFLICTING GOALS

The aim of the following discussion is to outline a way of viewing the
relationships among the numerous criteria that might be considered in

SOURCE: Reprinted by permission from the July 1965, issue of the *Michigan Business
Review*, published by the Graduate School of Business Administration, The University of
Michigan.

the evaluation of the performance of an organization. To understand such relationships we shall need to make some distinctions between different kinds of criterion measures. We shall need to create some encompassing conceptions that serve to aid the evaluation of performance when some desired measures are not available, or when the number of measures is inconveniently large.

The issues taken up here arise because most organizations have multiple goals rather than a single goal, and goal achievement may not be directly measurable. The formal objectives of the organization may themselves be multiple and, in any case, there are multiple short-run goals and subgoals that need to be examined. The matter would be simple if the various goals were all of similar priority and combinable in some simple additive way; but this is not the situation. The manager making decisions that rest upon multivariate assessments of the performance of his organization has to calculate the weights and the correlation values that he will apply when estimating the net outcome of a course of action.

A typical example would be the case of a manager who wishes his firm to obtain a substantial profit, and at the same time to grow in size, to insure future profit by product improvements, to avoid financial risk, to pay a substantial annual dividend to his investors, to have satisfied employees, and to have his firm respected in the community. He cannot maximize all of these simultaneously, as increasing one (e.g. dividends or risk avoidance) may imply reduced achievement on another (e.g. growth, product research). He must consider their trade-off value, their contingencies, and the presence of negative correlations among them. To estimate an optimum course of action he has to evaluate the dependability and relevance of the various measures and then estimate the way in which they combine to provide an overall evaluation of performance or a prediction of future change in performance. This task will be easier when we have for his use a theory to describe the performance of organizations. The following suggestions are a step in that direction.

CRITERIA AND THEIR USES

To begin with we need to make some distinctions among different kinds of criteria and their uses.

1. *Ends vs. means.* Some criteria are close to the formal objectives of the organization in the sense that they represent ends or goals that are valued in themselves; others have value mainly or only because they are thought to be necessary means or conditions for achieving the main goals of the organization. Substantial profit, for example, may be a goal sought by a business organization, while employee satisfaction may be valued because it is thought to be an aid in reaching the goal of substantial profit.

2. *Time reference.* Some criterion measures refer to a past time period (profit for the past year), others to current states (net worth), and

still others to anticipated future periods (projected growth). Whatever their time reference, all may be used for drawing inferences about past or future conditions or changes.

3. *Long vs. short run.* Some criterion measures refer to a relatively short period of time, others to a longer period; they may refer to performances that are relatively stable (do not change much in the short run) or relatively unstable (erratic or highly variable in the short run). The usefulness of a criterion measure is limited if the period covered is not appropriate to the usual or potential rate of change in the variable.[1]

4. *"Hard" vs. "soft."* Some criteria are measured by the characteristics of, or number or frequency of, physical objects and events, while others are measured by qualitative observation of behavior or by evaluative questions put to people. Dollar measures, for example, or tons of scrap, or number of grievances, are "hard" measures; while employee satisfaction, motivation to work, cooperation, product quality, customer loyalty, and many others are usually "soft." *The distinction is useful, but it contains a trap,* for we commonly think of the hard variables as being in some way inherently more valid, more reliable, and more relevant to the performance evaluation problem, when this is not necessarily true. Profit rate, for example—a popular hard variable—is a rather vague concept to begin with (accountants dispute about definition and about conventions for measurement) and it is often in the short run unreliable as a performance indicator and thus quite irrelevant to the evaluation problem, even for an organization whose long-run goals include making a profit. Similarly, a soft variable, such as one representing the intentions of key executives to stay with the organization, may be measured with high reliability in some circumstances and may be vital in the assessment of the organization's performance.

5. *Values.* Some variables appear to have a linear value scale (more is always better than less), while others have a curvilinear scale (some optimum is desired; more and less are both to be avoided). The shape of the curves determines in part the trade-off relationships among assessment variables under conditions where simultaneous optimization is not possible. Examples: profit rate is usually linear in value in the sense that more is better than less; maintenance costs, by contrast, are usually curvilinear in value in the sense that either excessively high or low costs may be judged to diminish overall firm performance.

THE HIERARCHY OF CRITERIA

A full accounting for the performance of an organization requires consideration for (1) achievement of the organization's main goals over a long span of time, (2) performance over shorter periods on each of those criteria that represent ends valued in themselves, and which, jointly, as a set, determine the net ultimate performance, and (3) performance on each of a number of subsidiary criteria that provide an immediate or current indication of the progress toward, or probability of achieving, success on end-result variables. The network of criteria of performance can be viewed as a pyramid shaped hierarchy:

1. *At the top* is the "ultimate criterion"—some conception of the net performance of the organization over a long span of time in achieving its formal objectives, whatever they may be, with optimum use of the organization's environmental resources and opportunities. The ultimate criterion is never measured (except possibly by historians); yet some concept of this kind is the basis for evaluation of lesser criteria of performance.

2. *In the middle* are the penultimate criteria. These are shorter run performance factors or dimensions comprised by the ultimate criterion. They are "output" or "results" criteria: things sought for their own value and having trade-off value[2] in relation to each other. Their sum, in some weighted mixture, determines the ultimate criterion. Typical variables of this class for business organizations are: sales volume, productive efficiency, growth rate, profit rate, and the like. There may be included some "soft" (usually behavioral) variables such as employee satisfaction or customer satisfaction. In the case of some nonbusiness organizations these penultimate criteria might be predominantly of the behavioral kind, as in the case of a school whose output is judged in terms of learning rates, proportion of students reaching some standard of personal growth or development, etc.

3. *At the bottom* of the hierarchy of assessment criteria are measures of the current organizational functioning according to some theory or some empirical system concerning the conditions associated with high achievement on each of the penultimate criteria.[3] These variables include those descriptive of the organization as a system and also those representing subgoals or means associated with penultimate criteria. The number of criteria in this class is very large (over 200 have been used in some studies without sensing that the limits were being approached), and they are interrelated in a complex network that includes causal, interactional, and modifier types of relationships. Included are some criteria that are not valued at all except for their power to reduce the amount of uncontrolled variance in the network. Among the "hard" criteria at this level, for a business organization, might be such as: scrappage, short-run profit, productivity against standards, meeting of production schedules, machine downtime, ratio of overtime to regular time, product return rate, rate of technological innovation, and the like. Among the "soft" criteria at this level may be such as these: employee morale, credit rating, communication effectiveness, absenteeism, turnover, group cohesiveness, customer loyalty, pride in firm, level of performance motivation, and others.

CHARACTERISTICS OF BEHAVIORAL CRITERIA

Such a model locates the behavioral criteria—those descriptive of the members (in this context, customers and clients are also "members") of the organization and of their values, attitudes, relationships, and activities—mainly in the lower regions of the network of assessment criteria, distant and perhaps only indirectly related to the ultimate goals by which the organization is eventually judged.

If behavioral criteria appear near the top of the network, it is because they are valued in themselves and have trade-off value in relation to other priority goals of the organization. In general, however, the hard—nonbehavioral—criteria are the preferred ones for most business organizations for the good reason that they are more relevant to the formal objectives of the organization.

The behavioral measures are presumed to have some stable relationships to the various nonbehavioral measures; these relationships may be causal, interactional, or merely one of covariance. It is further presumed that the criteria and their relationships are not entirely unique to each organization, nor transient, but are to some degree stable and to some extent common to all or many organizations. These presumptions appear to have some partial confirmation from analyses performed so far.[4]

We come now to the question of the role of behavioral criteria in the light of this broader conception of the evaluation of organizational performance. It appears that behavioral criteria are not likely, for most business organizations, to have a prominent place in the roster of penultimate criteria although they may and do appear there. Their chief role will arise from their power to improve the prediction of future changes in the preferred "hard" criteria, i.e., their power to give advance signals of impending problems or opportunities.

A second use that they may commonly have is to complement the available hard criteria in such a way as to give the manager a more balanced and more inclusive informational basis for his decisions in the case where the hard variable measures are incomplete or not reliable for short-run evaluation.[5]

In some rare instances, the behavioral criteria have to be used exclusively instead of the preferred hard criteria of organizational performance for the reason that measurements of hard criteria are not available at all or not at reasonable cost.

There are three basic strategies that may be applied in formulating a unique version of this general scheme that may be appropriate for a particular organization.

1. There exist several partially developed general theories concerning the survival requirements of organizations. These assumed requirements may be defined in performance terms and posited as the roster of penultimate criteria or organizational goals. From this starting point, a set of subsidiary goals and performance criteria may be constructed on empirical grounds, on theoretical grounds, or on some combination of the two.

2. The existing personal values of the owners of a firm, or of the managers as representatives, may be pooled to form an agreed upon

roster of penultimate criteria together with their corresponding performance indicators, and from this starting point the set of subsidiary goals and performance criteria can be constructed.

3. Comparative empirical study can be made of the performance characteristics of a set of organizations assumed to share the same ultimate criterion but clearly differing in their overall success as judged by competent observers (for example, such a study might be made of a set of insurance sales agencies, some clearly prospering and others clearly headed for business failure). Using factorial analysis methods and actual performance data to identify the sets of lower-order performance criteria, and using trend and correlational analyses to detect the relationships among these sets of criteria over time, one can, in principle, draw conclusions about the penultimate components of performance that bear upon organizational survival or failure in that particular line of business.

ALTERNATIVE THEORETICAL APPROACHES

These three approaches can and do produce strikingly different systems for describing the network of criteria to be used in evaluating organizational performance. One of the general theories, for example, proposes that there are nine basic requirements to be met, or problems to be continuously solved, for an organization to achieve its long run goals; these include such requirements as adequate input of resources, adequate normative integration, adequate means of moderation of organizational strain, adequate coordination among parts of the organization, etc. Theories of this kind are produced mainly by general organizational sociologists and stem from the view that an organization is a living system with intrinsic goals and requirements that may be unlike those of individual members. By contrast, the second mentioned approach stems from the personal values of managers. The resulting networks of criteria are different.[6]

A start has been made at the Institute for Social Research in exploring such alternative strategies. With respect to the first approach, two theoretical models have been tested against empirical data from a set of organizations in a service industry, using executive judgments of unit overall effectiveness as the ultimate criterion. Both models proved to be about equally valid, but of limited utility in explaining variance on the ultimate criterion: each "accounted for" about half of the ultimate criterion variance, with the unexplained portion arising from measurement errors and/or faulty theory. An attempt to apply the wholly empirical approach to the same set of data proved to be a failure in the sense that it was no more powerful in explaining variance on the ultimate criterion than were the simpler, theory based models, and furthermore the resulting roster of performance dimensions was not very satisfactory in common-sense terms.

A third effort is now in progress, using objective data about the performance of a set of insurance sales agencies over a span of twelve years;

the early results look very promising on first examination. It appears that there will be identified a roster of about ten penultimate criteria of agency performance, each independent of the others and of varying weight in relation to ultimate performance, and each associated with a roster of subsidiary criteria of kinds that lend themselves to ready measurement and statistical combination. It remains to be seen whether these criteria are unique to this particular line of business, or have some applicability to other kinds of organizations.

NOTES AND REFERENCES

1. Many firms' current operating and financial statistics, although appropriate for control and accounting purposes, prove to be of little value for performance evaluation for the reason that they are short-period measures of unstable performances. Monthly plant maintenance costs, for example, may be extremely variable (perhaps seasonal) and may be useful as a performance criterion measure only when applied to longer periods of time. In the short run, apart from other considerations, low maintenance costs may or may not be a favorable indicator.

2. By trade-off value we mean only that an amount of one kind of performance may be substituted for an amount of another; for example, an increase in sales volume may be judged to offset a decline in profit rate per sales unit.

3. One large U.S. firm has published what appears to be a carefully considered formulation of its own roster of assessment criteria at this penultimate level. It includes one behavioral category, "employee attitudes," which is further defined in operational terms in a manner compatible with the system outlined here.

4. See "Applying Modern Management Principles to Sales Organizations," Foundation for Research on Human Behavior seminar report, 1963, for an illustration of the similarity across three sales organizations in the relevance of behavioral measures to hard penultimate criteria of organizational performance. Also, "Models of Organization Performance," an unpublished manuscript by Basil Georgopoulos, Stanley Seashore, and Bernard Indik; and "Relationships Among Criteria of Job Performance," by Stanley Seashore, Bernard Indik, and Basil Georgopoulos, *Journal of Applied Psychology*, 44 (1960), pp. 195–202.

5. As an example, a decision to raise prices is likely to rest not only upon estimates of hard performances, past and future, but also upon estimates of political and economic climate, of customer loyalty, of the feasibility of alternatives such as employee collaboration in cost reduction, etc.

6. To illustrate, take the criterion of profit: in one case, profit is likely to be treated as one of a few penultimate criteria (ends valued in their own right), while in the other case profit is relegated to a subsidiary role as one of several alternative means for insuring adequate input of resources. If this seems implausible, note that some organizations—government, educational, and religious organizations, for example—have survived and prospered without profit from their own activities.

21

Human Organizational Measurements: Key to Financial Success

Rensis Likert

A significant objective of the control process is to identify deviations from planned objectives. Clearly the sooner a deviation is identified the more rapidly a correction can be made. In this article Rensis Likert suggests that we need no longer rely on "after-the-fact" measurements to tell us of problems. By measuring certain aspects of the human part of the organization, it may be possible to identify future problems in advance and greatly improve upon our control processes.—Eds.

Managers and administrators need no longer wait until "after-the-fact" measurements tell them that they are in trouble before taking corrective steps. All performance, accounting, and financial data are after-the-fact measurements. They reveal the state of a department or organization as it was *yesterday*. As a consequence, often before a problem becomes sufficiently clear to be recognized, it has reached serious proportions.

Recent research developments in the social sciences, however, now can enable any administrator to have data one or more years in advance of trouble. These data can reveal the operating and performance problems which his organization is likely to encounter, the probable causes of these problems, and the steps which if taken now will correct the situation and prevent the problem from developing.

SOURCE: Reprinted by permission from the May 1971, issue of the *Michigan Business Review,* published by the Graduate School of Business Administration, The University of Michigan.

These *lead time data* are measurements of the state of the human organization of an agency or department. They include such measurements as the leadership behavior of administrators and reveal the extent to which the agency is capable of performing in a highly efficient, productive manner. These measurements of the human organization are objective, impartial, and replicable. They can be used to:

1. Reveal the extent to which the organization as a whole and each of its administrators and supervisors are using managerial principles and practices which yield the highest productivity and the best performance. They will show how well each manager or administrator is building his subordinates into a highly motivated, highly effective unit.

2. Provide evidence concerning the condition for each firm, department, or subordinate unit of such variables as communication, decision making, attitudes and loyalty, motivation, performance goals, and commitment to the organization's success.

3. Increase the lead time by one to three years concerning awareness of operational and performance problems caused by deterioration of the human organization and its productive capability. Lead time measurements will reveal problems at their early stages, point to the major causes of each incipient problem, provide clues to the course of action most likely to correct the situation, show at an early stage how effective each attempt to solve a problem is proving to be, and indicate the further steps likely to bring additional improvement.

4. Reveal the extent to which greater productivity and better performance represent true improvement, in contrast to that achieved by costly liquidation of the human organization.

5. Establish the basis for improving the compensation of managers and supervisors by providing more objective and more accurate data concerning the effectiveness of each administrator's managerial practices.

6. Improve labor relations by facilitating early awareness of problem situations, more accurate diagnosis of their causes, and early action of a remedial character.

7. Detect at an early stage new innovative improvements in organizational structure or in managerial or supervisory behavior. This early detection of better principles and methods of administration will enable the more rapid dissemination of these principles and methods to other parts of the organization. In this manner, all managers and supervisors in the organization can be aided in rapidly adopting better practices.

MANAGEMENT AND ACHIEVEMENT

These and similar uses of lead time measurements are based on the capacity of these measurements to describe correctly the condition of the human organization of a firm and to predict the trends in the performance capability of that firm. A large number of studies of business firms and governmental agencies by the Institute for Social Research, involving thousands of managers and tens of thousands of employees, reveal a relatively consistent relationship between the leadership style and management system of a business firm and the extent to which the organization is able to achieve its objectives fully and efficiently. In widely different kinds of organizations, the managers who are achieving the greatest productivity, lowest cost, best quality of operation, and best labor relations are using the same basic principles of management. These principles differ significantly from those used by managers who achieve average or below average performance.

The kind of organization created by the most successful managers can be described briefly: This human system is made up of interlocking work groups with a high degree of group loyalty among members and favorable attitudes and trust between supervisors and subordinates. Sensitivity to others and relatively high levels of skill in personal interaction and the functioning of groups also are present. These skills permit effective participation in decisions on common problems. Participation is used, for example, to establish organizational objectives which are a satisfactory integration of the needs and desires of all members of the organization and of persons functionally related to it. High levels of reciprocal influence occur, and high levels of total coordinated influence are achieved in the organization. Responsibility for the organization's success is felt individually by the members and each initiates action, when necessary to assure that the organization accomplishes its objectives. Communication is efficient and effective. There is a flow from one part of the organization to another of all relevant information important for each decision and action. The leadership in the organization has developed what might well be called a highly effective social system for interaction and mutual influence.

The system of management based on this theory has been labelled "System 4" for convenient reference. Prevailing systems of management and administration which are more authoritarian in character will be referred to as "System 2." System 4 is an appreciably more effective management system than is System 2.

SIGNIFICANCE OF TRENDS

These relationships between the management systems of an organization and the excellence of its performance are, however, *much more marked if trends and relationships over time* are examined instead of using measurements made only at one point in time.

In a recent study of a continuous process plant, for example, the relationship was examined between managerial behavior and cost performance of 40 departments. When both measurements were obtained at the same point in time, the relationships were so slight as to be not statistically significant. But when these measurements of managerial behavior obtained in 1966 were related to cost performance by departments in 1967, i.e., one year later, one fourth of the variation in costs among departments was accounted for by the behavior of the managers one year earlier. When the time interval was two years, one-half of the variation in costs among departments could be attributed to managerial behavior two years earlier.

These findings and other recent studies reveal that measurements of such causal variables as the behavior of administrators and supervisors can be used to predict subsequent trends in organizational performance. As a consequence, these measurements are highly valuable for the uses suggested for lead time purposes.

Any business firm, governmental agency, or educational institution that wishes to do so can use both lead time human organizational measurements and System 4 to achieve excellent performance at low cost. A number of studies show that when an organization does this, productivity is higher and costs lower by 15 to 30 percent or more. The use of System 4 and human organizational measurements can pay off handsomely.

PLANNING-PROGRAMMING-BUDGETING

There are, moreover, other valuable uses of these human organizational measurements which reveal the productive capability of an agency and the probable trends in this capability. For example, these data can be used in conjunction with P.P.B. (Planning-Programming-Budgeting).

P.P.B. is a powerful administrative management tool but it can be effective only in situations where objectives and progress toward their achievement can be expressed in quantitative dimensions. For many governmental operations, it is very difficult, if not impossible, to state organizational objectives so that the extent to which they are being achieved can be measured quantitatively and at a reasonable cost. When this condition exists, it is still possible to make effective use of the powerful resources of P.P.B. This involves shifting the P.P.B activity from focusing on end-result variables to dealing with human organizational variables. For this purpose, all of the major human organizational variables should be used, including both *causal*—such as managerial behavior—and *intervening*—such as communication, motivation, and control.

This application of the human organizational variables as the fundamental dimension for P.P.B. is based on the substantial body of research findings which show that when an organization is functioning well, as revealed by measurements of its human organizational variables, it is, or soon will be, achieving its performance, service, and other end-result objectives well. This application of P.P.B. requires that objectives be stated and progress toward their achievement measured in terms of human organizational variables. To date, this combined use of P.P.B. and human organizational variables has not been tried. It is, however, perfectly feasible and is likely to yield highly profitable results.

P.P.B. is used commonly in situations where some, but not all, of the objectives of an organization can be dealt with quantitatively. In some of these situations, P.P.B. may work well. In many, however, it may give the appearance of working well when its use is actually producing costly adverse consequences. This occurs when P.P.B. causes an agency to focus its efforts on activities which, when carried out, may achieve the quantitatively stated subobjective, but with considerable adverse consequences so far as the total objectives of the organization are concerned.

IMPACTS OF COST REDUCTION PROGRAM

The typical cost reduction program can be used to illustrate this point. These cost reduction programs, like P.P.B., focused on a quantitatively defined subobjective, usually accomplish their immediate cost reduction goals, but with serious financial losses to the agency or firm. A study was made recently of a typical cost reduction program in a plant of about 700 persons. This cost reduction program employed the usual methods of "tightening up." The work was analyzed with the aid of outside consultants to see whether the work could be reorganized so as to require less labor. This analysis revealed that in some departments savings in labor could be achieved. For each of these departments, teams consisting of persons from other departments, staff and outside consultants were established to study the department and recommend how the estimated labor savings could be achieved. The manager of each affected department was ordered to introduce the specific changes and achieve the designated labor savings. The total annual savings amounted to approximately $250,000.

This saving, viewed by itself, was a nice reduction in costs. But measurements of the human organizational variables for this plant and especially for the departments most affected by the cost reduction effort, showed an appreciable drop. Leadership behavior, motivation, communication, control, coordination, and similar variables all showed an adverse shift. When scores on these variables worsen, research findings show that productivity and earnings drop subsequently. The unfavorable shift in these variables for this plant indicate that an annual drop in earnings of approximately one million dollars is likely to occur in each of the next several years.

Recent data from this plant concerning production, costs, quality, and labor relations indicate that the poorer results forecast by the adverse shift in the human organizational variables are occurring. Moreover, the estimated loss mentioned above understates the total drop since it ignores all losses due to downtime and any losses caused by customer dissatisfaction due to poor quality.

Long range survival and financial success are more important in this company's total objectives than are short range cash flows erroneously labelled "savings." This cash flow was accompanied in this plant by a liquidation of the firm's human assets far greater in amount than the increased cash flow reported as savings. This cost reduction program illustrates the unfavorable consequences to an organization of concentrating on those subobjectives which can be measured with traditional methods, ignoring the extent to which the total objectives are, or are not, being realized.

PROMISE AND PROBLEMS IN P.P.B.

Education is a good example of a situation where it is possible to deal with subobjectives quantitatively, but where it is virtually impossible at any reasonable cost to measure the extent to which each teacher, class, school, and school system is performing efficiently as an educational institution. It is extremely difficult to eliminate or partial out from measurements of educational achievement such influences as each student's native ability and the environment of his home. It is extremely difficult, consequently, and would be prohibitively costly to attempt to measure the overall effectiveness of a school system in achieving its total educational objectives efficiently. For these reasons, P.P.B. cannot be applied to the overall operation of a school system.

P.P.B. is used at present, however, for such specific educational subobjectives as teaching students to read or having a designated proportion of students achieve a specified score on a standardized achievement test. The danger of this use of P.P.B., when only a fractional part of an agency's total objectives is dealt with in quantitative dimensions, is that the subobjective may be accomplished but often serious adverse consequences for the organization's total objectives may ensue. The cost of teaching youngsters to read might be reduced, for example, by focusing intensive effort on it and by putting pressure on each teacher to achieve specified results and on each pupil to learn. Such a program could achieve the P.P.B. objective in reducing the costs of teaching students to read, but it could simultaneously create resentful attitudes in teachers and develop hostile attitudes among students toward reading, school, and education. Hostile attitudes toward schools and education lead to dropouts. If the least costly way of teaching reading led to dropouts years later, it would be a high cost to pay for a 5 percent reduction in the cost of learning to read. This would be as inefficient and undesirable as the typical cost reduction programs which yield immediate cash flows accompanied by financial losses over many subsequent years.

It is perfectly feasible for an organization to use P.P.B. to gain the benefit of achieving some of its subobjectives efficiently, without suffering overall adverse consequences. This requires measurements of both the causal and intervening human organizational variables and their use in conjunction with the P.P.B. effort focused on achieving the subobjective. If these human organizational variables are measured and examined regularly, trends in these variables can be used to prevent costly overall consequences while achieving the subobjective. Thus, when P.P.B. is used to reduce the costs of teaching students to read, measurements of the human organizational variables of the school system should be obtained. If the latter measurements reveal an adverse shift in the motivation, values, attitudes, and behavior of teachers and students, the effort to achieve the specified subobjective should be modified appropriately.

These are a few examples of the use of human organizational variables to improve the capacity of any agency or organization to achieve its objectives efficiently.

PART FIVE

Directing Processes in Management

The directing processes are those which involve guiding employees into activities which will accomplish organizational purposes. Directing is the primary aim of leadership and motivation activities, and therefore, directing activities are more concerned with interpersonal relationships than most other managerial processes. For this reason, directing is much more than telling people what to do; it is, in addition, the creation of an environment which is conducive to the development and utilization of employee resources. Direction is also planned. Directives must be consistent with the previously determined goals of the organization, and further, must be compatible with the structure or organization of the enterprise. And finally, direction must be compatible with and complementary to the control processes of the organization.

Clearly a major topic in directing is that of leadership. Probably no other area of managerial endeavor has received as much interest and emphasis for so long a time as leadership. The earliest writings bearing on leadership date back to approximately 1100 B.C. and the constitution of Chow, indicating the Chinese were cognizant of the importance of this process. Specific principles of leadership and the dysfunctinal consequences of ignoring them were addressed by Sun Tzu around 500 B.C. Since this time numerous writers have studied the process of leadership resulting in a myriad of many times confusing and sometimes contradictory approaches, schools, theories, and styles. Nonetheless, we have made significant studies in this period in understanding the dynamics of leadership.

Leadership is influence, and influence is what we are trying to exert when we talk about motivation. Motivation is an integral part of the directing process and is inseparably intertwined with leadership. Motivation may be thought of as external (something we do to someone) and typified by the carrot-and-stick approach, or it may be conceived as internal (something someone does to himself) and typified by the behavioral science approaches. In either case, how the manager chooses to approach the question of motivation is very much a function of his or her own leadership orientation interacting with the nature of (1) the task to be done, (2) the employees performing the task, and (3) the environment in which the work is taking place.

Questions of influence, leadership, authority, and motivation, then, are very much involved in the management processes of directing. The articles in this section reflect this fact. They also reflect the fact that while we still have much to learn about directing the activities of people in work organizations, we already have learned a great deal.

A. Motivating

22

A Theory of Human Motivation

Abraham H. Maslow

A classic among classics, Maslow's article sets forth the well known idea that all human needs may be grouped into five major categories which, in turn, are arranged into a hierarchy of importance so that the needs at one level must be minimally satisfied before higher level needs become active. This is important because, according to Maslow, only unsatisfied needs are motivators of behavior. The article includes an important discussion of the implications of the theory.—Eds.

In a previous paper (13) various propositions were presented which would have to be included in any theory of human motivation that could lay claim to being definitive. These conclusions may be briefly summarized as follows:

1. The integrated wholeness of the organism must be one of the foundation stones of motivation theory.

2. The hunger drive (or any other physiological drive) was rejected as a centering point or model for a definitive theory of motivation. Any drive that is somatically based and localizable was shown to be atypical rather than typical in human motivation.

3. Such a theory should stress and center itself upon ultimate or basic goals rather than partial or superficial ones, upon ends rather than means to these ends. Such a stress would imply a more central place for unconscious than for conscious motivations.

SOURCE: Abraham H. Maslow, "A Theory of Human Motivation," *Psychological Review,* Vol. 50 (1943), pp. 370–96. Copyright 1943 by the American Psychological Association. Reprinted by permission.

4. There are usually available various cultural paths to the same goal. Therefore conscious, specific, local-cultural desires are not as fundamental in motivation theory as the more basic, unconscious goals.

5. Any motivated behavior, either preparatory or consummatory, must be understood to be a channel through which many basic needs may be simultaneously expressed or satisfied. Typically an act has *more* than one motivation.

6. Practically all organismic states are to be understood as motivated and as motivating.

7. Human needs arrange themselves in hierarchies of prepotency. That is to say, the appearance of one need usually rests on the prior satisfaction of another, more prepotent need. Man is a perpetually wanting animal. Also no need or drive can be treated as if it were isolated or discrete; every drive is related to the state of satisfaction or dissatisfaction of other drives.

8. *Lists* of drives will get us nowhere for various theoretical and practical reasons. Furthermore any classification of motivations must deal with the problem of levels of specificity or generalization of the motives to be classified.

9. Classifications of motivations must be based upon goals rather than upon instigating drives or motivated behavior.

10. Motivation theory should be human-centered rather than animal-centered.

11. The situation or the field in which the organism reacts must be taken into account but the field alone can rarely serve as an exclusive explanation for behavior. Furthermore the field itself must be interpreted in terms of the organism. Field theory cannot be a substitute for motivation theory.

12. Not only the integration of the organism must be taken into account, but also the possibility of isolated, specific, partial or segmental reactions.

It has since become necessary to add to these another affirmation.

13. Motivation theory is not synonymous with behavior theory. The motivations are only one class of determinants of behavior. While behavior is almost always motivated, it is also almost always biologically, culturally and situationally determined as well.

The present paper is an attempt to formulate a positive theory of motivation which will satisfy these theoretical demands and at the same time conform to the known facts, clinical and observational as well as experimental. It derives most directly, however, from clinical experience. This theory is, I think, in the functionalist tradition of James and Dewey, and is fused with the holism of Wertheimer (19), Goldstein (6), and Gestalt Psychology, and with the dymamicism of Freud (4) and Adler (1). This fusion or synthesis may arbitrarily be called a 'general-dynamic' theory.

It is far easier to perceive and to criticize the aspects in motivation theory than to remedy them. Mostly this is because of the very serious lack of sound data in this area. I conceive this lack of sound facts to be due primarily to the absence of a valid theory of motivation. The present theory then must be considered to be a suggested program or framework for future research and must stand or fall, not so much on facts available or evidence presented, as upon researches yet to be done, researches suggested perhaps by the questions raised in this paper.

THE BASIC NEEDS

The 'Physiological' Needs

The needs that are usually taken as the starting point for motivation theory are the so-called physiological drives. Two recent lines of research make it necessary to revise our customary notions about these needs, first, the development of the concept of homeostasis, and second, the finding that appetites (preferential choices among foods) are a fairly efficient indication of actual needs or lacks in the body.

Homeostasis refers to the body's automatic efforts to maintain a constant, normal state of the blood stream. Cannon (2) has described this process for (1) the water content of the blood, (2) salt content, (3) sugar content, (4) protein content, (5) fat content, (6) calcium content, (7) oxygen content, (8) constant hydrogen-ion level (acid-base balance) and (9) constant temperature of the blood. Obviously this list can be extended to include other minerals, the hormones, vitamins, etc.

Young in a recent article (21) has summarized the work on appetite in its relation to body needs. If the body lacks some chemical, the individual will tend to develop a specific appetite or partial hunger for that food element.

Thus it seems impossible as well as useless to make any list of fundamental physiological needs for they can come to almost any number one might wish, depending on the degree of specificity of description. We cannot identify all physiological needs as homeostatic. That sexual desire, sleepiness, sheer activity and maternal behavior in animals, are homeostatic, has not yet been demonstrated. Furthermore, this list would not include the various sensory pleasures (tastes, smells, tickling, stroking) which are probably physiological and which may become the goals of motivated behavior.

In a previous paper (13) it has been pointed out that these physiological drives or needs are to be considered unusual rather than typical because they are isolable, and because they are localizable somatically. That is to say, they are relatively independent of each other, of other motivations and of the organism as a whole, and secondly, in many cases, it is possible to demonstrate a localized, underlying somatic base for the drive. This is true less generally than has been thought (exceptions are fatigue, sleepiness, maternal responses) but it is still true in the classic instances of hunger, sex, and thirst.

It should be pointed out again that any of the physiological needs and the consummatory behavior involved with them serve as channels for all sorts of other needs as well. That is to say, the person who thinks he is hungry may actually be seeking more for comfort, or dependence, than for vitamins or proteins. Conversely, it is possible to satisfy the hunger need in part by other activities such as drinking water or smoking cigarettes. In other words, relatively isolable as these physiological needs are, they are not completely so.

Undoubtedly these physiological needs are the most prepotent of all needs. What this means specifically is that in the human being who is missing everything in life in an extreme fashion, it is most likely that the major motivation would be the physiological needs rather than any others. A person who is lacking food, safety, love, and esteem would most probably hunger for food more strongly than for anything else.

If all the needs are unsatisfied, and the organism is then dominated by the physiological needs, all other needs may become simply nonexistent or be pushed into the background. It is then fair to characterize the whole organism by saying simply that it is hungry, for consciousness is almost completely preempted by hunger. All capacities are put into the service of hunger-satisfaction, and the organization of these capacities is almost entirely determined by the one purpose of satisfying hunger. The receptors and effectors, the intelligence, memory, habits, all may now be defined simply as hunger-gratifying tools. Capacities that are not useful for this purpose lie dormant, or are pushed into the background. The urge to write poetry, the desire to acquire an automobile, the interest in American history, the desire for a new pair of shoes are, in the extreme case, forgotten or become of secondary importance. For the man who is extremely and dangerously hungry, no other interests exist but food. He dreams food, he remembers food, he thinks about food, he emotes only about food, he perceives only food and he wants only food. The more subtle determinants that ordinarily fuse with the physiological drives in organizing even feeding, drinking or sexual behavior, may now be so completely overwhelmed as to allow us to speak at this time (but *only* at this time) of pure hunger drive and behavior, with the one unqualified aim of relief.

Another peculiar characteristic of the human organism when it is dominated by a certain need is that the whole philosophy of the future tends also to change. For our chronically and extremely hungry man, Utopia can be defined very simply as a place where there is plenty of food. He tends to think that if only he is guaranteed food for the rest of his life, he will be perfectly happy and will never want anything more. Life itself tends to be defined in terms of eating. Anything else will be defined as unimportant. Freedom, love, community feeling, respect, philosophy, may all be waved aside as fripperies which are useless since they fail to fill the stomach. Such a man may fairly be said to live by bread alone.

It cannot possibly be denied that such things are true but their *generality* can be denied. Emergency conditions are, almost by definition, rare in the normally functioning peaceful society. That this truism can be forgotten is due mainly to two reasons. First, rats have few motivations other than physiological ones, and since so much of the research upon motivation has been made with these animals, it is easy to carry the rat picture over to the human being. Secondly, it is too often not realized that culture itself is an adaptive tool, one of whose main functions is to make the physiological emergencies come less and less often. In most of the known societies, chronic extreme hunger of the emergency type is rare, rather than common. In any case, this is still true in the United States. The average American citizen is experiencing appetite rather than hunger when he says "I am hungry." He is apt to experience sheer life-and-death hunger only by accident and then only a few times through his entire life.

Obviously a good way to obscure the 'higher' motivations, and to get a lopsided view of human capacities and human nature, is to make the organism extremely and chronically hungry or thirsty. Anyone who attempts to make an emergency picture into a typical one, and who will measure all of man's goals and desires by his behavior during extreme physiological deprivation is certainly being blind to many things. It is quite true that man lives by bread alone—when there is no bread. But what happens to man's desires when there *is* plenty of bread and when his belly is chronically filled?

At once other (and 'higher') needs emerge and these, rather than physiological hungers, dominate the organism. And when these in turn are satisfied, again new (and still 'higher') needs emerge and so on. This is what we mean by saying that the basic human needs are organized into a hierarchy of relative prepotency.

One main implication of this phrasing is that gratification becomes as important a concept as deprivation in motivation theory, for it releases the organism from the domination of a relatively more physiological need, permitting thereby the emergence of other more social goals. The physiological needs, along with their partial goals, when chronically gratified cease to exist as active determinants or organizers of behavior. They now exist only in a potential fashion in the sense that they may emerge again to dominate the organism if they are thwarted. But a want that is satisfied is no longer a want. The organism is dominated and its behavior organized only by unsatisfied needs. If hunger is satisfied, it becomes unimportant in the current dynamics of the individual.

This statement is somewhat qualified by a hypothesis to be discussed more fully later, namely that it is precisely those individuals in whom a certain need has always been satisfied who are best equipped to tolerate deprivation of that need in the future, and that furthermore, those who have been deprived in the past will react differently to current satisfactions than the one who has never been deprived.

The Safety Needs

If the physiological needs are relatively well gratified, there then emerges a new set of needs, which we may categorize roughly as the safety needs. All that has been said of the physiological needs is equally true, although in lesser degree, of these desires. The organism may equally well be wholly dominated by them. They may serve as the almost exclusive organizers of behavior, recruiting all the capacities of the organism in their service, and we may then fairly describe the whole organism as a safety-seeking mechanism. Again we may say of the receptors, the effectors, of the intellect and the other capacities that they are primarily safety-seeking tools. Again, as in the hungry man, we find that the dominating goal is a strong determinant not only of his current world outlook and philosophy but also of his philosophy of the future. Practically everything looks less important than safety (even sometimes the physiological needs which, being satisfied, are now underestimated). A man, in this state, if it is extreme enough and chronic enough, may be characterized as living almost for safety alone.

Although in this paper we are interested primarily in the needs of the adult, we can approach an understanding of his safety needs perhaps more efficiently by observation of infants and children, in whom these needs are much more simple and obvious. One reason for the clearer appearance of the threat or danger reaction in infants is that they do not inhibit this reaction at all, whereas adults in our society have been taught to inhibit it at all costs. Thus even when adults do feel their safety to be threatened we may not be able to see this on the surface. Infants will react in a total fashion and as if they were endangered, if they are disturbed or dropped suddenly, startled by loud noises, flashing light, or other unusual sensory stimulation, by rough handling, by general loss of support in the mother's arms, or by inadequate support.[1]

In infants we can also see a much more direct reaction to bodily illnesses of various kinds. Sometimes these illnesses seem to be immediately and per se threatening and seem to make the child feel unsafe. For instance, vomiting, colic or other sharp pains seem to make the child look at the whole world in a different way. At such a moment of pain, it may be postulated that, for the child, the appearance of the whole world suddenly changes from sunniness to darkness, so to speak, and becomes a place in which anything at all might happen, in which previously stable things have suddenly become unstable. Thus a child who because of some bad food is taken ill may, for a day or two, develop fear, nightmares, and a need for protection and reassurance never seen in him before his illness.

Another indication of the child's need for safety is his preference for some kind of undisrupted routine or rhythm. He seems to want a predictable, orderly world. For instance, injustice, unfairness, or inconsistency in the parents seems to make a child feel anxious and unsafe. This attitude may be not so much because of the injustice per se or any particular pains involved, but rather because this treatment threatens to make the world look unreliable, or unsafe, or unpredictable. Young children seem to thrive better under a system which has at least a skeletal outline of rigidity, in which there is a schedule of a kind, some sort of routine, something that can be counted upon, not only for the present but also far into the future. Perhaps one could express this more accurately by saying that the child needs an organized world rather than an unorganized or unstructured one.

The central role of the parents and the normal family setup are indisputable. Quarreling, physical assault, separation, divorce or death within the family may be particularly terrifying. Also parental outbursts of rage or threats of punishment directed to the child, calling him names, speaking to him harshly, shaking him, handling him roughly, or actual physical punishment sometimes elicit such total panic and terror in the child that we must assume more is involved than the physical pain alone. While it is true that in some children this terror may represent also a fear of loss of parental love, it can also occur in completely rejected children, who seem to cling to the hating parents more for sheer safety and protection than because of hope of love.

Confronting the average child with new, unfamiliar, strange, unmanageable stimuli or situations will too frequently elicit the danger or terror reaction, as for example, getting lost or even being separated from the parents for a short time, being confronted with new faces, new situations or new tasks, the sight of strange, unfamiliar or uncontrollable objects, illness or death. Particularly at such times, the child's frantic clinging to his parents is eloquent testimony to their role as protectors (quite apart from their roles as food-givers and love-givers).

From these and similar observations, we may generalize and say that the average child in our society generally prefers a safe, orderly, predictable, organized world, which he can count on, and in which unexpected, unmanageable or other dangerous things do not happen, and in which, in any case, he has all-powerful parents who protect and shield him from harm.

That these reactions may so easily be observed in children is in a way a proof of the fact that children in our society feel too unsafe (or, in a word, are badly brought up). Children who are reared in an unthreatening, loving family do *not* ordinarily react as we have described above (17). In such children the danger reactions are apt to come mostly to objects or situations that adults too would consider dangerous.[2]

The healthy, normal, fortunate adult in our culture is largely satisfied in his safety needs. The peaceful, smoothly running, 'good' society ordinarily makes its members feel safe enough from wild animals, extremes of temperature, criminals, assault and murder, tyranny, etc. Therefore, in a very real sense, he no longer has any safety needs as active motivators. Just as a sated man no longer feels hungry, a safe man no longer feels endangered. If we wish to see these needs directly and clearly we must turn to neurotic or near-neurotic individuals, and to the economic and social underdogs. In between these extremes, we can perceive the expressions of safety needs only in such phenomena as, for instance, the common preference for a job with tenure and protection, the desire for a savings account, and for insurance of various kinds (medical, dental, unemployment, disability, old age).

Other broader aspects of the attempt to seek safety and stability in the world are seen in the very common preference for familiar rather than unfamiliar things, or for the known rather than the unknown. The tendency to have some religion or world-philosophy that organizes the universe and the men in it into some sort of satisfactorily coherent, meaningful whole is also in part motivated by safety-seeking. Here too we may list science and philosophy in general as partially motivated by the safety needs (we shall see later that there are also other motivations to scientific, philosophical or religious endeavor).

Otherwise the need for safety is seen as an active and dominant mobilizer of the organism's resources only in emergencies, e.g., war, disease, natural catastrophies, crime waves, societal disorganization, neurosis, brain injury, chronically bad situation.

Some neurotic adults in our society are, in many ways, like the unsafe child in their desire for safety, although in the former it takes on a somewhat special appearance. Their reaction is often to unknown, psychological dangers in a world that is perceived to be hostile, overwhelming and threatening. Such a person behaves as if a great catastrophe were almost always impending, i.e., he is usually responding as if to an emergency. His safety needs often find specific expression in a search for a protector, or a stronger person on whom he may depend, or perhaps, a Fuehrer.

The neurotic individual may be described in a slightly different way with some usefulness as a grownup person who retains his childish attitudes toward the world. That is to say, a neurotic adult may be said to behave 'as if' he were actually afraid of a spanking, or of his mother's disapproval, or of being abandoned by his parents, or having his food taken away from him. It is as if his childish attitudes of fear and threat reaction to a dangerous world had gone underground, and untouched by the growing up and learning processes, were now ready to be called out by any stimulus that would make a child feel endangered and threatened.[3]

The neurosis in which the search for safety takes its clearest form is in the compulsive-obsessive neurosis. Compulsive-obsessives try frantically to order and stabilize the world so that no unmanageable, unexpected or unfamiliar dangers will ever appear (14). They hedge themselves about with all sorts of ceremonials, rules and formulas so that every possible contingency may be provided for and so that no new contingencies may appear. They are much like the brain injured cases, described by Goldstein (6), who manage to maintain their equilibrium by avoiding everything unfamiliar and strange and by ordering their restricted world in such a neat, disciplined, orderly fashion that everything in the world can be counted upon. They try to arrange the world so that anything unexpected (dangers) cannot possibly occur. If, through no fault of their own, something unexpected does occur, they go into a panic reaction as if this unexpected occurrence constituted a grave danger. What we can see only as a none too strong preference in the healthy person, e.g., preference for the familiar, becomes a life-and-death necessity in abnormal cases.

The Love Needs

If both the physiological and the safety needs are fairly well gratified, then there will emerge the love and affection and belongingness needs, and the whole cycle already described will repeat itself with this new center. Now the person will feel keenly, as never before, the absence of friends, or a sweetheart, or a wife, or children. He will hunger for affectionate relations with people in general, namely, for a place in his group, and he will strive with great intensity to achieve this goal. He will want to attain such a place more than anything else in the world and may even forget that once, when he was hungry, he sneered at love.

In our society the thwarting of these needs is the most commonly found core in cases of maladjustment and more severe psychopathology. Love and affection, as well as their possible expression in sexuality, are generally looked upon with ambivalence and are customarily hedged about with many restrictions and inhibitions. Practically all theorists of psychopathology have stressed thwarting of the love needs as basic in the picture of maladjustment. Many clinical studies have therefore been made of this need and we know more about it perhaps than any of the other needs except the physiological ones (14).

One thing that must be stressed at this point is that love is not synonymous with sex. Sex may be studied as a purely physiological need. Ordinarily sexual behavior is multidetermined, that is to say, determined not only by sexual but also by other needs, chief among which are the love and affection needs. Also not to be overlooked is the fact that the love needs involve both giving *and* receiving love.[4]

The Esteem Needs

All people in our society (with a few pathological exceptions) have a need or desire for a stable, firmly based, (usually) high evaluation of themselves, for self-respect, or self-esteem, and for the esteem of others. By firmly based self-esteem, we mean that which is soundly based upon real capacity, achievement and respect from others. These needs may be classified into two subsidiary sets. These are, first, the desire for strength, for achievement, for adequacy, for confidence in the face of the world, and for independence and freedom.[5] Secondly, we have what we may call the desire for reputation or prestige (defining it as respect or esteem from other people), recognition, attention, importance or appreciation.[6] These needs have been relatively stressed by Alfred Adler and his followers, and have been relatively neglected by Freud and the psychoanalysts. More and more today however there is appearing widespread appreciation of their central importance.

Satisfaction of the self-esteem need leads to feelings of self-confidence, worth, strength, capability and adequacy of being useful and necessary in the world. But thwarting of these needs produces feelings of inferiority, of weakness and of helplessness. These feelings in turn give rise to either basic discouragement or else compensatory or neurotic trends. An appreciation of the necessity of basic self-confidence and an understanding of how helpless people are without it, can be easily gained from a study of severe traumatic neurosis (8).[7]

The Need for Self-Actualization

Even if all these needs are satisfied, we may still often (if not always) expect that a new discontent and restlessness will soon develop, unless the individual is doing what he is fitted for. A musician must make music, an artist must paint, a poet must write, if he is to be ultimately happy. What a man *can* be, he *must* be. This need we may call self-actualization.

This term, first coined by Kurt Goldstein, is being used in this paper in a much more specific and limited fashion. It refers to the desire for self-fulfillment, namely, to the tendency for him [a person] to become actualized in what he is potentially. This tendency might be phrased as the desire to become more and more what one is, to become everything that one is capable of becoming.

The specific form that these needs will take will of course vary greatly from person to person. In one individual it may take the form of the desire to be an ideal mother, in another it may be expressed athletically, and in still another it may be expressed in painting pictures or in inventions. It is not necessarily a creative urge although in people who have any capacities for creation it will take this form.

The clear emergence of these needs rests upon prior satisfaction of the physiological, safety, love and esteem needs. We shall call people who are satisfied in these needs, basically satisfied people, and it is from these that we may expect the fullest (and healthiest) creativeness.[8] Since, in our society, basically satisfied people are the exception, we do not know much about self-actualization, either experimentally or clinically. It remains a challenging problem for research.

The Preconditions for the Basic Need Satisfactions

There are certain conditions which are immediate prerequisites for the basic need satisfactions. Danger to these is reacted to almost as if it were a direct danger to the basic needs themselves. Such conditions as freedom to speak, freedom to do what one wishes so long as no harm is done to others, freedom to express one's self, freedom to investigate and seek for information, freedom to defend one's self, justice, fairness, honesty, orderliness in the group are examples of such preconditions for basic need satisfactions. Thwarting in these freedoms will be reacted to with a threat or emergency response. These conditions are not ends in themselves but they are *almost* so since they are so closely related to the basic needs, which are apparently the only ends in themselves. These conditions are defended because without them the basic satisfactions are quite impossible, or at least, very severely endangered.

If we remember that the cognitive capacities (perceptual, intellectual, learning) are a set of adjustive tools, which have among other functions, that of satisfaction of our basic needs, then it is clear that any danger to them, any deprivation or blocking of their free use, must also be indirectly threatening to the basic needs themselves. Such a statement is a partial solution of the general problems of curiosity, the search for knowledge, truth and wisdom, and the ever-persistent urge to solve the cosmic mysteries.

We must therefore introduce another hypothesis and speak of degrees of closeness to the basic needs, for we have already pointed out that *any* conscious desires (partial goals) are more or less important as they are more or less close to the basic needs. The same statement may be made for various behavior acts. An act is psychologically important if it contributes directly to satisfaction of basic needs. The less directly it so contributes, or the weaker this contribution is, the less important this act must be conceived to be from the point of view of dynamic psychology. A similar statement may be made for the various defense or coping mechanisms. Some are very directly related to the protection or attainment of the basic needs, others are only weakly and distantly related. Indeed if we wished, we could speak of more basic and less basic defense mechanisms, and then affirm that danger to the more basic defenses is more threatening than danger to less basic defenses (always remembering that this is so only because of their relationship to the basic needs).

The Desires to Know and to Understand

So far, we have mentioned the cognitive needs only in passing. Acquiring knowledge and systematizing the universe have been considered as, in part, techniques for the achievement of basic safety in the world, or, for the intelligent man, expressions of self-actualization. Also freedom of inquiry and expression have been discussed as preconditions of satisfactions of the basic needs. True though these formulations may be, they do not constitute definitive answers to the question as to the motivation role of curiosity, learning, philosophizing, experimenting, etc. They are, at best, no more than partial answers.

This question is especially difficult because we know so little about the facts. Curiosity, exploration, desire for the facts, desire to know may certainly be observed easily enough. The fact that they often are pursued even at great cost to the individual's safety is an earnest of the partial character of our previous discussion. In addition, the writer must admit that, though he has sufficient clinical evidence to postulate the desire to know as a very strong drive in intelligent people, no data are available for unintelligent people. It may then be largely a function of relatively high intelligence. Rather tentatively, then, and largely in the hope of stimulating discussion and research, we shall postulate a basic desire to know, to be aware of reality, to get the facts, to satisfy curiosity, or as Wertheimer phrases it, to see rather than to be blind.

This postulation, however, is not enough. Even after we know, we are impelled to know more and more minutely and microscopically on the one hand, and on the other, more and more extensively in the direction of a world philosophy, religion, etc. The facts that we acquire, if they are isolated or atomistic, inevitably get theorized about, and either analyzed or organized or both. This process has been phrased by some as the search for 'meaning.' We shall then postulate a desire to understand, to systematize, to organize, to analyze, to look for relations and meanings.

Once these desires are accepted for discussion, we see that they too form themselves into a small hierarchy in which the desire to know is prepotent over the desire to understand. All the characteristics of a hierarchy of prepotency that we have described above, seem to hold for this one as well.

We must guard ourselves against the too easy tendency to separate these desires from the basic needs we have discussed above, i.e., to make a sharp dichotomy between 'cognitive' and 'conative' needs. The desires to know and to understand are themselves conative, i.e., have a striving character, and are as much personality needs as the 'basic needs' we have already discussed (19).

FURTHER CHARACTERISTICS OF THE BASIC NEEDS

The Degree of Fixity of the Hierarchy of Basic Needs

We have spoken so far as if this hierarchy were a fixed order but actually it is not nearly as rigid as we may have implied. It is true that most of the people with whom we have worked have seemed to have these basic needs in about the order that has been indicated. However, there have been a number of exceptions.

(1) There are some people in whom, for instance, self-esteem seems to be more important than love. This most common reversal in the hierarchy is usually due to the development of the notion that the person who is most likely to be loved is a strong or powerful person, one who inspires respect or fear, and who is self-confident or aggressive. Therefore such people who lack love and seek it, may try hard to put on a front of aggressive, confident behavior. But essentially they seek high self-esteem and its behavior expressions more as a means to an end than for its own sake; they seek self-assertion for the sake of love rather than for self-esteem itself.

(2) There are other, apparently innately creative people in whom the drive to creativeness seems to be more important than any other counter-determinant. Their creativeness might appear not as self-actualization released by basic satisfaction, but in spite of lack of basic satisfaction.

(3) In certain people the level of aspiration may be permanently deadened or lowered. That is to say, the less prepotent goals may simply be lost, and may disappear forever, so that the person who has experienced life at a very low level, i.e., chronic unemployment, may continue to be satisfied for the rest of his life if only he can get enough food.

(4) The so-called psychopathic personality is another example of permanent loss of the love needs. These are people who, according to the best data available (9), have been starved for love in the earliest months of their lives and have simply lost forever the desire and the ability to give and to receive affection (as animals lose sucking or pecking reflexes that are not exercised soon enough after birth).

(5) Another cause of reversal of the hierarchy is that when a need has been satisfied for a long time, this need may be underevaluated. People who have never experienced chronic hunger are apt to underestimate its effects and to look upon food as a rather unimportant thing. If they are dominated by a higher need, this higher need will seem to be the most important of all. It then becomes possible, and indeed does actually happen, that they may, for the sake of this higher need, put themselves into the position of being deprived in a more basic need. We may expect that after a long-time deprivation of the more basic need there will be a tendency to reevaluate both needs so that the more prepotent need will actually become consciously prepotent for the individual who may have given it up very lightly. Thus, a man who has given up his job rather than lose his self-respect, and who then starves for six months or so, may be willing to take his job back even at the price of losing his self-respect.

(6) Another partial explanation of *apparent* reversals is seen in the fact that we have been talking about the hierarchy of prepotency in terms of consciously felt wants or desires rather than of behavior. Looking at behavior itself may give us the wrong impression. What we have claimed

is that the person will *want* the more basic of two needs when deprived in both. There is no necessary implication here that he will act upon his desires. Let us say again that there are many determinants of behavior other than the needs and desires.

(7) Perhaps more important than all these exceptions are the ones that involve ideals, high social standards, high values and the like. With such values people become martyrs; they will give up everything for the sake of a particular ideal, or value. These people may be understood, at least in part, by reference to one basic concept (or hypothesis) which may be called 'increased frustration-tolerance through early gratification.' People who have been satisfied in their basic needs throughout their lives, particularly in their earlier years, seem to develop exceptional power to withstand present or future thwarting of these needs simply because they have strong, healthy character structure as a result of basic satisfaction. They are the 'strong' people who can easily weather disagreement or opposition who can swim against the stream of public opinion and who can stand up for the truth at great personal cost. It is just the ones who have loved and been well loved, and who have had many deep friendships, who can hold out against hatred, rejection or persecution.

I say all this in spite of the fact that there is a certain amount of sheer habituation which is also involved in any full discussion of frustration tolerance. For instance, it is likely that those persons who have been accustomed to relative starvation for a long time, are partially enabled thereby to withstand food deprivation. What sort of balance must be made between these two tendencies, of habituation on the one hand, and of past satisfaction breeding present frustration tolerance on the other hand, remains to be worked out by further research. Meanwhile we may assume that they are both operative, side by side, since they do not contradict each other. In respect to this phenomenon of increased frustration tolerance, it seems probable that the most important gratifications come in the first two years of life. That is to say, people who have been made secure and strong in the earliest years, tend to remain secure and strong thereafter in the face of whatever threatens.

Degrees of Relative Satisfaction

So far, our theoretical discussion may have given the impression that these five sets of needs are somehow in a stepwise, all-or-none relationship to each other. We have spoken in such terms as the following: "If one need is satisfied, then another emerges." This statement might give the false impression that a need must be satisfied 100 percent before the next need emerges. In actual fact, most members of our society who are normal, are partially satisfied in all their basic needs and partially unsatisfied in all their basic needs at the same time. A more realistic description of the hierarchy would be in terms of decreasing percentages of satisfaction as we go up the hierarchy of prepotency. For instance, if I may assign arbitrary figures for the sake of illustration, it is as if the average citizen is satisfied perhaps 85 percent in his physiological needs, 70 percent in his safety needs, 50 percent in his love needs, 40 percent in his self-esteem needs, and 10 percent in his self-actualization needs.

As for the concept of emergence of a new need after satisfaction of the prepotent need, this emergence is not a sudden, saltatory phenomenon but rather a gradual emergence by slow degrees from nothingness. For instance, if prepotent need A is satisfied only 10 percent, then need B may not be visible at all. However, as this need A becomes satisfied 25 percent, need B may emerge 5 percent; as need A becomes satisfied 75 percent, need B may emerge 90 percent, and so on.

Unconscious Character of Needs

These needs are neither necessarily conscious nor unconscious. On the whole, however, in the average person, they are more often unconscious rather than conscious. It is not necessary at this point to overhaul the tremendous mass of evidence which indicates the crucial importance of unconscious motivation. It would by now be expected, on a priori grounds alone, that unconscious motivations would on the whole be rather more important than the conscious motivations. What we have called the basic needs are very often largely unconscious although they may, with suitable techniques, and with sophisticated people become conscious.

Cultural Specificity and Generality of Needs

This classification of basic needs makes some attempt to take account of the relative unity behind the superficial differences in specific desires from one culture to another. Certainly in any particular culture an individual's conscious motivational content will usually be extremely different from the conscious motivational content of an individual in another society. However, it is the common experience of anthropologists that people, even in different societies, are much more alike than we would think from our first contact with them, and that as we know them better we seem to find more and more of this commonness. We then recognize the most startling differences to be superficial rather than basic, e.g., differences in style of hairdress, clothes, tastes in food, etc. Our classification of basic needs is in part an attempt to account for this unity behind the apparent diversity from culture to culture. No claim is made that it is ultimate or universal for all cultures. The claim is made only that it is relatively *more* ultimate, more universal, more basic, than the superficial conscious desires from culture to culture, and makes a somewhat closer approach to common human characteristics. Basic needs are *more* common-human than superficial desires or behaviors.

Mutiple Motivations of Behavior

These needs must be understood *not* to be *exclusive* or single determiners of certain kinds of behavior. An example may be found in any behavior that seems to be physiologically motivated, such as eating, or sexual play or the like. The clinical psychologists have long since found that any behavior may be a channel through which flow various determinants. Or to say it in another way, most behavior is multimotivated. Within the sphere of motivational determinants any behavior tends to be determined by several or *all* of the basic needs simultaneously rather than by only one of them. The latter would be more an exception than the former. Eating may be partially for the sake of filling the stomach, and partially for the sake of comfort and amelioration of other needs. One may make love not only for pure sexual release, but also to convince one's self of one's masculinity, or to make a conquest, to feel powerful, or to win more basic affection. As an illustration, I may point out that it would be possible (theoretically if not practically) to analyze a single act of an individual and see in it the expression of his physiological needs, his safety needs, his love needs, his esteem needs and self-actualization. This contrasts sharply with the more naive brand of trait psychology in which one trait or one motive accounts for a certain kind of act, i.e., an aggressive act is traced solely to a trait of aggressiveness.

Multiple Determinants of Behavior

Not all behavior is determined by the basic needs. We might even say that not all behavior is motivated. There are many determinants of behavior other than motives.[9] For instance, one other important class of determinants is the so-called field determinants. Theoretically, at least, behavior may be determined completely by the field, or even by specific isolated external stimuli, as in association of ideas, or certain conditioned reflexes. If in response to the stimulus word "table," I immediately perceive a memory image of a table, this response certainly has nothing to do with my basic needs.

Secondly, we may call attention again to the concept of 'degree of closeness to the basic needs' or 'degree of motivation.' Some behavior is highly motivated, other behavior is only weakly motivated. Some is not motivated at all (but all behavior is determined).

Another important point[10] is that there is a basic difference between expressive behavior and coping behavior (functional striving, purposive goal seeking). An expressive behavior does not try to do anything; it is simply a reflection of the personality. A stupid man behaves stupidly, not because he wants to, or tries to, or is motivated to, but simply because he *is* what he is. The same is true when I speak in a bass voice rather than tenor or soprano. The random movements of a healthy child, the smile on the face of a happy man even when he is alone, the springiness of the healthy man's walk, and the erectness of his carriage are other examples of expressive, nonfunctional behavior. Also the *style* in which a man carries out almost all his behavior, motivated as well as unmotivated, is often expressive.

We may then ask, is *all* behavior expressive or reflective of the character structure? The answer is no. Rote, habitual, automatized, or conventional behavior may or may not be expressive. The same is true for most 'stimulus-bound' behaviors.

It is finally necessary to stress that expressiveness of behavior, and goal-directedness of behavior are not mutually exclusive categories. Average behavior is usually both.

Goals as Centering Principle in Motivation Theory

It will be observed that the basic principle in our classification has been neither the instigation nor the motivated behavior but rather the functions, effects, purposes, or goals of the behavior. It has been proven sufficiently by various people that this is the most suitable point for centering in any motivation theory.[11]

Animal- and Human-Centering

This theory starts with the human being rather than any lower and presumably 'simpler' animal. Too many of the findings that have been made in animals have been proven to be true for animals but not for the human being. There is no reason whatsoever why we should start with animals in order to study human motivation. The logic or rather illogic behind this general fallacy of 'pseudosimplicity' has been exposed often enough by philosophers and logicians as well as by scientists in each of the various fields. It is no more necessary to study animals before one can study man than it is to study mathematics before one can study geology or psychology or biology.

We may also reject the old, naive behaviorism which assumed that it was somehow necessary, or at least more 'scientific' to judge human beings by animal standards. One consequence of this belief was that the whole notion of purpose and goal was excluded from motivational psychology simply because one could not ask a white rat about his purposes. Tolman (18) has long since proven in animal studies themselves that this exclusion was not necessary.

Motivation and the Theory of Psychopathogenesis

The conscious motivational content of everyday life has, according to the foregoing, been conceived to be relatively important or unimportant accordingly as it is more or less closely related to the basic goals. A desire

for an ice cream cone might actually be an indirect expression of a desire
for love. If it is, then this desire for the ice cream cone becomes extremely
important motivation. If however the ice cream is simply something to
cool the mouth with, or a casual appetitive reaction, then the desire is
relatively unimportant. Everyday conscious desires are to be regarded as
symptoms, as surface indicators of more basic needs. If we were to take
these superficial desires at their face value we would find ourselves in a
state of complete confusion which could never be resolved, since we would
be dealing seriously with symptoms rather than with what lay behind the
symptoms.

Thwarting of unimportant desires produces no psychopathological
results; thwarting of a basically important need does produce such
results. Any theory of psychopathogenesis must then be based on a sound
theory of motivation. A conflict or a frustration is not necessarily pathogenic. It becomes so only when it threatens or thwarts the basic needs, or
partial needs that are closely related to the basic needs (10).

The Role of Gratified Needs

It has been pointed out above several times that our needs usually
emerge only when more prepotent needs have been gratified. Thus gratification has an important role in motivation theory. Apart from this, however, needs cease to play an active determining or organizing role as soon
as they are gratified.

What this means is that, e.g., a basically satisfied person no longer
has the needs for esteem, love, safety, etc. The only sense in which he
might be said to have them is in the almost metaphysical sense that a
sated man has hunger, or a filled bottle has emptiness. If we are interested in what *actually* motivates us, and not in what has, will, or might
motivate us, then a satisfied need is not a motivator. It must be considered for all practical purposes simply not to exist, to have disappeared.
This point should be emphasized because it has been either overlooked or
contradicted in every theory of motivation I know.[12] The perfectly
healthy, normal, fortunate man has no sex needs or hunger needs, or
needs for safety, or for love, or for prestige, or self-esteem, except in stray
moments of quickly passing threat. If we were to say otherwise, we
should also have to aver that every man had all the pathological reflexes,
e.g., Babinski, etc., because if his nervous system were damaged, these
would appear.

It is such considerations as these that suggest the bold postulation
that a man who is thwarted in any of his basic needs may fairly be
envisaged simply as a sick man. This is a fair parallel to our designation
as 'sick' of the man who lacks vitamins or minerals. Who is to say that a
lack of love is less important than a lack of vitamins? Since we know the
pathogenic effects of love starvation, who is to say that we are invoking
value-questions in an unscientific or illegitimate way, any more than the

physician does who diagnoses and treats pellagra or scurvy? If I were permitted this usage, I should then say simply that a healthy man is primarily motivated by his needs to develop and actualize his fullest potentialities and capacities. If a man has any other basic needs in any active, chronic sense, then he is simply an unhealthy man. He is as surely sick as if he had suddenly developed a strong salt hunger or calcium hunger.[13]

If this statement seems unusual or paradoxical the reader may be assured that this is only one among many such paradoxes that will appear as we revise our ways of looking at man's deeper motivations. When we ask what man wants of life, we deal with his very essence.

SUMMARY

1. There are at least five sets of goals, which we may call basic needs. These are briefly physiological, safety, love, esteem, and self-actualization. In addition, we are motivated by the desire to achieve or maintain the various conditions upon which these basic satisfactions rest and by certain more intellectual desires.

2. These basic goals are related to each other, being arranged in a hierarchy of prepotency. This means that the most prepotent goal will monopolize consciousness and will tend of itself to organize the recruitment of the various capacities of the organism. The less prepotent needs are minimized, even forgotten or denied. But when a need is fairly well satisfied, the next prepotent ("higher") need emerges, in turn to dominate the conscious life and to serve as the center of organization of behavior, since gratified needs are not active motivators.

Thus man is a perpetually wanting animal. Ordinarily the satisfaction of these wants is not altogether mutually exclusive, but only tends to be. The average member of our society is most often partially satisfied and partially unsatisfied in all of his wants. The hierarchy principle is usually empirically observed in terms of increasing percentages of nonsatisfaction as we go up the hierarchy. Reversals of the average order of the hierarchy are sometimes observed. Also it has been observed that an individual may permanently lose the higher wants in the hierarchy under special conditions. There are not only ordinarily multiple motivations for usual behavior, but in addition many determinants other than motives.

3. Any thwarting or possibility of thwarting of these basic human goals, or danger to the defenses which protect them, or to the conditions upon which they rest, is considered to be a psychological threat. With a few exceptions, all psychopathology may be partially traced to such threats. A basically thwarted man may actually be defined as a 'sick' man, if we wish.

4. It is such basic threats which bring about the general emergency reactions.

5. Certain other basic problems have not been dealt with because of limitations of space. Among these are *(a)* the problem of values in any definitive motivation theory, *(b)* the relation between appetites, desires, needs and what is 'good' for the organism, *(c)* the etiology of the basic needs and their possible derivation in early childhood, *(d)* redefinition of motivational concepts, i.e., drive, desire, wish, need, goal, *(e)* implication of our theory for hedonistic theory, *(f)* the nature of the uncompleted act, of success and failure, and of aspiration level, *(g)* the role of association, habit and conditioning, *(h)* relation to the theory of interpersonal relations, *(i)* implications for psychotherapy, *(j)* implication for theory of society, *(k)* the theory of selfishness, *(l)* the relation between needs and cultural patterns, *(m)* the relation between this theory and Allport's theory of functional autonomy. These as well as certain other less important questions must be considered as motivation theory attempts to become definitive.

NOTES

1. As the child grows up, sheer knowledge and familiarity as well as better motor development make these "dangers" less and less dangerous and more and more manageable. Throughout life it may be said that one of the main conative functions of education is this neutralizing of apparent dangers through knowledge, e.g., I am not afraid of thunder because I know something about it.

2. A "test battery" for safety might be confronting the child with a small exploding firecracker, or with a bewhiskered face, having the mother leave the room, putting him upon a high ladder, a hypodermic injection, having a mouse crawl up to him, etc. Of course I cannot seriously recommend the deliberate use of such "tests" for they might very well harm the child being tested. But these and similar situations come up by the score in the child's ordinary day-to-day living and may be observed. There is no reason why these stimuli should not be used with, for example, young chimpanzees.

3. Not all neurotic individuals feel unsafe. Neurosis may have at its core a thwarting of the affection and esteem needs in a person who is generally safe.

4. For further details see (12) and (16, Ch. 5).

5. Whether or not this particular desire is universal we do not know. The crucial question, especially important today, is "Will men who are enslaved and dominated inevitably feel dissatisfied and rebellious?" We may assume on the basis of commonly known clinical data that a man who has known true freedom (not paid for by giving up safety and security but rather built on the basis of adequate safety and security) will not willingly or easily allow his freedom to be taken away from him. But we do not know that this is true for the person born into slavery. The events of the next decade should give us our answer. See discussion of this problem in (5).

6. Perhaps the desire for prestige and respect from others is subsidiary to the desire for self-esteem or confidence in oneself. Observation of children seems

to indicate that this is so, but clinical data give no clear support for such a conclusion.

7. For more extensive discussion of normal self-esteem, as well as for reports of various researches, see (11).

8. Clearly creative behavior, like painting, is like any other behavior in having multiple determinants. It may be seen in "innately creative" people whether they are satisfied or not, happy or unhappy, hungry or sated. Also it is clear that creative activity may be compensatory, ameliorative or purely economic. It is my impression (as yet unconfirmed) that it is possible to distinguish the artistic and intellectual products of basically satisfied people from those of basically unsatisfied people by inspection alone. In any case, here too we must distinguish, in a dynamic fashion, the overt behavior itself from its various motivations or purposes.

9. I am aware that many psychologists and psychoanalysts use the term "motivated" and "determined" synonymously, e.g., Freud. But I consider this an obfuscating usage. Sharp distinctions are necessary for clarity of thought, and precision in experimentation.

10. Discussed fully in a subsequent publication.

11. The interested reader is referred to the very excellent discussion of this point in Murray's *Explorations in Personality* (15).

12. Note that acceptance of this theory necessitates basic revision of the Freudian theory.

13. If we were to use the word "sick" in this way, we should then also have to face squarely the relations of man to his society. One clear implication of our definition would be that (1) since a man is to be called sick who is basically thwarted, and (2) since such basic thwarting is made possible ultimately only by forces outside the individual, then (3) sickness in the individual must come ultimately from a sickness in the society. The "good" or healthy society would then be defined as one that permitted man's highest purposes to emerge by satisfying all his prepotent basic needs.

REFERENCES

(1) A. Adler, *Social Interest* (London: Faber & Faber, 1938).

(2) W. B. Cannon, *Wisdom of the Body* (New York: Norton, 1932).

(3) A. Freud, *The Ego and the Mechanisms of Defense* (London: Hogarth, 1937).

(4) S. Freud, *New Introductory Lectures on Psychoanalysis* (New York: Norton, 1933).

(5) E. Fromm, *Escape from Freedom* (New York: Farrar and Rinehart, 1941).

(6) K. Goldstein, *The Organism* (New York: American Book Co., 1939).

(7) K. Horney, *The Neurotic Personality of Our Time* (New York: Norton, 1937).

(8) A. Kardiner, *The Traumatic Neuroses of War* (New York: Hoeber, 1941).

(9) D. M. Levy, "Primary Affect Hunger," *American Journal of Psychiatry*, 94 (1937), pp. 643–652.

(10) A. H. Maslow, "Conflict, Frustration, and the Theory of Threat," *Journal of Abnormal (Social) Psychology,* 38 (1943), pp. 81–86.

(11) A. H. Maslow, "Dominance, Personality and Social Behavior in Women," *Journal of Social Psychology,* 10 (1939), pp. 3–39.

(12) A. H. Maslow, "The Dynamics of Psychological Security-Insecurity," *Character and Personality,* 10 (1942), pp. 331–344.

(13) A. H. Maslow, "A Preface to Motivation Theory," *Psychosomatic Medicine,* 5 (1943), pp. 85–92.

(14) A. H. Maslow and B. Mittelmann, *Principles of Abnormal Psychology* (New York: Harper & Brothers, 1941).

(15) H. A. Murray, et al., *Explorations in Personality* (New York: Oxford University Press, 1938).

(16) J. Plant, *Personality and the Cultural Pattern* (New York: Commonwealth Fund, 1937).

(17) M. Shirley, "Children's Adjustments to a Strange Situation," *Journal of Abnormal (Social) Psychology,* 37 (1942), pp. 201–217.

(18) E. C. Tolman, *Purposive Behavior in Animals and Men* (New York: Century, 1932).

(19) M. Wertheimer, Unpublished lectures at the New School for Social Research.

(20) P. T. Young, *Motivation of Behavior* (New York: John Wiley and Sons, 1936).

(21) P. T. Young, "The Experimental Analysis of Appetite," *Psychology Bulletin,* 38 (1941), pp. 129–164.

23

That Urge to Achieve

David C. McClelland

Foremost among the factors which serve to spur individuals to greater and greater efforts is thought by many to be the need to achieve. In this article, McClelland, who has devoted his professional life to understanding this need, describes what achievement motivation is, how it is measured, and most importantly, how it can be taught. McClelland argues that the urge to achieve is an essential ingredient in business success for individuals as well as for nations.—Eds.

Most people in this world, psychologically, can be divided into two broad groups. There is that minority which is challenged by opportunity and willing to work hard to achieve something, and the majority which really does not care all that much.

For nearly twenty years now, psychologists have tried to penetrate the mystery of this curious dichotomy. Is the need to achieve (or the absence of it) an accident, is it hereditary, or is it the result of environment? Is it a single, isolatable human motive, or a combination of motives—the desire to accumulate wealth, power, fame? Most important of all, is there some technique that could give this will to achieve to people, even whole societies, who do not now have it?

While we do not yet have complete answers for any of these questions, years of work have given us partial answers to most of them and insights into all of them. There is a distinct human motive, distinguishable from others. It can be found, in fact tested for, in any group.

SOURCE: From *THINK Magazine,* Vol. 32, No. 6 (November-December, 1966), pp. 19–23. Reprinted by permission from *THINK Magazine,* published by IBM, copyright 1966 by International Business Machines Corporation.

Let me give you one example. Several years ago, a careful study was made of 450 workers who had been thrown out of work by a plant shutdown in Erie, Pennsylvania. Most of the unemployed workers stayed home for a while and then checked back with the United States Employment Service to see if their old jobs or similar ones were available. But a small minority among them behaved differently; the day they were laid off, they started job-hunting.

They checked both the United States and the Pennsylvania Employment Office; they studied the "Help Wanted" sections of the papers; they checked through their union, their church, and various fraternal organizations; they looked into training courses to learn a new skill; they even left town to look for work, while the majority when questioned said they would not under any circumstances move away from Erie to obtain a job. Obviously the members of that active minority were differently motivated. All the men were more or less in the same situation objectively: they needed work, money, food, shelter, job security. Yet only a minority showed initiative and enterprise in finding what they needed. Why? Psychologists, after years of research, now believe they can answer that question. They have demonstrated that these men possessed in greater degree a specific type of human motivation. For the moment let us refer to this personality characteristic as "Motive A" and review some of the other characteristics of the men who have more of the motive than other men.

Suppose they are confronted by a work situation in which they can set their own goals as to how difficult a task they will undertake. In the psychological laboratory, such a situation is very simply created by asking them to throw rings over a peg from any distance they may choose. Most men throw more or less randomly, standing now close, now far away, but those with Motive A seem to calculate carefully where they are most likely to get a sense of mastery. They stand nearly always at moderate distances, not so close as to make the task ridiculously easy, nor so far away as to make it impossible. They set moderately difficult, but potentially achievable goals for themselves, where they objectively have only about a 1-in-3 chance of succeeding. In other words, they are always setting challenges for themselves, tasks to make them stretch themselves a little.

But they behave like this only if *they* can influence the outcome by performing the work themselves. They prefer not to gamble at all. Say they are given a choice between rolling dice with one in three chances of winning and working on a problem with a one-in-three chance of solving in the time allotted, they choose to work on the problem even though rolling the dice is obviously less work and the odds of winning are the same. They prefer to work at a problem rather than leave the outcome to chance or to others.

Obviously they are concerned with personal achievement rather than with the rewards of success *per se,* since they stand just as much chance of getting those rewards by throwing the dice. This leads to another characteristic the Motive A men show—namely, a strong preference for work situations in which they get concrete feedback on how well they are doing, as one does, say in playing golf, or in being a salesman, but as one does not in teaching, or in personnel counseling. A golfer always knows his score and can compare how well he is doing with par or with his own performance yesterday or last week. A teacher has no such concrete feedback on how well he is doing in "getting across" to his students.

The *n* Ach Men

But why do certain men behave like this? At one level the reply is simple: because they habitually spend their time thinking about doing things better. In fact, psychologists typically measure the strength of Motive A by taking samples of a man's spontaneous thoughts (such as making up a story about a picture they have been shown) and counting the frequency with which he mentions doing things better. The count is objective and can even be made these days with the help of a computer program for content analysis. It yields what is referred to technically as an individual's *n* Ach score (for "need for Achievement"). It is not difficult to understand why people who think constantly about "doing better" are more apt to do better at job-hunting, to set moderate, achievable goals for themselves, to dislike gambling (because they get no achievement satisfaction from success) and to prefer work situations where they can tell easily whether they are improving or not. But why some people and not others come to think this way is another question. The evidence suggests it is not because they are born that way, but because of special training they get in the home from parents who get moderately high achievement goals but who are warm, encouraging and nonauthoritarian in helping their children reach these goals.

Such detailed knowledge about one motive helps correct a lot of common sense ideas about human motivation. For example, much public policy (and much business policy) is based on the simpleminded notion that people will work harder "if they have to." As a first approximation, the idea isn't totally wrong, but it is only a half-truth. The majority of unemployed workers in Erie "had to" find work as much as those with higher *n* Ach, but they certainly didn't work as hard at it. Or again, it is frequently assumed that *any* strong motive will lead to doing things better. Wouldn't it be fair to say that most of the Erie workers were just "unmotivated"? But our detailed knowledge of various human motives shows that each one leads a person to behave in *different* ways. The contrast is not between being "motivated" or "unmotivated" but between being motivated toward A or B or C, etc.

A simple experiment makes the point nicely: subjects were told that they could choose as a working partner either a close friend or a stranger who was known to be an expert on the problem to be solved. Those with higher n Ach (more "need to achieve") chose the experts over their friends, whereas those with more n Aff (the "need to affiliate with others") chose friends over experts. The latter were not "unmotivated"; their desire to be with someone they liked was simply a stronger motive than their desire to excel at the task. Other such needs have been studied by psychologists. For instance, the need for Power is often confused with the need for Achievement because both may lead to "outstanding" activities. There is a distinct difference. People with a strong need for Power want to command attention, get recognition, and control others. They are more active in political life and tend to busy themselves primarily with controlling the channels of communication both up to the top and down to the people so that they are more "in charge." Those with high n Power are not as concerned with improving their work performance daily as those with high n Ach.

It follows, from what we have been able to learn, that not all "great achievers" score high n Ach. Many generals, outstanding politicians, great research scientists do not, for instance, because their work requires other personality characteristics, other motives. A general or a politician must be more concerned with power relationships, a research scientist must be able to go for long periods without the immediate feedback the person with high n Ach requires, etc. On the other hand, business executives, particularly if they are in positions of real responsibility or if they are salesmen, tend to score high in n Ach. This is true even in a Communist country like Poland: apparently there, as well as in a private enterprise economy, a manager succeeds if he is concerned about improving all the time, setting moderate goals, keeping track of his or the company's performance, etc.

Motivation and Half-Truths

Since careful study has shown that common sense notions about motivation are at best half-truths, it also follows that you cannot trust what people tell you about their motives. After all, they often get their own motives from common sense. Thus a general may say he is interested in achievement (because he has obviously achieved), or a businessman that he is interested only in making money (because he has made money), or one of the majority of unemployed in Erie that he desperately wants a job (because he knows he needs one); but a careful check of what each one thinks about and how he spends his time may show that each is concerned about quite different things. It requires special measurement techniques to identify the presence of n Ach and other such motives. Thus what people say and believe is not very closely related to these "hidden" motives which seem to affect a person's "style of life" more than his political, religious or social attitudes. Thus n Ach produces enterprising men among labor leaders or managers, Republicans or Democrats, Catholics or Protestants, capitalists or communists.

Wherever people begin to think often in *n* Ach terms things begin to move. Men with higher *n* Ach get more raises and are promoted more rapidly, because they keep actively seeking ways to do a better job. Companies with many such men grow faster. In one comparison of two firms in Mexico, it was discovered that all but one of the top executives of a fast growing firm had higher *n* Ach scores than the highest scoring executive in an equally large but slow-growing firm. Countries with many such rapidly growing firms tend to show above-average rates of economic growth. This appears to be the reason why correlations have regularly been found between the *n* Ach content in popular literature (such as popular songs or stories in children's textbooks) and subsequent rates of national economic growth. A nation which is thinking about doing better all the time (as shown in its popular literature) actually does do better economically speaking. Careful quantitative studies have shown this to be true in Ancient Greece, in Spain in the Middle Ages, in England from 1400–1800, as well as among contemporary nations, whether capitalist or communist, developed or underdeveloped.

Contrast these two stories for example. Which one contains more *n* Ach? Which one reflects a state of mind which ought to lead to harder striving to improve the way things are?

Excerpt from story A (4th grade reader): "Don't Ever Owe a Man— The world is an illusion. Wife, children, horses, and cows are all just ties of fate. They are ephemeral. Each after fulfilling his part in life disappears. So we should not clamour after riches which are not permanent. As long as we live it is wise not to have any attachments and just think of God. We have to spend our lives without trouble, for is it not time that there is an end to grievances? So it is better to live knowing the real state of affairs. Don't get entangled in the meshes of family life."

Excerpt from story B (4th grade reader): "How I Do Like to Learn—I was sent to an accelerated technical high school. I was so happy I cried. Learning is not very easy. In the beginning I couldn't understand what the teacher taught us. I always got a red cross mark on my papers. The boy sitting next to me was very enthusiastic and also an outstanding student. When he found I couldn't do the problems he offered to show me how he had done them. I could not copy his work. I must learn through my own reasoning. I gave his paper back and explained I had to do it myself. Sometimes I worked on a problem until midnight. If I couldn't finish, I started early in the morning. The red cross marks on my work were getting less common. I conquered my difficulties. My marks rose. I graduated and went on to college."

Most readers would agree without any special knowledge of the *n* Ach coding system, that the second story shows more concern with improvement than the first, which comes from a contemporary reader used in Indian public schools. In fact the latter has a certain Horatio Alger quality that is reminiscent of our own McGuffey readers of several generations ago. It appears today in the textbooks of Communist China. It should not, therefore, come as a surprise if a nation like Communist China, obsessed as it is with improvement, tended in the long run to outproduce a nation like India, which appears to be more fatalistic.

The n Ach level is obviously important for statesmen to watch and in many instances to try to do something about, particularly if a nation's economy is lagging. Take Britain, for example. A generation ago (around 1925) it ranked fifth among 25 countries where children's readers were scored for n Ach—and its economy was doing well. By 1950 the n Ach level had dropped to 27th out of 39 countries—well below the world average—and today, its leaders are feeling the severe economic effects of this loss in the spirit of enterprise.

Economics and n Ach

If psychologists can detect n Ach levels in individuals or nations, particularly before their effects are widespread, can't the knowledge somehow be put to use to foster economic development? Obviously detection or diagnosis is not enough. What good is it to tell Britain (or India for that matter) that it needs more n Ach, a greater spirit of enterprise? In most such cases, informed observers of the local scene know very well that such a need exists, though they may be slower to discover it than the psychologist hovering over n Ach in individuals or nations.

Since about 1960, psychologists in my research group at Harvard have been experimenting with techniques designed to accomplish this goal, chiefly among business executives whose work requires the action characteristics of people with high n Ach. Initially, we had real doubts as to whether we could succeed, partly because like most American psychologists we had been strongly influenced by the psychoanalytic view that basic motives are laid down in childhood and cannot really be changed later, and partly because many studies of intensive psychotherapy and counseling have shown minor if any long-term personality effects. On the other hand we were encouraged by the nonprofessionals: those enthusiasts like Dale Carnegie, the communist ideologue or the church missionary, who felt they could change adults and in fact seemed to be doing so. At any rate we ran some brief (7 to 10 days) "total push" training courses for businessmen, designed to increase their n Ach.

Four Main Goals

In broad outline the courses had four main goals: (1) They were designed to teach the participants how to think, talk and act like a person with high n Ach, based on our knowledge of such people gained through 17 years of research. For instance, men learned how to make up stories that would code high in n Ach (i.e., how to think in n Ach terms), how to set moderate goals for themselves in the ring toss game (and in life). (2) The courses stimulated the participants to set higher but carefully planned and realistic work goals for themselves over the next two years. Then we checked back with them every six months to see how well they were doing in terms of their own objectives. (3) The courses also utilized techniques for giving the participants knowledge about themselves. For instance, in playing the ring toss game, they could observe that they behaved differently from others—perhaps in refusing to adjust a goal downward after failure. This would then become a matter for group discussion and the man would have to explain what he had in mind in setting such unrealistic goals. Discussion could then lead on to what a man's ultimate goals in life were, how much he cared about actually improving performance versus making a good impression or having many friends. In this way the participants would be freer to realize their achievement goals without being blocked by old habits and attitudes. (4) The courses also usually created a group *esprit de corps* from learning about each other's hopes and fears, successes and failures, and from going through an emotional experience together, away from everyday life, in a retreat setting. This membership in a new group helps a man achieve his goals, partly because he knows he has their sympathy and support and partly because he knows they will be watching to see how well he does. The same effect has been noted in other therapy groups like Alcoholics Anonymous. We are not sure which of these course "inputs" is really absolutely essential—that remains a research question—but we were taking no chances at the outset in view of the general pessimism about such efforts, and we wanted to include any and all techniques that were thought to change people.

The courses have been given: to executives in a large American firm, and in several Mexican firms; to underachieving high school boys; and to businessmen in India from Bombay and from a small city—Kakinada in the state of Andhra Pradesh. In every instance save one (the Mexican case), it was possible to demonstrate statistically, some two years later, that the men who took the course had done better (made more money, got promoted faster, expanded their businesses faster) than comparable men who did not take the course or who took some other management course.

Consider the Kakinada results, for example. In the two years preceding the course 9 men, 18 percent of the 52 paticipants, had shown "unusual" enterprise in their businesses. In the 18 months following the course 25 of the men, in other words nearly 50 percent, were unusually active. And this was not due to a general upturn of business in India. Data from a control city some forty-five miles away, show the same base rate of "unusually active" men as in Kakinada before the course—namely, about 20 percent. Something clearly happened in Kakinada: the owner of a small radio shop started a chemical plant; a banker was so successful in making commercial loans in an enterprising way that he was promoted to a much larger branch of his bank in Calcutta; the local political leader accomplished his goal (it was set in the course) to get the federal government to deepen the harbor and make it into an all-weather port; plans are far along for establishing a steel rolling mill, etc. All this took place without any substantial capital input from outside. In fact, the only costs were for four 10-day courses plus some brief follow-up visits every six months. The men are raising their own capital and using their own resources for getting business and industry moving in a city that had been considered stagnant and unenterprising.

The promise of such a method of developing achievement motivation seems very great. It has obvious applications in helping underdeveloped countries, or "pockets of poverty" in the United States, to move faster economically. It has great potential for businesses that need to "turn around" and take a more enterprising approach toward their growth and development. It may even be helpful in developing more n Ach among low-income groups. For instance, data show that lower-class Negro Americans have a very low level of n Ach. This is not surprising. Society has systematically discouraged and blocked their achievement striving. But as the barriers to upward mobility are broken down, it will be necessary to help stimulate the motivation that will lead them to take advantage of new opportunities opening up.

Extreme Reactions

But a word of caution: Whenever I speak of this research and its great potential, audience reaction tends to go to opposite extremes. Either people remain skeptical and argue that motives can't really be changed, that all we are doing is dressing Dale Carnegie up in fancy "psychologese," or they become converts and want instant course descriptions by return mail to solve their local motivational problems. Either response is unjustified. What I have described here in a few pages has taken 20 years of patient research effort, and hundreds of thousands of dollars in basic research costs. What remains to be done will involve even larger sums or more time for development to turn a promising idea into something of wide practical utility.

Encouragement Needed

To take only one example, we have not learned to develop n Ach really well among low-income groups. In our first effort—a summer course for bright underachieving 14-year-olds—we found that boys from the middle class improved steadily in grades in school over a two-year period, but boys from the lower class showed an improvement after the first year followed by a drop back in their beginning low grade average. (See the accompanying chart.) Why? We speculate that it was because they moved back into an environment in which neither parents nor friends encouraged achievement or upward mobility. In other words, it isn't enough to change a man's motivation if the environment in which he lives doesn't support at least to some degree his new efforts. Negroes striving to rise

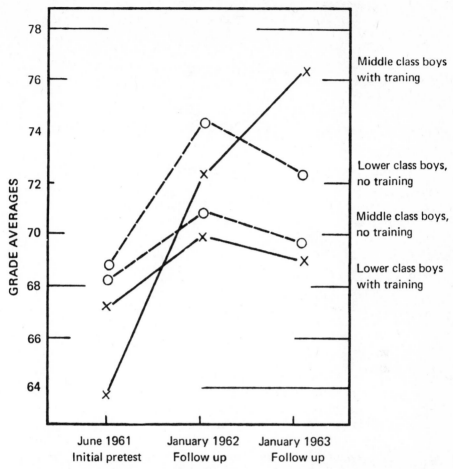

Middle class boys with traning

Lower class boys, no training

Middle class boys, no training

Lower class boys with training

In a Harvard study, a group of underachieving 14 year-olds was given a six-week course designed to help them do better in school. Some of the boys were also given training in achievement motivation, or *n* Ach (solid lines). As graph reveals, the only boys who continued to improve after a two-year period were the middle-class boys with the special *n* Ach training. Psychologists suspect the lower-class boys dropped back, even with *n* Ach training, because they returned to an environment in which neither parents nor friends encouraged achievement.

out of the ghetto frequently confront this problem: they are faced by skepticism at home and suspicion on the job, so that even if their *n* Ach is raised, it can be lowered again by the heavy odds against their success. We must learn not only to raise *n* Ach but also to find methods of instructing people in how to manage it, to create a favorable environment in which it can flourish.

Many of these training techniques are now only in the pilot testing stage. It will take time and money to perfect them, but society should be willing to invest heavily in them in view of their tremendous potential for contributing to human betterment.

24

One More Time: How Do You Motivate Employees?

Frederick Herzberg

The approach to work motivation described in this article has probably stimulated more research, more attempts to implement it in organizations, and more controversy than any other motivation theory. Herzberg explores some common myths about work motivation and then describes how his motivator-hygiene theory builds motivation directly into the job itself by enriching the activities which define the job. Provocative is perhaps the best single-word description of this article.—Eds.

How many articles, books, speeches, and workshops have pleaded plaintively, "How do I get an employee to do what I want him to do?"

The psychology of motivation is tremendously complex, and what has been unraveled with any degree of assurance is small indeed. But the dismal ratio of knowledge to speculation has not dampened the enthusiasm for new forms of snake oil that are constantly coming on the market, many of them with academic testimonials. Doubtless this article will have no depressing impact on the market for snake oil, but since the ideas expressed in it have been tested in many corporations and other organizations, it will help—I hope—to redress the imbalance in the aforementioned ratio.

"MOTIVATING" WITH KITA

In lectures to industry on the problem, I have found that the audiences are anxious for quick and practical answers, so I will begin with a straightforward, practical formula for moving people.

What is the simplest, surest, and most direct way of getting someone to do something? Ask him? But if he responds that he does not want to do it, then that calls for a psychological consultation to determine the reason for his obstinacy. Tell him? His response shows that he does not understand you, and now an expert in communications methods has to be brought in to show you how to get through to him. Give him a monetary incentive? I do not need to remind the reader of the complexity and difficulty involved in setting up and administering an incentive system. Show him? This means a costly training program. We need a simple way.

Every audience contains the "direct action" manager who shouts, "Kick him!" And this type of manager is right. The surest and least circumlocuted way of getting someone to do something is to kick him in the pants—give him what might be called the KITA.

Negative physical KITA. This is a literal application of the term and was frequently used in the past. It has, however, three major drawbacks: (1) it is inelegant; (2) it contradicts the precious image of benevolence that most organizations cherish; and (3) since it is a physical attack, it directly stimulates the autonomic nervous system, and this often results in negative feedback—the employee may just kick you in return. These factors give rise to certain taboos against negative physical KITA.

The psychologist has come to the rescue of those who are no longer permitted to use negative physical KITA. He has uncovered infinite sources of psychological vulnerabilities and the appropriate methods to play tunes on them. "He took my rug away"; "I wonder what he meant by that"; "The boss is always going around me"—These symptomatic expressions of ego sores that have been rubbed raw are the result of application of:

Negative psychological KITA. This has several advantages over negative physical KITA. First, the cruelty is not visible; the bleeding is internal and comes much later. Second, since it affects the higher cortical centers of the brain with its inhibitory powers, it reduces the possibility of physical backlash. Third, since the number of psychological pains that a person can feel is almost infinite, the direction and site possibilities of the KITA are increased many times. Fourth, the person administering the kick can manage to be above it all and let the system accomplish the dirty work. Fifth, those who practice it receive some ego satisfaction (one-upmanship), whereas they would find drawing blood abhorrent. Finally, if the employee does complain, he can always be accused of being paranoid, since there is no tangible evidence of an actual attack.

Now what does negative KITA accomplish? If I kick you in the rear (physically or psychologically), who is motivated? *I* am motivated; *you* move! Negative KITA does not lead to motivation, but to movement. So:

Positive KITA. Let us consider motivation. If I say to you, "Do this for me or the company, and in return I will give you a reward, an incentive, more status, a promotion, all the quid pro quos that exist in the industrial organization," am I motivating you? The overwhelming opinion I receive from management people is, "Yes, this is motivation."

I have a year-old Schnauzer. When it was a small puppy and I wanted it to move, I kicked it in the rear and it moved. Now that I have finished its obedience training, I hold up a dog biscuit when I want the Schnauzer to move. In this instance, who is motivated—I or the dog? The dog wants the biscuit, but it is I who want it to move. Again, I am the one who is motivated, and the dog is the one who moves. In this instance all I did was apply KITA frontally; I exerted a pull instead of a push. When industry wishes to use such positive KITAs, it has available an incredible number and variety of dog biscuits (jelly beans for humans) to wave in front of the employee to get him to jump.

Why is it that managerial audiences are quick to see that negative KITA is *not* motivation, while they are almost unanimous in their judgment that positive KITA *is* motivation? It is because negative KITA is rape, and positive KITA is seduction. But it is infinitely worse to be seduced than to be raped; the latter is an unfortunate occurrence, while the former signifies that you were a party to your own downfall. This is why positive KITA is so popular: it is a tradition; it is in the American way. The organization does not have to kick you; you kick yourself.

Myths about Motivation

Why is KITA not motivation? If I kick my dog (from the front or the back), he will move. And when I want him to move again, what must I do? I must kick him again. Similarly, I can charge a man's battery, and then recharge it, and recharge it again. But it is only when he has his own generator that we can talk about motivation. He then needs no outside stimulation. He *wants* to do it.

With this in mind, we can review some positive KITA personnel practices that were developed as attempts to instill "motivation":

1. *Reducing time spent at work*—This represents a marvelous way of motivating people to work—getting them off the job! We have reduced (formally and informally) the time spent on the job over the last 50 or 60 years until we are finally on the way to the "6½-day weekend." An interesting variant of this approach is the development of off-hour recreation programs. The philosophy here seems to be that those who play together, work together. The fact is that motivated people seek more hours of work, not fewer.

2. *Spiraling wages*—Have these motivated people? Yes, to seek the next wage increase. Some medievalists still can be heard to say that a

good depression will get employees moving. They feel that if rising wages don't or won't do the job, perhaps reducing them will.

3. *Fringe benefits*—Industry has outdone the most welfare-minded of welfare states in dispensing cradle-to-the-grave succor. One company I know of had a informal "fringe benefit of the month club" going for a while. The cost of fringe benefits in this country has reached approximately 25% of the wage dollar, and we still cry for motivation.

People spend less time working for more money and more security than ever before, and the trend cannot be reversed. These benefits are no longer rewards; they are rights. A 6-day week is inhuman, a 10-hour day is exploitation, extended medical coverage is a basic decency, and stock options are the salvation of American initiative. Unless the ante is continuously raised, the psychological reaction of employees is that the company is turning back the clock.

When industry began to realize that both the economic nerve and the lazy nerve of their employees had insatiable appetites, it started to listen to the behavioral scientists who, more out of a humanist tradition than from scientific study, criticized management for not knowing how to deal with people. The next KITA easily followed.

4. *Human relations training*—Over 30 years of teaching and, in many instances, of practicing psychological approaches to handling people have resulted in costly human relations programs and, in the end, the same question: How do you motivate workers? Here too, escalations have taken place. Thirty years ago it was necessary to request, "Please don't spit on the floor." Today the same admonition requires three "please's" before the employee feels that his superior has demonstrated the psychologically proper attitudes toward him.

The failure of human relations training to produce motivation led to the conclusion that the supervisor or manager himself was not psychologically true to himself in his practice of interpersonal decency. So an advanced form of human relations KITA, sensitivity training, was unfolded.

5. *Sensitivity training*—Do you really, really understand yourself? Do you really, really, really trust the other man? Do you really, really, really, really cooperate? The failure of sensitivity training is now being explained, by those who have become opportunistic exploiters of the technique, as a failure to really (five times) conduct proper sensitivity training courses.

With the realization that there are only temporary gains from comfort and economic and interpersonal KITA, personnel managers concluded that the fault lay not in what they were doing, but in the employee's failure to appreciate what they were doing. This opened up the field of communications, a whole new area of "scientifically" sanctioned KITA.

6. *Communications*—The professor of communications was invited to join the faculty of management training programs and help in making employees understand what management was doing for them. House

organs, briefing sessions, supervisory instruction on the importance of communication, and all sorts of propaganda have proliferated until today there is even an International Council of Industrial Editors. But no motivation resulted, and the obvious thought occurred that perhaps management was not hearing what the employees were saying. That led to the next KITA.

7. *Two-way communication*—Management ordered morale surveys, suggestion plans, and group participation programs. Then both employees and management were communicating and listening to each other more than ever, but without much improvement in motivation.

The behavioral scientists began to take another look at their conceptions and their data, and they took human relations one step further. A glimmer of truth was beginning to show through in the writings of the so-called higher-order-need psychologists. People, so they said, want to actualize themselves. Unfortunately, the "actualizing" psychologists got mixed up with the human relations psychologists, and a new KITA emerged.

8. *Job participation*—Though it may not have been the theoretical intention, job participation often became a "give them the big picture" approach. For example, if a man is tightening 10,000 nuts a day on an assembly line with a torque wrench, tell him he is building a Chevrolet. Another approach had the goal of giving the employee a *feeling* that he is determining, in some measure, what he does on his job. The goal was to provide a *sense* of achievement rather than a substantive achievement in his task. Real achievement, of course, requires a task that makes it possible.

But still there was no motivation. This led to the inevitable conclusion that the employees must be sick, and therefore to the next KITA.

9. *Employee counseling*—The initial use of this form of KITA in a systematic fashion can be credited to the Hawthorne experiment of the Western Electric Company during the early 1930's. At that time, it was found that the employees harbored irrational feelings that were interfering with the rational operation of the factory. Counseling in this instance was a means of letting the employees unburden themselves by talking to someone about their problems. Although the counseling techniques were primitive, the program was large indeed.

The counseling approach suffered as a result of experiences during World War II, when the programs themselves were found to be interfering with the operation of the organizations; the counselors had forgotten their role of benevolent listeners and were attempting to do something about the problems that they heard about. Psychological counseling, however, has managed to survive the negative impact of World War II experiences and today is beginning to flourish with renewed sophistication. But, alas, many of these programs, like all the others, do not seem to have lessened the pressure of demands to find out how to motivate workers.

Since KITA results only in short-term movement, it is safe to predict that the cost of these programs will increase steadily and new varieties will be developed as old positive KITAs reach their satiation points.

HYGIENE VS. MOTIVATORS

Let me rephrase the perennial question this way: How do you install a generator in an employee? A brief review of my motivation-hygiene theory of job attitudes is required before theoretical and practical suggestions can be offered. The theory was first drawn from an examination of events in the lives of engineers and accountants. At least 16 other investigations, using a wide variety of populations (including some in the Communist countries), have since been completed making the original research one of the most replicated studies in the field of job attitudes.

The findings of these studies, along with corroboration from many other investigations using different procedures, suggest that the factors involved in producing job satisfaction (and motivation) are separate and distinct from the factors that lead to job dissatisfaction. Since separate factors need to be considered, depending on whether job satisfaction or job dissatisfaction is being examined, it follows that these two feelings are not opposites of each other. The opposite of job satisfaction is not job dissatisfaction but, rather, *no* job satisfaction; and, similarly, the opposite of job dissatisfaction is not job satisfaction, but *no* job dissatisfaction.

Stating the concept presents a problem in semantics, for we normally think of satisfaction and dissatisfaction as opposites—i.e., what is not satisfying must be dissatisfying, and vice versa. But when it comes to understanding the behavior of people in their jobs, more than a play on words is involved.

Two different needs of man are involved here. One set of needs can be thought of as stemming from his animal nature—the built-in drive to avoid pain from the environment, plus all the learned drives which become conditioned to the basic biological needs. For example, hunger, the basic biological drive, makes it necessary to earn money, and then money becomes a specific drive. The other set of needs relates to that unique human characteristic, the ability to achieve and, through achievement, to experience psychological growth. The stimuli for the growth needs are tasks that induce growth; in the industrial setting, they are the *job content*. Contrariwise, the stimuli inducing pain-avoidance behavior are found in the *job environment*.

The growth or *motivator* factors that are intrinsic to the job are: achievement, recognition of achievement, the work itself, responsibility, and growth or advancement. The dissatisfaction-avoidance or *hygiene* (KITA) factors that are extrinsic to the job include: company policy and administration, supervision, interpersonal relationships, working conditions, salary, status, and security.

A composite of the factors that are involved in causing job satisfaction and job dissatisfaction, drawn from samples of 1,685 employees, is shown in Exhibit 1. The results indicate that motivators were the primary cause of satisfaction, and hygiene factors the primary cause of unhappiness on the job. The employees, studied in 12 different investigations, included lower-level supervisors, professional women, agricultural administrators, men about to retire from management positions, hospital maintenance personnel, manufacturing supervisors, nurses, food handlers, military officers, engineers, scientists, housekeepers, teachers, technicians, female assemblers, accountants, Finnish foremen, and Hungarian engineers.

They were asked what job events had occurred in their work that had led to extreme satisfaction or extreme dissatisfaction on their part. Their responses are broken down in the exhibit into percentages of total "positive" job events and of total "negative" job events. (The figures total more than 100% on both the "hygiene" and "motivators" sides because often at least two factors can be attributed to a single event; advancement, for instance, often accompanies assumption of responsibility.)

To illustrate, a typical response involving achievement that had a negative effect for the employee was, "I was unhappy because I didn't do the job successfully." A typical response in the small number of positive job events in the Company Policy and Administration grouping was, "I was happy because the company reorganized the section so that I didn't report any longer to the guy I didn't get along with."

As the lower right-hand part of the exhibit shows, of all the factors contributing to job satisfaction, 81% were motivators. And of all the factors contributing to the employees' dissatisfaction over their work, 69% involved hygiene elements.

Eternal Triangle

There are three general philosophies of personnel management. The first is based on organizational theory, the second on industrial engineering, and the third on behavioral science.

The organizational theorist believes that human needs are either so irrational or so varied and adjustable to specific situations that the major function of personnel management is to be as pragmatic as the occasion demands. If jobs are organized in a proper manner, he reasons, the result will be the most efficient job structure, and the most favorable job attitudes will follow as a matter of course.

The industrial engineer holds that man is mechanistically oriented and economically motivated and his needs are best met by attuning the individual to the most efficient work process. The goal of personnel management therefore should be to concoct the most appropriate incentive system and to design the specific working conditions in a way that facilitates the most efficient use of the human machine. By structuring jobs in a manner that leads to the most efficient operation, the engineer believes

EXHIBIT 1 Factors Affecting Job Attitudes, as Reported in Twelve Investigations

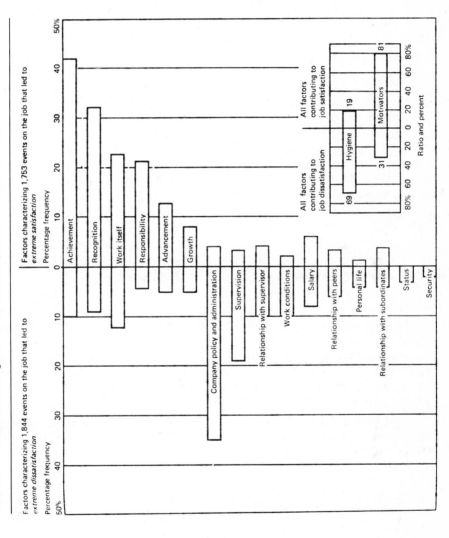

EXHIBIT 2 "Triangle" of Philosophies of Personnel Management

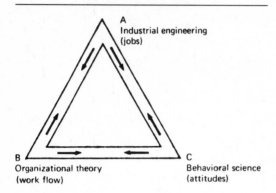

that he can obtain the optimal organization of work and the proper work attitudes.

The behavioral scientist focuses on group sentiments, attitudes of individual employees, and the organization's social and psychological climate. According to his persuasion, he emphasizes one or more of the various hygiene and motivator needs. His approach to personnel management generally emphasizes some form of human relations education, in the hope of instilling healthy employee attitudes and an organizational climate which he considers to be felicitous to human values. He believes that proper attitudes will lead to efficient job and organizational structure.

There is always a lively debate as to the overall effectiveness of the approaches of the organizational theorist and the industrial engineer. Manifestly they have achieved much. But the nagging question for the behavioral scientist has been: What is the cost in human problems that eventually cause more expense to the organization—for instance, turnover, absenteeism, errors, violation of safety rules, strikes, restriction of output, higher wages, and greater fringe benefits? On the other hand, the behavioral scientist is hard put to document much manifest improvement in personnel management, using his approach.

The three philosophies can be depicted as a triangle, as is done in Exhibit 2, with each persuasion claiming the apex angle. The motivation-hygiene theory claims the same angle as industrial engineering, but for opposite goals. Rather than rationalizing the work to increase efficiency, the theory suggests that work be *enriched* to bring about effective utilization of personnel. Such a systematic attempt to motivate employees by manipulating the motivator factors is just beginning.

The term *job enrichment* describes this embryonic movement. An older term, job enlargement, should be avoided because it is associated with past failures stemming from a misunderstanding of the problem.

Job enrichment provides the opportunity for the employee's psychological growth, while job enlargement merely makes a job structurally bigger. Since scientific job enrichment is very new, this article only suggests the principles and practical steps that have recently emerged from several successful experiments in industry.

Job Loading

In attempting to enrich an employee's job, management often succeeds in reducing the man's personal contribution, rather than giving him an opportunity for growth in his accustomed job. Such an endeavor, which I shall call horizontal job loading (as opposed to vertical loading, or providing motivator factors), has been the problem of earlier job enlargement programs. This activity merely enlarges the meaninglessness of the job. Some examples of this approach, and their effect, are:

- Challenging the employee by increasing the amount of production expected of him. If he tightens 10,000 bolts a day, see if he can tighten 20,000 bolts a day. The arithmetic involved shows that multiplying zero by zero still equals zero.
- Adding another meaningless task to the existing one, usually some routine clerical activity. The arithmetic here is adding zero to zero.
- Rotating the assignments of a number of jobs that need to be enriched. This means washing dishes for a while, then washing silverware. The arithmetic is substituting one zero for another zero.
- Removing the most difficult parts of this assignment in order to free the worker to accomplish more of the less challenging assignments. This traditional industrial engineering approach amounts to substraction in the hope of accomplishing addition.

These are common forms of horizontal loading that frequently come up in preliminary brainstorming sessions on job enrichment. The principles of vertical loading have not all been worked out as yet, and they remain rather general, but I have furnished seven useful starting points for consideration in Exhibit 3.

A Successful Application

An example from a highly successful job enrichment experiment can illustrate the distinction between horizontal and vertical loading of a job. The subjects of this study were the stockholder correspondents employed by a very large corporation. Seemingly, the task required of these carefully selected and highly trained correspondents was quite complex and challenging. But almost all indexes of performance and job attitudes were low, and exit interviewing confirmed that the challenge of the job existed merely as words.

EXHIBIT 3 Principles of Vertical Job Loading

Principle	Motivators Involved
A. Removing some controls while retaining accountability	Responsibility and personal achievement
B. Increasing the accountability of individuals for own work	Responsibility and recognition
C. Giving a person a complete natural unit of work (module, division, area, and so on)	Responsibility, achievement, and recognition
D. Granting additional authority to an employee in his activity; job freedom	Responsibility, achievement, and recognition
E. Making periodic reports directly available to the worker himself rather than to the supervisor	Internal recognition
F. Introducing new and more difficult tasks not previously handled	Growth and learning
G. Assigning individuals specific or specialized tasks, enabling them to become experts	Responsibility, growth, and advancement

A job enrichment project was initiated in the form of an experiment with one group, designated as an achieving unit, having its job enriched by the principles described in Exhibit 3. A control group continued to do its job in the traditional way. (There were also two "uncommitted" groups of correspondents formed to measure the so-called Hawthorne Effect—that is, to gauge whether productivity and attitudes toward the job changed artificially merely because employees sensed that the company was paying more attention to them in doing something different or novel. The results for these groups were substantially the same as for the control group, and for the sake of simplicity I do not deal with them in this summary.) No changes in hygiene were introduced for either group other than those that would have been made anyway, such as normal pay increases.

The changes for the achieving unit were introduced in the first two months, averaging one per week of the seven motivators listed in Exhibit 3. At the end of six months the members of the achieving unit were found to be outperforming their counterparts in the control group, and in addition indicated a marked increase in their liking for their jobs. Other results showed that the achieving group had lower absenteeism and, subsequently, a much higher rate or promotion.

Exhibit 4 illustrates the changes in performance, measured in February and March, before the study period began, and at the end of each month of the study period. The shareholder service index represents quality of letters, including accuracy of information, and speed of response to stockholders' letters of inquiry. The index of a current month was aver-

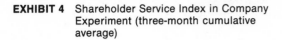

EXHIBIT 4 Shareholder Service Index in Company Experiment (three-month cumulative average)

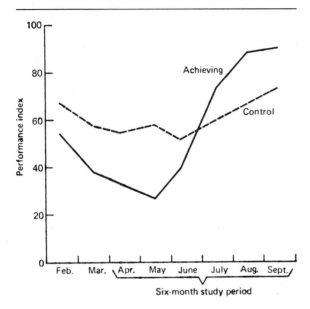

aged into the average of the two prior months, which means that improvement was harder to obtain if the indexes of the previous months were low. The "achievers" were performing less well before the six-month period started, and their performance service index continued to decline after the introduction of the motivators, evidently because of uncertainty over their newly granted responsibilities. In the third month, however, performance improved, and soon the members of this group had reached a high level of accomplishment.

Exhibit 5 shows the two groups' attitudes toward their job, measured at the end of March, just before the first motivator was introduced, and again at the end of September. The correspondents were asked 16 questions, all involving motivation. A typical one was, "As you see it, how many opportunities do you feel that you have in your job for making worthwhile contributions?" The answers were scaled from 1 to 5, with 80 as the maximum possible score. The achievers became much more positive about their job, while the attitude of the control unit remained about the same (the drop is not statistically significant).

How was the job of these correspondents restructured? Exhibit 6 lists the suggestions made that were deemed to be horizontal loading, and the actual vertical loading changes that were incorporated in the job of the achieving unit. The capital letters under "Principle" after "Vertical loading" refer to the corresponding letters in Exhibit 3. The reader will note

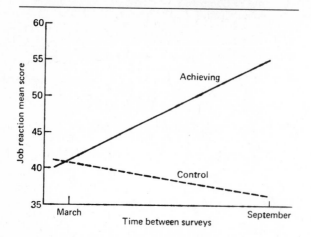

Horizontal Loading Suggestions (Rejected)	Vertical Loading Suggestions (Adopted)	Principle
Firm quotas could be set for letters to be answered each day, using a rate which would be hard to reach.	Subject matter experts were appointed within each unit for other members of the unit to consult with before seeking supervisory help. (The supervisor had been answering all specialized and difficult questions.)	G
The women could type the letters themselves, as well as compose them, or take on any other clerical functions.	Correspondents signed their own names on letters. (The supervisor had been signing all letters.)	B
All difficult or complex inquiries could be channeled to a few women so that the remainder could achieve high rates of output. These jobs could be exchanged from time to time.	The work of the more experienced correspondents was proofread less frequently by supervisors and was done at the correspondents' desks, dropping verification from 100% to 10%. (Previously, all correspondents' letters had been checked by the supervisor.)	A
	Production was discussed, but only in terms such as "a full day's work is expected." As time went on, this was no longer mentioned. (Before, the group had been constantly reminded of the number of letters that needed to be answered.)	D
The women could be rotated through units handling different customers, and then sent back to their own units.	Outgoing mail went directly to the mailroom without going over supervisor's desks. (The letters had always been routed through the supervisors.)	A
	Correspondents were encouraged to answer letters in a more personalized way. (Reliance on the form-letter approach had been standard practice.)	C
	Each correspondent was held personally responsible for the quality and accuracy of letters. (This responsibility had been the province of the supervisor and the verifier.)	B, E

that the rejected forms of horizontal loading correspond closely to the list of common manifestations of the phenomenon on page 292, right column.

STEPS TO JOB ENRICHMENT

Now that the motivator idea has been described in practice, here are the steps that managers should take in instituting the principle with their employees:

1. Select those jobs in which (a) the investment in industrial engineering does not make changes too costly, (b) attitudes are poor, (c) hygiene is becoming very costly, and (d) motivation will make a difference in performance.

2. Approach these jobs with the conviction that they can be changed. Years of tradition have led managers to believe that the content of the jobs is sacrosanct and the only scope of action that they have is in the ways of stimulating people.

3. Brainstorm a list of changes that may enrich the jobs, without concern for their practicality.

4. Screen the list to eliminate suggestions that involve hygiene, rather than actual motivation.

5. Screen the list of generalities, such as "give them more responsibility," that are rarely followed in practice. This might seem obvious, but the motivator words have never left industry; the substance has just been rationalized and organized out. Words like "responsibility," "growth," "achievement," and "challenge," for example, have been elevated to the lyrics of the patriotic anthem for all organizations. It is the old problem typified by the pledge of allegiance to the flag being more important than contributions to the country—of following the form, rather than the substance.

6. Screen the list to eliminate any *horizontal* loading suggestions.

7. Avoid direct participation by the employees whose jobs are to be enriched. Ideas they have expressed previously certainly constitute a valuable source for recommended changes, but their direct involvement contaminates the process with human relations *hygiene* and, more specifically, gives them only a *sense* of making a contribution. The job is to be changed, and it is the content that will produce the motivation, not attitudes about being involved or the challenge inherent in setting up a job. That process will be over shortly, and it is what the employees will be doing from then on that will determine their motivation. A sense of participation will result only in short-term movement.

8. In the initial attempts at job enrichment, set up a controlled experiment. At least two equivalent groups should be chosen, one an experimental unit in which the motivators are systematically introduced over a period of time, and the other one a control group in which no changes are made. For both groups, hygiene should be allowed to follow its natural

course for the duration of the experiment. Pre- and post-installation tests of performance and job attitudes are necessary to evaluate the effectiveness of the job enrichment program. The attitude test must be limited to motivator items in order to divorce the employee's view of the job he is given from all the surrounding hygiene feelings that he might have.

9. Be prepared for a drop in performance in the experimental group the first few weeks. The changeover to a new job may lead to a temporary reduction in efficiency.

10. Expect your first-line supervisors to experience some anxiety and hostility over the changes you are making. The anxiety comes from their fear that the changes will result in poorer performance for their unit. Hostility will arise when the employees start assuming what the supervisors regard as their own responsibility for performance. The supervisor without checking duties to perform may then be left with little to do.

After a successful experiment, however, the supervisor usually discovers the supervisory and managerial functions he has neglected, or which were never his because all his time was given over to checking the work of his subordinates. For example, in the R&D division of one large chemical company I know of, the supervisors of the laboratory assistants were theoretically responsible for their training and evaluation. These functions, however, had come to be performed in a routine, unsubstantial fashion. After the job enrichment program, during which the supervisors were not merely passive observers of the assistants' performance, the supervisors actually were devoting their time to reviewing performance and administering thorough training.

What has been called an employee-centered style of supervision will come about not through education of supervisors, but by changing the jobs that they do.

CONCLUDING NOTE

Job enrichment will not be a one-time proposition, but a continuous management function. The initial changes, however, should last for a very long period of time. Thee are a number of reasons for this:

- The changes should bring the job up to the level of challenge commensurate with the skill that was hired.
- Those who have still more ability eventually will be able to demonstrate it better and win promotion to higher-level jobs.
- The very nature of motivators, as opposed to hygiene factors, is that they have a much longer-term effect on employees' attitudes. Perhaps the job will have to be enriched again, but this will not occur as frequently as the need for hygiene.

Not all jobs can be enriched, nor do all jobs need to be enriched. If only a small percentage of the time and money that is now devoted to hygiene, however, were given to job enrichment efforts, the return in human satis-faction and economic gain would be one of the largest dividends that industry and society have ever reaped through their efforts at better personnel management.

The argument for job enrichment can be summed up quite simply: If you have someone on a job, use him. If you can't use him on the job, get rid of him, either via automation or by selecting someone with lesser ability. If you can't use him and you can't get rid of him, you will have a motiva-tion problem.

25

On the Folly of Rewarding A, while Hoping for B

Steven Kerr

Supposedly, we reward people for doing what we want them to and don't reward them when they do something else. While it sounds very simple and straightforward, this article by Steven Kerr suggests that it isn't that way at all. He notes that all too often organizations create motivational forces which lead to unwanted and unintended consequences by rewarding behaviors that are not desired and by discouraging behaviors that are desired.—Eds.

Whether dealing with monkeys, rats, or human beings, it is hardly controversial to state that most organisms seek information concerning what activities are rewarded, and then seek to do (or at least pretend to do) those things, often to the virtual exclusion of activities not rewarded. The extent to which this occurs of course will depend on the perceived attractiveness of the rewards offered, but neither operant nor expectancy theorists would quarrel with the essence of this notion.

Nevertheless, numerous examples exist of reward systems that are fouled up in that behaviors which are rewarded are those which the rewarder is trying to *discourage,* while the behavior he desires is not being rewarded at all.

In an effort to understand and explain this phenomenon, this paper presents examples from society, from organizations in general, and from profit-making firms in particular. Data from a manufacturing company and information from an insurance firm are examined to demonstrate the consequences of such reward systems for the organizations involved, and

SOURCE: Reprinted from *Academy of Management Journal,* 1975, *18,* pp. 769–83.

possible reasons why such reward systems continue to exist are considered.

SOCIETAL EXAMPLES

Politics

Official goals are "purposely vague and general and do not indicate . . . the host of decisions that must be made among alternative ways of achieving official goals and the priority of multiple goals . . ." (8, p. 66). They usually may be relied on to offend absolutely no one, and in this sense can be considered high-acceptance, low-quality goals. An example might be "build better schools." Operative goals are higher in quality but lower in acceptance, since they specify where the money will come from, what alternative goals will be ignored, etc.

The American citzenry supposedly wants its candidates for public office to set forth operative goals, making their proposed programs "perfectly clear," specifying sources and uses of funds, etc. However, since operative goals are lower in acceptance, and since aspirants to public office need acceptance (from at least 50.1 percent of the people), most politicians prefer to speak only of official goals, at least until after the election. They of course would agree to speak at the operative level if "punished" for not doing so. The electorate could do this by refusing to support candidates who do not speak at the operative level.

Instead, however, the American voter typically punishes (withholds support from) candidates who frankly discuss where the money will come from, rewards politicians who speak only of official goals, but hopes that candidates (despite the reward system) will discuss the issues operatively. It is academic whether it was moral for Nixon, for example, to refuse to discuss his 1968 "secret plan" to end the Vietnam war, his 1972 operative goals concerning the lifting of price controls, the reshuffling of his cabinet, etc. The point is that the reward system made such refusal rational.

It seems worth mentioning that no manuscript can adequately define what is "moral" and what is not. However, examination of costs and benefits, combined with knowledge of what motivates a particular individual, often will suffice to determine what for him is "rational."[1] If the reward system is so designed that it is irrational to be moral, this does not necessarily mean that immorality will result. But is this not asking for trouble?

War

If some oversimplification may be permitted, let it be assumed that the primary goal of the organization (Pentagon, Luftwaffe, or whatever) is to win. Let it be assumed further that the primary goal of most individuals on the front lines is to get home alive. Then there appears to be an important conflict in goals—personally rational behavior by those at the bottom will endanger goal attainment by those at the top.

But not necessarily! It depends on how the reward system is set up. The Vietnam war was indeed a study of disobedience and rebellion, with terms such as "fragging" (killing one's own commanding officer) and "search and evade" becoming part of the military vocabulary. The difference in subordinates' acceptance of authority between World War II and Vietnam is reported to be considerable, and veterans of the Second World War often have been quoted as being outraged at the mutinous actions of many American soldiers in Vietnam.

Consider, however, some critical differences in the reward system in use during the two conflicts. What did the GI in World War II want? To go home. And when did he get to go home? When the war was won! If he disobeyed the orders to clean out the trenches and take the hills, the war would not be won and he would not go home. Furthermore, what were his chances of attaining his goal (getting home alive) if he obeyed the orders compared to his chances if he did not? What is being suggested is that the rational soldier in World War II, *whether patriotic or not,* probably found it expedient to obey.

Consider the reward system in use in Vietnam. What did the man at the bottom want? To go home. And when did he get to go home? When his tour of duty was over! This was the case *whether or not* the war was won. Furthermore, concerning the relative chance of getting home alive by obeying orders compared to the chance if they were disobeyed, it is worth noting that a mutineer in Vietnam was far more likely to be assigned rest and rehabilitation (on the assumption that fatigue was the cause) than he was to suffer any negative consequence.

In his description of the "zone of indifference," Barnard stated that "a person can and will accept a communication as authoritative only when . . . at the time of his decision, he believes it to be compatible with his personal interests as a whole" (1, p. 165). In light of the reward system used in Vietnam, would it not have been personally irrational for some orders to have been obeyed? Was not the military implementing a system which *rewarded* disobedience, while *hoping* that soldiers (despite the reward system) would obey orders?

Medicine

Theoretically, a physician can make either of two types of error, and intuitively one seems as bad as the other. A doctor can pronounce a patient sick when he is actually well, thus causing him needless anxiety and expense, curtailment of enjoyable foods and activities, and even physical danger by subjecting him to needless medication and surgery. Alternately, a doctor can label a sick person well, and thus avoid treating what may be a serious, even fatal ailment. It might be natural to conclude that physicians seek to minimize both types of error.

Such a conclusion would be wrong.[2] It is estimated that numerous Americans are presently afflicted with iatrogenic (physician *caused*) illnesses (9). This occurs when the doctor is approached by someone complaining of a few stray symptoms. The doctor classifies and organizes these symptoms, gives them a name, and obligingly tells the patient what further symptoms may be expected. This information often acts as a self-fulfilling prophecy, with the result that from that day on the patient for all practical purposes is sick.

Why does this happen? Why are physicians so reluctant to sustain a type 2 error (pronouncing a sick person well) that they will tolerate many type 1 errors? Again, a look at the reward system is needed. The punishments for a type 2 error are real: guilt, embarrassment, and the threat of lawsuit and scandal. On the other hand, a type 1 error (labeling a well person sick) "is sometimes seen as sound clinical practice, indicating a healthy conservative approach to medicine" (9, p. 69). Type 1 errors also are likely to generate increased income and a stream of steady customers who, being well in a limited physiological sense, will not embarrass the doctor by dying abruptly.

Fellow physicians and the general public therefore are really *rewarding* type 1 errors and at the same time *hoping* fervently that doctors will try not to make them.

GENERAL ORGANIZATIONAL EXAMPLES

Rehabilitation Centers and Orphanages

In terms of the prime beneficiary classification (2, p. 42) organizations such as these are supposed to exist for the "public-in-contact," that is, clients. The orphanage therefore theoretically is interested in placing as many children as possible in good homes. However, often orphanages surround themselves with so many rules concerning adoption that it is nearly impossible to pry a child out of the place. Orphanages may deny adoption unless the applicants are a married couple, both of the same religion as the child, without history of emotional or vocational instability, with a specified minimum income and a private room for the child, etc.

If the primary goal is to place children in good homes, then the rules ought to constitute means toward that goal. Goal displacement results when these "means become ends-in-themselves that displace the original goals" (2, p. 229).

To some extent these rules are required by law. But the influence of the reward system on the orphanage's management should not be ignored. Consider, for example, that the:

1. Number of children enrolled often is the most important determinant of the size of the allocated budget.

2. Number of children under the director's care also will affect the size of his staff.

3. Total organizational size will determine largely the director's prestige at the annual conventions, in the community, etc.

Therefore, to the extent that staff size, total budget, and personal prestige are valued by the orphanage's executive personnel, it becomes rational for them to make it difficult for children to be adopted. After all, who wants to be the director of the smallest orphanage in the state?

If the reward system errs in the opposite direction, paying off only for placements, extensive goal displacement again is likely to result. A common example of vocational rehabilitation in many states, for example, consists of placing someone in a job for which he has little interest and few qualifications, for two months or so, and then "rehabilitating" him again in another position. Such behavior is quite consistent with the prevailing reward system, which pays off for the number of individuals placed in any position for 60 days or more. Rehabilitation counselors also confess to competing with one another to place relatively skilled clients, sometimes ignoring persons with few skills who would be harder to place. Extensively disabled clients find that counselors often prefer to work with those whose disabilities are less severe.[3]

Universities

Society *hopes* that teachers will not neglect their teaching responsibilities but *rewards* them almost entirely for research and publications. This is most true at the large and prestigious universities. Clichés such as "good research and good teaching go together" notwithstanding, professors often find that they must choose between teaching and research-oriented activities when allocating their time. Rewards for good teaching usually are limited to outstanding teacher awards, which are given to only a small percentage of good teachers and which usually bestow little money and fleeting prestige. Punishments for poor teaching also are rare.

Rewards for research and publications, on the other hand, and punishments for failure to accomplish these, are commonly administered by universities at which teachers are employed. Furthermore, publication-oriented resumés usually will be well received at other universities, whereas teaching credentials, harder to document and quantify, are much less transferable. Consequently it is rational for university teachers to concentrate on research, even if to the detriment of teaching and at the expense of their students.

By the same token, it is rational for students to act based upon the goal displacement which has occurred within universities concerning what they are rewarded for. If it is assumed that a primary goal of a university is to transfer knowledge from teacher to student, then grades become identifiable as a means toward that goal, serving as motivational, control, and feedback devices to expedite the knowledge transfer. Instead, however, the grades themselves have become much more important for entrance to graduate school, successful employment, tuition refunds, parental respect, etc., than the knowledge or lack of knowledge they are supposed to signify.

It therefore should come as no surprise that information has surfaced in recent years concerning fraternity files for examinations, term-paper writing services, organized cheating at the service academies, and the like. Such activities constitute a personally rational response to a reward system which pays off for grades rather than knowledge.

BUSINESS-RELATED EXAMPLES

Ecology

Assume that the president of XYZ Corporation is confronted with the following alternatives:

1. Spend $11 million for antipollution equipment to keep from poisoning fish in the river adjacent to the plant; or
2. Do nothing, in violation of the law, and assume a one in ten chance of being caught, with a resultant $1 million fine plus the necessity of buying the equipment.

Under this not unrealistic set of choices it requires no linear program to determine that XYZ Corporation can maximize its probabilities by flouting the law. Add the fact that XYZ's president is probably being rewarded (by creditors, stockholders, and other salient parts of his task environment) according to criteria totally unrelated to the number of fish poisoned, and his probable course of action becomes clear.

Evaluation of Training

It is axiomatic that those who care about a firm's well-being should insist that the organization get fair value for its expenditures. Yet it is commonly known that firms seldom bother to evaluate a new GRID, MBO, job enrichment program, or whatever, to see if the company is getting its money's worth. Why? Certainly it is not because people have not pointed out that this situation exists; numerous practitioner-oriented articles are written each year to just this point.

The individuals (whether in personnel, manpower planning, or wherever) who normally would be responsible for conducting such evaluations are the same ones often charged with introducing the change effort in the first place. Having convinced top management to spend the money, they usually are quite animated afterwards in collecting rigorous vignettes and anecdotes about how successful the program was. The last thing many desire is a formal, systematic, and revealing evaluation. Although members of top management may actually *hope* for such systematic evaluation, their reward systems continue to *reward* ignorance in this area. And if the personnel department abdicates its responsibility, who is to step into the breach? The change agent himself? Hardly! He is likely to be too busy collecting anecdotal "evidence" of his own, for use with his next client.

Miscellaneous

Many additional examples could be cited of systems which in fact are rewarding behaviors other than those supposedly desired by the rewarder. A few of these are described briefly below.

Most coaches disdain to discuss individual accomplishments, preferring to speak of teamwork, proper attitude, and a one-for-all spirit. Usually, however, rewards are distributed according to individual performance. The college basketball player who feeds his teammates instead of shooting will not compile impressive scoring statistics and is less likely to be drafted by the pros. The ballplayer who hits to right field to advance the runners will win neither the batting nor home run titles, and will be offered smaller raises. It therefore is rational for players to think of themselves first, and the team second.

In business organizations where rewards are dispensed for unit performance or for individual goals achieved, without regard for overall effectiveness, similar attitudes often are observed. Under most Management by Objectives (MBO) systems, goals in areas where quantification is difficult often go unspecified. The organization therefore often is in a position where it *hopes* for employee effort in the areas of team building, interpersonal relations, creativity, etc., but it formally *rewards* none of these. In cases where promotions and raises are formally tied to MBO, the system itself contains a paradox in that it "asks employees to set challenging, risky goals, only to face smaller paychecks and possibly damaged careers if these goals are not accomplished" (5, p. 40).

It is *hoped* that administrators will pay attention to long-run costs and opportunities and will institute programs which will bear fruit later on. However, many organizational reward systems pay off for short-run sales and earnings only. Under such circumstances it is personally rational for officials to sacrifice long-term growth and profit (by selling off equipment and property, or by stifling research and development) for short-term advantages. This probably is most pertinent in the public sector, with the result that many public officials are unwilling to implement programs which will not show benefits by election time.

As a final, clear-cut example of a fouled-up reward system, consider the cost-plus contract or its next of kin, the allocation of next year's budget as a direct function of this year's expenditures. It probably is conceivable that those who award such budgets and contracts really hope for economy and prudence in spending. It is obvious, however, that adopting the proverb "to him who spends shall more be given," rewards not economy, but spending itself.

TWO COMPANIES' EXPERIENCES

A Manufacturing Organization

A midwest manufacturer of industrial goods had been troubled for some time by aspects of its organizational climate it believed dysfunctional. For research purposes, interviews were conducted with many employees and a questionnaire was administered on a company-wide basis, including plants and offices in several American and Canadian locations. The company strongly encouraged employee participation in the survey, and made available time and space during the workday for completion of the instrument. All employees in attendance during the day of the survey completed the questionnaire. All instruments were collected directly by the researcher, who personally administered each session. Since no one employed by the firm handled the questionnaires, and since respondent names were not asked for, it seems likely that the pledge of anonymity given was believed.

A modified version of the Expect Approval scale (7) was included as part of the questionnaire. The instrument asked respondents to indicate the degree of approval or disapproval they could expect if they performed each of the described actions. A seven-point Likert scale was used, with 1 indicating that the action would probably bring strong disapproval and 7 signifying likely strong approval.

Although normative data for this scale from studies of other organizations are unavailable, it is possible to examine fruitfully the data obtained from this survey in several ways. First, it may be worth noting that the questionnaire data corresponded closely to information gathered through interviews. Furthermore, as can be seen from the results summarized in Table 1, sizable differences between various work units, and between employees at different job levels within the same work unit, were obtained. This suggests that response bias effects (social desirability in particular loomed as a potential concern) are not likely to be severe.

Most importantly, comparisons between scores obtained on the Expect Approval scale and a statement of problems which were the reason for the survey revealed that the same behaviors which managers in each division thought dysfunctional were those which lower level employees claimed were rewarded. As compared to job levels 1 to 8 in Division B (see Table 1), those in Division A claimed a much higher acceptance by management of "conforming" activities. Between 31 and 37 percent of Division A employees at levels 1–8 stated that going along with the majority, agreeing with the boss, and staying on everyone's good side brought

TABLE 1 Summary of Two Divisions' Data Relevant to Conforming and Risk-Avoidance Behaviors (extent to which subjects expect approval)

				Percentage of Workers Responding		
Dimension	Item	Division and Sample	Total Responses	1, 2, or 3 (Disapproval)	4	5, 6, or 7 (Approval)
Risk avoidance	Making a risky decision based on the best information available at the time, but which turns out wrong.	A, levels 1–4 (lowest)	127	61	25	14
		A, levels 5–8	172	46	31	23
		A, levels 9 and above	17	41	30	30
		B, levels 1–4 (lowest)	31	58	26	16
		B, levels 5–8	19	42	42	16
		B, levels 9 and above	10	50	20	30
Risk	Setting extremely high and challenging standards and goals, and then narrowly failing to make them.	A, levels 1–4	122	47	28	25
		A, levels 5–8	168	33	26	41
		A, levels 9+	17	24	6	70

	B, levels 1–4	31	48	23	29
	B, levels 5–8	18	17	33	50
	B, levels 9+	10	30	0	70
Setting goals which are extremely easy to make and then making them.	A, levels 1–4	124	35	30	35
	A, levels 5–8	171	47	27	26
	A, levels 9+	17	70	24	6
	B, levels 1–4	31	58	26	16
	B, levels 5–8	19	63	16	21
	B, levels 9+	10	80	0	20
Being a "yes man" and always agreeing with the boss.	A, levels 1–4	126	46	17	37
	A, levels 5–8	180	54	14	31
	A, levels 9+	17	88	12	0
	B, levels 1–4	32	53	28	19
	B, levels 5–8	19	68	21	11
	B, levels 9+	10	80	10	10

TABLE 1 *(concluded)*

Dimension	Item	Division and Sample	Total Responses	Percentage of Workers Responding		
				1, 2, or 3 (Disapproval)	4	5, 6, or 7 (Approval)
	Always going along with the majority.	A, levels 1–4	125	40	25	35
		A, levels 5–8	173	47	21	32
		A, levels 9+	17	70	12	18
		B, levels 1–4	31	61	23	16
		B, levels 5–8	19	68	11	21
		B, levels 9+	10	80	10	10
	Being careful to stay on the good side of everyone, so that everyone agrees that you are a great guy.	A, levels 1–4	124	45	18	37
		A, levels 5–8	173	45	22	33
		A, levels 9+	17	64	6	30
		B, levels 1–4	31	54	23	23
		B, levels 5–8	19	73	11	16
		B, levels 9+	10	80	10	10

approval; only once (level 5–8 responses to one of the three items) did a majority suggest that such actions would generate disapproval.

Furthermore, responses from Division A workers at levels 1–4 indicate that behaviors geared toward risk avoidance were as likely to be rewarded as to be punished. Only at job levels 9 and above was it apparent that the reward system was positively reinforcing behaviors desired by top management. Overall, the same "tendencies toward conservatism and apple-polishing at the lower levels" which divisional management had complained about during the interviews were those claimed by subordinates to be the most rational course of action in light of the existing reward system. Management apparently was not getting the behaviors it was *hoping* for, but it certainly was getting the behaviors it was perceived by subordinates to be *rewarding*.

An Insurance Firm

The Group Health Claims Division of a large eastern insurance company provides another rich illustration of a reward system which reinforces behaviors not desired by top management.

Attempting to measure and reward accuracy in paying surgical claims, the firm systematically keeps track of the number of returned checks and letters of complaint received from policyholders. However, underpayments are likely to provoke cries of outrage from the insured, while overpayments often are accepted in courteous silence. Since it often is impossible to tell from the physician's statement which of two surgical procedures, with different allowable benefits, was performed, and since writing for clarifications will interfere with other standards used by the firm concerning "percentage of claims paid within two days of receipt," the new hire in more than one claims section is soon acquainted with the informal norm: "When in doubt, pay it out!"

The situation would be even worse were it not for the fact that other features of the firm's reward system tend to neutralize those described. For example, annual "merit" increases are given to all employees, in one of the following three amounts:

1. If the worker is "outstanding" (a select category, into which no more than two employees per section may be placed): 5 percent
2. If the worker is "above average" (normally all workers not "outstanding" are so rated): 4 percent
3. If the worker commits gross acts of negligence and irresponsibility for which he might be discharged in many other companies: 3 percent.

Now, since *(a)* the difference between the 5 percent theoretically attainable through hard work and the 4 percent attainable merely by living until the review date is small and *(b)* since insurance firms seldom dispense much of a salary increase in cash (rather, the worker's insurance benefits increase, causing him to be further overinsured), many employees are rather indifferent to the possibility of obtaining the extra one percent reward and therefore tend to ignore the norm concerning indiscriminant payments.

However, most employees are not indifferent to the rule which states that, should absences or latenesses total three or more in any six-month period, the entire 4 or 5 percent due at the next "merit" review must be forfeited. In this sense the firm may be described as *hoping* for performance, while *rewarding* attendance. What it gets, of course, is attendance. (If the absence-lateness rule appears to the reader to be stringent, it really is not. The company counts "times" rather than "days" absent, and a ten-day absence therefore counts the same as one lasting two days. A worker in danger of accumulating a third absence within six months merely has to remain ill [away from work] during his second absence until his first absence is more than six months old. The limiting factor is that at some point his salary ceases, and his sickness benefits take over. This usually is sufficient to get the younger workers to return, but for those with 20 or more years' service, the company provides sickness benefits of 90 percent of normal salary, tax-free! Therefore . . .)

CAUSES

Extremely diverse instances of systems which reward behavior A although the rewarder apparently hopes for behavior B have been given. These are useful to illustrate the breadth and magnitude of the phenomenon, but the diversity increases the difficulty of determining commonalities and establishing causes. However, four general factors may be pertinent to an explanation of why fouled-up reward systems seem to be so prevelant.

Fascination with an "Objective" Criterion

It has been mentioned elsewhere that:

> Most "objective" measures of productivity are objective only in that their subjective elements are (a) determined in advance, rather than coming into play at the time of the formal evaluation, and (b) well concealed on the rating instrument itself. Thus industrial firms seeking to devise objective rating systems first decide, in an arbitrary manner, what dimensions are to be rated, . . . usually including some items having little to do with organizational effectiveness while excluding others that do. Only then does Personnel Division churn out official-looking documents on which all dimensions chosen to be rated are assigned point values, categories, or whatever (6, p. 92).

Nonetheless, many individuals seek to establish simple, quantifiable standards against which to measure and reward performance. Such efforts may be successful in highly predictable areas within an organization, but are likely to cause goal displacement when applied anywhere else. Overconcern with attendance and lateness in the insurance firm and with number of people placed in the vocational rehabilitation division may have been largely responsible for the problems described in those organizations.

Overemphasis on Highly Visible Behaviors

Difficulties often stem from the fact that some parts of the task are highly visible while other parts are not. For example, publications are easier to demonstrate than teaching, and scoring baskets and hitting home runs are more readily observable than feeding teammates and advancing base runners. Similarly, the adverse consequences of pronouncing a sick person well are more visible than those sustained by labeling a well person sick. Team-building and creativity are other examples of behaviors which may not be rewarded simply because they are hard to observe.

Hypocrisy

In some of the instances described the rewarder may have been getting the desired behavior, notwithstanding claims that the behavior was not desired. This may be true, for example, of management's attitude toward apple-polishing in the manufacturing firm (a behavior which subordinates felt was rewarded, despite management's avowed dislike of the practice). This also may explain politicians' unwillingness to revise the penalties for disobedience of ecology laws, and the failure of top management to devise reward systems which would cause systematic evaluation of training and development programs.

Emphasis on Morality or Equity Rather than Efficiency

Some consideration of other factors prevents the establishment of a system which rewards behaviors desired by the rewarder. The felt obligation of many Americans to vote for one candidate or another, for example, may impair their ability to withhold support from politicians who refuse to discuss the issues. Similarly, the concern for spreading the risks and costs of wartime military service may outweigh the advantage to be obtained by committing personnel to combat until the war is over.

It should be noted that only with respect to the first two causes are reward systems really paying off for other than desired behaviors. In the case of the third and fourth causes the system *is* rewarding behaviors desired by the rewarder, and the systems are fouled up only from the standpoints of those who believe the rewarder's public statements (cause 3), or those who seek to maximize efficiency rather than other outcomes (cause 4).

CONCLUSIONS

Modern organization theory requires a recognition that the members of organizations and society possess divergent goals and motives. It therefore is unlikely that managers and their subordinates will seek the same outcomes. Three possible remedies for this potential problem are suggested.

Selection

It is theoretically possible for organizations to employ only those individuals whose goals and motives are wholly consonant with those of management. In such cases the same behaviors judged by subordinates to be rational would be perceived by management as desirable. State-of-the-art reviews of selection techniques, however, provide scant grounds for hope that such an approach would be successful (for example, see 12).

Training

Another theoretical alternative is for the organization to admit those employees whose goals are not consonant with those of management and then, through training, socialization, or whatever, alter employee goals to make them consonant. However, research on the effectiveness of such training programs, though limited, provides further grounds for pessimism (for example, see 3).

Altering the Reward System

What would have been the result if:

1. Nixon had been assured by his advisors that he could not win reelection except by discussing the issues in detail?
2. Physicians' conduct was subjected to regular examination by review boards for type 1 errors (calling healthy people ill) and to penalties (fines, censure, etc.) for errors of either type?
3. The President of XYZ Corporation had to choose between (a) spending $11 million for antipollution equipment, and (b) incurring a 50-50 chance of going to jail for five years?

Managers who complain that their workers are not motivated might do well to consider the possibility that they have installed reward systems which are paying off for behaviors other than those they are seeking. This, in part, is what happened in Vietnam, and this is what regularly frustrates societal efforts to bring about honest politicians, civic-minded managers, etc. This certainly is what happened in both the manufacturing and the insurance companies.

A first step for such managers might be to find out what behaviors currently are being rewarded. Perhaps an instrument similar to that used in the manufacturing firm could be useful for this purpose. Chances are excellent that these managers will be surprised by what they find— that their firms are not rewarding what they assume they are. In fact, such undesirable behavior by organizational members as they have observed may be explained largely by the reward systems in use.

This is not to say that all organizational behavior is determined by formal rewards and punishments. Certainly it is true that in the absence of formal reinforcement some soldiers will be patriotic, some presidents will be ecology-minded, and some orphanage directors will care about children. The point, however, is that in such cases the rewarder is not *causing* the behaviors desired but is only a fortunate bystander. For an organization to *act* upon its members, the formal reward system should positively reinforce desired behaviors, not constitute an obstacle to be overcome.

It might be wise to underscore the obvious fact that there is nothing really new in what has been said. In both theory and practice these matters have been mentioned before. Thus in many states Good Samaritan laws have been installed to protect doctors who stop to assist a stricken motorist. In states without such laws it is commonplace for doctors to refuse to stop, for fear of involvement in a subsequent lawsuit. In college basketball additional penalties have been instituted against players who foul their opponents deliberately. It has long been argued by Milton Friedman and others that penalties should be altered so as to make it irrational to disobey the ecology laws, and so on.

By altering the reward system the organization escapes the necessity of selecting only desirable people or of trying to alter undesirable ones. In Skinnerian terms (as described in 11, p. 704), "As for responsibility and goodness—as commonly defined—no one . . . would want or need them. They refer to a man's behaving well despite the absence of positive reinforcement that is obviously sufficient to explain it. Where such reinforcement exists, 'no one needs goodness.'"

NOTES

1. In Simon's (10, pp. 76–77) terms, a decision is "subjectively rational" if it maximizes an individual's valued outcomes so far as his knowledge permits. A decision is "personally rational" if it is oriented toward the individual's goals.

2. In one study (4) of 14,867 films for signs of tuberculosis, 1,216 positive readings turned out to be clinically negative; only 24 negative readings proved clinically active, a ratio of 50 to 1.

3. Personal interviews conducted during 1972–73.

REFERENCES

1. Barnard, Chester I. *The functions of the executive.* Cambridge, Mass.: Harvard University Press, 1968. [First published in 1936.]

2. Blau, Peter M., & Scott, W. Richard. *Formal organizations.* San Francisco: Chandler, 1962.

3. Fiedler, Fred E. Predicting the effects of leadership training and experience from the contingency model. *Journal of Applied Psychology,* 1972, *56,* 114–119.

4. Garland, L. H. Studies of the accuracy of diagnostic procedures. *American Journal Roentgenological, Radium Therapy Nuclear Medicine,* 1959, *82,* 25–28.

5. Kerr, Steven. Some modifications in MBO as an OD strategy. *Academy of Management Proceedings,* 1973, pp. 39–42.

6. Kerr, Steven. What price objectivity? *American Sociologist,* 1973, *8,* 92–93.

7. Litwin, G. H., & Stringer, R. A., Jr. *Motivation and organizational climate.* Cambridge, Mass.: Harvard University Press, 1968.

8. Perrow, Charles. The analysis of goals in complex organizations. In A. Etzioni (Ed.), *Readings on Modern Organizations.* Englewood Cliffs, N.J.: Prentice-Hall, 1969.

9. Scheff, Thomas J. Decision rules, types of error, and their consequences in medical diagnosis. In F. Massarik & P. Ratoosh (Eds.), *Mathematical Explorations in Behavioral Science.* Homewood, Ill.: Richard D. Irwin, 1965.

10. Simon, Herbert A. *Administrative behavior.* New York: Free Press, 1957.

11. Swanson, G. E. Review symposium: Beyond freedom and dignity. *American Journal of Sociology,* 1972, *78,* 702–705.

12. Webster, E. *Decision making in the employment interview.* Montreal: Industrial Relations Center, McGill University, 1964.

B. Leading

26

The Human Side of Enterprise

Douglas M. McGregor

*In this, one of the most widely reprinted articles in the management litera-
ture, Douglas McGregor introduces the notion that under proper conditions, unimagined resources of creative human energy could become available within organizational settings. Designating the conventional view of
managing as Theory X and the social science based approach as Theory Y,
McGregor discusses the advantages of decentralization, job enlargement,
participation, and performance appraisal.*—Eds.

It has become trite to say that industry has the fundamental know-how to
utilize physical science and technology for the material benefit of mankind, and that we must now learn how to utilize the social sciences to
make our human organizations truly effective.

To a degree, the social sciences today are in a position like that of the
physical sciences with respect to atomic energy in the thirties. We know
that past conceptions of the nature of man are inadequate and, in many
ways, incorrect. We are becoming quite certain that, under proper conditions, unimagined resources of creative human energy could become
available within the organizational setting.

We cannot tell industrial management how to apply this new knowledge in simple, economic ways. We know it will require years of exploration, much costly development research, and a substantial amount of
creative imagination on the part of management to discover how to apply
this growing knowledge to the organization of human effort in industry.

SOURCE: Reprinted by permission of the publisher from *Management Review,* November
1957, © 1957 by American Management Association, Inc.

MANAGEMENT'S TASK: THE CONVENTIONAL VIEW

The conventional conception of management's task in harnessing human energy to organizational requirements can be stated broadly in terms of three propositions. In order to avoid the complications introduced by a label, let us call this set of propositions "Theory X":

1. Management is responsible for organizing the elements of productive enterprise—money, materials, equipment, people—in the interest of economic ends.
2. With respect to people, this is a process of directing their efforts, motivating them, controlling their actions, modifying their behavior to fit the needs of the organization.
3. Without this active intervention by management, people would be passive—even resistant—to organizational needs. They must therefore be persuaded, rewarded, punished, controlled—their activities must be directed. This is management's task. We often sum it up by saying that management consists of getting things done through other people.

Behind this conventional theory there are several additional beliefs—less explicit, but widespread:

4. The average man is by nature indolent—he works as little as possible.
5. He lacks ambition, dislikes responsibility, prefers to be led.
6. He is inherently self-centered, indifferent to organizational needs.
7. He is by nature resistant to change.
8. He is gullible, not very bright, the ready dupe of the charlatan and the demagogue.

The human side of economic enterprise today is fashioned from propositions and beliefs such as these. Conventional organization structures and managerial policies, practices, and programs reflect these assumptions.

In accomplishing its task—with these assumptions as guides—management has conceived of a range of possibilities.

At one extreme, management can be "hard" or "strong." The methods for directing behavior involve coercion and threat (usually disguised), close supervision, tight controls over behavior. At the other extreme, management can be "soft" or "weak." The methods for directing behavior involve being permissive, satisfying people's demands, achieving harmony. Then they will be tractable, accept direction.

This range has been fairly completely explored during the past half century, and management has learned some things from the exploration. There are difficulties in the "hard" approach. Force breeds counterforces: restriction of output, antagonism, militant unionism, subtle but effective sabotage of management objectives. This "hard" approach is especially difficult during times of full employment.

There are also difficulties in the "soft" approach. It leads frequently to the abdication of management—to harmony, perhaps, but to indifferent performance. People take advantage of the soft approach. They continually expect more, but they give less and less.

Currently, the popular theme is "firm but fair." This is an attempt to gain the advantages of both the hard and the soft approaches. It is reminiscent of Teddy Roosevelt's "speak softly and carry a big stick."

IS THE CONVENTIONAL VIEW CORRECT?

The findings which are beginning to emerge from the social sciences challenge this whole set of beliefs about man and human nature and about the task of management. The evidence is far from conclusive, certainly, but it is suggestive. It comes from the laboratory, the clinic, the schoolroom, the home, and even to a limited extent from industry itself.

The social scientist does not deny that human behavior in industrial organization today is approximately what management perceives it to be. He has, in fact, observed it and studied it fairly extensively. But he is pretty sure that this behavior is *not* a consequence of man's inherent nature. It is a consequence rather of the nature of industrial organizations, of management philosophy, policy, and practice. The conventional approach of Theory X is based on mistaken notions of what is cause and what is effect.

Perhaps the best way to indicate why the conventional approach of management is inadequate is to consider the subject of motivation.

PHYSIOLOGICAL NEEDS

Man is a wanting animal—as soon as one of his needs is satisfied, another appears in its place. This process is unending. It continues from birth to death.

Man's needs are organized in a series of levels—a hierarchy of importance. At the lowest level, but preeminent in importance when they are thwarted, are his *physiological needs*. Man lives for bread alone, when there is no bread. Unless the circumstances are unusual, his needs for love, for status, for recognition are inoperative when his stomach has been empty for a while. But when he eats regularly and adequately, hunger ceases to be an important motivation. The same is true of the other physiological needs of man—for rest, exercise, shelter, protection from the elements.

A satisfied need is not a motivator of behavior! This is a fact of profound significance that is regularly ignored in the conventional approach to the management of people. Consider your own need for air: Except as you are deprived of it, it has no appreciable motivating effect upon your behavior.

SAFETY NEEDS

When the physiological needs are reasonably satisfied, needs at the next higher level begin to dominate man's behavior—to motivate him. These are called *safety* needs. They are needs for protection against danger, threat, deprivation. Some people mistakenly refer to these as needs for security. However, unless man is in a dependent relationship where he fears arbitrary deprivation, he does not demand security. The need is for the "fairest possible break." When he is confident of this, he is more than willing to take risks. But when he feels threatened or dependent, his greatest need is for guarantees, for protection, for security.

The fact needs little emphasis that, since every industrial employee is in a dependent relationship, safety needs may assume considerable importance. Arbitrary management actions, behavior which arouses uncertainty with respect to continued employment or which reflects favoritism or discrimination, unpredictable administration of policy—these can be powerful motivators of the safety needs in the employment relationship *at every level,* from worker to vice-president.

SOCIAL NEEDS

When man's physiological needs are satisfied and he is no longer fearful about his physical welfare, his *social needs* become important motivators of his behavior—needs for belonging, for association, for acceptance by his fellows, for giving and receiving friendship and love.

Management knows today of the existence of these needs, but it often assumes quite wrongly that they represent a threat to the organization. Many studies have demonstrated that the tightly knit, cohesive work group may, under proper conditions, be far more effective than an equal number of separate individuals in achieving organizational goals.

Yet management, fearing group hostility to its own objectives, often goes to considerable lengths to control and direct human efforts in ways that are inimical to the natural "groupiness" of human beings. When man's social needs—and perhaps his safety needs, too—are thus thwarted, he behaves in ways which tend to defeat organizational objectives. He becomes resistant, antagonistic, uncooperative. But this behavior is a consequence, not a cause.

EGO NEEDS

Above the social needs—in the sense that they do not become motivators until lower needs are reasonably satisfied—are the needs of greatest significance to management and to man himself. They are the *egoistic needs,* and they are of two kinds:

1. Those needs that relate to one's self-esteem—needs for self-confidence, for independence, for achievement, for competence, for knowledge.
2. Those needs that relate to one's reputation—needs for status, for recognition, for appreciation, for the deserved respect of one's fellows.

Unlike the lower needs, these are rarely satisfied; man seeks indefinitely for more satisfaction of these needs once they have become important to him. But they do not appear in any significant way until physiological, safety, and social needs are all reasonably satisfied.

The typical industrial organization offers few opportunities for the satisfaction of these egoistic needs to people at lower levels in the hierarchy. The conventional methods of organizing work, particularly in mass production industries, give little heed to these aspects of human motivation. If the practices of scientific management were deliberately calculated to thwart these needs, they could hardly accomplish this purpose better than they do.

SELF-FULFILLMENT NEEDS

Finally—a capstone, as it were, on the hierarchy of man's needs—there are what we may call the *needs for self-fulfillment.* These are the needs for realizing one's own potentialities, for continued self-development, for being creative in the broadest sense of that term.

It is clear that the conditions of modern life give only limited opportunity for these relatively weak needs to obtain expression. The deprivation most people experience with respect to other lower level needs diverts their energies into the struggle to satisfy *those* needs, and the needs for self-fulfillment remain dormant.

MANAGEMENT AND MOTIVATION

We recognize readily enough that a man suffering from a severe dietary deficiency is sick. The deprivation of physiological needs has behavioral consequences. The same is true—although less well recognized—of deprivation of higher level needs. The man whose needs for safety, association, independence, or status are thwarted is sick just as surely as the man who has rickets. And his sickness will have behavioral consequences. We will be mistaken if we attribute his resultant passivity, his hostility, his refusal to accept responsibility to his inherent "human nature." These forms of behavior are *symptoms of* illness—of deprivation of his social and egoistic needs.

The man whose lower level needs are satisfied is not motivated to satisfy those needs any longer. For practical purposes they exist no longer. Management often asks, "Why aren't people more productive? We pay good wages, provide good working conditions, have excellent fringe benefits and steady employment. Yet people do not seem to be willing to put forth more than minimum effort."

The fact that management has provided for these physiological and safety needs has shifted the motivational emphasis to the social and perhaps to the egoistic needs. Unless there are opportunities *at work* to satisfy these higher level needs, people will be deprived; and their behavior will reflect this deprivation. Under such conditions, if management continues to focus its attention on physiological needs, its efforts are bound to be ineffective.

People *will* make insistent demands for more money under these conditions. It becomes more important than ever to buy the material goods and services which can provide limited satisfaction of the thwarted needs. Although money has only limited value in satisfying many higher level needs, it can become the focus of interest if it is the *only* means available.

THE CARROT-AND-STICK APPROACH

The carrot-and-stick theory of motivation (like Newtonian physical theory) works reasonably well under certain circumstances. The *means* for satisfying man's physiological and (within limits) his safety needs can be provided or withheld by management. Employment itself is such a means, and so are wages, working conditions, and benefits. By these means the individual can be controlled so long as he is struggling for subsistence.

But the carrot-and-stick theory does not work at all once man has reached an adequate subsistence level and is motivated primarily by higher needs. Management cannot provide a man with self-respect, or with the respect of his fellows, or with the satisfaction of needs for self-fulfillment. It can create such conditions that he is encouraged and enabled to seek such satisfactions for *himself,* or it can thwart him by failing to create those conditions.

But this creation of conditions is not "control." It is not a good device for directing behavior. And so management finds itself in an odd position. The high standard of living created by our modern technological know-how provides quite adequately for the satisfaction of physiological and safety needs. The only significant exception is where management practices have not created confidence in a "fair break"—and thus where safety needs are thwarted. But by making possible the satisfaction of low level needs, management has deprived itself of the ability to use as motivators the devices on which conventional theory has taught it to rely—rewards, promises, incentives, or threats and other coercive de-vices.

The philosophy of management by direction and control—*regardless of whether it is hard or soft*—is inadequate to motivate because the hu-man needs on which this approach relies are today unimportant motiva-tors of behavior. Direction and control are essentially useless in motivat-ing people whose important needs are social and egoistic. Both the hard and the soft approach fail today because they are simply irrelevant to the situation.

People, deprived of opportunities to satisfy at work the needs which are now important to them, behave exactly as we might predict—with indolence, passivity, resistance to change, lack of responsibility, willing-ness to follow the demagogue, unreasonable demands for economic bene-fits. It would seem that we are caught in a web of our own weaving.

A NEW THEORY OF MANAGEMENT

For these and many other reasons, we require a different theory of the task of managing people based on more adequate assumptions about human nature and human motivation. I am going to be so bold as to suggest the broad dimensions of such a theory. Call it "Theory Y," if you will.

1. Management is responsible for organizing the elements of produc-tive enterprise—money, materials, equipment, people—in the in-terest of economic ends.

2. People are *not* by nature passive or resistant to organizational needs. They have become so as a result of experience in organiza-tions.

3. The motivation, the potential for development, the capacity for assuming responsibility, the readiness to direct behavior toward organizational goals are all present in people. Management does not put them there. It is a responsibility of management to make it possible for people to recognize and develop these human charac-teristics for themselves.

4. The essential task of management is to arrange organizational conditions and methods of operation so that people can achieve their own goals *best* by directing *their own* efforts toward organiza-tional objectives.

This is a process primarily of creating opportunities, releasing poten-tial, removing obstacles, encouraging growth, providing guidance. It is what Peter Drucker has called "management by objectives" in contrast to "management by control." It does *not* involve the abdication of manage-ment, the absence of leadership, the lowering of standards, or the other characteristics usually associated with the "soft" approach under Theory X.

SOME DIFFICULTIES

It is no more possible to create an organization today which will be a full, effective application of this theory than it was to build an atomic power plant in 1945. There are many formidable obstacles to overcome.

The conditions imposed by conventional organization theory and by the approach of scientific management for the past half century have tied men to limited jobs which do not utilize their capabilities, have discouraged the acceptance of responsibility, have encouraged passivity, have eliminated meaning from work. Man's habits, attitudes, expectations—his whole conception of membership in an industrial organization—have been conditioned by his experience under these circumstances.

People today are accustomed to being directed, manipulated, controlled in industrial organizations and to finding satisfaction for their social, egoistic, and self-fulfillment needs away from the job. This is true of much of management as well as of workers. Genuine "industrial citizenship"—to borrow again a term from Drucker—is a remote and unrealistic idea, the meaning of which has not even been considered by most members of industrial organizations.

Another way of saying this is that Theory X places exclusive reliance upon external control of human behavior, while Theory Y relies heavily on self-control and self-direction. It is worth noting that this difference is the difference between treating people as children and treating them as mature adults. After generations of the former, we cannot expect to shift to the latter overnight.

STEPS IN THE RIGHT DIRECTION

Before we are overwhelmed by the obstacles, let us remember that the application of theory is always slow. Progress is usually achieved in small steps. Some innovative ideas which are entirely consistent with Theory Y are today being applied with some success.

Decentralization and Delegation

These are ways of freeing people from the too-close control of conventional organization, giving them a degree of freedom to direct their own activities, to assume responsibility, and, importantly, to satisfy their egoistic needs. In this connection, the flat organization of Sears, Roebuck and Company provides an interesting example. It forces "management by objectives," since it enlarges the number of people reporting to a manager until he cannot direct and control them in the conventional manner.

Job Enlargement

This concept, pioneered by IBM and Detroit Edison, is quite consistent with Theory Y. It encourages the acceptance of responsibility at the bottom of the organization; it provides opportunities for satisfying social and egoistic needs. In fact, the reorganization of work at the factory level offers one of the more challenging opportunities for innovation consistent with Theory Y.

Participation and Consultative Management

Under proper conditions, participation and consultative management provide encouragement to people to direct their creative energies toward organizational objectives, give them some voice in decisions that affect them, provide significant opportunities for the satisfaction of social and egoistic needs. The Scanlon Plan is the outstanding embodiment of these ideas in practice.

Performance Appraisal

Even a cursory examination of conventional programs of performance appraisal within the ranks of management will reveal how completely consistent they are with Theory X. In fact, most such programs tend to treat the individual as though he were a product under inspection on the assembly line.

A few companies—among them General Mills, Ansul Chemical, and General Electric—have been experimenting with approaches which involve the individual in setting "targets" or objectives *for himself* and in a *self*-evaluation of performance semiannually or annually. Of course, the superior plays an important leadership role in this process—one, in fact, which demands substantially more competence than the conventional approach. The role is, however, considerably more congenial to many managers than the role of "judge" or "inspector" which is usually forced upon them. Above all, the individual is encouraged to take a greater responsibility for planning and appraising his own contribution to organizational objectives; and the accompanying effects on egoistic and self-fulfillment needs are substantial.

APPLYING THE IDEAS

The not infrequent failure of such ideas as these to work as well as expected is often attributable to the fact that a management has "bought the idea" but applied it within the framework of Theory X and its assumptions.

Delegation is not an effective way of exercising management by control. Participation becomes a farce when it is applied as a sales gimmick or a device for kidding people into thinking they are important. Only the management that has confidence in human capacities and is itself directed toward organizational objectives rather than toward the preservation of personal power can grasp the implications of this emerging theory. Such management will find and apply successfully other innovative ideas as we move slowly toward the full implementation of a theory like Y.

THE HUMAN SIDE OF ENTERPRISE

It is quite possible for us to realize substantial improvements in the effectiveness of industrial organizations during the next decade or two. The social sciences can contribute much to such developments; we are only beginning to grasp the implications of the growing body of knowledge in these fields. But if this conviction is to become a reality instead of a pious hope, we will need to view the process much as we view the process of releasing the energy of the atom for constructive human ends—as a slow, costly, sometimes discouraging approach toward a goal which would seem to many to be quite unrealistic.

The ingenuity and the perseverance of industrial management in the pursuit of economic ends have changed many scientific and technological dreams into commonplace realities. It is now becoming clear that the application of these same talents to the human side of enterprise will not only enhance substantially these materialistic achievements, but will bring us one step closer to "the good society."

27

How to Choose a Leadership Pattern

Robert Tannenbaum
and
Warren H. Schmidt

Tannenbaum and Schmidt see the leadership problem as being one of how managers can be democratic and still retain necessary control. By looking at forces in the manager, forces in the subordinates and forces in the situation they present a guide for making appropriate leadership decisions. It is interesting to note that this article written thirty years ago anticipates modern-day contingency theory.—Eds.

- "I put most problems into my group's hands and leave it to them to carry the ball from there. I serve merely as a catalyst, mirroring back the people's thoughts and feelings so that they can better understand them."
- "It's foolish to make decisions oneself on matters that affect people. I always talk things over with my subordinates, but I make it clear to them that I'm the one who has to have the final say."
- "Once I have decided on a course of action, I do my best to sell my ideas to my employees."
- "I'm being paid to lead. If I let a lot of other people make the decisions I should be making, then I'm not worth my salt."
- "I believe in getting things done. I can't waste time calling meetings. Someone has to call the shots around here, and I think it should be me."

SOURCE: Robert Tannenbaum and Warren H. Schmidt, "How to Choose a Leadership Pattern," *Harvard Business Review* (May-June 1973), pp. 162–164, 168, 170, 173, 175, 178–180. © 1973 by the President and Fellows of Harvard College; all rights reserved. This article, an "HBR Classic," was originally published in 1958.

Each of these statements represents a point of view about "good leadership." Considerable experience, factual data, and theoretical principles could be cited to support each statement, even though they seem to be inconsistent when placed together. Such contradictions point up the dilemma in which the modern manager frequently finds himself.

NEW PROBLEMS

The problem of how the modern manager can be "democratic" in his relations with subordinates and at the same time maintain the necessary authority and control in the organization for which he is responsible has come into focus increasingly in recent years.

Earlier in the century this problem was not so acutely felt. The successful executive was generally pictured as possessing intelligence, imagination, initiative, the capacity to make rapid (and generally wise) decisions, and the ability to inspire subordinates. People tended to think of the world as being divided into "leaders" and "followers."

New Focus

Gradually, however, from the social sciences emerged the concept of "group dynamics" with its focus on *members* of the group rather than solely on the leader. Research efforts of social scientists underscored the importance of employee involvement and participation in decision making. Evidence began to challenge the efficiency of highly directive leadership, and increasing attention was paid to problems of motivation and human relations.

Through training laboratories in group development that sprang up across the country, many of the newer notions of leadership began to exert an impact. These training laboratories were carefully designed to give people a first-hand experience in full participation and decision making. The designated "leaders" deliberately attempted to reduce their own power and to make group members as responsible as possible for setting their own goals and methods within the laboratory experience.

It was perhaps inevitable that some of the people who attended the training laboratories regarded this kind of leadership as being truly "democratic" and went home with the determination to build fully participative decision making into their own organizations. Whenever their bosses made a decision without convening a staff meeting, they tended to perceive this as authoritarian behavior. The true symbol of democratic leadership to some was the meeting—and the less directed from the top, the more democratic it was.

Some of the more enthusiastic alumni of these training laboratories began to get the habit of categorizing leader behavior as "democratic" *or* "authoritarian." The boss who made too many decisions himself was thought of as an authoritarian, and his directive behavior was often attributed solely to his personality.

New Need

The net result of the research findings and of the human relations training based upon them has been to call into question the stereotype of an effective leader. Consequently, the modern manager often finds himself in an uncomfortable state of mind.

Often he is not quite sure how to behave; there are times when he is torn between exerting "strong" leadership and "permissive" leadership. Sometimes new knowledge pushes him in one direction ("I should really get the group to help make this decision"), but at the same time his experience pushes him in another direction ("I really understand the problem better than the group and therefore I should make the decision"). He is not sure when a group decision is really appropriate or when holding a staff meeting serves merely as a device for avoiding his own decision-making responsibility.

The purpose of our article is to suggest a framework which managers may find useful in grappling with this dilemma. First, we shall look at the different patterns of leadership behavior that the manager can choose from in relating himself to his subordinates. Then, we shall turn to some of the questions suggested by this range of patterns. For instance, how important is it for a manager's subordinates to know what type of leadership he is using in a situation? What factors should he consider in deciding on a leadership pattern? What difference do his long-run objectives make as compared to his immediate objectives?

RANGE OF BEHAVIOR

Figure 1 presents the continuum or range of possible leadership behavior available to a manager. Each type of action is related to the degree of authority used by the boss and to the amount of freedom available to his subordinates in reaching decisions. The actions seen on the extreme left characterize the manager who maintains a high degree of control while those seen on the extreme right characterize the manager who releases a high degree of control. Neither extreme is absolute; authority and freedom are never without their limitations.

Now let us look more closely at each of the behavior points occurring along this continuum.

- The manager makes the decision and announces it.

In this case the boss identifies a problem, considers alternative solutions, chooses one of them, and then reports this decision to his subordinates for implementation. He may or may not give consideration to what he believes his subordinates will think or feel about his decision; in any

FIGURE 1 Continuum of Leadership Behavior

Boss-centered leadership ← → Subordinate-centered leadership

Use of authority by the manager

Area of freedom for subordinates

| Manager makes decision and announces it. | Manager "sells" decision. | Manager presents ideas and invites questions. | Manager presents tentative decision subject to change. | Manager presents problem, gets suggestions, makes decision. | Manager defines limits; asks group to make decision. | Manager permits subordinates to function within limits defined by superior. |

case, he provides no opportunity for them to participate directly in the decision-making process. Coercion may or may not be used or implied.

• The manager "sells" his decision.

Here the manager, as before, takes responsibility for identifying the problem and arriving at a decision. However, rather than simply announcing it, he takes the additional step of persuading his subordinates to accept it. In doing so, he recognizes the possibility of some resistance among those who will be faced with the decision, and seeks to reduce this resistance by indicating, for example, what the employees have to gain from his decision.

• The manager presents his ideas, invites questions.

Here the boss who has arrived at a decision and who seeks acceptance of his ideas provides an opportunity for his subordinates to get a fuller explanation of his thinking and his intentions. After presenting the ideas, he invites questions so that his associates can better understand what he is trying to accomplish. This "give and take" also enables the manager and the subordinates to explore more fully the implications of the decision.

• The manager presents a tentative decision subject to change.

This kind of behavior permits the subordinates to exert some influence on the decision. The initiative for identifying and diagnosing the problem remains with the boss. Before meeting with his staff, he has thought the problem through and arrived at a decision—but only a tentative one. Before finalizing it, he presents his proposed solution for the reaction of those who will be affected by it. He says in effect, "I'd like to hear what you have to say about this plan that I have developed. I'll appreciate your frank reactions, but will reserve for myself the final decision."

• The manager presents the problem, gets suggestions, and then makes his decision.

Up to this point the boss has come before the group with a solution of his own. Not so in this case. The subordinates now get the first chance to suggest solutions. The manager's initial role involves identifying the problem. He might, for example, say something of this sort: "We are faced with a number of complaints from newspapers and the general public on our service policy. What is wrong here? What ideas do you have for coming to grips with this problem?"

The function of the group becomes one of increasing the manager's repertory of possible solutions to the problem. The purpose is to capitalize on the knowledge and experience of those who are on the "firing line." From the expanded list of alternatives developed by the manager and his subordinates, the manager then selects the solution that he regards as most promising.[1]

- The manager defines the limits and requests the group to make a decision.

At this point the manager passes to the group (possibly including himself as a member) the right to make decisions. Before doing so, however, he defines the problem to be solved and the boundaries within which the decision must be made.

An example might be the handling of a parking problem at a plant. The boss decides that this is something that should be worked on by the people involved, so he calls them together and points up the existence of the problem. Then he tells them:

"There is the open field just north of the main plant which has been designated for additional employee parking. We can build underground or surface multilevel facilities as long as the cost does not exceed $100,000. Within these limits we are free to work out whatever solution makes sense to us. After we decide on a specific plan, the company will spend the available money in whatever way we indicate."

- The manager permits the group to make decisions within prescribed limits.

This represents an extreme degree of group freedom only occasionally encountered in formal organizations, as, for instance, in many research groups. Here the team of managers or engineers undertakes the identification and diagnosis of the problem, develops alternative procedures for solving it, and decides on one or more of these alternative solutions. The only limits directly imposed on the group by the organization are those specified by the superior of the team's boss. If the boss participates in the decision-making process, he attempts to do so with no more authority than any other member of the group. He commits himself in advance to assist in implementing whatever decision the group makes.

Key Questions

As the continuum in Figure 1 demonstrates, there are a number of alternative ways in which a manager can relate himself to the group or individuals he is supervising. At the extreme left of the range, the emphasis is on the manager—on what *he* is interested in, how *he* sees things, how *he* feels about them. As we move toward the subordinate-centered end of the continuum, however, the focus is increasingly on the subordinates— on what *they* are interested in, how *they* look at things, how *they* feel about them.

When business leadership is regarded in this way, a number of questions arise. Let us take four of especial importance:

1. Can a boss ever relinquish his responsibility by delegating it to someone else?

Our view is that the manager must expect to be held responsible by his superior for the quality of the decisions made, even though operationally these decisions may have been made on a group basis. He should, therefore, be ready to accept whatever risk is involved whenever he delegates decision-making power to his subordinates. Delegation is not a way of "passing the buck." Also, it should be emphasized that the amount of freedom the boss gives to his subordinates cannot be greater than the freedom which he himself has been given by his own superior.

2. Should the manager participate with his subordinates once he has delegated responsibility to them?

The manager should carefully think over this question and decide on his role prior to involving the subordinate group. He should ask if his presence will inhibit or facilitate the problem-solving process. There may be some instances when he should leave the group to let it solve the problem for itself. Typically, however, the boss has useful ideas to contribute, and should function as an additional member of the group. In the latter instance, it is important that he indicate clearly to the group that he sees himself in a *member* role rather than in an authority role.

3. How important is it for the group to recognize what kind of leadership behavior the boss is using?

It makes a great deal of difference. Many relationship problems between boss and subordinate occur because the boss fails to make clear how he plans to use his authority. If, for example, he actually intends to make a certain decision himself, but the subordinate group gets the impression that he has delegated this authority, considerable confusion and resentment are likely to follow. Problems may also occur when the boss uses a "democratic" facade to conceal the fact that he has already made a decision which he hopes the group will accept as its own. The attempt to "make them think it was their idea in the first place" is a risky one. We believe that it is highly important for the manager to be honest and clear in describing what authority he is keeping and what role he is asking his subordinates to assume in solving a particular problem.

4. Can you tell how "democratic" a manager is by the number of decisions his subordinates make?

The sheer *number* of decisions is not an accurate index of the amount of freedom that a subordinate group enjoys. More important is the *significance* of the decisions which the boss entrusts to his subordinates. Obviously a decision on how to arrange desks is of an entirely different order from a decision involving the introduction of new electronic data-processing equipment. Even though the widest possible limits are given in dealing with the first issue, the group will sense no particular degree of responsibility. For a boss to permit the group to decide equipment policy, even within rather narrow limits, would reflect a greater degree of confidence in them on his part.

Deciding How to Lead

Now let us turn from the types of leadership which are possible in a company situation to the question of what types are *practical* and *desirable*. What factors or forces should a manager consider in deciding how to manage? Three are of particular importance:

- Forces in the manager.
- Forces in the subordinates.
- Forces in the situation.

We should like briefly to describe these elements and indicate how they might influence a manager's action in a decision-making situation.[2] The strength of each of them will, of course, vary from instance to instance, but the manager who is sensitive to them can better assess the problems which face him and determine which mode of leadership behavior is most appropriate for him.

Forces in the manager. The manager's behavior in any given instance will be influenced greatly by the many forces operating within his own personality. He will, of course, perceive his leadership problems in a unique way on the basis of his background, knowledge, and experience. Among the important internal forces affecting him will be the following:

1. His value system.

How strongly does he feel that individuals should have a share in making the decisions which affect them? Or, how convinced is he that the official who is paid to assume responsibility should personally carry the burden of decision making? The strength of his convictions on questions like these will tend to move the manager to one end or the other of the continuum shown in Figure 1. His behavior will also be influenced by the relative importance that he attaches to organizational efficiency, personal growth of subordinates, and company profits.[3]

2. His confidence in his subordinates.

Managers differ greatly in the amount of trust they have in other people generally, and this carries over to the particular employees they supervise at a given time. In viewing his particular group of subordinates, the manager is likely to consider their knowledge and competence with respect to the problem. A central question he might ask himself is: "Who is best qualified to deal with this problem?" Often he may, justifiably or not, have more confidence in his own capabilities than in those of his subordinates.

3. His own leadership inclinations.

There are some managers who seem to function more comfortably and naturally as highly directive leaders. Resolving problems and issuing orders come easily to them. Other managers seem to operate more comfortably in a team role, where they are continually sharing many of their functions with their subordinates.

4. His feelings of security in an uncertain situation.

The manager who releases control over the decision-making process thereby reduces the predictability of the outcome. Some managers have a greater need than others for predictability and stability in their environment. This "tolerance for ambiguity" is being viewed increasingly by psychologists as a key variable in a person's manner of dealing with problems.

The manager brings these and other highly personal variables to each situation he faces. If he can see them as forces which, consciously or unconsciously, influence his behavior, he can better understand what makes him prefer to act in a given way. And understanding this, he can often make himself more effective.

Forces in the subordinate.   Before deciding how to lead a certain group, the manager will also want to consider a number of forces affecting his subordinates' behavior. He will want to remember that each employee, like himself, is influenced by many personality variables. In addition, each subordinate has a set of expectations about how the boss should act in relation to him (the phrase "expected behavior" is one we hear more and more often these days at discussions of leadership and teaching). The better the manager understands these factors, the more accurately he can determine what kind of behavior on his part will enable his subordinates to act most effectively.

Generally speaking, the manager can permit his subordinates greater freedom if the following essential conditions exist:

- If the subordinates have relatively high needs for independence. (As we all know, people differ greatly in the amount of direction that they desire.)
- If the subordinates have a readiness to assume responsibility for decision making. (Some see additional responsibility as a tribute to their ability; others see it as "passing the buck.")
- If they have a relatively high tolerance for ambiguity. (Some employees prefer to have clear-cut directives given to them; others prefer a wider area of freedom.)
- If they are interested in the problem and feel that it is important.
- If they understand and identify with the goals of the organization.
- If they have the necessary knowledge and experience to deal with the problem.
- If they have learned to expect to share in decision making. (Persons who have come to expect strong leadership and are then suddenly confronted with the request to share more fully in decision making are often upset by this new experience. On the other hand, persons who have enjoyed a considerable amount of freedom resent the boss who begins to make all the decisions himself.)

The manager will probably tend to make fuller use of his own authority if the above conditions do *not* exist; at times there may be no realistic alternative to running a "one-man show."

The restrictive effect of many of the forces will, of course, be greatly modified by the general feeling of confidence which subordinates have in the boss. Where they have learned to respect and trust him, he is free to vary his behavior. He will feel certain that he will not be perceived as an authoritarian boss on those occasions when he makes decisions by himself. Similarly, he will not be seen as using staff meetings to avoid his decision-making responsibility. In a climate of mutual confidence and respect, people tend to feel less threatened by deviations from normal practice, which in turn makes possible a higher degree of flexibility in the whole relationship.

Forces in the situation. In addition to the forces which exist in the manager himself and in his subordinates, certain characteristics of the general situation will also affect the manager's behavior. Among the more critical environmental pressures that surround him are those which stem from the organization, the work group, the nature of the problem, and the pressures of time. Let us look briefly at each of these:

1. Type of organization.

Like individuals, organizations have values and traditions which inevitably influence the behavior of the people who work in them. The manager who is a newcomer to a company quickly discovers that certain kinds of behavior are approved while others are not. He also discovers that to deviate radically from what is generally accepted is likely to create problems for him.

These values and traditions are communicated in numerous ways—through job descriptions, policy pronouncements, and public statements by top executives. Some organizations, for example, hold to the notion that the desirable executive is one who is dynamic, imaginative, decisive, and persuasive. Other organizations put more emphasis upon the importance of the executive's ability to work effectively with people—his human relations skills. The fact that his superiors have a defined concept of what the good executive should be will very likely push the manager toward one end or the other of the behavioral range.

In addition to the above, the amount of employee participation is influenced by such variables as the size of the working units, their geographical distribution, and the degree of inter- and intra-organizational security required to attain company goals. For example, the wide geographical dispersion of an organization may preclude a practical system of participative decision making, even though this would otherwise be desirable. Similarly, the size of the working units or the need for keeping plans confidential may make it necessary for the boss to exercise more control than would otherwise be the case. Factors like these may limit considerably the manager's ability to function flexibly on the continuum.

2. Group effectiveness.

Before turning decision-making responsibility over to a subordinate group, the boss should consider how effectively its members work together as a unit.

One of the relevant factors here is the experience the group has had in working together. It can generally be expected that a group which has functioned for some time will have developed habits of cooperation and thus be able to tackle a problem more effectively than a new group. It can also be expected that a group of people with similar backgrounds and interests will work more quickly and easily than people with dissimilar backgrounds, because the communication problems are likely to be less complex.

The degree of confidence that the members have in their ability to solve problems as a group is also a key consideration. Finally, such group variables as cohesiveness, permissiveness, mutual acceptance, and commonality of purpose will exert subtle but powerful influence on the group's functioning.

3. The problem itself.

The nature of the problem may determine what degree of authority should be delegated by the manager to his subordinates. Obviously he will ask himself whether they have the kind of knowledge which is needed. It is possible to do them a real disservice by assigning a problem that their experience does not equip them to handle.

Since the problems faced in larger or growing industries increasingly require knowledge of specialists from many different fields, it might be inferred that the more complex a problem, the more anxious a manager will be to get some assistance in solving it. However, this is not always the case. There will be times when the very complexity of the problem calls for one person to work it out. For example, if the manager has most of the background and factual data relevant to a given issue, it may be easier for him to think it through himself than to take the time to fill in his staff on all the pertinent background information.

The key question to ask, of course, is: "Have I heard the ideas of everyone who has the necessary knowledge to make a significant contribution to the solution of this problem?"

4. The pressure of time.

This is perhaps the most clearly felt pressure on the manager (in spite of the fact that it may sometimes be imagined). The more that he feels the need for an immediate decision, the more difficult it is to involve other people. In organizations which are in a constant state of "crisis" and "crash programming" one is likely to find managers personally using a high degree of authority with relatively little delegation to subordinates. When the time pressure is less intense, however, it becomes much more possible to bring subordinates in on the decision-making process.

These, then, are the principal forces that impinge on the manager in any given instance and that tend to determine his tactical behavior in relation to his subordinates. In each case his behavior ideally will be that which makes possible the most effective attainment of his immediate goal within the limits facing him.

Long-Run Strategy

As the manager works with his organization on the problems that come up day by day, his choice of a leadership pattern is usually limited. He must take account of the forces just described and within the restrictions they impose on him, do the best that he can. But as he looks ahead months or even years, he can shift his thinking from tactics to large-scale strategy. No longer need he be fettered by all of the forces mentioned, for he can view many of them as variables over which he has some control. He can, for example, gain new insights or skills for himself, supply training for individual subordinates, and provide participative experiences for his employee group.

In trying to bring about a change in these variables, however, he is faced with a challenging question: At which point along the continuum *should* he act?

Attaining objectives. The answer depends largely on what he wants to accomplish. Let us suppose that he is interested in the same objectives that most modern managers seek to attain when they can shift their attention from the pressure of immediate assignments:

1. To raise the level of employee motivation.
2. To increase the readiness of subordinates to accept change.
3. To improve the quality of all managerial decisions.
4. To develop teamwork and morale.
5. To further the individual development of employees.

In recent years the manager has been deluged with a flow of advice on how best to achieve these longer-run objectives. It is little wonder that he is often both bewildered and annoyed. However, there are some guidelines which he can usefully follow in making a decision.

Most research and much of the experience of recent years give a strong factual basis to the theory that a fairly high degree of subordinate-centered behavior is associated with the accomplishment of the five purposes mentioned.[4] This does not mean that a manager should always leave all decisions to his assistants. To provide the individual or the group with greater freedom than they are ready for at any given time may very well tend to generate anxieties and therefore inhibit rather than facilitate the attainment of desired objectives. But this should not keep the manager from making a continuing effort to confront his subordinates with the challenge of freedom.

CONCLUSION

In summary, there are two implications in the basic thesis that we have been developing. The first is that the successful leader is one who is keenly aware of those forces which are most relevant to his behavior at any given time. He accurately understands himself, the individuals and group he is dealing with, and the company and broader social environment in which he operates. And certainly he is able to assess the present readiness for growth of his subordinates.

But this sensitivity or understanding is not enough, which brings us to the second implication. The successful leader is one who is able to behave appropriately in the light of these perceptions. If direction is in order, he is able to direct; if considerable participative freedom is called for, he is able to provide such freedom.

Thus, the successful manager of men can be primarily characterized neither as a strong leader nor as a permissive one. Rather, he is one who maintains a high batting average in accurately assessing the forces that determine what his most appropriate behavior at any given time should be and in actually being able to behave accordingly. Being both insightful and flexible, he is less likely to see the problems of leadership as a dilemma.

RETROSPECTIVE COMMENTARY

Since this HBR Classic was first published in 1958, there have been many changes in organizations and in the world that have affected leadership patterns. While the article's continued popularity attests to its essential validity, we believe it can be reconsidered and updated to reflect subsequent societal changes and new management concepts.

The reasons for the article's continued relevance can be summarized briefly:

- The article contains insights and perspectives which mesh well with, and help clarify, the experiences of managers, other leaders, and students of leadership. Thus it is useful to individuals in a wide variety of organizations—industrial, governmental, educational, religious, and community.
- The concept of leadership the article defines is reflected in a continuum of leadership behavior (see Figure 1 in original article). Rather than offering a choice between two styles of leadership, democratic or authoritarian, it sanctions a range of behavior.
- The concept does not dictate to managers but helps them to analyze their own behavior. The continuum permits them to review their behavior within a context of other alternatives, without any style being labeled right or wrong.

(We have sometimes wondered if we have, perhaps, made it too easy for anyone to justify his or her style of leadership. It may be a small step between being nonjudgmental and giving the impression that all behavior is equally valid and useful. The latter was not our intention. Indeed, the thrust of our endorsement was for the manager who is insightful in assessing relevant forces within himself, others, and the situation, and who can be flexible in responding to these forces.)

In recognizing that our article can be updated, we are acknowledging that organizations do not exist in a vacuum but are affected by changes that occur in society. Consider, for example, the implications for organizations of these recent social developments:

- The youth revolution that expresses distrust and even contempt for organizations identified with the establishment.
- The civil rights movement that demands all minority groups be given a greater opportunity for participation and influence in the organizational processes.
- The ecology and consumer movements that challenge the right of managers to make decisions without considering the interest of people outside the organization.
- The increasing national concern with the quality of working life and its relationship to worker productivity, participation, and satisfaction.

These and other societal changes make effective leadership in this decade a more challenging task, requiring even greater sensitivity and flexibility than was needed in the 1950s. Today's manager is more likely to deal with employees who resent being treated as subordinates, who may be highly critical of any organizational system, who expect to be consulted and to exert influence, and who often stand on the edge of alienation from the institution that needs their loyalty and commitment. In addition, he is frequently confronted by a highly turbulent, unpredictable environment.

In response to these social pressures, new concepts of management have emerged in organizations. Open-system theory, with its emphasis on subsystems' interdependency *and* on the interaction of an organization with its environment, has made a powerful impact on managers' approach to problems. Organization development has emerged as a new behavioral science approach to the improvement of individual, group, organizational, and interorganizational performance. New research has added to our understanding of motivation in the work situation. More and more executives have become concerned with social responsibility and have explored the feasibility of social audits. And a growing number of organizations, in Europe and in the United States, have conducted experiments in industrial democracy.

In light of these developments, we submit the following thoughts on how we would rewrite certain points in our original article.

The article described forces in the manager, subordinates, and the situation as givens, with the leadership pattern a resultant of these forces. We would now give more attention to the *interdependency* of these forces. For example, such interdependency occurs in: (a) the interplay between the manager's confidence in his subordinates, their readiness to assume responsibility, and the level of group effectiveness; and (b) the impact of the behavior of the manager on that of his subordinates, and vice versa.

In discussing the forces in the situation, we primarily identified organizational phenomena. We would now include forces lying outside the organization, and would explore the relevant interdependencies between the organization and its environment.

In the original article, we presented the size of the rectangle in Figure 1 as a given, with its boundaries already determined by external forces—in effect, a closed system. We would now recognize the possibility of the manager and/or his subordinates taking the initiative to change those boundaries through interaction with relevant external forces—both within their own organization and in the larger society.

The article portrayed the manager as the principal and almost unilateral actor. He initiated and determined group functions, assumed responsibility, and exercised control. Subordinates made inputs and assumed power only at the will of the manager. Although the manager might have taken into account forces outside himself, it was *he* who decided where to operate on the continuum—that is, whether to announce a decision instead of trying to sell his idea to his subordinates, whether to invite questions, to let subordinates decide an issue, and so on. While the manager has retained this clear prerogative in many organizations, it has been challenged in others. Even in situations where he has retained it, however, the balance in the relationship between manager and subordinates at any given time is arrived at by interaction—direct or indirect—between the two parties.

Although power and its use by the manager played a role in our article, we now realize that our concern with cooperation and collaboration, common goals, commitment, trust, and mutual caring limited our vision with respect to the realities of power. We did not attempt to deal with unions, other forms of joint worker action, or with individual workers' expressions of resistance. Today, we would recognize much more clearly the power available to *all* parties, and the factors that underlie the interrelated decisions on whether to use it.

In the original article, we used the terms "manager" and "subordinate." We are now uncomfortable with "subordinate" because of its demeaning, dependency-laden connotations and prefer "nonmanager." The titles "manager" and "nonmanager" make the terminological difference functional rather than hierarchical.

FIGURE 2 Continuum of Manager-Nonmanager Behavior

Manager power and influence

Nonmanager power and influence

Area of freedom for manager

Area of freedom for nonmanagers

Manager able to make decision which nonmanagers accept.

Manager must "sell" decision before gaining acceptance.

Manager presents decision but must respond to questions from nonmanagers.

Manager presents tentative decision subject to change after nonmanager inputs.

Manager presents problem, gets inputs from nonmanagers, then decides.

Manager defines limits within which nonmanagers make decision.

Manager and nonmanagers jointly make decision within limits defined by organizational constraints.

Resultant manager and nonmanager behavior

THE ORGANIZATIONAL ENVIRONMENT

THE SOCIETAL ENVIRONMENT

We assumed fairly traditional organizational structures in our original article. Now we would alter our formulation to reflect newer organizational modes which are slowly emerging, such as industrial democracy, intentional communities, and "phenomenarchy."[5] These new modes are based on observations such as the following:

- Both managers and nonmanagers may be governing forces in their group's environment, contributing to the definition of the total area of freedom.
- A group can function without a manager, with managerial functions being shared by group members.
- A group, as a unit, can be delegated authority and can assume responsibility within a larger organizational context.

Our thoughts on the question of leadership have prompted us to design a new behavior continuum (see Figure 2) in which the total area of freedom shared by manager and nonmanagers is constantly redefined by interactions between them and the forces in the environment.

The arrows in the figure indicate the continual flow of interdependent influence among systems and people. The points on the continuum designate the types of manager and nonmanager behavior that become possible with any given amount of freedom available to each. The new continuum is both more complex and more dynamic than the 1958 version, reflecting the organizational and societal realities of 1973.

NOTES AND REFERENCES

1. For a fuller explanation of this approach, see Leo Moore, "Too Much Management, Too Little Change," *Harvard Business Review,* January-February, 1956, p. 41.

2. See also Robert Tannenbaum and Fred Massarik, "Participation by Subordinates in the Managerial Decision-Making Process," *Canadian Journal of Economics and Political Science,* August, 1950, p. 413.

3. See Chris Argyris, "Top Management Dilemma: Company Needs vs. Individual Development," *Personnel,* September, 1955, pp. 123–134.

4. For example, see Warren H. Schmidt and Paul C. Buchanan, *Techniques that Produce Teamwork* (New London: Arthur C. Croft Publications, 1954); and Morris S. Viteles, *Motivation and Morale in Industry* (New York: W. W. Norton and Co., Inc., 1953).

5. For a description of phenomenarchy, see Will McWhinney, "Phenomenarchy: A Suggestion for Social Redesign," *Journal of Applied Behavioral Science,* May, 1973.

28

The Contingency Model—New Directions for Leadership Utilization

Fred E. Fiedler

An early proponent of the contingency approach, Fiedler suggests that what constitutes effective leadership is dependent upon the situation in which the leadership attempt is made. Fiedler goes on to clearly spell out what aspects of the situation are important, namely the state of leader-member relations, task structure and the leader's formal power. These three factors combine to determine situational favorableness, a key variable in the model. While the theory has its problems, it is a classical example of the contingency approach.—Eds.

Leadership research has come a long way from the simple concepts of earlier years which centered on the search for the magic leadership trait. We have had to replace the old cherished notion that "leaders are born and not made." These increasingly complex formulations postulate that some types of leaders will behave and perform differently in a given situation than other types. The Contingency Model is one of the earliest and most articulated of these theories;[1] taking into account the personality of the leader as well as aspects of the situation which affect the leader's behavior and performance. This model has given rise to well over one-hundred empirical studies. This article briefly reviews the current status of the Contingency Model and then discusses several new developments which promise to have considerable impact on our thinking about leadership as well as on the management of executive manpower.

SOURCE: From the *Journal of Contemporary Business*, Vol. 3, No. 4, pp. 65–80 (Autumn, 1974). Reprinted by permission of the publisher.

THE CONTINGENCY MODEL

The theory holds that the effectiveness of a task group or of an organization depends on two main factors: the personality of the leader and the degree to which the situation gives the leader power, control and influence over the situation or, conversely, the degree to which the situation confronts the leader with uncertainty[2]

Leader personality. The first of these factors distinguishes leader personality in terms of two different motivational systems, i.e., the basic or primary goals as well as the secondary goals which people pursue once their more pressing needs are satisfied. One type of person, whom we shall call "relationship-motivated," primarily seeks to maintain good interpersonal relationships with coworkers. These basic goals become very apparent in uncertain and anxiety provoking situations in which we try to make sure that the important needs are secured. Under these conditions the relationship-motivated individual will seek out others and solicit their support; however, under conditions in which he or she feels quite secure and relaxed—because this individual has achieved the major goals of having close relations with subordinates—he or she will seek the esteem and admiration of others. In a leadership situation where task performance results in esteem and admiration from superiors, this leader will tend to concentrate on behaving in a task-relevant manner, sometimes to the detriment of relations with immediate subordinates.

The relationship-motivated leader's counterpart has as a major goal the accomplishment of some tangible evidence of his or her worth. This person gets satisfaction from the task itself and from knowing that he or she has done well. In a leadership situation which is uncertain and anxiety provoking, this person will, therefore, put primary emphasis on completing the task. However, when this individual has considerable control and influence and knows, therefore, the task will get done, he or she will relax and be concerned with subordinates' feelings and satisfactions. In other words, business before pleasure, but business *with* pleasure whenever possible.

Of course, these two thumbnail sketches are oversimplified, but they do give a picture which tells us, first, that we are dealing with different types of people and, second, that they differ in their primary and secondary goals and, consequently, in the way they behave under various conditions. Both the relationship-motivated and the task-motivated persons may be pleasant and considerate toward their members. However, the task-motivated leader will be considerate in situations in which he or she is secure, i.e., in which the individual's power and influence are high; the relationship-motivated leader will be considerate when his or her control and influence are less assured, when some uncertainty is present.

These motivational systems are measured by the Least Preferred Coworker score (LPC) which is obtained by first asking an individual to think of all people with whom he or she has ever worked, and then to describe the one person with whom this individual has been able to work least well. The description of the least preferred coworker is made on a short, bipolar eight-point scale, from 16 to 22 item-scale of the semantic differential format. The LPC score is the sum of the item scores; e.g.:

Friendly

:___:___:___:___:___:___:___:___:
  1   2   3   4   5   6   7   8

                           Unfriendly

Cooperative

:___:___:___:___:___:___:___:___:
  1   2   3   4   5   6   7   8

                         Uncooperative

High-LPC persons, i.e., individuals who describe their LPC in relatively positive terms, seem primarily relationship-motivated. Low-LPC persons, those who describe their least preferred coworker in very unfavorable terms, are basically task-motivated. Therefore, as can be seen, the LPC score is not a description of leader behavior because the behavior of high- and low-LPC people changes with different situations.

Relationship-motivated people seem more open, more approachable and more like McGregor's "Theory Y" managers, while the task-motivated leaders tend to be more controlled and more controlling persons, even though they may be as likeable and pleasant as their relationship-motivated colleagues.[3]

Current evidence suggests that the LPC scores and the personality attributes they reflect are almost as stable as most other personality measures. (For example, test-retest reliabilities for military leaders have been .72 over an 8-month period[4] and .67 over a 2-year period for faculty members.)[5] Changes do occur, but in the absence of major upsets in the individual's life, they tend to be gradual and relatively small.

The leadership situation. The second variable, "situational favorableness,"[6] indicates the degree to which the situation gives the leader control and influence and the ability to predict the consequences of his or her behavior.[7] A situation in which the leader cannot predict the consequences of the decision tends to be stressful and anxiety arousing.

One rough but useful method for defining situational favorableness is based on three subscales. These are the degree to which (a) the leader is, or feels, accepted and supported by his or her members (leader-member relations); (b) the task is clear-cut, programmed and structured as to goals, procedures and measurable progress and success (task structure); and (c) the leader's position provides power to reward and punish and, thus, to obtain compliance from subordinates (position power).

Groups then can be categorized as being high or low on each of these three dimensions by dividing them at the median or, on the basis of

FIGURE 1

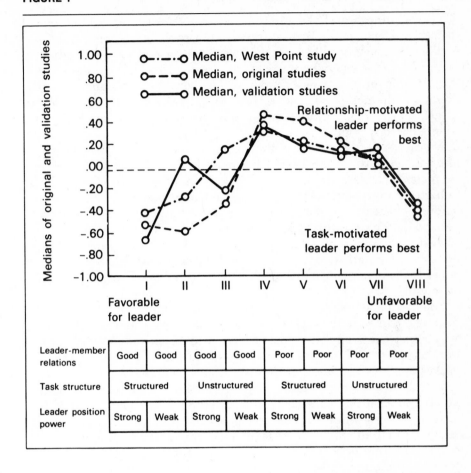

normative scores, into those with good and poor leader-member relations, task structure and position power. This leads to an eight-celled classification shown on the horizontal axis of Figure 1. The eight cells or "octants" are scaled from "most favorable" (octant I) to the left of the graph to "least favorable" (octant VIII) to the right. A leader obviously will have the most control and influence in groups that fall into octant I; i.e., in which this leader is accepted, has high position power and a structured task. The leader will have somewhat less control and influence in octant II, where he or she is accepted and has a structured task, but little position power, and so on to groups in octant VIII where control and influence will be relatively small because the leader is not accepted by his or her group, has a vague, unstructured task and little position power. Situational favorableness and LPC are, of course, neither empirically nor logically related to each other.

The Personality-Situation Interaction

The basic findings of the Contingency Model are that task-motivated leaders perform generally best in very "favorable" situations, i.e., either under conditions in which their power, control and influence are very high (or, conversely, where uncertainty is very low) or where the situation is unfavorable, where they have low power, control and influence. Relationship-motivated leaders tend to perform best in situations in which they have moderate power, control and influence. The findings are summarized in Figure 1. The horizontal axis indicates the eight cells of the situational favorableness dimension, with the most favorable end on the left side of the graph's axis. The vertical axis indicates the *correlation coefficients* between the leader's LPC score and the group's performance. A high correlation in the positive direction, indicated by a point above the midline of the graph, shows that the relationship-motivated leaders performed better than the task-motivated leaders. A negative correlation, shown by a point which falls below the midline of the graph, indicates that the task-motivated leaders performed better than relationship-motivated leaders, i.e., the higher the LPC score, the lower the group's performance.

The solid curve connects the median correlations within each of the octants obtained in the original studies (before 1963) on which the model was based. The broken line connects the median correlations obtained in various validation studies from 1964-1971.[8] As can be seen, the two curves are very similar, and the points on the curves correlate .76 (p < .01). Only in octant 2 is there a major discrepancy. However, it should be pointed out that there are very few groups in real life which have a highly structured task while the leader has low position power, e.g., in high school basketball teams and student surveying parties. Most of the validation evidence for octant II comes from laboratory studies in which this type of situation may be difficult to reproduce. However, the field study results for this octant are in the negative direction, just as the model predicts.

The most convincing validation evidence comes from a well-controlled experiment conducted by Chemers and Skrzypek at the U.S. Military Academy at West Point.[9] LPC scores as well as sociometric performance ratings to predict leader-member relations were obtained several weeks *prior* to the study, and groups then were assembled in advance, based on having the leader's LPC score and the expressed positive or negative feelings of group members about one another. The results of the Chemers and Skrzypek study are shown in the figure as a dotted line and give nearly a point-for-point replication of the original model with a correlation of .86 (p < .01). A subsequent reanalysis of the Chemers and Skrzypek data by Shiflett showed that the Contingency Model accounted for no less than 28 percent of the variance in group performance.[10] This is a very high degree of prediction, especially in a study in which variables

FIGURE 2   The Performance of Relationship- and Task-Motivated Leaders in Different Situational-Favorableness Conditions

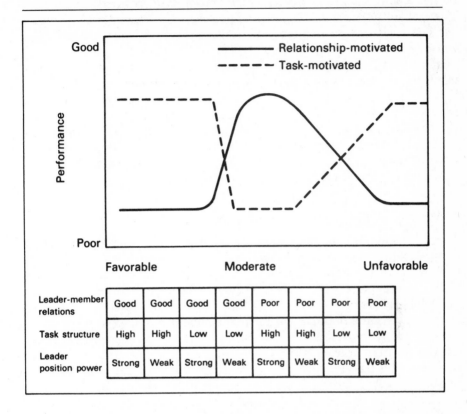

such as the group members' intelligence, the leader's ability, the motivational factors of participants and similar effects were uncontrolled. Of course, it is inconceivable that data of this nature could be obtained by pure chance.

A different and somewhat clearer description of the Contingency Model is presented schematically in Figure 2. As before, the situational favorableness dimension is indicated on the horizontal axis, extending from the most favorable situation on the left to the relatively least favorable situation on the right. However, here the vertical axis indicates the group or organizational performance; the solid line on the graph is the schematic performance curve of relationship-motivated (high-LPC) leaders, while the dashed line indicates the performance of task-motivated (low-LPC) leaders.

These curves show, first of all, that both the relationship- and the task-motivated leaders perform well under some situations but not under others. Therefore, it is not accurate to speak of a "good" or a "poor" leader, rather, a leader may perform well in one type of situation but not in another. Outstanding directors of research teams do not necessarily make good production foremen or military leaders, and outstanding battle field commanders, like General Patton, do not necessarily make good chiefs of staff or good chairmen of volunteer school picnic committees.

The second major implication of Figure 2 is that leader performance depends as much on the situation to which the organization assigns him (her) as on his or her own personality. Hence, organizational improvement can be achieved either by changing the leader's personality and motivational system—which is at best a very difficult and uncertain process—or by modifying the degree to which the situation provides the leader with power and influence. It should be obvious from the graph that certain leaders perform better with less rather than more power, i.e., some leaders let the power "go to their heads," they become cocky and arrogant, while others need security to function well.

Extensions of the Contingency Model

Two important tests of any theory are the degree to which it allows us to understand phenomena which do not follow common-sense expectations and, second, the extent to which it predicts nonobvious findings. In both of these respects, the Contingency Model has demonstrated its usefulness. We present here several important findings from recent studies, and then discuss some implications for management.

Effects of experience and training.   One of the major research efforts in the area of leadership and management has been the attempt to develop training methods which will improve organizational performance. However, until now the various training programs have failed to live up to their expectations. Stogdill concluded that:

> The research on leadership training is generally inadequate in both design and execution. It has failed to address itself to the most crucial problem of leadership—. . . [the] effects of leadership on group performance and member satisfaction.[11]

The Contingency Model would predict that training should increase the performance of some leaders and also decrease the performance of others. However, it raises the question of whether any current method of training logically can result in an across-the-board increase in organizational leadership performance.[12]

As pointed out before, a group's performance depends on the leader's personality as well as the degree to which the situation provides him or her with control, power and influence. If the leader's power and influence are increased by experience and training, the "match" between leader personality and situational favorableness would change. However, increasing the leader's power and influence is exactly the goal of most leadership training. For example, technical training increases the leader's expert power; coaching and orthodox training programs which use the case study and lecture method are designed to increase the structure of the task by providing the leader with methods for dealing with problems which, otherwise, would require him or her to think of new solutions. Human relations training is designed to develop better relations with group members, thus enabling the leader to exert more personal influence or "referent power."

For example, let us take a newly promoted supervisor of a production department in which he has not worked before. As he begins his new job, some of the tasks may seem unfamiliar and he will be unsure of his exact duties and responsibilities. He also may be uncertain of the power his position provides—how, for example, will the group react if he tries to dock an old, experienced worker who had come in late? Is this type of disciplinary measure acceptable to the group even though it may be allowed by the union contract? He may wonder how he should handle a problem with a fellow supervisor in the plant on whom he has to depend for parts and supplies. Should he file a formal complaint or should he talk to him personally?

After several years on the job, our supervisor will have learned the ropes; he will know how far he can go in disciplining his workers, how to troubleshoot various machines and how to deal with other managers in the organization. Thus, for the experienced supervisor the job is structured, his position power is high and his relations with his group are probably good. In other words, his situation is very favorable.

When he first started on the job, his leadership situation probably was only moderately favorable. If you will recall, relationship-motivated leaders tend to perform best in moderately favorable situations, while task-motivated leaders perform better in very favorable situations. Therefore, a relationship-motivated leader will perform well at first before gaining experience (e.g., by using the resources of group members and inviting their participation); a task-motivated leader will perform well after becoming experienced. In other words, the relationship-motivated leader actually should perform less well after gaining experience, while the task-motivated leader's performance should increase with greater experience.

A substantial number of studies now support this prediction.[13] A good example comes from a longitudinal study of infantry squad leaders who were assigned to newly organized units.[14] Their performance was evaluated by the same judges shortly after they joined their squads and, again, approximately 5 months later after their squads had passed the combat readiness test. As Figure 3 shows, the data are exactly as predicted by the Contingency Model. Similar results have been obtained in studies on the effects of training and experience of post office managers, managers of consumer cooperatives, police patrol supervisors and leaders of various military units.

The effect of leadership training on performance also was demonstrated by a very ingenious experiment conducted at the University of

FIGURE 3 Performance of High- and Low-LPC Leaders as a Function of Increased Experience and More Structured Task Assignment Over Five Months

Utah.[15] ROTC cadets and students were assembled *a priori* into four-man teams with high and low-LPC leaders. One-half of the team leaders were given training in decoding cryptographic messages, i.e., they were shown how to decode simple messages easily by first counting all the letters in the message and considering the most frequent letter an "e." A three-letter word, ending with the supposed "e" is then likely to be a "the," etc. The other half of the leaders were given no training of this type. All teams operated under a fairly high degree of tension, as indicated by subsequent ratings of the group atmosphere. Because the task is by definition unstructured, the situation was moderately favorable for the trained leaders but unfavorable for the untrained leaders. Therefore, we would expect that the relationship-motivated leaders would perform bet-

FIGURE 4 Interaction of Training and LPC on Group Productivity

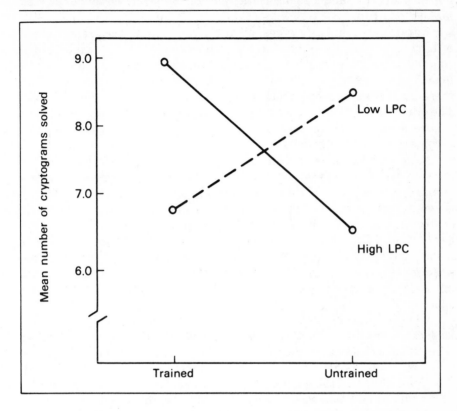

ter with training, while the task-motivated leaders would perform more effectively in the unfavorable situation, i.e., without the benefit of training. As can be seen in Figure 4, the findings support the predictions of the model.

FURTHER IMPLICATIONS

Selection. It seems highly likely from these and similar findings that we need to reconsider our management selection strategies. Obviously, the old adage calling for "the right man for the right job" is not as simple as it once appeared. The right person for a particular job today may be the wrong person in 6 months or in 1 or 2 years. As we have seen, the job which presents a very favorable leadership situation for the experienced leader presents a moderately favorable situation for the leader who is new and inexperienced or untrained. Hence, under these conditions a relationship-motivated leader should be chosen for the long run. The job which is moderately favorable for the experienced and trained leader is likely to represent an unfavorable leadership situation for the inexperienced leader. Hence, a task-motivated leader should be selected for the short run, and a relationship-motivated leader should be selected for the long run.

Rotation. Figure 4 suggests that certain types of leaders will reach a "burn-out point" after they have stayed on the job for a given length of time. They will become bored, stale, disinterested and no longer challenged. A rational rotation policy obviously must be designed to rotate these leaders at the appropriate time to new and more challenging jobs. The other types of leaders, e.g., the task-motivated leaders represented in Figure 4, should be permitted to remain on the job so that they can become maximally efficient.

Most organizations and, in particular, the military services, have a rotation system which (at least in theory) moves all officers to new jobs after a specified period of time. Such a rigid system is likely to be dysfunctional because it does not properly allow for individual differences which determine the time required by different types of people to reach their best performance. Recent research by Bons also has shown that the behavior and performance of leaders is influenced by such other organizational changes as the transfer of a leader from one unit to a similar unit and by a reorganization which involves the reassignment of the leader's superiors.[16]

The Contingency Model clearly is a very complex formulation of the leadership problem. Whether it is more complex than is necessary, as some of its critics have claimed, or whether it is still not sufficiently complex, as others have averred, remains an open question. It is clear at this point that the theory not only predicts leadership performance in field studies and laboratory experiments, but also that it serves as a very important and fruitful source of new hypotheses in the area of leadership.

NOTES AND REFERENCES

1. F. E. Fiedler, "A Contingency Model of Leadership Effectiveness," in L. Berkowitz, ed., *Advances in Experimental Social Psychology* (Academic Press, 1964); Also *A Theory of Leadership Effectiveness* (New York: McGraw-Hill, 1967); F. E. Fiedler and M. M. Chemers, *Leadership and Effective Management* (Glenview, Ill.: Scott, Foresman & Co., 1974).

2. D. Nebeker, "Situational Favorability and Environmental Uncertainty: An Integrative Study," *Administrative Science Quarterly* (1974).

3. L. K. Michaelsen, "Leader Orientation, Leader Behavior, Group Effectiveness and Situational Favorability: An Empirical Extension of the Contingency Model," *Organizational Behavior and Human Performance*, 9 (1973), pp. 226–245.

4. P. M. Bons, "The Effect of Changes in Leadership Environment on the Behavior of Relationship- and Task-Motivated Leaders" (Ph.D. diss., University of Washington, 1974).

5. Joyce Prothero, "Personality and Situational Effects on the Job-Related Behavior of Faculty Members" (Honors thesis, University of Washington, 1974).

6. F. E. Fiedler, *Leadership Effectiveness*.

7. D. Nebeker, "Situational Favorability."

8. F. E. Fiedler, "Validation and Extension of the Contingency Model of Leadership Effectiveness: A Review of Empirical Findings," *Psychological Bulletin,* 76 (1971), pp. 128–148.

9. M. M. Chemers and G. J. Skrzypek, "Experimental Test of the Contingency Model of Leadership Effectiveness, *Journal of Personality and Social Psychology,* 24 (1972), pp. 172–177.

10. S. C. Shiflett, "The Contingency Model of Leadership Effectiveness: Some Implications of Its Statistical and Methodological Properties," *Behavioral Science,* 18 (1973), pp. 429–441.

11. R. M. Stogdill, *Handbook of Leadership: A Survey of Theory and Research* (New York: Free Press, 1974).

12. F. E. Fiedler, "The Effects of Leadership Training and Experience: A Contingency Model Interpretation," *Administrative Science Quarterly,* 17 (1972), pp. 453–470.

13. *Ibid.*

14. F. E. Fiedler, P. M. Bons and L. L. Hastings, "New Strategies for Leadership Utilization," in W. T. Singleton and P. Spurgeon, eds., *Defense Psychology* NATO, Division of Scientific Affairs (1974).

15. M. M. Chemers et al., "Leader LPC, Training and Effectiveness: An Experimental Examination," *Journal of Personality and Social Psychology* (1974).

16. P. M. Bons, "Changes in Leadership."

29

Participative Management: Time for a Second Look

Robert C. Albrook

Participative management might not be for everyone cautions this article. Albrook calls for a reexamination of some of the notions we have about the democratic approach to management, noting that some assumptions about the utility of participation in decision making and the showing of authority are not always valid. Note particularly the discussion of the special difficulties involved in moving a traditionally authoritarian organization toward a participative style.—Eds.

The management of change has become a central preoccupation of U.S. business. When the directors have approved the record capital budget and congratulated themselves on "progress," when the banquet speaker has used his last superlative to describe the "world of tomorrow," the talk turns, inevitably, to the question: "Who will make it all work?" Some people resist change. Some hold the keys to it. Some admit the need for new ways but don't know how to begin. The question becomes what kind of management can ease the inevitable pains, unlock the talent, energy, and knowledge where they're needed, help valuable men to contribute to and shape change rather than be flattened by it.

The recipe is elusive, and increasingly business has turned to the academic world for help, particularly to the behavioral scientists—the psychologists, sociologists, and anthropologists whose studies have now become the showpieces of the better business schools. A number of major corporations, such as General Electric, Texas Instruments, and Standard

SOURCE: Reprinted by permission of the publisher from "Participative Management: Time for a Second Look," *Fortune* (May 1967), pp. 166–70, 197–200.

Oil (N.J.), have brought social scientists onto their staffs. Some companies collaborate closely with university based scholars and are contributing importantly to advanced theoretical work, just as industry's physicists, chemists, and engineers have become significant contributors of new knowledge in their respective realms. Hundreds of companies, large and small, have tried one or another formulation of basic behavioral theory, such as the many schemes for sharing their savings with employees and actively soliciting their ideas for improved efficiency.

For forty years the quantity and quality of academic expertise in this field have been steadily improving, and there has lately been a new burst of ideas which suggest that the researchers in the business schools and other centers of learning are really getting down to cases. The newest concepts already represent a considerable spin off from the appealingly simple notions on which the behavioral pioneers first concentrated. The essential message these outriders had for business was this: recognize the social needs of employees in their work, as well as their need for money; they will respond with a deeper commitment and better performance, help to shape the organization's changing goals and make them their own. To blue-collar workers this meant such steps as organizing work around tasks large enough to have meaning and inviting workers' ideas; for middle and upper management it meant more participation in decision making, more sharing of authority and responsibility, more open and more candid communication, up, down, and sideways.

The new work suggests that neither the basic philosophy nor all of the early prescriptions of this management style were scientifically sound or universally workable. The word from the behavioral scientists is becoming more specific and "scientific," less simple and moralistic. At Harvard, M.I.T., the University of Michigan, Chicago, U.C.L.A., Stanford, and elsewhere, they are mounting bigger, longer, and more rigorous studies of the human factors in management than ever before undertaken.

One conclusion is that the "participative" or "group" approach doesn't seem to work with all people and in all situations. Research has shown that satisfied, happy workers are sometimes more productive—and sometimes merely happy. Some managers and workers are able to take only limited responsibility, however much the company tries to give them. Some people will recognize the need to delegate but "can't let go." In a profit squeeze the only way to get costs under control fast enough often seems to be with centralized, "get tough" management.

Few, if any, behaviorists espouse a general return to authoritarian management. Instead, they are seeking a more thorough, systematic way to apply participative principles on a sustained schedule that will give the theory a better chance to work. Others are insisting that management must be tailor-made, suited to the work or the people, rather than packaged in a standard mixture. Some people aren't and never will be suited for "democracy" on the job, according to one viewpoint, while others insist that new kinds of psychological training can fit most executives for the rugged give-and-take of successful group management.

As more variables are brought into their concepts, and as they look increasingly at the specifics of a management situation, the behaviorists are also being drawn toward collaboration with the systems designers and the theorists of data processing. Born in reaction to the cold scientism of the earlier "scientific management" experts with their stopwatches and measuring tapes, the "human relations" or behavioral school of today may be getting ready at last to bury that hatchet in a joint search for a broadly useful "general theory" of management.

WHY EXECUTIVES DON'T PRACTICE WHAT THEY PREACH

Before any general theory can be evolved, a great deal more has to be known about the difficulty of putting theory into practice—i.e., of transforming a simple managerial attitude into an effective managerial style. "There are plenty of executives," observes Stanley Seashore, a social psychologist at the University of Michigan's Institute for Social Research, "who'll decide one morning they're going to be more participative and by the afternoon have concluded it doesn't work."

What's often lacking is an understanding of how deeply and specifically management style affects corporate operations. The executive who seeks a more effective approach needs a map of the whole terrain of management activity. Rensis Likert, director of the Michigan institute, has developed a chart to assist managers in gaining a deeper understanding of the way they operate. A simplified version appears [in Table 1]. By answering the questions in the left-hand column of the chart (e.g., "Are subordinates' ideas sought and used?"), an executive sketches a profile of the way his company is run and whether it leans to the "authoritative" or the "participative." Hundreds of businessmen have used the chart, under Likert's direction, and many have discovered a good deal they didn't realize about the way they were handling people.

Likert leads his subjects in deliberate steps to a conclusion that most of them do not practice what they say they believe. First, the executive is asked to think of the most successful company (or division of a company) he knows intimately. He then checks off on the chart his answers as they apply to that company. When the executive has finished this exercise, he has nearly always traced the profile of a strongly "participative" management system, well to the right on Likert's chart. He is next asked to repeat the procedure for the least successful company (or division) he knows well. Again, the profiles are nearly always the same, but this time they portray a strongly "authoritative" system, far to the left on the chart.

Then comes the point of the exercise. The executive is asked to describe his own company or division. Almost always, the resulting profile is that of a company somewhere in the middle, a blend of the "benevolent authoritative" and the "consultative"—well to the left of what the executive had previously identified as the most successful style. To check out the reliability of this self-analysis, Likert sometimes asks employees in the same company or division to draw its profile, too. They tend to rate it as slightly more "authoritative" than the boss does.

Likert believes that the predominant management style in U.S. industry today falls about in the middle of his chart, even though most managers seem to know from personal observation of other organizations that a more participative approach works better. What accounts for their consistent failure to emulate what they consider successful? Reaching for a general explanation, Likert asks his subjects one final question: "In your experience, what happens when the senior officer becomes concerned about earnings and takes steps to cut costs, increase productivity, and improve profits?" Most reply that the company's management profile shifts left, toward the authoritarian style. General orders to economize—and promptly—often result in quick, across-the-board budget cuts. Some programs with high potential are sacrificed along with obvious losers. Carefully laid, logical plans go down the drain. Some people are laid off—usually the least essential ones. But the best people in the organization sooner or later rebel at arbitrary decisions, and many of them leave.

At the outset, the arbitrary cost cutting produces a fairly prompt improvement in earnings, of course. But there is an unrecognized trade-off in the subsequent loss of human capital, which shows up still later in loss of business. In due course, management has to "swing right" again, rebuilding its human assets at great expense in order to restore good performance. Yet the manager who puts his firm through this dreary cycle, Likert observes, is often rewarded with a bonus at the outset, when things still look good. Indeed, he may be sent off to work his magic in another division!

Likert acknowledges that there are emergencies when sharp and sudden belt-tightening is inescapable. The trouble, he says, is that it is frequently at the expense of human assets and relationships that have taken years to build. Often it would make more sense to sell off inventory or dispose of a plant. But such possibilities are overlooked because human assets do not show up in the traditional balance sheet the way physical assets do. A company can, of course, lose $100,000 worth of talent and look better on its statement than if it sells off $10,000 worth of inventory at half price.

A dollars-and-cents way of listing the value of a good engineering staff, an experienced shop crew, or an executive group with effective, established working relations might indeed steady the hand of a hard-pressed president whose banker is on the phone. Likert believes he is now on the trail of a way to assign such values—values that should be at least as realistic as the often arbitrary and outdated figures given for real estate and plant. It will take some doing to get the notion accepted by

TABLE 1

	System 1 Exploitative Authoritative	System 2 Benevolent Authoritative	System 3 Consultative	System 4 Participative Group
LEADERSHIP				
How much confidence is shown in subordinates?	None	Condescending	Substantial	Complete
How free do they feel to talk to superiors about job?	Not at all	Not very	Rather free	Fully free
Are subordinates' ideas sought and used, if worthy?	Seldom	Sometimes	Usually	Always
MOTIVATION				
Is predominant use made of (1) fear, (2) threats, (3) punishment, (4) rewards, (5) involvement?	1, 2, 3, occasionally 4	4, some 3	4, some 3 and 5	5, 4, based on group set goals
Where is responsibility felt for achieving organization's goals?	Mostly at top	Top and middle	Fairly general	At all levels
COMMUNICATION				
How much communication is aimed at achieving organization's objectives?	Very little	Little	Quite a bit	A great deal
What is the direction of information flow?	Downward	Mostly downward	Down and up	Down, up, and sideways
How is downward communication accepted?	With suspicion	Possibly with suspicion	With caution	With an open mind
How accurate is upward communication?	Often wrong	Censored for the boss	Limited accuracy	Accurate

	Know little	Some knowledge	Quite well	Very well
How well do superiors know problems faced by subordinates?	Know little	Some knowledge	Quite well	Very well
DECISIONS				
At what level are decisions formally made?	Mostly at top	Policy at top, some delegation	Broad policy at top, more delegation	Throughout but well integrated
What is the origin of technical and professional knowledge used in decision making?	Top management	Upper and middle	To a certain extent, throughout	To a great extent, throughout
Are subordinates involved in decisions related to their work?	Not at all	Occasionally consulted	Generally consulted	Fully involved
What does decision-making process contribute to motivation?	Nothing, often weakens it	Relatively little	Some contribution	Substantial contribution
GOALS				
How are organizational goals established?	Orders issued	Orders, some comment invited	After discussion, by orders	By group action (except in crisis)
How much covert resistance to goals is present?	Strong resistance	Moderate resistance	Some resistance at times	Little or none
CONTROL				
How concentrated are review and control functions?	Highly at top	Relatively highly at top	Moderate delegation to lower levels	Quite widely shared
Is there an informal organization resisting the formal one?	Yes	Usually	Sometimes	No—same goals as formal
What are cost, productivity, and other control data used for?	Policing, punishment	Reward and punishment	Reward, some self-guidance	Self-guidance, problem solving

Adapted, with permission, from *The Human Organization: Its Management and Value*, by Rensis Likert. Published in April 1967, by McGraw-Hill.

bankers and accountants, however sophisticated his method turns out to be. But today's executives are hardly unaware that their long payrolls of expensive scientific and managerial talent represent an asset as well as an expense. Indeed, it is an asset that is often bankable. A merely more regular, explicit recognition of human assets in cost-cutting decisions would help to ensure that human assets get at least an even break with plant and inventory in time of trouble.

Likert and his institute colleagues are negotiating with several corporations to enlist them in a systematic five-year study, in effect a controlled experiment, that should put a firmer footing under tentative conclusions and hypotheses. This study will test Likert's belief that across-the-board participative management, carefully developed, sustained through thick and thin, and supported by a balance sheet that somehow reckons the human factor, will show better long-run results than the cyclical swing between authoritarian and participative styles reflected in the typical middle-ground profile on his chart.

CONVERSION IN A PAJAMA FACTORY

Already there's enough evidence in industry experience to suggest that participative management gets in trouble when it is adopted too fast. In some cases, an authoritarian management has abruptly ordered junior executives or employees to start taking on more responsibility, not recognizing that the directive itself reasserted the fact of continuing centralized control. Sometimes, of course, a hard shove may be necessary, as in the recent experience of Harwood Manufacturing Corp. of Marion, Virginia, which has employed participative practices widely for many years. When it acquired a rival pajama maker, Weldon Manufacturing Co., the latter's long-held authoritarian traditions were hard to crack. With patient but firm prodding by outside consultants, who acknowledge an initial element of "coercion," the switch in style was finally accomplished.

Ideally, in the view of Likert and others, a move of this kind should begin with the patient education of top executives, followed by the development of the needed skills in internal communication, group leadership, and the other requisites of the new system. Given time, this will produce better employee attitudes and begin to harness personal motivation to corporate goals. Still later, there will be improved productivity, less waste, lower turnover and absence rates, fewer grievances and slowdowns, improved product quality, and, finally, better customer relations.

The transformation may take several years. A checkup too early in the game might prove that participative management, even when thoroughly understood and embraced at the top, doesn't produce better results. By the same token, a management that is retreating from the new style in a typical cost squeeze may still be nominally participative, yet may already have thrown away the fruits of the system. Some research findings do indicate that participation isn't producing the hoped-for results. In Likert's view, these were spot checks, made without regard to which way the company was tending and where it was in the cycle of change.

A growing number of behaviorists, however, have begun to question whether the participative style is an ideal toward which all management should strive. If they once believed it was, more as a matter of faith in their long struggle against the "scientific" manager's machine-like view of man than as a finding from any new science of their own, they are now ready to take a second look at the proposition.

It seems plain enough that a research scientist generally benefits from a good deal of freedom and autonomy, and that top executives, confronted every day by new problems that no routine can anticipate, operate better with maximum consultation and uninhibited contributions from every member of the team. If the vice-president for finance can't talk candidly with the vice-president for production about financing the new plant, a lot of time can be wasted. In sales, group effort—instead of the usual competition—can be highly productive. But in the accounting department, things must go by the book. "Creative accounting" sounds more like a formula for jail than for the old behaviorists' dream of personal self-fulfillment on the job. And so with quality control in the chemical plant. An inspired adjustment here and there isn't welcome, thank you; just follow the specifications.

In the production department, automation has washed out a lot of the old problem of man as a prisoner of the assembly line, the kind of problem that first brought the "human relations" experts into the factories in the 1920s and 1930s. If a shop is full of computer-controlled machine tools busily reproducing themselves, the boy with the broom who sweeps away the shavings may be the only one who can put a personal flourish into his work. The creativity is all upstairs in the engineering and programing departments. But then, so are most of the people.

"Look what's happened in the last twenty years," says Harold J. Leavitt, a social psychologist who recently moved to Stanford after some years at Carnegie Tech. "Originally the concern of the human relations people was with the blue-collar worker. Then the focus began to shift to foremen and to middle management. Now it's concentrated in special areas like research and development and in top management. Why? Because the 'group' style works best where nobody knows exactly and all the time what they're supposed to be doing, where there's a continuous need to change and adapt."

DEMOCRACY WORKS BETTER IN PLASTICS

One conclusion that has been drawn from this is that management style has to be custom designed to fit the particular characteristics of each industry. The participative approach will work best in those industries that are in the vanguard of change. A Harvard Business School study has compared high performance companies in three related, but subtly different, fields: plastics, packaged food, and standard containers. The plastics company faced the greatest uncertainties and change in research, new products, and market developments. The food company's business was somewhat more stable, while the container company encountered little or no requirement for innovation. The three achieved good results using markedly different management styles. The plastics firm provided for wide dispersal of responsibility for major decisions, the food company for moderate decentralization of authority, and the container company operated with highly centralized control.

Less successful enterprises in each of the three industries were also examined, and their managements were compared with those of the high performance companies. From this part of the study, Harvard researchers Paul Lawrence and Jay Lorsch drew another conclusion; not only may each industry have its own appropriate management style, but so may the individual operations within the same company. The companies that do best are those which allow for variations among their departments and know how to take these variations into account in coordinating the whole corporate effort.

Both the sales and the research departments in a fast-moving plastics company, for example, may adopt a style that encourages employees to participate actively in departmental decision making. But in special ways the two operations still need to differ. The research worker, for example, thinks in long-range terms, focusing on results expected in two or three years. The sales executive has his sights set on results next week or next month. This different sense of time may make it hard for the two departments to understand each other. But if top management recognizes the reasons and the need for such differences, each department will do its own job better, and they can be better coordinated. On the other hand, if top management ignores the differences and insists for example, on rigidly uniform budgeting and planning timetables, there will be a loss of effectiveness.

It seems an obvious point that sales must be allowed to operate like sales, accounting like accounting, and production like production. But as Lawrence comments, "The mark of a good idea in this field is that as soon as it is articulated, it does seem obvious. People forget that, five minutes before, it wasn't. One curse of the behavioral scientist is that anything he comes up with is going to seem that way, because anything that's good *is* obvious."

PEOPLE, TOO, HAVE THEIR STYLES

Other behavioral scientists take the view that management style should be determined not so much by the nature of the particular business operation involved, but by the personality traits of the people themselves. There may be some tendency for certain kinds of jobs to attract certain kinds of people. But in nearly any shop or office a wide range of personality types may be observed. There is, for example, the outgoing, socially oriented scientist as well as the supposedly more typical introverted recluse. There are mature, confident managers, and there are those who somehow fill the job despite nagging self-doubt and a consuming need for reassurance.

For a long time, personality tests seemed to offer a way to steer people lnto the psychologically right kind of work. Whether such testing for placement is worth while is now a matter of some dispute. In any case, the whole question of individual differences is often reduced to little more than an office guessing game. Will Sue cooperate with Jane? Can Dorothy stand working for Jim? Will Harry take suggestions?

The participative approach to management may be based upon a greatly oversimplified notion about people, in the view of psychologist Clare Graves of Union College in Schenectady, New York. On the basis of limited samplings, he tentatively concludes that as many as half the people in the northeastern U.S., and a larger proportion nationwide, are not and many never will be the eager beaver workers on whom the late Douglas McGregor of M.I.T. based his "Theory Y." Only some variation of old-style authoritarian management will meet their psychological needs, Graves contends.

Graves believes he has identified seven fairly distinct personality types, although he acknowledges that many people are not "purebreds" who would fit his abstractions perfectly and that new and higher personality forms may still be evolving. At the bottom of his well-ordered hierarchy he places the childlike "autistic" personality, which requires "close care and nurturing." Next up the scale are the "animistic" type, which must be dealt with by sheer force or enticement; the "ordered" personality that responds best to a moralistic management; and the "materialistic" individual who calls for pragmatic, hard bargaining. None of these are suited for the participative kind of management.

At the top of Graves's personality ladder are the "sociocentric," the "cognitive," and the "apprehending" types of people. They are motivated, respectively, by a need for "belonging," for "information," and for an "understanding" of the total situation in which they are involved. For each of these levels some form of participative management will work. However, those at the very top, the unemotional "apprehending" individuals, must be allowed pretty much to set their own terms for work. Management can trust such people to contribute usefully only according to their own cool perception of what is needed. They will seldom take the trouble to fight authority when they disagree with it, but merely withdraw, do a passable but not excellent job, and wait for management to see things their way. In that sense, these highest-level people are probably not ideal participators.

Graves believes most adults are stuck at one level throughout their lifetimes or move up a single notch, at best. He finds, incidentally, that there can be bright or dull, mature or immature behavior at nearly all levels. The stages simply represent psychological growth toward a larger and larger awareness of the individual's relationship to society.

If a company has a mixture of personality types, as most do, it must somehow sort them out. One way would be to place participative-type managers in charge of some groups, and authoritarian managers in charge of others. Employees would then be encouraged to transfer into sections where the management style best suits them. This would hardly simplify corporate life. But companies pushing the group approach might at least avoid substituting harmful new rigidities—"participate, or else!"—for the old ones.

THE ANTHROPOLOGICAL VIEW

Behaviorists who have been studying management problems from an anthropological viewpoint naturally stress cultural rather than individual differences. Manning Nash, of the University of Chicago's business school, for example, observes that the American emphasis on egalitarianism and performance has always tempered management style in the U.S. "No matter what your role is, if you don't perform, no one in this country will defer to you," he says. "Americans won't act unless they respect you. You couldn't have an American Charge of the Light Brigade." But try to export that attitude to a country with a more autocratic social tradition, and, in the words of Stanley Davis of Harvard, "it won't be bought and may not be workable."

Within the U.S. there are many cultural differences that might provide guides to managerial style if they could be successfully analyzed. Recent research by Lawrence and Arthur N. Turner at the Harvard Business School hints at important differences between blue-collar workers in cities and those in smaller towns, although religious and other factors fog the results. Town workers seem to seek "a relatively large amount of variety, autonomy, interaction, skill and responsibility" in their work, whereas city workers "find more simple tasks less stress-producing and more satisfying."

In managerial areas where democratic techniques *are* likely to work, the problem is how to give managers skill and practice in participation. The National Education Association's National Training Laboratories twenty years ago pioneered a way of doing this called "sensitivity training" (see "Two Weeks in a T-Group," *Fortune*, August 1961). Small groups of men, commonly drawn from the executive ranks, sit down with a professional trainer but without agenda or rule book and "see what happens." The "vacuum" draws out first one and then another participant, in a way that tends to expose in fairly short order how he comes across to others.

The technique has had many critics, few more vocal than William Gomberg of the University of Pennsylvania's Wharton School. Renewing his assault recently, he called the "training" groups "titillating therapy, management development's most fashionable fad." When people from the same company are in the group, he argues, the whole exercise is an invasion of privacy, an abuse of the therapeutic technique to help the company, not the individual. For top executives in such groups, Gomberg and others contend, the technique offers mainly a catharsis for their loneliness or insecurity.

"PSYCHING OUT THE BOSS"

Undoubtedly the T-group can be abused, intentionally or otherwise. But today's sensitivity trainers are trying to make sure the experience leads to useful results for both the individual and his firm. They realize that early groups, made up of total strangers gathered at some remote "cultural island," often gave the executive little notion of how to apply his new knowledge back on the job. To bring more realism to the exercise, the National Training Laboratories began ten years ago to make up groups of executives and managers from the same company, but not men who had working relationships with one another. These "cousin labs" have led, in turn, to some training of actual management "families," a boss and his subordinates. At the West Coast headquarters of the T-group movement, the business school at U.C.L.A., some now call such training "task-group therapy."

Many businessmen insist T-groups have helped them. Forty-three presidents and chairmen and hundreds of lesser executives are National Training Laboratories alumni. U.C.L.A. is besieged by applicants, and many are turned away.

Sensitivity training is supposed to help most in business situations where there is a great deal of uncertainty, as there is in the training sessions themselves. In such situations in the corporate setting there is sometimes a tendency for executives to withdraw, to defer action, to play a kind of game with other people in the organization to see who will climb out on a limb first. A chief ploy is "psyching out the boss," which means trying to anticipate the way the winds of ultimate decision will blow and to set course accordingly.

The aim of sensitivity training is to stop all this, to get the executive's nerve up so that he faces facts, or, in the words of U.C.L.A.'s James V. Clark, to "lay bare the stress and strain faster and get a resolution of the problem." In that limited sense, such therapy could well serve any style of management. In Clark's view, this kind of training, early in the game, might save many a company a costly detour on the road to company-wide "democracy." He cites the experience of Non-Linear Systems, Inc., of Del Mar, California, a manufacturer of such electronic gear as digital voltmeters and data-logging equipment and an important supplier to aerospace contractors. The company is headed by Andrew Kay, a leading champion of the participative style. At the lower levels, Kay's application of participative concepts worked well. He gave workers responsibility for "the whole black box" instead of for pieces of his complex finished products. Because it was still a box, with some definite boundaries, the workers seized the new opportunity without fear or hesitation. The psychological magic of meaningful work, as opposed to the hopelessly specialized chore, took hold. Productivity rose.

VICE-PRESIDENTS IN MIDAIR

But at the executive level, Kay moved too quickly, failing to prepare his executives for broad and undefined responsibilities—or failing to choose men better suited for the challenge. One vice president was put in charge of "innovation." Suspended in midair, without the support of departments or functional groups and lacking even so much as a job description, most of the V.P.'s became passive and incapable of making decisions. "They lost touch with reality—including the reality of the market," recalls Clark. When the industry suffered a general slump and new competition entered the field, Non-Linear wasn't ready. Sales dropped 16 percent, according to Kay. In time he realized he was surrounded with dependent men, untrained to participate in the fashion he had peremptorily commanded. He trimmed his executive group and expects to set a new sales record this year.

Sheldon Davis of TRW Systems in Redondo Beach, California, blames the behavioral scientists themselves for breakdowns like Non-Linear's. Too often, he argues, "their messages come out sounding soft and easy, as if what we are trying to do is build happy teams of employees who feel 'good' about things, rather than saying we're trying to build effective organizations with groups that function well and that can zero in quickly on their problems and deal with them rationally."

To Davis, participation should mean "tough, open exchange," focused on the problem, not the organizational chart. Old-style managers who simply dictate a solution are wrong, he argues, and so are those new-style managers who think the idea is simply to go along with a subordinate's proposals if they're earnestly offered. Neither approach taps the full potential of the executive group. When problems are faced squarely, Davis believes, the boss—who should remain boss—gets the best solution because all relevant factors are thoroughly considered. And because everyone has contributed to the solution and feels responsible for it, it is also the solution most likely to be carried out.

One of the most useful new developments in the behavioral study of management is a fresh emphasis on collaboration with technology. In the early days of the human-relations movement in industry, technology was often regarded as "the enemy," the source of the personal and social problems that the psychologists were trying to treat. But from the beginning, some social scientists wanted to move right in and help fashion machines and industrial processes so as to reduce or eliminate their supposedly antihuman effects. Today this concept is more than mere talk. The idea is to develop so-called "sociotechnical" systems that permit man and technology *together* to produce the best performance.

Some early experimentation in the British coal mines, by London's Tavistock Institute, as well as scattered work in this country and in Scandinavia, have already demonstrated practical results from such a collaboration. Tavistock found that an attempt to apply specialized factory-style technology to coal mining had isolated the miners from one another. They missed the sense of group support and self-direction that had helped them cope with uncertainty and danger deep in the coal faces. Productivity suffered. In this case, Tavistock's solution was to redesign the new system so that men could still work in groups.

In the U.S. a manufacturer of small household appliances installed some highly sophisticated new technical processes that put the company well in the front of its field. But the engineers had broken down the jobs to such an extent that workers were getting no satisfaction out of their performance and productivity declined. Costs went up and, in the end, some of the new machinery had to be scrapped.

Some technologists seem more than ready to welcome a partnership with the human-relations expert. Louis Davis, a professor of engineering, has joined the U.C.L.A. business-school faculty to lead a six-man sociotechnical research group that includes several behaviorists. Among them is Eric Trist, a highly respected psychologist from the Tavistock Institute. Davis hopes today's collaboration will lead in time to a new breed of experts knowledgeable in both the engineering and the social disciplines.

"IT'S TIME WE STOPPED BUILDING RIVAL DICTIONARIES"

The importance of time, the nature of the task, the differences within a large organization, the nature of the people, the cultural setting, the psychological preparation of management, the relationship to technology—all these and other variables are making the search for effective managerial style more and more complex. But the growing recognition of these complexities has drained the human-relations movement of much of its antagonism toward the "superrationalism" of management science. Humanists must be more systematic and rational if they are to make some useful sense of the scattered and half-tested concepts they have thus far developed, and put their new theories to a real test.

A number of behaviorists believe it is well past time to bury the hatchet and collaborate in earnest with the mathematicians and economists. Some business schools and commercial consulting groups are already realigning their staffs to encourage such work. It won't be easy. Most "systems" thinkers are preoccupied with bringing all the relevant knowledge to bear on a management problem in a systematic way, seeking the theoretically "best" solution. Most behaviorists have tended to assume that the solution which is *most likely to be carried out* is the best one, hence their focus on involving lots of people in the decision-making so that they will follow through. Where the "experts" who shape decisions are also in charge of getting the job done, the two approaches sometimes blend, in practice. But in many organizations, it is a long, long road from a creative and imaginative decision to actual performance. A general theory of management must show how to build systematic expertise into a style that is also well suited to people.

The rapprochement among management theorists has a distinguished herald, Fritz J. Roethlisberger of Harvard Business School, one of the human-relations pioneers who first disclosed the potential of the "small group" in industrial experiments forty years ago. He laughs quickly at any suggestion that a unified approach will come easily. "But after all, we are all looking at the same thing," he says. "It's time we stopped building rival dictionaries and learned to make some sentences that really say something."

PART SIX

Decision-Making Processes in Management

Of all the management processes, decision making is in many respects the most complex. In view of this, it is somewhat surprising that decision making has received the least attention as an important management process in its own right. Clearly, decision making is a crucial part of the other processes we have discussed—planning, organizing, controlling, and directing. But it is also much more than that and deserves to be examined as a critical and unique process of its own. It has been said, in fact, that management *is* decision making, and because it is, the very essence of the entire managerial process is to be found in its study.

Historically, all of the functions of management have undergone changes. As we have learned more, as managerial responsibilities have increased, as technology has advanced, we have evolved better and more efficient systems of performing managerial functions. Probably no process, however, has undergone greater change than that of decision making. The earlier managers made decisions on the basis of hunch, guesswork, intuition, and, in some cases, palmists and the phases of the moon. Frederick Taylor was one of the first to attempt to move decision making away from intuition and superstition and toward the use of logic and the scientific method. Today's managers have at their disposal a variety of decision-making tools and techniques their predecessors lacked. The most significant of these, because of its impact, is the computer. The computer literally revolutionized information processing and its effect on decision making was of an equal magnitude. In addition to the computer, the development of quantitative techniques such as decision theory, linear programming, queuing theory, inventory control, and simulation have greatly enhanced the manager's ability to assemble and process large amounts of information.

The process of decision making involves (1) gathering information, (2) defining the problem, (3) determining various alternatives, (4) evaluating each of the alternatives according to the relevant objectives, (5) deciding upon a course of action, (6) implementing that course, and (7) following up to determine the consequences. The last two steps in that process are of critical importance but are often overlooked in the study of decision making.

Decisions are often categorized by type or class. A Class I decision involves a routine problem for which the manager knows or can find out the solution method, but does not know the actual solution. Class II decisions are those in which the manager knows the results he wishes to achieve, but does not know how to achieve those results. The articles in this section deal with aspects of both these classes of decisions.

30

The Myth of Management

C. West Churchman

The myth, according to the author, is that of believing that the really great manager has a special ability to solve the puzzling problems found in large, complex organizations. Effective managerial decision making is seen not as a result of hidden special abilities but as a reasoned logical approach to problem analysis.—Eds.

Making decisions is, on the one hand, one of the most fascinating manifestations of biological activity and, on the other hand, a matter of terrifying implications for the whole of the human race. Although this activity is both fascinating and awesome, it is difficult to find a satisfactory name for it in any of the common languages. In English we use such terms as *manager, administrator, executive,* or simply *decision maker.* Yet each of these terms fails somehow to capture the true significance of this important activity of the human being. Because we need a label to conduct our discussion, I shall risk choosing the term *manager* and begin to say some things that will generalize on this term beyond its ordinary usage in English.

The manager is the man who decides among alternative choices. He must decide which choice he believes will lead to a certain desired objective or set of objectives. But his decision is not an abstract one, because it creates a type of reality. The manager is the man with the magic that enables him to create in the world a state of affairs that would not have occurred except for him. We say that the manager is one who has the authority to make such choices. He is also a person who has the responsi-

SOURCE: From *Challenge to Reason,* by C. West Churchman. Copyright © 1968 by McGraw-Hill, Inc. Used with permission of McGraw-Hill Book Company.

bility for the choices he has made in the sense that the rest of his fellow men may judge whether he should be rewarded or punished for his choices; he is the person who justifiably is the object of praise or blame.

So broad a description of the manager makes managers of us all. It is a common failing of the labels that language applies to things that they may be generalized to encompass everything, as philosophers have long recognized in the case of such labels as *matter* and *mind*. It takes no great sophomoric talent to see that the world is basically matter and that everything could be reduced thereto. Nor does it take any great astuteness to see that everything a human being recognizes as natural reality is the product of some mind or collection of minds. So, too, the label *manager* may become appropriately applied to practically everything or at least to every human, once we describe the manager as someone having the authority and responsibility for making choices. I am interested in the broad aspects of decision making, but for present purposes I want to add one more stipulation that makes the label *manager* less general. This is the stipulation that managerial activity take place within a "system": The manager must concern himself with interrelated parts of a complex organization of activities, and he is responsible for the effectiveness of the whole system. . . .

But even this further stipulation concerning the use of the label *manager* permits us to describe many activities as management. It is true that in the history of England and the United States, the term *management* has often been narrowed to mean the managing of industrial activities, especially for the purpose of generating profit for an enterprise. In this connection management is contrasted with labor. In government activities our use of the term *manager* is often labelled *administrator*, and the term *executive* is often used to describe people who are given the legal authority to put into practice the laws of the land. All these activities, whether they be at the level of government or industry or education or health, or whatever, have a common ground which we wish to explore. The common ground is the burden of making choices about system improvement and the responsibility of responding to the choices made in a human environment in which there is bound to be opposition to what the manager has decided. Thus the head of a labor union, the state legislator, the head of a government agency, the foreman of a shop are all managers in our sense. So is a man in his own family a manager; so is the captain of a football team. Probably all of us at some time or other in our lives become managers when, because of appointment to a committee or because of our political activities, we take on the authority and responsibility of making decisions in complex systems. Managing is an activity of which we are all aware, and its consequences concern each one of us.

I said that managers must bear the burden of the decisions they make. I could have added, in a more optimistic tone, that they enjoy the pleasures accompanying the power to make decisions. And certainly many managers in today's society do find a great deal of psychic satisfaction in the roles they play which society so clearly recognizes as important and which it credits with a great deal of prestige.

Now managing is a type of behavior, and since it's a very important type of behavior, you might expect that we know a great deal about it. But we don't at all. We could also explore the many ways in which managers often think they know how they manage, but observers of their behavior often differ from them quite radically. The manager is frequently astonished to hear a sociologist's description of his activities, which he believes he himself knows so well, and he resents the inclination on the part of the "detached" scientist to try to describe the activity that he performs.

Imagine an observer carefully trained to study such activities as bees in a hive, or fish in a school, or birds in a flock, and suppose such a student of nature becomes curious about the behavior of judges during a trial. How might such a scientist describe what the judge actually does? He might learn a little bit from some of the reflective judges, and perhaps a little bit more from the sociologists and other scientists who have attempted to describe legal behavior, but he would find that most of the activity remains a huge mystery to the whole of humanity—a mystery that no one has ever felt inclined to investigate in detail.

The whole activity of managing, important as it is for the human race, is still largely an unknown aspect of the natural world. When man detaches himself and tries to observe what kind of living animal he is, he finds that he knows very little about the things most important to him and precious little about his role as a decision maker. Few managers are capable of describing how they reach their decisions in a way that someone else can understand; few can tell us how they feel about the decisions once they have been made. Of course, despite our ignorance about managerial phenomena, a great deal is written on the subject in popular magazines and managerial journals. It appears that the less we know about a subject, the more we are inclined to write extensively about it with great conviction. Some writings describe the various rituals followed in organizations prior and posterior to the actual managerial decision. But most of these descriptions pay little attention to the very puzzling question of *when* a decision actually occurred and *who* made it. A great deal is said about committee deliberations and other aspects of organizational rationality that go into the making of a decision, and the many checks and controls that are exerted to determine whether the decisions have been made properly. Much attention is paid to these aspects of organizational decision making, because they show up on the surface, so to speak. But the facts that a committee deliberated for three hours and then a decision emerged do not tell us *who* made the decision, *how* it was made, or *when* it was made. It might be added that the verbal assertions of the committee often do not tell us *what* decision is made.

So there is a great mystery of the natural world: the *who, when, how,* and *what* of man's decision making.

But even if we were to succeed in discovering a great deal more than we have about management, the result would be at best descriptive. It would be merely the background of the basic problem before us, namely, the question of how the manager *should* decide.

Am I right in claiming that we know so little about management? After all, most of us are quite willing, even eager, to express an opinion about managers, because we love to praise and complain. We don't hesitate to say that some men are better managers than others. We are constantly criticizing our political leaders. Biographers are accustomed to choose the most "outstanding" leaders of the age as the subject of their texts. These leaders may be great political leaders, leaders of industry, leaders of social movements, of religion, and so on. What is the quality these men of success have that their less successful colleagues lack? Since we believe we can identify "successful" leaders, surely we also believe we know a great deal about what a manager *should* decide. For example, in the case of the Presidents of the United States, we are told in our schoolboy texts that we can readily recognize that some of these Presidents were "great" and some of them far from great. What is the quality of greatness that we are led to ascribe to some of these Presidents?

A ready answer is at hand—the successful and great Presidents were those who made decisions that today we clearly recognize to be correct, and those who made these decisions in the face of severe opposition. We are led to believe that the activity of great Presidents is a marvelous example of successful decision making in large complex systems.

But the skeptics among us will find this answer quite unsatisfactory as an explanation of what constitutes greatness in a President. In the first place, history has no record of what would have happened had the opposition's point of view succeeded or if serious modifications had been made in the choices of the so-called great Presidents. What if the Union had *not* been saved, or our independence declared? History seems only to have recorded the episodes that followed upon the particular decision that was made and does not provide us with an analysis of events that might have occurred if an alternative had been adopted.

More curious still is the implicit assumption that a successful President made his great decisions on the basis of his own particular abilities. Since evidence is so often lacking that great Presidents of the past had these abilities, there is a natural inclination on the part of many of us to ascribe either determinism or randomness to the activities of so-called successful managers. In the case of determinism, we might argue that the events of the world occur by the accidental conglomeration of many forces unknown to man, and that these forces produce "decisions" that man in his innocence believes that he himself makes. The decision of independence in 1776 was, according to this view, simply the outgrowth of many complex human and physical interrelationships. Those who adopt the idea of randomness simply add to the physical determinism of events a random fluctuation of the sort occurring in a roulette wheel or in the shuffling of cards. They would then be willing to admit that other decisions might have been made in 1776 or later, but that these decisions would be very much like the outcome of another spin of the roulette wheel. In either event, whether we choose to describe the world of decision making as determinism or as randomness, we conclude that ascribing greatness to the decision makers in Independence Hall would be a mistake unless one meant by greatness some recognizable features of the determined or random events occurring in the world. By analogy one might say that the man who spins the roulette wheel is its "manager" who decides nothing about the outcome of his spins; a multitude of hidden physical forces determine where the wheel will stop. Calling a President great is like calling the spinner of a roulette wheel that happens to have a satisfactory result a great spinner.

This is certainly a crass and impolite way to describe the great managerial minds of the past. Surely we can do more for their memories than to describe them as irrelevant aspects of the history of society. We might try to look into the story of their lives to find evidence that they really had superior methods of deliberation. We might try to show that they had the sort of brilliance and courage that creates an ability to handle confusing pieces of information and to reach appropriate decisions. Perhaps the great manager is an extremely adept information processor who can act so rapidly that he himself is not even aware of the comparisons and computations he has made.

Indeed, this last is more or less the popular image of the great manager. For example, many scientists who advise politicians, corporate managers, and other decision makers often state that they cannot possibly attempt to tell such men what decisions *should* be made. At best they believe they can merely tell the decision maker about certain outcomes if the decisions are adopted. Thus the more modest among the advisers believe that they have no intent of "replacing" the managers they advise. And yet if these scientific advisers are capable of discerning at least some aspects of the managerial decision, what is it they lack? What are they incapable of doing that the politician and corporate manager are so successful in accomplishing? What is this secret ingredient of the great presidents of corporations, universities, and countries that no scientist or ordinary man could ever hope to acquire?

The answer usually given is that the President has information about many different aspects of the world and has an ability to put these aspects together in a way that no analysis could possibly do. In other words, he has a vision of the whole system and can relate the effectiveness of the parts to the effectiveness of the whole. The hidden secret of the great manager, so goes the myth, is his ability to solve the puzzling problems of whole systems that we have been discussing so far.

This answer is a myth, because it is totally unsatisfactory to the reasoning of an intellectually curious person. Are "great" managers fantastically high-speed data processors? Do great managerial minds outstrip any machinery now on the market or contemplated for decades to come? From what we know of the brain and its capabilities, the answer seems to be no. Indeed, it is doubtful whether the great manager in reaching decisions uses very much of the information he has received from various sources. It is also doubtful whether the manager scans many of the alternatives open to him. . . . we described how the scientist, when he comes to grips with the problems of decision making, discovers that they can only be represented by fairly complicated mathematical models. Even in fairly simple decision-making situations we have come to learn how complicated is the problem of developing a sensible way of using available information. It seems incredible that the so-called successful managers really have inbuilt models that are rich and complicated enough to include the subtleties of large-scale systems.

Suppose for the moment we descend from the lofty heights of the decision makers in Independence Hall and the White House and begin to describe a very mundane and easily recognized managerial problem concerning the number of tellers that should be available to customers in a bank. All of us have experienced the annoyance of going into a bank in a hurry and spending a leisurely but frustrating half hour behind the wrong line. How should the bank manager decide on the allocation of tellers at various times of the day?

This is a fairly simple managerial problem and its like is encountered by thousands of middle managers every day. Furthermore, this problem has been studied quite extensively in operations research and its "solution" is often found in the elementary texts. The texts say that the scientist should try to answer the managerial question by considering both the inconvenience of the customers who wait in the lines and the possible idle time of the tellers who wait at their stations when no customers are there. Thus the "successful" manager can be identified in an objective way, and we need not take a poll of greatness or lack thereof to ascertain whether the manager has performed well. The successful manager will be someone who has properly balanced the two costs of the operation of servicing customers in a bank: the cost of waiting customers and the cost of idle tellers. He will insist that the cost of a minute's waiting of a customer in a line must be compared to a minute's idle time of the teller. On the basis of this comparison, together with suitable evidence concerning the arrival rate of customers and the time required to service each customer, the successful manager will determine the policy concerning allocation of tellers to various stations during the day. Perhaps no one will feel inclined to write the biography of so ordinary a man as the manager of a branch of a local bank, but in any case if this manager decides according to the rational methods just outlined, his biographer may at least be honest about his "greatness."

Nevertheless, the analysis just outlined leaves much unanswered. For example, an idle teller need not be idle while waiting at a station where there are no customers. Instead he may be occupied with other routine matters requiring attention in the administration of the bank. Consequently, if the manager can design the entire operation of his bank's many functions properly, he may be able to decrease the cost of idle time of personnel who are servicing customers. If we look on the other side of the picture, that is, the inconvenience to a customer, we may find that in fact waiting in line is not an inconvenience at all if the customer happens to meet an acquaintance there. Perhaps the manager should serve coffee and doughnuts to waiting customers. Furthermore, if the manager could somehow or other hope to control the behavior of his customers, he might be able to recognize their arrivals in such a way that inconvenience costs are vastly reduced. Add to these considerations other innovations that might be introduced: For example, in many cases banks set up Express Windows to handle customers who would normally have very low service times. Hence, an overall average waiting time may not make sense if there are different types of service tailored to the various needs of the customers.

But then another, broader consideration occurs to us: Handling the public's financial matters by branch banking methods may be completely wrong. Modern technology may provide ways of developing financial servicing methods far cheaper for both bank and customer. After all, handling cash and checks is an extremely awkward way for a person to acquire goods at a price. With adequately designed information centers, the retail markets need only input information about a customer purchase, and the customer's employers need only input information about his income. Thus every purchase would become simply a matter of centralized information processing, as would a man's weekly or monthly paycheck. There would therefore be no real need for any of us to carry money about and no need to go to a bank and stand patiently in line. But this idea of automated purchasing and income recording is followed by another thought. We realize that any such automated financial system would probably end in eliminating a number of clerical and managerial jobs. Consequently we must examine the social problems of displaced personnel and the need for retraining, otherwise total social costs of automated banking might be far greater than the convenience gained by introducing new technology.

Before we can decide whether the manager of the branch bank is performing "satisfactorily," we must decide a much broader issue—whether the particular system that the manager operates is an appropriate one. This question leads to deeper considerations concerning the potentials of modern technology and their implications with respect to automation, job training, and the future economics of many lives.

The simple illustration with which we started has now driven us to an almost absurd concept of the "great" manager of even so little a system as a branch bank. The really successful manager must be able to understand the optimal design of the whole bank, as well as the optimal behavior patterns of his customers, and the optimal development of the technology of automation. The great manager of a little enterprise needs to be the great manager of the great enterprise.

This is a curious concept of human behavior that we have been developing. The manager cannot manage well unless he in some sense manages all. Specifically, he must have some idea of what the whole relevant world is like to be able to justify that what he manages is managed correctly.

At the present time we understand very little about managerial behavior, because in all studies of behavior we concentrate our attention on what the observer sees the manager doing; even if we broaden our perspective of his behavior to include the manager's objectives, we usually narrow the scope of these objectives so we are capable of understanding them, that is, of representing them in some kind of analytical form. We have no apparatus in our scientific kit that enables us to observe an activity which must encompass so broad a scope as managerial activity actually implies.

In other words, when we undertake studies to assist managers, or when we try to understand how managers themselves behave, we are incapable of deciding what the behavior of the manager really means because we are incapable of understanding or observing the manager's whole system. When a system scientist tries to solve a production problem or a government agency problem, he feels there are symptoms of trouble and he wishes to remove them. But he has no means by which he can decide whether the entire activity ought to be redesigned, thereby eliminating both the trouble and the far more serious loss entailed in a useless set of activities. This is true whether or not he claims he has used the "systems approach."

We have certainly failed to live up to the lessons that Greek philosophy tried to teach mankind, namely, that knowledge of oneself is the most important knowledge man can gain. We have undoubtedly done much in biology and psychology to study certain properties of living organisms and their minds. Our efforts in sociology have been mainly of a descriptive nature, since the sociologist typically does not try to judge that which he observes, nor even to understand what the characteristics of an excellent or healthy decision maker might be. Hence there is a serious question whether what is observed by the "behavioral sciences" is really relevant at all with respect to the healthy life of the organization. The study of the health of organizations is thus largely neglected, even though it is the most important health problem that exists.

The heritage of Western science with its emphasis on observation and logic seems to have provided us with no tools to study managerial activity, even though this is undoubtedly the most important problem ever faced by man. We simply do not understand the part of the natural world that is of most concern to us. At best we are able to say that the good manager is one who has a faith of a proper sort in what will happen in the world, a faith that he does not attempt to examine or control. Abraham

Lincoln, for example, had the faith that, by trying to preserve the Union through war, an excellent democracy would result. No matter that he failed to understand or have any evidence concerning the implications of the Civil War in the late decades of the nineteenth and early twentieth centuries. No matter either that Lincoln's whole concept of political activity might have been wrong. No matter that today we have no adequate information about what other courses of action were available in the 1860s and what their implications might have been. We too have a simple faith that Lincoln was a "great" President, or else—south of the Mason-Dixon line—an equally simple faith that he was not.

If we are to be honest about our ignorance, we will have to admit that some managers become great simply because there is common agreement that they are great. The scientist, the public, and the manager all agree that the decisions made by these great managers were correct, and they agree that there were no other alternatives that would have led to far better results. They also agree that the enterprise in which the manager was engaged was a meaningful one. The scientist might contribute to this agreement by using whatever resources he has available to study the alternatives that were open to the great manager; the public can recognize the benefits they have received from the great manager's activities because they "worked out" well, and the managers themselves through their experience can appreciate what the great manager has accomplished. The public, science, and management come to agree that certain managerial activities are beneficial to the whole system. What results is a judgment of excellence of management based upon such common agreement—not too bad a basis after all in view of the powerful role that common agreement often plays.

We must admit, though, that agreement is a dangerous basis for rational conclusions. Agreement always has its opposite side and often becomes disagreement in the next generation, especially in healthy societies where social change is bound to occur. A rational mind will want to find a far better basis for the judgment of excellence. He will want to find the rational basis in whose terms he can really prove the excellence of managerial decisions, based on an accurate account of the whole system.

Actually, we humans are quite incapable of understanding the agreements we reach. We often take common agreement as expressed in majority opinion to be the end of the matter, even though we frankly recognize that our own judgments are so often inadequate, no matter how strong the agreement behind them.

It may be that as men become politically more astute, they will begin to develop that part of their mentality which enables them to so look at themselves that they can examine the common agreements they hold and adopt a critical attitude toward them. Instead of gaining moral support from the agreements of his fellow man, a person may instead begin to regard agreement as a kind of evidence of danger ahead. He will then be on his way toward what we may call a theory of management, that is, a knowledge about what management really is and not what it is merely perceived to be.

We have been discussing the manager as though he were an object of study of the scientist, and we have been using as an analogy the way in which the scientist observes any kind of living activity. We have seen, however, that science is incapable as yet of generating an adequate science of management simply because it has no basis or technique by which it can adequately judge the difference between good and bad, or healthy and unhealthy, types of managerial behavior. We recognize that there must be such things as a good and a bad manager, but we have no basis on which to decide whether a specific activity falls in one category or the other.

We have also been speaking as though the scientist's interest in management is based mainly on the kind of intellectual curiosity that motivates him to discover the meaning of various mysteries of nature, that is, to transform myth into objectivity.

There is, however, another way in which we should look at the matter: We should realize that science itself is an organized activity, that is, a complex system, and we should examine what the management characteristics of this system are. The typical scientist regards the manager as someone who provides resources and creates the kind of environment in which "high-level" intellectual activity can occur. The scientist has failed to see that the whole problem of management is fundamental to every aspect of his own activities. Rather, he did see this three centuries ago, but saw it in a way that for later science turned out to be unsatisfactory. Thus the idea that management is fundamental to science disappeared in favor of other types of foundations of science. But the scientist is clearly a manager in the broad sense of the term. . . . If the concept of a great manager is a myth or a mystery, cannot the same be said of the great scientist?

31

New Perspectives in Managerial Decision Making

Ernest Dale

In this article, the author traces the development of decision making in recent years and concludes a number of important changes have occurred. Dale compares differences in the locus of decision making and finds three different types of control: control by one person, control by a few, and control by many. He concludes the article by discussing rebuttal power as related to the managerial decision making function.—Eds.

Studies in managerial decision making have become increasingly popular in the last few years. This is due partly to the growing interest in applied economics and in training for practical business affairs. It also stems from a widespread concern about the concentration of economic and managerial power in the hands of a few individuals. Finally, it is realized that the studies of economists have frequently reached a point of rapidly diminishing returns, that they have carried their refinements beyond the point which the social metallurgist would consider profitable. As it has been well put: "In the alloy of human behavior the economic motive may be as significant as the carbon content of steel, but a more adequate understanding of human behavior requires some knowledge of iron as well as carbon."

For the purpose of better analysis and prediction of businessmen's decisions, new sets of questions need to be devised and many more empirical studies of human behavior in industry and commerce undertaken. The result of such studies may be that the present structure of economic

SOURCE: Reprinted by permission of the author and The University of Chicago Press from "New Perspectives in Managerial Decision Making," *Journal of Business*, Vol. 26, No. 1 (January 1953), pp. 1–8.

theory can provide at best only a partial explanation and sometimes gives quite an incorrect explanation, because it omits some factors altogether and weights others incorrectly. In this connection many of the studies of wage determination, labor mobility, and occupational choice have shown the importance of noneconomic factors.

While most economists pay lip service to the influence of these noneconomic factors, they usually ignore them in their writings or relegate them to the bag of "assuming other things being equal." Or they may establish some arbitrary rate of exchange between the economic and the noneconomic influences. On the whole, the economist appears to assume far more certainty and rationality in decision making than is actually the case.

TYPES OF DECISIONS

A major reason for the influence of noneconomic forces is the factor of uncertainty in businessmen's decisions. In order to study the impact of uncertainty more effectively, decisions might be divided into different classes, the various categories depending on the degree of uncertainty involved. There are, first of all, the routine decisions, such as the operation of a payroll procedure or a cafeteria; such decisions often affect only one department and can be handled by precedent and habit. Even though decisions may be difficult to make because of the uncertainty involved, if they are repeated frequently, such as similar price decisions, they can be routinized. The aim of companies is frequently to increase the area of routine decisions in order to reduce the high expenses of continually making new decisions (and mistakes). Next there is the decision which affects several departments, such as the choice between a hand-operated and a mechanical system of bookkeeping. The relevant factors can be estimated with a fair degree of accuracy. In the third area uncertainty may be considered to be one of the major factors involved, as, for example, in the hiring of a top executive or the decision to force a strike. The final area may be described as one in which uncertainty predominates, such as company action on a wage demand which will be decided by a government board. We might conclude from this series of categories that the greater the knowledge of the future and the greater the influence of economic forces, the greater the degree of the company's control.

REASONS FOR UNCERTAINTY

Inaccuracy of the Data

The nature of most economic data is not precise in the sense that they can be defined, measured, and verified accurately. Hence judgement is involved in determining the data to be used and how to use them. At the level of the firm this is evident in the use of financial statements, because there is an arbitrary cutoff point before the actual value of many items is finally determined, such as, for example, the expiration of fixed assets. Important differences arise, depending on whether acquisition value or replacement value is used, especially during these last twelve years of continuous price increases. There are also important differences regarding the definition of accounting concepts, such as, for example, the profit and loss figure indicating a company's ability to pay. For instance, one writer has shown how for

> a group of companies, over the eight-year period reviewed the most restrictive application of these [general accounting] principles with relation to profits would have produced an aggregate net profit for all the companies combined of about $125 million, while the most liberal application, if consistently followed, would have produced an aggregate profit of about $275 million. It is noteworthy that none of these differences results from the difficulties of the measurement of values (which play such a role in accounting and are a major reason for inaccurate data); they arise exclusively from differences of opinion as to what constitutes a profit.[1]

There are many other important areas of disagreement about economic and business data, such as, for example, the productivity of labor (and how to separate it from other factors of production), and, in the national field, the aggregate measures about the economy as a whole, such as the national income and its components.[2] This area of uncertainty is only gradually being reduced.

The Influence of the Past and Future

A second major factor which is not readily adaptable to rigorous economic theorizing is the hidden effect of past events and traditions and the uncertainty of the future. Custom, experience, background, folklore, and subconscious memories and drives may exercise an important influence on decisions, even though that influence may not be apparent on the surface. And, even if complete knowledge of all the essential economic, technical, and administrative factors within the company could be assumed, many decisions still would involve interpretation of the unknown requiring the use of intuition, the "hunch," speculation, and extrapolation.

For major policy decisions, the chief unknowns may well be the great underlying secular trends (to which one may merely be able to adapt oneself), the reactions of consumers and competitors, the actions of government (in turn influenced by the vagaries of foreign policy), the availability of outside technical and administrative ability, the provision of a steady labor supply, and the sources of financial funds. In comparison to these unknowns, the rate of wages which must be paid and the rate of interest on capital are in many cases probably of minor importance.

Thus the likelihood of error about the past and the future increases the weight of intuitive judgment. This second major noneconomic influence on decision making can probably be best studied through a detailed examination and cross-checking of a number of major decisions.

Personality and Status

Finally, there is the influence of personality and status. The major significance which this factor may assume in company decision making is evident if one thinks of the dominating influence which the chief executive of the firm may exercise and how entirely different are the decisions that may be made in similar situations—for instance, Henry Ford, Sr., and Henry Ford II. The influence of the personality of the chief may be particularly strong in times of prosperity and in companies with a surplus revenue. Under conditions that do not demand economic rationality for the survival of the firm, the possibly irrational influence of personalities (irrational from the economic point of view) is not necessarily catastrophic for the firm. Costly decisions and mistakes not only are possible but are also tolerated—if made by the right people. This is also one reason why experiences of one firm cannot be exactly copied by other firms.

This last noneconomic factor in decision making—personality—is perhaps the most important and most inscrutable of all these factors in decision making by one man or by a small group of executives. It may therefore be worth while to explore in some more detail the role of personality in business decision making. We might investigate more specifically the locus of decision making: Which executives make the major decisions? What decisions do they make? How do they make these decisions— from what point of view, with short- or long-run considerations in mind, with what degree of participation, and with what results?

THE LOCUS OF DECISION MAKING

An attempt was made to find the locus of decision making in twenty large companies, varying in size from 4,000 to 20,000 employees. Typical decisions were selected, and each level of management was asked for the nature of its authority on the particular subject, such as, for example, the level on which various salary changes could be initiated or the amount of capital expenditures which could be incurred at different levels. In this way the authority limitations were ascertained for the chairman of the board of directors, the president, the executive vice-president, the various vice-presidents, and so on down the line to the foreman. Inquiry at these different levels also served as a check. Emphasis was placed principally on decisions dealing with money expenditures, since these can be ascertained more accurately than, say, grievances.

The result of this limited inquiry was that there tends to be a high degree of centralization of major decision making in most of the companies studied. This is particularly so in regard to decisions which are concerned with financial, legal, and industrial relations problems and to a lesser extent in manufacturing and marketing. Decisions are centralized at the top directly by requiring a check before a decision is made or indirectly by such devices as the use of manuals; detailed spelling out of all executives' limitations; training and indoctrination in line with the wishes of the chief executive; a rather complete knowledge of what the chief would do and would like to have done if he were there; central controls and group approvals; sanctions to enforce centralization.

To illustrate from the special field of industrial relations, a high degree of centralization of final decision making by the chief or the group around him was found in the following matters:

a) Determination of and changes in salaries above $4,000–$6,000 per annum and all bonus, pension, and stock purchase arrangements. A widely held view was that recognition of managerial merit and the equitable distribution of salaries are so vital to the maintenance and improvement of managerial efficiency that it needs to be left to the chief executive who may be most nearly in the position of an "impartial umpire" and who should be most concerned with managerial succession and development. Decision on salaries by the chief executive also seemed to be a device for keeping salaries within the company's ability to pay and in line with its other obligations, as well as to prevent unmerited increases. If it is merely known that the chief executive may examine any one request for a salary increase, it encourages care in presenting only those requests which can be justified if challenged.

b) Basic provisions in the union contract. The wage-rate increase, fringe benefits, and the costs of job evaluation were considered major cost factors affecting future profits and hence requiring the chief's approval in many instances. This was especially true where labor costs formed a considerable proportion of total costs, where the profit margin was narrow, or where competitive factors were important. Basic changes regarding union or management security, job assignments, technological changes, output standards, and arbitration provisions are considered to be of such vital import in the business—for reasons of cost or power relationships—that they required approval by the chief executive.

c) Hiring, development, and promotion of executives. Since sums involved in the hiring and training of executives are heavy and responsibility for succession is urgent, this function was often considered a basic responsibility of the chief.

d) Precedent-setting grievances. These grievances may have to be checked with the chief executive.

DIFFERENT TYPES OF CHIEF EXECUTIVES

From this analysis of the locus of decision-making, different types of control emerge—control by one man, control by a few, control by many.

One-Man Control

First, there is the "one-man business" which appears to be considerably more widespread than is believed by many writers and observers. In many firms there is one-man control not only of most major decisions but also of a host of minor ones.

Among the major reasons for the one-man business may be mentioned principally tradition and necessity.

Tradition. In many businesses that have grown up under one-man direction, it is frequently difficult for the founder to give up his responsibilities to someone else. He may have the personal problem of not being able or willing to relinquish one of his major activities. He may fear that others would be less competent than he in exercising them. He may be concerned with a possible loss of prestige or of power. To the chief executive delegation may threaten undue dependence on others, while centralized power may seem to suggest unlimited personal capacity. He also may fear that extended delegation of powers will lead to the establishment of a rival organization within his own empire.

The chief also faces the problem of personnel. Those who grew up with him in the business may not be able (or willing) to shoulder any additional responsibility, yet may expect to receive it. If he brings in outside personnel, capable of taking on additional responsibilities, the newcomers may be thwarted by uncooperative old-timers.

The chief finally faces the problem that the power of vested ideas may well be stronger than the power of vested economic interests. It is hard for the one man in control to jettison all his intellectual investments.

If the founder's successor is one of his sons, the new chief may be reluctant to give up powers of decision making for reasons of pride, desire to carry on the family tradition, or lack of stature to acknowledge that others, too, can make a contribution. If the successor is not a member of the family, he may want to imitate his old chief, to compensate for his previous lack of power, or to defend his newly won power against all insiders and outsiders.

Necessity. Delegation of decision making may be costly. There are the expense of training and the cost of mistakes by junior executives. Costly duplication of functions may result; for example, additional personnel men may have to be hired for the various divisions or branches, in addition to the central personnel department. The talents of these men may not be fully utilized. Moreover, there may be friction, jealousy, and lack of uniformity among semi-independent and divergent sections.

Closer personal supervision may seem to be required in hard times resulting from increased competition, a downturn of the business cycle, or long-run decline of the industry. Yet, as more decisions are centralized, often less time and thought can be given to problems lower down in the management hierarchy. Because at the top there is less familiarity with the circumstances, decisions may be delayed by the necessity for gathering information or may be made hastily without all relevant data, and the action decided upon may be less sound and the expense greater than if the responsibility had been delegated.

Continued failure of effective decision making because of overcentralization may lead to even more centralization than before, with increasingly adverse results. This vicious circle may contribute to the deterioration of an already depressed business condition.

Control by the Few

Not so different from one-man control is what may be described as "control by the few" or "oligarchic" control. In this case the major decisions of the firm are made, more or less exclusively, by a group of persons ranging in number from two to more than half a dozen, most often three or four. Usually each of these men has an area of decision making of his own in which he has the final say, such as finance, production, or marketing. However, on vital matters that go beyond his area of jurisdiction, other members of the top group may participate in the decision. This appears to be the situation in an increasing number of firms.

The distinguishing characteristic of oligarchic control is that each member of the group has equality in making important decisions for the firm. Such an arrangement may lead to considerable delay in making decisions and even to a complete deadlock on important matters if the top executives cannot agree among themselves and none of them has the power of final decision making.

In one large corporation three executives have had approximately equal powers of decision making. Each is supreme in his own field—public relations, production, or finance. On several important labor questions there recently was a serious split, the production specialist urging agreement with the union, largely for the sake of continued operations, while the other two opposed an agreement, chiefly on the basis of the principles involved. The deadlock was resolved only when a competitive firm signed with the union, thus forcing the two dissenters to capitulate. Since this event the company has moved steadily toward one-man control by the production executive. The management feels that there must be one final, decisive vote if complete standstill and breakdown are to be avoided.

Another type of oligarchic control is that exercised by financial interests, sometimes operated from a distance and based largely on narrow financial considerations, with little regard for the local people. This situation may result in a bitter struggle between a human relations-conscious local management and the outside financial interests which lack this consideration.

Oligarchic control often is a passing phenomenon that may either regress to one-man control or progress toward greater participation by an increasing number of executives. The latter tendency develops as the members of the oligarchy attempt to arrive at genuine joint decisions, better than those that any one individual could reach alone and involving an increasing number of the persons affected by them. In formal or informal meetings these executives seeking this goal tend to confine themselves to contributions that will advance group thinking, without necessarily advancing the individuals making them, into channels and procedures that tend to produce integration rather than domination or conflict.

Control by Many

The control-by-many type of decision making may be called "integrative" or "participative" (these probably are better terms than "democratic," because the latter, taken from political science, assumes an equality of men that usually does not exist in this context, certainly not in terms of status and income and normally not in terms of the power to influence business decisions). Most frequently this participation takes the form of informal, friendly consultation among the leading executives and possibly their subordinates.

The criterion of real delegation or participation is the extent to which the individual can differ from the opinions of others, especially those of his superiors, and the extent to which he can really influence decisions. In many firms this participation exists to some extent for the staff specialists and staff assistants. Their power is conferred principally by technical competence and such necessities as those resulting from the superior's lack of time to consider the problems thoroughly, as, for example, capital expenditures. Thus in many companies the advisability of highly complex capital expenditures is passed to the engineering department to decide on the basis of the technical possibilities, the availability of capital and skilled labor, the potential market. The participation of the technical staff is likely to be greater, the more certain and tangible the considerations involved and the smaller the area of intuition and shadowy judgment.

Another use of staff participation is in cases where divergent personalities are involved at the top. Their subordinate staff members are required to resolve the problems among themselves at a level where there is less possibility of "loss of face" and more chance for open discussion and differences of opinion. Sometimes the staffs can enforce a decision on the strength of their reputation for technical competence because the higher-ups are afraid to mix in technical matters.

The line more frequently is handled on a military basis, and, as a consequence, participation is less frequent. When participation does occur, it is ordinarily through consultation or conferences.

Sometimes participation is haphazard. The chief executive may be influenced by a chance event, such as an unforeseen conversation with an employee far down the line or a chance remark heard at a party or on a train ride to the office. For example, one railroad is said to have converted from steam to diesel engines because the chief executive on one of his trips happened to talk to the engineer of his train and the latter was enthusiastic about diesel engines.

Sometimes such a chance decision may be reached during an enforced period of rest. Charles E. Wilson, until recently president of the General Motors Corporation, says that the idea of the wage escalator clause and the linkage of wage rates to a national productivity index came to him when he was confined to his bed for several weeks after a skating accident.

At the top level of management, participation may occur through a series of stepup conferences, in which members of each level of management jointly formulate suggested solutions to company problems. More frequently real power to disagree rests with a top company committee consisting of the heads of all the major functions, deliberating on a basis of real equality. In this type of participation the chief executive has a vote merely as one member of the committee.

Control by "Rebuttal Power"

One-man control may be modified by participation above the chief executive. The board of directors has the power to remove the chief executive if he no longer adequately carries out the objectives of the corporation. However, the chief may be able to "pack" the board with his own friends or achieve the same effect through superior knowledge or persuasiveness.

An important "rebuttal" power may exist in one of the committees of the board of directors or on the board itself through the appointment of specialists or former company executives. They may serve as a check on unsound proposals, either because their presence and competence discourage presentation of such proposals or because they have the power to veto them. In addition, the power of the chief executive may be modified through the appointment of outside directors from other industries; public institutions; or consumer, supplier, or banking interests.

The power of the chief executive also may be limited by "monopsony," the counterbargaining power of other concerns, labor unions, and government officials. Some have suggested that the chiefs term of office may be confined to a certain period of years, also as a means of avoiding the possible exhaustion of his ideas and the vitality of his leadership.

Finally, certain important control functions may be transferred from the chief executive to the board of directors. For instance, the chief financial official in a number of companies reports directly to the finance committee of the board, which in this way has an independent financial check. Many chief executives welcome such effective "rebuttal power" because they feel it helps them to a more effective performance of their duties.

CONCLUSIONS

From our brief survey of the current status of decision making in American industry, it is clear that important changes have taken place since the traditional concepts of management were formulated. We have moved from the owner-manager to the professional manager in a large number of companies. This may have resulted in some important changes of businessmen's objectives, possibly a shift from the emphasis on profits to that of power, to the improvement of status and professional performance, to more rationalized and responsible policies. The essential nature of the decision making of the owner-manager may not have been modified too radically by the professional manager. The great economist Alfred Marshall's conception of the employer as "himself exercising a general control over everything and preserving unity in the main plan of business" may still apply to the professional heads of many businesses today. To some extent, however, one-man control may still be buttressed by financial control (though this is relatively rare). Sometimes this leads to a return of one-man control, sometimes to an extension of participation, through formal or informal participation in major decisions by a number of top executives, by the board of directors, or by staff specialists. These groups may have some veto power, either through their legal position (as representatives of the shareholders) or through technical competence. It may be that the newer tendencies toward participation in decision making may lead to an important modification of the concept of the chief executive: he may change from an absolute ruler to a constitutional monarch who merely listens or gives advice and makes the final decision only in exceptional circumstances. But the road of such a development is not likely to be smooth. For the ideals of participation may well be used by the tyrant-entrepreneur as a more effective means of keeping control: his subordinates are made to think that they are participating in his decisions, whereas, in fact, they merely conform to the goals of the chief without even realizing it. On the contrary, they may believe that they are genuinely participating, and when something irks them they may be unable to find the source of the trouble—as they could do with the old, outspoken entrepreneur. On the other hand, a number of companies appear to have pioneered rather successfully in increasing participation by their executives in a constructive effort. Such may be the powers for good or ill of the new studies and techniques of psychology and sociology.

NOTES AND REFERENCES

1. Howard C. Greer, "What Are Accepted Principles of Accounting?" *Accounting Review*, March 1938.

2. Oskar Morgenstern, *On the Inaccuracy of Economic Observations* (Princeton, N.J.: Princeton University Press, 1950).

32

Administrative Decision Making

Herbert A. Simon

This article surveys the broad area of managerial decisions in organizations and summarizes the current state of the art with respect to decision making concepts and language. Of particular importance is the discussion of the role played in advancing our knowledge by (1) developments in management science, (2) the application of the experimental method to the investigation of decision making and (3) the computer.—Eds.

There is no need, at this late date, to justify the study of organization and administration in terms of the decision-making process, for decision-making concepts and language have become highly popular in writing about administration.[1] This paper will describe some of the progress that has been made over the past quarter century, employing this approach, toward deepening our scientific knowledge—what new facts have been learned about human behavior in organizations, what new scientific procedures for ascertaining facts, what new concepts for describing them, and what new generalizations for explaining them. This progress extends both to descriptive and normative matters: to the pure science of administration, and its application to the practical business of managing.

To satisfy limits on . . . space, your patience, and my time, the account will be highly selective. Only a few notable and significant advances have been selected; others for which equally plausible claims might be made are ignored. A frequent practice in the social sciences is to

SOURCE: Reprinted by permission of the author and the American Society for Public Administration from *Public Administration Review* (March 1965), pp. 31–37.

bemoan our present ignorance while making optimistic predictions about future knowledge. It is a pleasure to survey an area of social science where, by contrast, we can speak without blushing about our present knowledge—indeed, where only a small sample of the gains in knowledge that have been achieved in the past quarter century can be presented.

OPERATIONS RESEARCH AND MANAGEMENT SCIENCE

One obvious answer to the question "What's new?" is the spectacular development in the normative theory of decision making that goes under the labels of "operations research" and "management science." Through these activities, many classes of administrative decisions have been formalized, mathematics has been applied to determine the characteristics of the "best" or "good" decisions, and myriads of arithmetic calculations are carried out routinely in many business and governmental organizations to reach the actual decisions from day to day. A number of sophisticated mathematical tools—linear programming, queuing theory, dynamic programming, combinatorial mathematics, and others—have been invented or developed to this end.

Like all scientific developments, this one has a long intellectual history, and did not spring, full-grown, from the brow of Zeus. Nevertheless, the state of the art today is so remarkably advanced beyond its position before World War II that the difference of degree becomes one of kind.[2]

The quantitative decision-making tools of operations research have perhaps had more extensive application in business than in governmental organizations. It is worth recalling, however, that many of these tools underwent their early development in the American and British military services during and just after the Second World War (where the terms "operations research" and "operations analysis" were coined). Among the inventors of linear programming, for example, were Tjalling Koopmans, seeking, as statistician with the Combined Shipping Adjustment Board, a means for scheduling tanker operations efficiently; and George B. Dantzig and Marshall K. Wood, in the Office of the Air Force Controller, who used as one of their first (hypothetical) programming problems the scheduling of the Berlin Airlift.

Operations research, particularly in its governmental applications, has retained close intellectual ties with classical economic theory, and has sought to find effective ways of applying that theory to public budgeting and expenditure decisions. This has been a central preoccupation of the RAND Corporation effort, as exemplified by such works as Charles J. Hitch and Roland N. McKean, *The Economics of Defense in the Nuclear Age.*[3] In the past several years, Hitch, as Controller of the Department of Defense, and a number of his former RAND associates have played major roles in bringing the new tools to bear on Defense Department budget decisions. Thus, while the quarter century begins with V. O. Key's plaint about "The Lack of a Budgetary Theory,"[4] it ends with a distinct revitalization of the whole field of public expenditure theory, and with a burgeoning of new analytic tools to assist in allocating public resources.

OPTIMALITY AND ALL THAT

In many ways the contributions of operations research and management science to decision-making theory have been very pragmatic in flavor. The goal, after all, is to devise tools that will help management make better decisions. One example of a pragmatic technique that has proved itself very useful and has been rapidly and widely adopted over the past five years, is the scheduling procedure variously called PERT, or critical path scheduling. This technique does not use any very deep or sophisticated mathematics (which may account partly for the speed of its adoption), but is mainly an improvement of the common sense underlying the traditional Gantt Chart.

Contrasting with this pragmatic flavor, advances in operations research have been paralleled by developments in the pure theory of rational choice—a theory that has reached a very high level of mathematical and logical elegance and rigor. Among these developments perhaps the most important are: (1) rigorous, formal axiom systems for defining the concept of utility in operational terms, (2) extension of the theory of rational choice to encompass the maximization of expected utility under conditions of uncertainty, (3) extension of the theory to repeated choices over time—dynamic optimization, and (4) extension of the theory to competitive "gaming" situations. These formal advances have had an important influence, in turn, on directions of work in theoretical statistics (statistical decision theory, Bayesian statistics), and on the kinds of models that are preferred by operations researchers—or at least by the theorists among their number.[5]

An evaluation of these contributions on the pure theory of rational choice would return a mixed verdict. On the positive side, they have provided enormous conceptual clarification for discussions of "rationality." For example, it has always been unclear what rationality meant in a pure outwitting or bargaining situation, where each party is trying to outguess, and perhaps bluff, the other. If the theory of games, due to von Neumann and Morgenstern, did not solve this problem for all situations, it at least made painfully clear exactly what the problem is.

On the negative side, fascination with the pure theory of rational choice has sometimes distracted attention from the problems of decision makers who possess modest calculating powers in the face of a world of enormous complexity. (In the real world, the calculating powers of electronic computers as well as men must be described as "modest.") A normative theory, to be useful, must call only for information that can be obtained and only for calculations that can be performed. The classical theory of rational choice has generally ignored these information-processing limitations. It has assumed that rationality was concerned with choice among alternatives that were already specified, and whose consequences were known or were readily calculable. It has assumed, also, comparability of consequences—that is, a practically measurable utility index.

Since these conditions, on which the classical theory rests, are so seldom satisfied in the real world, great interest attaches to procedures that make less heroic assumptions about the "givens" and the knowns; and, there is considerable progress in devising less than optimal decision procedures for situations where the optimum is unknown and practically undiscoverable. These procedures, often called *heuristic methods,* are distinguishable from optimizing techniques in three respects: they grapple, as most optimizing techniques do not, with the problems of designing and discovering alternatives, as well as with choosing among given alternatives; they frequently "satisfice," or settle for good-enough answers in despair at finding best answers; they commonly do not guarantee the qualities of the solutions they provide, and often do not even guarantee they will find a solution. The second and third of these characteristics are, of course, not virtues, but are the price that must be paid for extending our theory and tools for decision making to the wide range of real-world situations not encompassed by the classical models.

By way of illustration, a common problem of business and governmental management involves locating a system of warehouses over a country so that products can be distributed from production points to ultimate users as economically as possible. Attempts to formulate the warehousing problem so that the optimizing methods known as linear programming can be used have failed because the computations become too lengthy. However, heuristic techniques have been applied successfully to find "good" solutions to the problem where "best" solutions are unattainable.[6]

It is traditional to observe, in any discussion of the modern decision-making tools, that knowledge of these tools runs far in advance of application, and that the domain of application has been limited largely to decisions that are well-structured or "programmed," and quantitative in character. The warehousing problem described above has both of these characteristics. Whether this limitation on applications is inherent or temporary is a more controversial question. One of the important tasks before us now is to see how far we can go in extending the applicability of the new decision-making tools to areas that are ill structured, and qualitative, calling for "judgment," "experience," and even "creativity." To do this, we shall presumably have to understand what "judgment," "experience," and "creativity" are, a topic discussed later.

EXPERIMENTS ON DECISION MAKING

A second area of significant advance has been in applying the experimental method to the investigation of decision making. This has been done both by arranging for experiments on live real-world organizations—on the model of the Hawthorne experiments—and/or by bringing organizations, or organizationoid systems into the laboratory. For obvious reasons, the latter has been done more often than the former.

The first volume of the *Public Administration Review* contained a report of a large-scale field experiment on the decision-making processes of social workers,[7] but similar experiments have been exceedingly rare in the succeeding twenty-five years. One of the few other examples to which I can refer is the study done in the Prudential Life Insurance Company by the Survey Research Center of the University of Michigan.[8] Either researchers on organizations decided that the information attainable from field experiments was not worth the trouble and cost of carrying out such experiments, or they found it difficult to secure the cooperation of business and governmental organizations in arranging such experiments—or both. Whatever the reason, field experiments have not been an important procedure for learning about organizational decision making.

In a few cases researchers have tried to import relatively sizeable organizations into the laboratory—hence, their studies lie on the boundary line between field and laboratory experiments. The Systems Research Laboratory of the RAND Corporation, for example, studied decision making by simulating, under controlled conditions, an entire air defense control center and associated early warning stations, manned on a full-time basis over a period of several months by a staff of some thirty subjects. While the studies conducted by the Systems Research Laboratory had as their direct outgrowth a major Air Force training program, the laboratory proved less tractable as a setting for obtaining data for testing theories of the decision-making process, and there has been no subsequent rash of studies of this kind.[9]

In contrast to the dearth of field experiments and large-scale laboratory experiments, laboratory experimentation with relatively small groups has been a thriving enterprise. Several examples of methodological advances in the art of small-group experimentation can be mentioned. Fred Bales, with his interaction process analysis, developed a scheme of data processing useful for studying the interaction of task-oriented and social-system oriented behavior in small problem-solving groups. Alex Bavelas devised a small-group task that permitted the experimenter to alter the decision-making process by opening or closing particular channels of communication between members of the group. In succeeding years, the Bales coding scheme and the Bavelas small-group task have both been used in a substantial number of studies, manipulating a great many different independent variables. Both have proved exceedingly valuable in permitting the cumulation of comparable knowledge from a whole series of experiments carried out by different investigators in different laboratories.

It is impossible to summarize here, or even to reference, the numerous contributions to the substantive knowledge of decision making that have been contributed by the small-group experiments. A single example will convey the flavor of such work. Cyert and March were able to produce bias in the estimates of members of a simulated organization by creating partial conflict of interest among them, but showed that under certain circumstances this bias did not affect organizational performance.[10]

New knowledge about organizational decision making can be obtained from appropriately planned experiments on individuals as well as from small-group experiments. Andrew Stedry, for example, has tested in this way theories about how budget controls affect behavior in organizations.[11] The series of studies of influence processes carried out at Yale by the late Carl Hovland and his associates belong in the same category.[12]

PERSUASION AND EVOCATION

Mention of the Yale research on influence processes marks a good point in our discussion to turn to several substantive developments in the theory of decision making. The notion that a decision is like a conclusion derived from a set of premises has been a useful metaphor for analyzing the decision-making process. Following the metaphor a step further, we can view each member of an organization as "inputting" certain premises, and "outputting" certain conclusions, or decisions. But each member's conclusions become, in turn, the inputs, that is to say, the premises, for other members. For one person to influence another involves inducing him to use appropriate premises in his decision making.

What happens in an organization, or in any kind of social system, when there are conflicting premises pushing a particular decision in different directions? Much of the research on influence processes has been aimed at answering this question. In much of this research, influence has been conceived as a kind of "force," so that when several influences are brought to bear simultaneously, the outcome is interpreted as a "resultant" of the impinging forces. Persuasion is then a process of exerting such a force.

An important advance in understanding decision making has been to complement the notion of persuasion with the notion of evocation. When we want someone to carry out a particular action, we may think of our task as one of inducing him to *accept* latent decision premises favorable to the action that he already possesses. Thus, writing about food will often make a reader hungry, but we would hardly say that we had "persuaded" him that he was hungry; it would be better to say that we had "reminded" him.

Processes of persuasion play their largest role in decision making in conflict situations—where the issue is already posed, and the alternatives present. This is the framework within which most of the Yale studies on attitude change were carried out. It is also the framework for the important and well-known study of *Voting* by Berelson, Lazarsfeld, and McPhee.[13]

On the other hand, in studies of decision making where the focus of attention of the participants is one of the main independent variables, the evoking processes take on larger importance. The recent study of the Trade Agreements Act renewal, by Raymond Bauer, Ithiel Pool, and Lewis Dexter indicates that these processes played a major role in deciding the issue.[14] The authors describe the setting of their study thus (p. 5): "We are interested in the sources of information for each of these populations, the bases of its attitudes on the trade issue, *and the circumstances which lead some individuals to take active roles in the making of policy.*" (Emphasis supplied.) They demonstrate convincingly that the behavior of particular Congressmen on the trade issue depended as much on the alternative claims on their time and attention as on the distribution of interests of their constituents.

To the extent that the mechanism of evocation is important for decision making, many new ways arise in which organizational arrangements may affect behavior. As example, one of the findings of the study just mentioned (p. 229) can be cited:

> In summary, we would suggest that most significant of all to an understanding of what communication went out from business on foreign trade was neither self-interest nor ideology, but the institutional structure which facilitated or blocked the production of messages. Whether a letter to a congressman would get written depended on whether organization facilitated it, whether the writer's round of daily conversations would lead up to it, whether a staff was set up to produce it, and whether the writer conceived writing this letter to be part of his job.

Evoking mechanisms take on special prominence wherever dynamic change is occurring. Studies of the diffusion of innovations show that the timing of adoption of an innovation depends critically on the means for getting people to attend to it.[15] From every point of view, the new knowledge gained about evoking and attention-directing processes is a major substantive advance in our understanding of organizational decision making.

THE STRUCTURE OF DECISIONS

A decision is not a simple, unitary event, but the product of a complex social process generally extending over a considerable period of time. As noted, decision making includes attention-directing or intelligence processes that determine the occasions of decision, processes for discovering and designing possible courses of action, and processes for evaluating alternatives and choosing among them. The complexity of decision making has posed grave difficulties in its study and description, difficulties only now being overcome by recent methodological innovations.

Traditionally, a decision-making process was captured and recorded by the common sense tools of the historian using everyday language. The notion that a decision might be viewed as a conclusion drawn from premises—a notion mentioned earlier—introduced a modicum of system into the description of decision making. According to this view, in order to record a decision-making process it was necessary to discover the sources of the decision premises, and the channels of communication they followed through the organization to the point where they became the raw materials of decision.

Studies that adopted this general approach to the description of decisions, while remaining within the traditional case study framework, became increasingly frequent during the period under discussion. One example is Herbert Kaufman's excellent study of *The Forest Ranger,* aimed at analyzing "the way their decisions and behavior are influenced within and by the Service."[16] Another is the study by the Carnegie Tech group of the influence of accounting information on operating decisions in large companies.[17]

The method of these studies is best described as "systematized common sense." The decision premise concept provides an ordering and organizing principle; it reduces somewhat the subjectivity of the description and the dangers of observer bias; but it falls far short of allowing complete formalization of the description. And it cannot, of course, solve the problem of how to validate generalizations with data from single cases.

The invention of the modern digital computer radically changed the situation. As gradually became apparent to those who came into contact with computers, the computer is a device that is capable of making decisions. (One demonstration of this is its use to implement the analytic decision-making schemes introduced by operations research.) Hence, a language suitable for describing the processes going on in computers might well be appropriate for describing decision making in organizations. At least the notion appeared to be worth a trial: to equate "decision premise" with the concepts of data input and program of instructions in a computer, and to equate the concept of a conclusion with the concept of the output of a computer program.

An early, and rather primitive, attempt to describe an organization decision-making process in computer programming terms appeared in 1956.[18] In this study the authors recounted the steps taken by a business firm to reach a decision about the installation of an electronic computer. They then showed how this sequence of events could be explained by a program composed of an organized system of relatively simple and general information gathering, searching, problem solving, and evaluating processes. Of particular interest was the fact that the decision examined in this study was not a highly structured, quantitative one, but one that called for large amounts of professional and administrative judgment.

Encouraging results from early studies of this kind raised hopes that it might be possible to use computer programming languages formally as well as informally to construct theories of organizational decision making, and to test those theories by simulating the decision process on the computer. Computer programs seeking to explain several kinds of organizational decision-making situations have, in fact, been constructed, and have shown themselves adequate to simulate important aspects of the human behavior in these situations. The decisions that have been simulated in this way to date are still relatively simple ones, but they encompass behavior that would generally be regarded as professional, and as involving judgment. Two of the best-developed examples are a simulation of a department store buyer and a simulation of a bank trust investment officer.[19]

I am not aware that any single comparable simulation of a decision-making process in the area of public administration has yet been carried out, but it appears that several are under way in current research. Perhaps the most likely target for initial attempts is public budgeting. If we examine the strategies described in recent empirical studies, like those of Wildavsky,[20] we will see that they can be rather directly translated into components of computer programs.

Parallel with these simulations of administrative decision making there has been a considerable exploration of individual thinking and problem solving processes, also using computer simulation as the tool of theory formulation and theory testing.[21] Today, we have a considerable specific knowledge on how human beings accomplish complex cognitive tasks. We have reasons for optimism, too, that this body of knowledge will increase rapidly, for in the digital computer language we have an analytic tool and a means for accurate expression whose powers are commensurate with the complexity of the phenomena we wish to describe and understand.

LANDMARKS AND NEW ROADS

These, then, are some of the more prominent landmarks along the road of decision-making research over the past twenty-five years. On the normative side, the analytic tools of modern operations research have secured an important place in the practical work of management. Their role in everyday decision making promises to be much enlarged as present techniques are supplemented by new heuristic approaches.

On the side of the pure science of administration, there have been equally fruitful developments. The experimental method, in the small-group laboratory, can now be used to study a wide range of decision-making behaviors that are relevant to organizations. We have introduced the concept of evocation into our theories of influence, and have used it to gain new understanding of the decision-making process in changing environments. Finally, the modern digital computer, a powerful new tool, has provided both a language for expressing our theories of decision making and an engine for calculating their empirical implications. Theories can now be compared with data of the real world of organizations.

The attention-directing mechanisms so important in decision making also have played their part in determining the particular developments sampled in this paper. Another scientist, with a different set of research concerns, would choose a different sample. The fact that even one such sample exists shows how far we have come during the past twenty-five years toward understanding human behavior in organizations.

NOTES AND REFERENCES

1. The term "decision making" occurred three times in the titles of articles in the first fifteen volumes of the *Public Administration Review*—that is, through 1955; it occurred ten times in the next eight volumes, or about six times as often per annum as in the earlier period.

2. Some notion of the state of proto-operations-research just before World War II, as it applied to municipal administration, can be obtained from Ridley and Simon, *Measuring Municipal Activities* (Chicago: International City Managers' Association, first edition, 1938).

3. Cambridge, Mass.: Harvard University Press, 1960.

4. *American Political Science Review*, December, 1940, p. 1142. Labels have an unfortunate tendency to compartmentalize knowledge. Thus, the literature of "budgeting" has been only partly informed by the literature on "decision making," and vice versa, and both of these have sometimes been isolated from the economics literature on resources allocation and public expenditure theory. Variants on the same basic sets of ideas are rediscovered each generation: "measurement of public services," "program budgeting," "performance budgeting," "engineering economy," "cost-benefit analysis," "operations analysis." What is genuinely new in this area in the past decade is the power and sophistication of the analytic and computational tools. Some impression of these tools may be gained from the Hitch and McKean book previously mentioned; from Roland N. McKean, *Efficiency in Government through Systems Analysis* (New York: John Wiley and Sons, 1958); Arthur Maass, et al., *Design of Water Resource Systems* (Cambridge, Mass.: Harvard University Press, 1962); or Allen V. Kneese, *The Economics of Regional Water Quality Management* (Baltimore: Johns Hopkins University Press, 1964), and the references cited therein.

5. Since I have discoursed at length on these matters elsewhere, I shall be brief here. See "Theories of Decision Making in Economics and Behavioral Science," *American Economic Review*, 49 (June, 1959), pp. 253–283, and Part 4 of *Models of Man* (New York: John Wiley and Sons, 1957).

6. Alfred A. Kuehn and Michael J. Hamberger, "A Heuristic Program for Locating Warehouses," *Management Science*, July 1963.

7. Herbert A. Simon and William R. Divine, "Human Factors in an Administrative Experiment," *Public Administration Review*, 1 (Autumn, 1941), pp. 485–492.

8. N. C. Morse and E. Reimer, "Experimental Change of a Major Organizational Variable," *Journal of Abnormal and Social Psychology*, 52 (1955), pp. 120–129.

9. Robert L. Chapman, et al., "The System Research Laboratory's Air Defense Experiments," *Management Science*, 5 (April, 1959), pp. 250–269.

10. Richard M. Cyert and James G. March, *The Behavioral Theory of the Firm* (Englewood Cliffs, N.J.: Prentice-Hall, Inc., 1963), pp. 67–77.

11. *Budget Control and Cost Behavior* (Englewood Cliffs, N.J.: Prentice-Hall, Inc., 1960), Ch. 4.

12. See the "Yale Studies in Attitude and Communication," edited by Hovland and Rosenberg, and published by the Yale University Press.

13. Chicago: University of Chicago Press, 1954.

14. *American Business and Public Policy: The Politics of Foreign Trade* (Atherton Press, 1963).

15. See J. Coleman, E. Katz, and H. Menzel, "Diffusion of an Innovation Among Physicians," *Sociometry,* 20 (1957), pp. 253–270; also, H. A. Simon and J. G. March, *Organizations* (New York: John Wiley and Sons, 1957), Ch. 7.

16. Johns Hopkins University Press, 1960, p. 4.

17. *Centralization versus Decentralization in Organizing the Controller's Department* (New York: The Controllership Foundation, 1954). The study is summarized in John M. Pfiffner and Frank P. Sherwood, *Administrative Organization* (Englewood Cliffs, N.J.: Prentice-Hall, Inc., 1960), Ch. 21.

18. R. M. Cyert, H. A. Simon, and D. B. Trow, "Observation of a Business Decision," *Journal of Business,* 29 (1956), pp. 237–248.

19. Descriptions of these two simulations may be found in Chapters 7 and 10, respectively, of Cyert and March, *Behavioral Theory of the Firm* (see note 10).

20. Aaron Wildavsky, *The Politics of the Budgetary Process* (Boston: Little, Brown and Company, 1964).

21. For a survey, and numerous examples, see Edward Feigenbaum and Julian Feldman, *Computers and Thought* (New York: McGraw-Hill, 1963).

33

The Science of "Muddling Through"

Charles E. Lindblom

It is frequently argued that people operate by experience and go with what they know will "work." In so doing they tend to arrive not at optimal solutions to problems, but satisfactory ones. In this article, Lindblom advances the notion that not only is this an accurate description of the way problems are solved, but that, all things considered, it is probably the best way.—Eds.

Suppose an administrator is given responsibility for formulating policy with respect to inflation. He might start by trying to list all related values in order of importance, e.g., full employment, reasonable business profit, protection of small savings, prevention of a stock market crash. Then all possible policy outcomes could be rated as more or less efficient in attaining a maximum of these values. This would of course require a prodigious inquiry into values held by members of society and an equally prodigious set of calculations on how much of each value is equal to how much of each other value. He could then proceed to outline all possible policy alternatives. In a third step, he would undertake systematic comparison of his multitude of alternatives to determine which attains the greatest amount of values.

In comparing policies, he would take advantage of any theory available that generalized about classes of policies. In considering inflation, for example, he would compare all policies in the light of the theory of prices. Since no alternatives are beyond his investigation, he would consider strict central control and the abolition of all prices and markets on the one hand and elimination of all public controls with reliance com-

---

SOURCE: Reprinted by permission of the author and the American Society for Public Administration from *Public Administration Review*, Vol. 19, No. 2 (1959), pp. 79–88.

pletely on the free market on the other, both in the light of whatever theoretical generalizations he could find on such hypothetical economies.

Finally, he would try to make the choice that would in fact maximize his values.

An alternative line of attack would be to set as his principal objective, either explicitly or without conscious thought, the relatively simple goal of keeping prices level. This objective might be compromised or complicated by only a few other goals, such as full employment. He would in fact disregard most other social values as beyond his present interest, and he would for the moment not even attempt to rank the few values that he regarded as immediately relevant. Were he pressed, he would quickly admit that he was ignoring many related values and many possible important consequences of his policies.

As a second step, he would outline those relatively few policy alternatives that occurred to him. He would then compare them. In comparing his limited number of alternatives, most of them familiar from past controversies, he would not ordinarily find a body of theory precise enough to carry him through a comparison of their respective consequences. Instead he would rely heavily on the record of past experience with small policy steps to predict the consequences of similar steps extended into the future.

Moreover, he would find that the policy alternatives combined objectives or values in different ways. For example, one policy might offer price level stability at the cost of some risk of unemployment; another might offer less price stability but also less risk of unemployment. Hence, the next step in his approach—the final selection—would combine into one the choice among values and the choice among instruments for reaching values. It would not, as in the first method of policy making, approximate a more mechanical process of choosing the means that best satisfied goals that were previously clarified and ranked. Because practitioners of the second approach expect to achieve their goals only partially, they would expect to repeat endlessly the sequence just described, as conditions and aspirations changed and as accuracy of prediction improved.

BY ROOT OR BY BRANCH

For complex problems, the first of these two approaches is of course impossible. Although such an approach can be described, it cannot be practiced except for relatively simple problems and even then only in a somewhat modified form. It assumes intellectual capacities and sources of information that men simply do not possess, and it is even more absurd as an approach to policy when the time and money that can be allocated to a policy problem is limited, as is always the case. Of particular importance to public administrators is the fact that public agencies are in effect usually instructed not to practice the first method. That is to say, their prescribed functions and constraints—the politically or legally possible—restrict their attention to relatively few values and relatively few alternative policies among the countless alternatives that might be imagined. It is the second method that is practiced.

Curiously, however, the literatures of decision making, policy formulation, planning, and public administration formalize the first approach rather than the second, leaving public administrators who handle complex decisions in the position of practicing what few preach. For emphasis I run some risk of overstatement. True enough, the literature is well aware of limits on man's capacities and of the inevitability that policies will be approached in some such style as the second. But attempts to formalize rational policy formulation—to lay out explicitly the necessary steps in the process—usually describe the first approach and not the second.[1]

The common tendency to describe policy formulation even for complex problems as though it followed the first approach has been strengthened by the attention given to, and successes enjoyed by, operations research, statistical decision theory, and systems analysis. The hallmarks of these procedures, typical of the first approach, are clarity of objective, explicitness of evaluation, a high degree of comprehensiveness of overview, and, wherever possible, quantification of values for mathematical analysis. But these advanced procedures remain largely the appropriate techniques of relatively small-scale problem solving where the total number of variables to be considered is small and value problems restricted. Charles Hitch, head of the Economics Division of RAND Corporation, one of the leading centers for application of these techniques, has written:

> I would make the empirical generalization from my experience at RAND and elsewhere that operations research is the art of suboptimizing, i.e., of solving some lower level problems, and that difficulties increase and our special competence diminishes by an order of magnitude with every level of decision making we attempt to ascend. The sort of simple explicit model which operations researchers are so proficient in using can certainly reflect most of the significant factors influencing traffic control on the George Washington Bridge, but the proportion of the relevant reality which we can represent by any such model or models in studying, say, a major foreign policy decision, appears to be almost trivial.[2]

Accordingly, I propose in this paper to clarify and formalize the second method, much neglected in the literature. This might be described as the method of *successive limited comparisons*. I will contrast it with the first approach, which might be called the rational comprehensive method.[3] More impressionistically and briefly—and therefore generally used in this article—they could be characterized as the branch method and root method, the former continually building out from the current situation, step-by-step and by small degrees; the latter starting from fundamentals anew each time, building on the past only as experience is embodied in a theory, and always prepared to start completely from the ground up.

TABLE 1

Rational Comprehensive (Root)	*Successive Limited Comparisons (Branch)*
1a. Clarification of values or objectives distinct from and usually prerequisite to empirical analysis of alternative policies.	1b. Selection of value goals and empirical analysis of the needed action are not distinct from one another but are closely intertwined.
2a. Policy formulation is therefore approached through means-end analysis: First the ends are isolated, then the means to achieve them are sought:	2b. Since means and ends are not distinct, means-end analysis is often inappropriate or limited.
3a. The test of a "good" policy is that it can be shown to be the most appropriate means to desired ends.	3b. The test of a "good" policy is typically that various analysts find themselves directly agreeing on a policy (without their agreeing that it is the most appropriate means to an agreed objective).
4a. Analysis is comprehensive; every important relevant factor is taken into account.	4b. Analysis is drastically limited: i) Important possible outcomes are neglected. ii) Important alternative potential policies are neglected. iii) Important affected values are neglected.
5a. Theory is often heavily relied upon.	5b. A succession of comparisons greatly reduces or eliminates reliance on theory.

Let us put the characteristics of the two methods side by side in simplest terms. [See Table 1.]

Assuming that the root method is familiar and understandable, we proceed directly to clarification of its alternative by contrast. In explaining the second, we shall be describing how most administrators do in fact approach complex questions, for the root method, the "best" way as a blueprint or model, is in fact not workable for complex policy questions, and administrators are forced to use the method of successive limited comparisons.

INTERTWINING EVALUATION AND EMPIRICAL ANALYSIS (1b)

The quickest way to understand how values are handled in the method of successive limited comparisons is to see how the root method often breaks down in *its* handling of values or objectives. The idea that values should be clarified, and in advance of the examination of alternative policies, is appealing. But what happens when we attempt it for complex social problems? The first difficulty is that on many critical values or objectives, citizens disagree, congressmen disagree, and public administrators disagree. Even where a fairly specific objective is prescribed for the administrator, there remains considerable room for disagreement on subobjectives. Consider, for example, the conflict with respect to locating public housing, described in Meyerson and Banfield's study of the Chicago Housing Authority[4]—disagreement which occurred despite the clear objective of providing a certain number of public housing units in the city. Similarly conflicting are objectives in highway location, traffic control, minimum wage administration, development of tourist facilities in national parks, or insect control.

Administrators cannot escape these conflicts by ascertaining the majority's preference, for preferences have not been registered on most issues; indeed, there often *are* no preferences in the absence of public discussion sufficient to bring an issue to the attention of the electorate. Furthermore, there is a question of whether intensity of feeling should be considered as well as the number of persons preferring each alternative. By the impossibility of doing otherwise, administrators often are reduced to deciding policy without clarifying objectives first.

Even when an administrator resolves to follow his own values as a criterion for decisions, he often will not know how to rank them when they conflict with one another, as they usually do. Suppose, for example, that an administrator must relocate tenants living in tenements scheduled for destruction. One objective is to empty the buildings fairly promptly, another is to find suitable accommodation for persons displaced, another is to avoid friction with residents in other areas in which a large influx would be unwelcome, another is to deal with all concerned through persuasion if possible, and so on.

How does one state even to himself the relative importance of these partially conflicting values? A simple ranking of them is not enough; one needs ideally to know how much of one value is worth sacrificing for some of another value. The answer is that typically the administrator chooses—and must choose—directly among policies in which these values are combined in different ways. He cannot first clarify his values and then choose among policies.

A more subtle third point underlies both the first two. Social objectives do not always have the same relative values. One objective may be highly prized in one circumstance, another in another circumstance. If, for example, an administrator values highly both the dispatch with which his agency can carry through its projects *and* good public relations, it matters little which of the two possibly conflicting values he favors in some abstract or general sense. Policy questions arise in forms which put to administrators such a question as: Given the degree to which we are or are not already achieving the values of dispatch and the values of good public relations, is it worth sacrificing a little speed for a happier clientele, or is it better to risk offending the clientele so that we can get on with our work? The answer to such a question varies with circumstances.

The value problem is, as the example shows, always a problem of adjustments at a margin. But there is no practicable way to state marginal objectives or values except in terms of particular policies. That one value is preferred to another in one decision situation does not mean that it will be preferred in another decision situation in which it can be had only at great sacrifice of another value. Attempts to rank or order values in general and abstract terms so that they do not shift from decision to decision end up by ignoring the relevant marginal preferences. The significance of this third point thus goes very far. Even if all administrators had at hand an agreed set of values, objectives, and constraints, and an agreed ranking of these values, objectives, and constraints, their marginal values in actual choice situations would be impossible to formulate.

Unable consequently to formulate the relevant values first and then choose among policies to achieve them, administrators must choose directly among alternative policies that offer different marginal combinations of values. Somewhat paradoxically, the only practicable way to disclose one's relevant marginal values even to oneself is to describe the policy one chooses to achieve them. Except roughly and vaguely, I know of no way to describe—or even to understand—what my relative evaluations are for, say, freedom and security, speed and accuracy in governmental decisions, or low taxes and better schools than to describe my preferences among specific policy choices that might be made between the alternatives in each of the pairs.

In summary, two aspects of the process by which values are actually handled can be distinguished. The first is clear: evaluation and empirical analysis are intertwined; that is, one chooses among values and among policies at one and the same time. Put a little more elaborately, one simultaneously chooses a policy to attain certain objectives and chooses the objectives themselves. The second aspect is related but distinct: the administrator focuses his attention on marginal or incremental values. Whether he is aware of it or not, he does not find general formulations of objectives very helpful and in fact makes specific marginal or incremental comparisons. Two policies, X and Y, confront him. Both promise the same degree of attainment of objectives a, b, c, d, and e. But X promises him somewhat more of f than does Y, while Y promises him somewhat more of g than does X. In choosing between them, he is in fact offered the alternative of a marginal or incremental amount of f at the expense of a marginal or incremental amount of g. The only values that are relevant to his choice are these increments by which the two policies differ; and, when he finally chooses between the two marginal values, he does so by making a choice between policies.[5]

As to whether the attempt to clarify objectives in advance of policy selection is more or less rational than the close intertwining of marginal evaluation and empirical analysis, the principal difference established is that for complex problems the first is impossible and irrelevant, and the second is both possible and relevant. The second is possible because the administrator need not try to analyze any values except the values by which alternative policies differ and need not be concerned with them except as they differ marginally. His need for information on values or objectives is drastically reduced as compared with the root method; and his capacity for grasping, comprehending, and relating values to one another is not strained beyond the breaking point.

RELATIONS BETWEEN MEANS AND ENDS (2b)

Decision making is ordinarily formalized as a means-ends relationship: means are conceived to be evaluated and chosen in the light of ends finally selected independently of and prior to the choice of means. This is the means-ends relationship of the root method. But it follows from all that has just been said that such a means-ends relationship is possible only to the extent that values are agreed upon, are reconcilable, and are stable at the margin. Typically, therefore, such a means-ends relationship is absent from the branch method, where means and ends are simultaneously chosen.

Yet any departure from the means-ends relationship of the root method will strike some readers as inconceivable. For it will appear to them that only in such a relationship is it possible to determine whether one policy choice is better or worse than another. How can an administrator know whether he has made a wise or foolish decision if he is without prior values or objectives by which to judge his decisions? The answer to this question calls up the third distinctive difference between root and branch methods: how to decide the best policy.

THE TEST OF "GOOD" POLICY (3b)

In the root method, a decision is "correct," "good," or "rational" if it can be shown to attain some specified objective, where the objective can be specified without simply describing the decision itself. Where objectives are defined only through the marginal or incremental approach to values described above, it is still sometimes possible to test whether a policy does in fact attain the desired objectives; but a precise statement of the objectives takes the form of a description of the policy chosen or some alternative to it. To show that a policy is mistaken one cannot offer an abstract argument that important objectives are not achieved; one must instead argue that another policy is more to be preferred.

So far, the departure from customary ways of looking at problem solving is not troublesome, for many administrators will be quick to agree that the most effective discussion of the correctness of policy does take the form of comparison with other policies that might have been chosen. But what of the situation in which administrators cannot agree on values or objectives, either abstractly or in marginal terms? What then is the test of "good" policy? For the root method, there is no test.

Agreement on objectives failing, there is no standard of "correctness." For the method of successive limited comparisons, the test is agreement on policy itself, which remains possible even when agreement on values is not.

It has been suggested that continuing agreement in Congress on the desirability of extending old age insurance stems from liberal desires to strengthen the welfare programs of the federal government and from conservative desires to reduce union demands for private pension plans. If so, this is an excellent demonstration of the ease with which individuals of different ideologies often can agree on concrete policy. Labor mediators report a similar phenomenon: the contestants cannot agree on criteria for settling their disputes but can agree on specific proposals. Similarly, when one administrator's objective turns out to be another's means, they often can agree on policy.

Agreement on policy thus becomes the only practicable test of the policy's correctness. And for one administrator to seek to win the other over to agreement on ends as well would accomplish nothing and create quite unnecessary controversy.

If agreement directly on policy as a test for "best" policy seems a poor substitute for testing the policy against its objectives, it ought to be remembered that objectives themselves have no ultimate validity other than they are agreed upon. Hence agreement is the test of "best" policy in both methods. But where the root method requires agreement on what elements in the decision constitute objectives and on which of these objectives should be sought, the branch method falls back on agreement wherever it can be found.

In an important sense, therefore, it is not irrational for an administrator to defend a policy as good without being able to specify what it is good for.

NONCOMPREHENSIVE ANALYSIS (4b)

Ideally, rational comprehensive analysis leaves out nothing important. But it is impossible to take everything important into consideration unless "important" is so narrowly defined that analysis is in fact quite limited. Limits on human intellectual capacities and on available information set definite limits to man's capacity to be comprehensive. In actual fact, therefore, no one can practice the rational comprehensive method for really complex problems, and every administrator faced with a sufficiently complex problem must find ways drastically to simplify.

An administrator assisting in the formulation of agricultural economic policy cannot in the first place be competent on all possible policies. He cannot even comprehend one policy entirely. In planning a soil bank program, he cannot successfully anticipate the impact of higher or lower farm income on, say, urbanization—the possible consequent loosening of family ties, possible consequent eventual need for revisions in social security and further implications for tax problems arising out of new federal responsibilities for social security and municipal responsibilities for urban services. Nor, to follow another line of repercussions, can he work through the soil bank program's effects on prices for agricultural products in foreign markets and consequent implications for foreign relations, including those arising out of economic rivalry between the United States and the U.S.S.R.

In the method of successive limited comparisons, simplification is systematically achieved in two principal ways. First, it is achieved through limitation of policy comparisons to those policies that differ in relatively small degree from policies presently in effect. Such a limitation immediately reduces the number of alternatives to be investigated and also drastically simplifies the character of the investigation of each. For it is not necessary to undertake fundamental inquiry into an alternative and its consequences; it is necessary only to study those respects in which the proposed alternative and its consequences differ from the status quo. The empirical comparison of marginal differences among alternative policies that differ only marginally is, of course, a counterpart to the incremental or marginal comparison of values discussed above.[6]

Relevance as Well as Realism

It is a matter of common observation that in Western democracies public administrators and policy analysts in general do largely limit their analyses to incremental or marginal differences in policies that are chosen to differ only incrementally. They do not do so, however, solely because they desperately need some way to simplify their problems; they also do so in order to be relevant. Democracies change their policies almost entirely through incremental adjustments. Policy does not move in leaps and bounds.

The incremental character of political change in the United States has often been remarked. The two major political parties agree on fundamentals; they offer alternative policies to the voters only on relatively small points of difference. Both parties favor full employment, but they define it somewhat differently; both favor the development of water power resources, but in slightly different ways; and both favor unemployment compensation, but not the same level of benefits. Similarly, shifts of policy within a party take place largely through a series of relatively small changes, as can be seen in their only gradual acceptance of the idea of governmental responsibility for support of the unemployed, a change in party positions beginning in the early thirties and culminating in a sense in the Employment Act of 1946.

Party behavior is in turn rooted in public attitudes, and political theorists cannot conceive of democracy's surviving in the United States in the absence of fundamental agreement on potentially disruptive issues, with consequent limitation of policy debates to relatively small differences in policy.

Since the policies ignored by the administrator are politically impossible and so irrelevant, the simplification of analysis achieved by concentrating on policies that differ only incrementally is not a capricious kind of simplification. In addition, it can be argued that, given the limits on knowledge within which policy makers are confined, simplifying by limiting the focus to small variations from present policy makes the most of available knowledge. Because policies being considered are like present and past policies, the administrator can obtain information and claim some insight. Nonincremental policy proposals are therefore typically not only politically irrelevant but also unpredictable in their consequences.

The second method of simplification of analysis is the practice of ignoring important possible consequences of possible policies, as well as the values attached to the neglected consequences. If this appears to disclose a shocking shortcoming of successive limited comparisons, it can be replied that, even if the exclusions are random, policies may nevertheless be more intelligently formulated than through futile attempts to achieve a comprehensiveness beyond human capacity. Actually, however, the exclusions, seeming arbitrary or random from one point of view, need be neither.

Achieving a Degree of Comprehensiveness

Suppose that each value neglected by one policy making agency were a major concern of at least one other agency. In that case, a helpful division of labor would be achieved, and no agency need find its task beyond its capacities. The shortcomings of such a system would be that one agency might destroy a value either before another agency could be activated to safeguard it or in spite of another agency's efforts. But the possibility that important values may be lost is present in any form of organization, even where agencies attempt to comprehend in planning more than is humanly possible.

The virtue of such a hypothetical division of labor is that every important interest or value has its watchdog. And these watchdogs can protect the interests in their jurisdiction in two quite different ways: first, by redressing damages done by other agencies; and, second, by anticipating and heading off injury before it occurs.

In a society like that of the United States in which individuals are free to combine to pursue almost any possible common interest they might have and in which government agencies are sensitive to the pressures of these groups, the system described is approximated. Almost every interest has its watchdog. Without claiming that every interest has a sufficiently powerful watchdog, it can be argued that our system often can assure a more comprehensive regard for the values of the whole society than any attempt at intellectual comprehensiveness.

In the United States, for example, no part of government attempts a comprehensive overview of policy on income distribution. A policy nevertheless evolves, and one responding to a wide variety of interests. A process of mutual adjustment among farm groups, labor unions, municipalities and school boards, tax authorities, and government agencies with responsibilities in the fields of housing, health, highways, national parks, fire, and police accomplishes a distribution of income in which particular income problems neglected at one point in the decision processes become central at another point.

Mutual adjustment is more pervasive than the explicit forms it takes in negotiation between groups; it persists through the mutual impacts of groups upon each other even where they are not in communication. For all the imperfections and latent dangers in this ubiquitous process of mutual adjustment, it will often accomplish an adaptation of policies to a wider range of interests than could be done by one group centrally.

Note, too, how the incremental pattern of policy making fits with the multiple pressure pattern. For when decisions are only incremental—closely related to known policies, it is easier for one group to anticipate the kind of moves another might make and easier too for it to make correction for injury already accomplished.[7]

Even partisanship and narrowness, to use pejorative terms, will sometimes be assets to rational decision making, for they can doubly insure that what one agency neglects, another will not; they specialize personnel to distinct points of view. The claim is valid that effective rational coordination of the federal administration, if possible to achieve at all, would require an agreed set of values[8]—if "rational" is defined as the practice of the root method of decision making. But a high degree of administrative coordination occurs as each agency adjusts its policies to the concerns of the other agencies in the process of fragmented decision making I have just described.

For all the apparent shortcomings of the incremental approach to policy alternatives with its arbitrary exclusion coupled with fragmentation, when compared to the root method, the branch method often looks far superior. In the root method, the inevitable exclusion of factors is accidental, unsystematic, and not defensible by any argument so far developed, while in the branch method the exclusions are deliberate, systematic, and defensible. Ideally, of course, the root method does not exclude; in practice it must.

Nor does the branch method necessarily neglect long-run considerations and objectives. It is clear that important values must be omitted in considering policy, and sometimes the only way long-run objectives can be given adequate attention is through the neglect of short-run considerations. But the values omitted can be either long-run or short-run.

SUCCESSIONS OF COMPARISONS (5b)

The final distinctive element in the branch method is that the comparisons, together with the policy choice, proceed in a chronological series. Policy is not made once and for all; it is made and remade endlessly.

Policy making is a process of successive approximation of some desired objectives in which what is desired itself continues to change under reconsideration.

Making policy is at best a very rough process. Neither social scientists, nor politicians nor public administrators yet know enough about the social world to avoid repeated error in predicting the consequences of policy moves. A wise policy maker consequently expects that his policies will achieve only part of what he hopes and at the same time will produce unanticipated consequences he would have preferred to avoid. If he proceeds through a *succession* of incremental changes, he avoids serious lasting mistakes in several ways.

In the first place, past sequences of policy steps have given him knowledge about the probable consequences of further similar steps. Second, he need not attempt big jumps toward his goals that would require predictions beyond his or anyone else's knowledge, because he never expects his policy to be a final resolution of a problem. His decision is only one step, one that if successful can quickly be followed by another. Third, he is in effect able to test his previous predictions as he moves on to each further step. Lastly, he often can remedy a past error fairly quickly—more quickly than if policy proceeded through more distinct steps widely spaced in time.

Compare this comparative analysis of incremental changes with the aspiration to employ theory in the root method. Man cannot think without classifying, without subsuming one experience under a more general category of experiences. The attempt to push categorization as far as possible and to find general propositions which can be applied to specific situations is what I refer to with the word "theory." Where root analysis often leans heavily on theory in this sense, the branch method does not.

The assumption of root analysts is that theory is the most systematic and economical way to bring relevant knowledge to bear on a specific problem. Granting the assumption, an unhappy fact is that we do not have adequate theory to apply to problems in any policy area, although theory is more adequate in some areas—monetary policy, for example—than in others. Comparative analysis, as in the branch method, is sometimes a systematic alternative to theory.

Suppose an administrator must choose among a small group of policies that differ only incrementally from each other and from present policy. He might aspire to "understand" each of the alternatives—for example, to know all the consequences of each aspect of each policy. If so, he would indeed require theory. In fact, however, he would usually decide that, *for policy-making purposes,* he need know, as explained above, only the consequences of each of those aspects of the policies in which they differed from one another. For this much more modest aspiration, he requires no theory (although it might be helpful, if available), for he can proceed to isolate probable differences by examining the differences in consequences associated with past differences in policies, a feasible program because he can take his observations from a long sequence of incremental changes.

For example, without a more comprehensive social theory about juvenile delinquency than scholars have yet produced, one cannot possibly understand the ways in which a variety of public policies—say on education, housing, recreation, employment, race relations, and policing—might encourage or discourage delinquency. And one needs such an understanding if he undertakes the comprehensive overview of the problem prescribed in the models of the root method. If, however, one merely wants to mobilize knowledge sufficient to assist in a choice among a small group of similar policies—alternative policies on juvenile court procedures, for example—he can do so by comparative analysis of the results of similar past policy moves.

THEORISTS AND PRACTITIONERS

This difference explains—in some cases at least—why the administrator often feels that the outside expert or academic problem solver is sometimes not helpful and why they in turn often urge more theory on him. And it explains why an administrator often feels more confident when "flying by the seat of his pants" than when following the advice of theorists. Theorists often ask the administrator to go the long way round to the solution of his problems, in effect ask him to follow the best canons of the scientific method, when the administrator knows that the best available theory will work less well than more modest incremental comparisons. Theorists do not realize that the administrator is often in fact practicing a systematic method. It would be foolish to push this explanation too far, for sometimes practical decision makers are pursuing neither a theoretical approach nor successive comparisons, nor any other systematic method.

It may be worth emphasizing that theory is sometimes of extremely limited helpfulness in policy making for at least two rather different reasons. It is greedy for facts; it can be constructed only through a great collection of observations. And it is typically insufficiently precise for application to a policy process that moves through small changes. In contrast, the comparative method both economizes on the need for facts and directs the analyst's attention to just those facts that are relevant to the fine choices faced by the decision maker.

With respect to precision of theory, economic theory serves as an example. It predicts that an economy without money or prices would in certain specified ways misallocate resources, but this finding pertains to an alternative far removed from the kind of policies on which administrators need help. On the other hand, it is not precise enough to predict the consequences of policies restricting business mergers, and this is the kind of issue on which the administrators need help. Only in relatively restricted areas does economic theory achieve sufficient precision to go far in resolving policy questions; its helpfulness in policy making is always so limited that it requires supplementation through comparative analysis.

SUCCESSIVE COMPARISON AS A SYSTEM

Successive limited comparisons is, then, indeed a method or system; it is not a failure of method for which administrators ought to apologize. None the less, its imperfections, which have not been explored in this paper, are many. For example, the method is without a built-in safeguard for all relevant values, and it also may lead the decision maker to overlook excellent policies for no other reason than that they are not suggested by the chain of successive policy steps leading up to the present. Hence, it ought to be said that under this method, as well as under some of the most sophisticated variants of the root method—operations research, for example—policies will continue to be as foolish as they are wise.

Why then bother to describe the method in all the above detail? Because it is in fact a common method of policy formulation, and is, for complex problems, the principal reliance of administrators as well as of other policy analysts.[9] And because it will be superior to any other decision-making method available for complex problems in many circumstances, certainly superior to a futile attempt at superhuman comprehensiveness. The reaction of the public administrator to the exposition of method doubtless will be less a discovery of a new method than a better acquaintance with an old. But by becoming more conscious of their practice of this method, administrators might practice it with more skill and know when to extend or constrict its use. (That they sometimes practice it effectively and sometimes not may explain the extremes of opinion on "muddling through," which is both praised as a highly sophisticated form of problem solving and denounced as no method at all. For I suspect that insofar as there is a system in what is known as "muddling through," this method is it.)

One of the noteworthy incidental consequences of clarification of the method is the light it throws on the suspicion an administrator sometimes entertains that a consultant or adviser is not speaking relevantly and responsibly when in fact by all ordinary objective evidence he is. The trouble lies in the fact that most of us approach policy problems within a framework given by our view of a chain of successive policy choices made up to the present. One's thinking about appropriate policies with respect, say, to urban traffic control is greatly influenced by one's knowledge of the incremental steps taken up to the present. An administrator enjoys an intimate knowledge of his past sequences that "outsiders" do not share, and his thinking and that of the "outsider" will consequently be different in ways that may puzzle both. Both may appear to be talking intelligently, yet each may find the other unsatisfactory. The relevance of the policy chain of succession is even more clear when an American tries to discuss, say, antitrust policy with a Swiss, for the chains of policy in the two countries are strikingly different and the two individuals consequently have organized their knowledge in quite different ways.

If this phenomenon is a barrier to communication, an understanding of it promises an enrichment of intellectual interaction in policy formulation. Once the source of difference is understood, it will sometimes be stimulating for an administrator to seek out a policy analyst whose recent experience is with a policy chain different from his own.

This raises again a question only briefly discussed above on the merits of like-mindedness among government administrators. While much of organization theory argues the virtues of common values and agreed organizational objectives, for complex problems in which the root method is inapplicable, agencies will want among their own personnel two types of diversification: administrators whose thinking is organized by reference to policy chains other than those familiar to most members of the organization and, even more commonly, administrators whose professional or personal values or interests create diversity of view (perhaps coming from different specialties, social classes, geographical areas) so that, even within a single agency, decision making can be fragmented and parts of the agency can serve as watchdogs for other parts.

NOTES AND REFERENCES

1. James G. March and Herbert A. Simon similarly characterize the literature. They also take some important steps, as have Simon's recent articles, to describe a less heroic model of policy making. See *Organizations* (New York: John Wiley and Sons, 1938), p. 137.

2. "Operations Research and National Planning—A Dissent," *Operations Research*, 5 (October, 1957), p. 718. Hitch's dissent is from particular points made in the article to which his paper is a reply; his claim that operations research is for low level problems is widely accepted.

   For examples of the kind of problems to which operations research is applied, see C. W. Churchman, R. L. Ackoff, and E. L. Arnoff, *Introduction to Operations Research* (New York: John Wiley and Sons, 1957); and J. F. McCloskey and J. M. Coppinger, eds., *Operations Research for Management* (Baltimore: Johns Hopkins Press, 1956), Vol. 2.

3. I am assuming that administrators often make policy and advise in the making of policy and am treating decision making and policy making as synonymous for purposes of this paper.

4. Martin Meyerson and Edward C. Banfield, *Politics, Planning and the Public Interest* (Glencoe, Ill.: Free Press, 1955).

5. The line of argument is, of course, an extension of the theory of market choice, especially the theory of consumer choice, to public policy choices.

6. A more precise definition of incremental policies and a discussion of whether a change that appears "small" to one observer might be seen differently by another is to be found in my "Policy Analysis," *American Economic Review*, 48 (June, 1958), p. 298.

7. The link between the practice of the method of successive limited comparisons and mutual adjustment of interests in a highly fragmented decision-making process adds a new facet to pluralist theories of government and administration.

8. Herbert Simon, Donald W. Smithburg, and Victor A. Thompson, *Public Administration* (New York: Alfred A. Knopf, 1950), p. 434.

9. Elsewhere I have explored this same method of policy formulation as practiced by academic analysts of policy ("Policy Analysis," *American Economic Review*, 48). Although it has been here presented as a method for public administrators, it is no less necessary to analysts more removed from immediate policy questions, despite their tendencies to describe their own analytical efforts as though they were the rational comprehensive method with an especially heavy use of theory. Similarly, this same method is inevitably resorted to in personal problem solving, where means and ends are sometimes impossible to separate, where aspirations or objectives undergo constant development, and where drastic simplification of the complexity of the real world is urgent if problems are to be solved in the time that can be given to them. To an economist accustomed to dealing with the marginal or incremental concept in market processes, the central idea in the method is that both evaluation and empirical analysis are incremental. Accordingly I have referred to the method elsewhere as "the incremental method."

34

Assets and Liabilities in Group Problem Solving: The Need for an Integrative Function

Norman R. F. Maier

One of the long-standing debates in management has centered on the pros and cons of individual versus group decision making. Norman Maier examines this question in this article and in so doing considers three forces which operate in group decision situations: forces that are assets, forces that are liabilities, and forces that can be either, depending upon the skills of the members of the group.—Eds.

A number of investigations have raised the question of whether group problem solving is superior, inferior, or equal to individual problem solving. Evidence can be cited in support of each position so that the answer to this question remains ambiguous. Rather than pursue this generalized approach to the question, it seems more fruitful to explore the forces that influence problem solving under the two conditions (see reviews by Hoffman, 1965; Kelly & Thibaut, 1954). It is hoped that a better recognition of these forces will permit clarification of the varied dimensions of the problem-solving process, especially in groups.

The forces operating in such groups include some that are assets, some that are liabilities, and some that can be either assets or liabilities, depending upon the skills of the members, especially those of the discussion leader. Let us examine these three sets of forces.

SOURCE: Reprinted from *Psychological Review*, 1967, *74*, 239–49. Copyright 1967 by the American Psychological Association. Reprinted by permission.

GROUP ASSETS

Greater Sum Total of Knowledge and Information

There is more information in a group than in any of its members. Thus problems that require the utilization of knowledge should give groups an advantage over individuals. Even if one member of the group (e.g., the leader) knows much more than anyone else, the limited unique knowledge of lesser-informed individuals could serve to fill in some gaps in knowledge. For example, a skilled machinist might contribute to an engineer's problem solving and an ordinary workman might supply information on how a new machine might be received by workers.

Greater Number of Approaches to a Problem

It has been shown that individuals get into ruts in their thinking (Duneker, 1945; Maier, 1930; Wertheimer, 1959). Many obstacles stand in the way of achieving a goal, and a solution must circumvent these. The individual is handicapped in that he tends to persist in his approach and thus fails to find another approach that might solve the problem in a simpler manner. Individuals in a group have the same failing, but the approaches in which they are persisting may be different. For example, one researcher may try to prevent the spread of a disease by making man immune to the germ, another by finding and destroying the carrier of the germ, and still another by altering the environment so as to kill the germ before it reaches man. There is no way of determining which approach will best achieve the desired goal, but undue persistence in any one will stifle new discoveries. Since group members do not have identical approaches, each can contribute by knocking others out of ruts of thinking.

Participation in Problem Solving Increases Acceptance

Many problems require solutions that depend upon the support of others to be effective. Insofar as group problem solving permits participation and influence, it follows that more individuals accept solutions when a group solves the problem than when one person solves it. When one individual solves a problem he still has the task of persuading others. It follows, therefore, that when groups solve such problems, a greater number of persons accept and feel responsible for making the solution work. A low-quality solution that has good acceptance can be more effective than a higher-quality solution that lacks acceptance.

Better Comprehension of the Decision

Decisions made by an individual, which are to be carried out by others, must be communicated from the decision-maker to the decision-executors. Thus individual problem solving often requires an additional stage—that of relaying the decision reached. Failure in this communication process detracts from the merits of the decision and can even cause its failure or create a problem of greater magnitude than the initial problem that was solved. Many organizational problems can be traced to inadequate communication of decisions made by superiors and transmitted to subordinates, who have the task of implementing the decision.

The chances for communication failures are greatly reduced when the individuals who must work together in executing the decision have participated in making it. They not only understand the solution because they saw it develop, but they are also aware of the several other alternatives that were considered and the reasons why they were discarded. The common assumption that decisions supplied by superiors are arbitrarily reached therefore disappears. A full knowledge of goals, obstacles, alternatives, and factual information is essential to communication, and this communication is maximized when the total problem-solving process is shared.

GROUP LIABILITIES

Social Pressure

Social pressure is a major force making for conformity. The desire to be a good group member and to be accepted tends to silence disagreement and favors consensus. Majority opinions tend to be accepted regardless of whether or not their objective quality is logically and scientifically sound. Problems requiring solutions based upon facts, regardless of feelings and wishes, can suffer in group problem-solving situations.

It has been shown (Maier & Solem, 1952) that minority opinions in leaderless groups have little influence in the solution reached, even when these opinions are the correct ones. Reaching agreement in a group often is confused with finding the right answer, and it is for this reason that the dimensions of decision's acceptance and its objective quality must be distinguished (Maier, 1963).

Valence of Solutions

When leaderless groups (made up of three or four persons) engage in problem solving, they propose a variety of solutions. Each solution may receive both critical and supportive comments, as well as descriptive and explorative comments from other participants. If the number of negative and positive comments for each solution are algebraically summed, each may be given a *valence index* (Hoffman & Maier, 1964). The first solution that receives a positive valence value of .15 tends to be adopted to the satisfaction of all participants about 85 percent of the time, regardless of its quality. Higher quality solutions introduced after the critical value for one of the solutions has been reached have little chance of achieving real consideration. Once some degree of consensus is reached, the jelling process seems to proceed rather rapidly.

The critical valence value of .15 appears not to be greatly altered by the nature of the problem or the exact size of the group. Rather, it seems to designate a turning point between the idea-getting process and the decision-making process (idea evaluation). A solution's valence index is not a measure of the number of persons supporting the solution, since a vocal minority can build up a solution's valence by actively pushing it. In this sense, valence becomes an influence in addition to social pressure in determining an outcome.

Since a solution's valence is independent of its objective quality, this group factor becomes an important liability in group problem solving, even when the value of a decision depends upon objective criteria (facts and logic). It becomes a means whereby skilled manipulators can have more influence over the group process than their proportion of membership deserves.

Individual Domination

In most leaderless groups a dominant individual emerges and captures more than his share of influence on the outcome. He can achieve this end through a greater degree of participation (valence), persuasive ability, or stubborn persistence (fatiguing the opposition). None of these factors is related to problem-solving ability, so that the best problem solver in the group may not have the influence to upgrade the quality of the group's solution (which he would have had if left to solve the problem by himself).

Hoffman and Maier (1967) found that the mere fact of appointing a leader causes this person to dominate a discussion. Thus, regardless of his problem-solving ability a leader tends to exert a major influence on the outcome of a discussion.

Conflicting Secondary Goal: Winning the Argument

When groups are confronted with a problem, the initial goal is to obtain a solution. However, the appearance of several alternatives causes individuals to have preferences and once these emerge the desire to support a position is created. Converting those with neutral viewpoints and refuting those with opposed viewpoints now enter into the problem-solving process. More and more the goal becomes that of winning the decision rather than finding the best solution. This new goal is unrelated to the quality of the problem's solution and therefore can result in lowering the quality of the decision (Hoffman & Maier, 1967).

FACTORS THAT SERVE AS ASSETS OR LIABILITIES, DEPENDING LARGELY UPON THE SKILL OF THE DISCUSSION LEADER

Disagreement

The fact that discussion may lead to disagreement can serve either to create hard feelings among members or lead to a resolution of conflict and hence to an innovative solution (Hoffman, 1961; Hoffman, Harburg, & Maier, 1962; Hoffman & Maier, 1961; Maier, 1958, 1963; Maier & Hoffman, 1965). The first of these outcomes of disagreement is a liability, especially with regard to the acceptance of solutions; while the second is an asset, particularly where innovation is desired. A leader can treat disagreement as undesirable and thereby reduce the probability of both hard feelings and innovation, or he can maximize disagreement and risk hard feelings in his attempts to achieve innovation. The skill of a leader requires his ability to create a climate for disagreement which will permit innovation without risking hard feelings. The leader's perception of disagreement is one of the critical factors in this skill area (Maier & Hoffman, 1965). Others involve permissiveness (Maier, 1953), delaying the reaching of a solution (Maier & Hoffman, 1960b; Maier & Solem, 1962), techniques for processing information and opinions (Maier, 1963; Maier & Hoffman, 1960b; Maier & Maier, 1957), and techniques for separating idea-getting from idea-evaluation (Maier, 1960, 1963; Osborn, 1953).

Conflicting Interests versus Mutual Interests

Disagreement in discussion may take many forms. Often participants disagree with one another with regard to solutions, but when issues are explored one finds that these conflicting solutions are designed to solve different problems. Before one can rightly expect agreement on a solution, there should be agreement on the nature of the problem. Even before this, there should be agreement on the goal, as well as on the various obstacles that prevent the goal from being reached. Once distinctions are made between goals, obstacles, and solutions (which represent ways of overcoming obstacles), one finds increased opportunities for cooperative problem solving and less conflict (Hoffman & Maier, 1959; Maier, 1960, 1963; Maier & Solem, 1962; Solem, 1965).

Often there is also disagreement regarding whether the objective of a solution is to achieve quality or acceptance (Maier & Hoffman, 1964b), and frequently a stated problem reveals a complex of separate problems, each having separate solutions so that a search for a single solution is impossible (Maier, 1963). Communications often are inadequate because the discussion is not synchronized and each person is engaged in discussing a different aspect. Organizing discussion to synchronize the exploration of different aspects of the problem and to follow a systematic procedure increases solution quality (Maier & Hoffman, 1960a; Maier & Maier, 1957). The leadership function of influencing discussion procedure is quite distinct from the function of evaluating or contributing ideas (Maier, 1950, 1953).

When the discussion leader aids in the separation of the several aspects of the problem-solving process and delays the solution-mindedness of the group (Maier, 1958, 1963; Maier & Solem, 1962), both solution quality and acceptance improve; when he hinders or fails to facilitate the isolation of these varied processes, he risks a deterioration in the group process (Solem, 1965). His skill thus determines whether a discussion drifts toward conflicting interests or whether mutual interests are located. Cooperative problem solving can only occur after the mutual interests have been established and it is surprising how often they can be found when the discussion leader makes this his task (Maier, 1952, 1963; Maier & Hayes, 1962).

Risk Taking

Groups are more willing than individuals to reach decisions involving risks (Wallach & Kogan, 1965; Wallach, Kogan, & Bem, 1962). Taking risks is a factor in acceptance of change, but change may represent either a gain or a loss. The best guard against the latter outcome seems to be primarily a matter of a decision's quality. In a group situation this depends upon the leader's skill in utilizing the factors that represent group assets and avoiding those that make for liabilities.

Time Requirements

In general, more time is required for a group to reach a decision than for a single individual to reach one. Insofar as some problems require quick decisions, individual decisions are favored. In other situations acceptance and quality are requirements, but excessive time without sufficient returns also represents a loss. On the other hand, discussion can resolve conflicts, whereas reaching consensus has limited value (Wallach & Kogan, 1965). The practice of hastening a meeting can prevent full discussion, but failure to move a discussion forward can lead to boredom and fatigue-type solutions, in which members agree merely to get out of the meeting. The effective utilization of discussion time (a delicate balance between permissiveness and control on the part of the leader), therefore, is needed to make the time factor an asset rather than a liability. Unskilled leaders tend to be too concerned with reaching a solution and therefore terminate a discussion before the group potential is achieved (Maier & Hoffman, 1960b).

Who Changes

In reaching consensus or agreement, some members of a group must change. Persuasive forces do not operate in individual problem solving in the same way they operate in a group situation; hence, the changing of someone's mind is not an issue. In group situations, however, who changes can be an asset or a liability. If persons with the most constructive views are induced to change, the end-product suffers; whereas if persons with the least constructive point of view change, the end-product is upgraded. The leader can upgrade the quality of a decision because his position permits him to protect the person with a minority view and increase his opportunity to influence the majority position. This protection is a constructive factor because a minority viewpoint influences only when facts favor it (Maier, 1950, 1952; Maier & Solem, 1952).

The leader also plays a constructive role insofar as he can facilitate communications and thereby reduce misunderstandings (Maier, 1952; Solem, 1965). The leader has an adverse effect on the end-product when he suppresses minority views by holding a contrary position and when he uses his office to promote his own views (Maier & Hoffman, 1960b, 1962; Maier & Solem, 1952). In many problem-solving discussions the untrained leader plays a dominant role in influencing the outcome, and when he is more resistant to changing his views than are the other participants, the quality of the outcome tends to be lowered. This negative leader-influence was demonstrated by experiments in which untrained leaders were asked to obtain a second solution to a problem after they had obtained their first one (Maier & Hoffman, 1960a). It was found that the second solution tended to be superior to the first. Since the dominant individual had influenced the first solution, he had won his point and therefore ceased to dominate the subsequent discussion which led to the second solution. Acceptance of a solution also increases as the leader sees disagreement as idea-producing rather than as a source of difficulty or trouble (Maier & Hoffman, 1965). Leaders who see some of their participants as troublemakers obtain fewer innovative solutions and gain less acceptance of decisions made than leaders who see disagreeing members as persons with ideas.

THE LEADER'S ROLE FOR
INTEGRATED GROUPS

Two Differing Types of Group Process

In observing group problem solving under various conditions it is rather easy to distinguish between cooperative problem-solving activity and persuasion or selling approaches. Problem-solving activity includes searching, trying out ideas on one another, listening to understand rather than to refute, making relatively short speeches, and reacting to differences in opinion as stimulating. The general pattern is one of rather complete participation, involvement. Persuasion activity includes the selling of opinions already formed, defending a position held, either not listening at all or listening in order to be able to refute, talking dominated by a few members, unfavorable reactions to disagreement, and a lack of involvement of some members. During problem solving the behavior observed seems to be that of members interacting as segments of a group. The interaction pattern is not between certain individual members, but with the group as a whole. Sometimes it is difficult to determine who should be credited with an idea. "It just developed," is a response often used to describe the solution reached. In contrast, discussions involving selling or persuasive behavior seem to consist of a series of interpersonal interactions with each individual retaining his identity. Such groups do not function as integrated units but as separate individuals, each with an agenda. In one situation the solution is unknown and is sought; in the other, several solutions exist and conflict occurs because commitments have been made.

The Starfish Analogy

The analysis of these two group processes suggests an analogy with the behavior of the rays of a starfish under two conditions; one with the nerve ring intact, the other with the nerve ring sectioned (Hamilton, 1922; Moore, 1924; Moore & Doudoroff, 1939; Schneirla & Maier, 1940). In the intact condition, locomotion and righting behavior reveal that the behavior of each ray is not merely a function of local stimulation. Locomotion and righting behavior reveal a degree of coordination and interdependence that is centrally controlled. However, when the nerve ring is sectioned, the behavior of one ray still can influence others, but internal coordination is lacking. For example, if one ray is stimulated, it may step forward, thereby exerting pressure on the sides of the other four rays. In response to these external pressures (tactile stimulation), these rays show stepping responses on the stimulated side so that locomotion successfully occurs without the aid of neural coordination. Thus integrated behavior can occur on the basis of external control. If, however, stimulation is applied to opposite rays, the specimen may be "locked" for a time, and in some species the conflicting locomotions may divide the animal, thus destroying it (Crozier, 1920; Moore & Doudoroff, 1939).

Each of the rays of the starfish can show stepping responses even when sectioned and removed from the animal. Thus each may be regarded as an individual. In a starfish with a sectioned nerve ring the five rays become members of a group. They can successfully work together for locomotion purposes by being controlled by the dominant ray. Thus if uniformity of action is desired, the group of five rays can sometimes be more effective than the individual ray in moving the group toward a source of stimulation. However, if "locking" or the division of the organism occurs, the group action becomes less effective than individual action. External control, through the influence of a dominant ray, therefore can lead to adaptive behavior for the starfish as a whole, but it can also result in a conflict that destroys the organism. Something more than external influence is needed.

In the animal with an intact nerve ring, the function of the rays is coordinated by the nerve ring. With this type of internal organization the group is always superior to that of the individual actions. When the rays function as a part of an organized unit, rather than as a group that is physically together, they become a higher type of organization—a single intact organism. This is accomplished by the nerve ring, which in itself does not do the behaving. Rather, it receives and processes the data which the rays relay to it. Through this central organization, the responses of the rays become part of a larger pattern so that together they constitute a single coordinated total response rather than a group of individual responses.

The Leader as the Group's Central Nervous System

If we now examine what goes on in a discussion group we find that members can problem-solve as individuals, they can influence others by external pushes and pulls, or they can function as a group with varying degrees of unity. In order for the latter function to be maximized, however, something must be introduced to serve the function of nerve ring. In our conceptualization of group problem solving and group decision (Maier, 1963), we see this as the function of the leader. Thus the leader does not serve as a dominant ray and produce the solution. Rather, his function is to receive information, facilitate communications between the individuals, relay messages, and integrate the incoming responses so that a single unified response occurs.

Solutions that are the product of good group discussions often come as surprises to discussion leaders. One of these is unexpected generosity. If there is a weak member, this member is given less to do, in much the same way as an organism adapts to an injured limb and alters the function of other limbs to keep the locomotion on course. Experimental evidence supports the point that group decisions award special consideration to needy members of groups (Hoffman & Maier, 1959). Group decisions in industrial groups often give smaller assignments to the less gifted (Maier, 1952). A leader could not effectually impose such differential treatment on group members without being charged with discriminatory practices.

Another unique aspect of group discussion is the way fairness is resolved. In a simulated problem situation involving the problem of how to introduce a new truck into a group of drivers, the typical group solution involves a trading of trucks so that several or all members stand to profit. If the leader makes the decision the number of persons who profit is often confined to one (Maier & Hoffman, 1962; Maier & Zerfoss, 1952). In industrial practice, supervisors assign a new truck to an individual member of a crew after careful evaluation of needs. This practice results in dissatisfaction, with the charge of *unfair* being leveled at him. Despite those repeated attempts to do justice, supervisors in the telephone industry never hit upon the notion of a general reallocation of trucks, a solution that crews invariably reach when the decision is theirs to make.

In experiments involving the introduction of change, the use of group discussion tends to lead to decisions that resolve differences (Maier, 1952, 1953; Maier & Hoffman, 1961, 1964a, 1964b). Such decisions tend to be different from decisions reached by individuals because of the very fact that disagreement is common in group problem solving. The process of resolving difference in a constructive setting causes the exploration of additional areas and leads to solutions that are integrative rather than compromises.

Finally, group solutions tend to be tailored to fit the interests and personalities of the participants; thus group solutions to problems involving fairness, fears, face-saving, etc., tend to vary from one group to another. An outsider cannot process these variables because they are not subject to logical treatment.

If we think of the leader as serving a function in the group different from that of its membership, we might be able to create a group that can function as an intact organism. For a leader, such functions as rejecting or promoting ideas according to his personal needs are out of bounds. He must be receptive to information contributed, accept contributions without evaluating them (posting contributions on a chalk board to keep them alive), summarize information to facilitate integration, stimulate exploratory behavior, create awareness of problems of one member by others, and detect when the group is ready to resolve differences and agree to a unified solution.

Since higher organisms have more than a nerve ring and can store information, a leader might appropriately supply information, but according to our model of a leader's role, he must clearly distinguish between supplying information and promoting a solution. If his knowledge indicates the desirability of a particular solution, sharing this knowledge might lead the group to find this solution, but the solution should be the group's discovery. A leader's contributions do not receive the same treatment as those of a member of the group. Whether he likes it or not, his position is different. According to our conception of the leader's contribution to discussion, his role not only differs in influence, but gives him an entirely different function. He is to serve much as the nerve ring in the starfish and to further refine this function so as to make it a higher type of nerve ring.

This model of a leader's role in group process has served as a guide for many of our studies in group problem solving. It is not our claim that this will lead to the best possible group function under all conditions. In sharing it we hope to indicate the nature of our guidelines in exploring group leadership as a function quite different and apart from group membership. Thus the model serves as a stimulant for research problems and as a guide for our analyses of leadership skills and principles.

CONCLUSIONS

On the basis of our analysis, it follows that the comparison of the merits of group versus individual problem solving depends on the nature of the problem, the goal to be achieved (high quality solution, highly accepted solution, effective communication and understanding of the solution, innovation, a quickly reached solution, or satisfaction), and the skill of the discussion leader. If liabilities inherent in groups are avoided, assets capitalized upon, and conditions that can serve either favorable or unfavorable outcomes are effectively used, it follows that groups have a potential which in many instances can exceed that of a superior individual functioning alone, even with respect to creativity.

This goal was nicely stated by Thibaut and Kelley (1961) when they

> . . . wonder whether it may not be possible for a rather small, intimate group to establish a problem solving process that capitalizes upon the total pool of information and provides for great interstimulation of ideas without any loss of innovative creativity due to social restraints (p. 268).

In order to accomplish this high level of achievement, however, a leader is needed who plays a role quite different from that of the members. His role is analogous to that of the nerve ring in the starfish which permits the rays to execute a unified response. If the leader can contribute the integrative requirement, group problem solving may emerge as a unique type of group function. This type of approach to group processes places the leader in a particular role in which he must cease to contribute, avoid evaluation, and refrain from thinking about solutions or group *products.* Instead he must concentrate on the group *process,* listen in order to understand rather than to appraise or refute, assume responsibility for accurate communication between members, be sensitive to unexpressed feelings, protect minority points of view, keep the discussion moving, and develop skills in summarizing.

NOTES AND REFERENCES

1. Crozier, W. J. Notes on some problems of adaptation. *Biological Bulletin,* 1920, 39, 116–129.

2. Dunkeker, K. On problem solving. *Psychological Monographs,* 1945, 58 (5, Whole No. 270).

3. Hamilton, W. F. Coordination in the starfish. III. The righting reaction as a phase of locomotion (righting and locomotion). *Journal of Comparative Psychology,* 1922, 2, 81–94.

4. Hoffman, L. R. Conditions for creative problem solving. *Journal of Psychology*, 1961, 52, 429–444.

5. Hoffman, L. R. Group problem solving. In L. Berkowitz (ed.), *Advances in Experimental Social Psychology*, Vol. 2. New York: Academic Press, 1965, pp. 99–132.

6. Hoffman, L. R., Harburg, E., & Maier, N. R. F. Differences and disagreement as factors in creative group problem solving. *Journal of Abnormal and Social Psychology*, 1962, 64, 206–214.

7. Hoffman, L. R. & Maier, N. R. F. The use of group decision to resolve a problem of fairness. *Personnel Psychology*, 1959, 12, 545–559.

8. Hoffman, L. R., & Maier, N. R. F. Quality and acceptance of problem solutions by members of homogeneous and heterogeneous groups. *Journal of Abnormal and Social Psychology*, 1961, 62, 401–407.

9. Hoffman, L. R., & Maier, N. R. F. Valence in the adoption of solutions by problem-solving groups: I. Concept, method, and results. *Journal of Abnormal and Social Psychology*, 1964, 69, 264–271.

10. Hoffman, L. R., & Maier, N. R. F. Valence in the adoption of solutions by problem-solving groups: II. Quality and acceptance as goals of leaders and members. Unpublished manuscript, 1967 (Mimeo).

11. Kelley, H. H., & Thibaut, J. W. Experimental studies of group problem solving and process. In G. Lindzey (ed.), *Handbook of Social Psychology*, Cambridge, Mass.: Addison Wesley, 1954, pp. 735–785.

12. Maier, N. R. F. Reasoning in humans. I. On direction. *Journal of Comparative Psychology*, 1930, 10, 115–143.

13. Maier, N. R. F. The quality of group decisions as influenced by the discussion leader. *Human Relations*, 1950, 3, 155–174.

14. Maier, N. R. F. *Principles of Human Relations*. New York: Wiley, 1952.

15. Maier, N. R. F. An experimental test of the effect of training on discussion leadership. *Human Relations*, 1953, 6, 161–173.

16. Maier, N. R. F. *The Appraisal Interview*. New York: Wiley, 1958.

17. Maier, N. R. F. Screening solutions to upgrade quality: A new approach to problem solving under conditions of uncertainty. *Journal of Psychology*, 1960, 49, 217–231.

18. Maier, N. R. F. *Problem solving discussions and conferences: Leadership methods and skills*. New York: McGraw-Hill, 1963.

19. Maier, N. R. F., & Hayes, J. A. *Creative Management*, New York: Wiley, 1962.

20. Maier, N. R. F., & Hoffman, L. R. Using trained "developmental" discussion leaders to improve further the quality of group decisions. *Journal of Applied Psychology*, 1960, 44, 274–251. (a)

21. Maier, N. R. F., & Hoffmann, L. R. Quality of first and second solutions in group decisions. *Journal of Applied Psychology*, 1960, 44, 278–283. (b)

22. Maier, N. R. F., & Hoffman, L. R. Organization and creative problem solving. *Journal of Applied Psychology*, 1961, 45, 277–280.

23. Maier, N. R. F., & Hoffman, L. R. Group decision in England and the United States. *Personnel Psychology*, 1962, 15, 78–87.

24. Maier N. R. F., & Hoffman, L. R. Financial incentives and group decision in motivation change. *Journal of Social Psychology,* 1964, 64, 369–378. (a)

25. Maier, N. R. F., & Hoffman, L. R. Types of problems confronting managers. *Personnel Psychology,* 1964, 17, 261–269. (b)

26. Maier, N. R. F., & Hoffman, L. R. Acceptance and quality of solutions as related to leaders' attitudes toward disagreement in group problem solving. *Journal of Applied Behavioral Science,* 1965, 1, 273–386.

27. Maier, N. R. F., & Maier, R. A. An experimental test of the effects of "developmental" vs. "free" discussions on the quality of group decisions. *Journal of Applied Psychology,* 1957, 41, 320–323.

28. Maier, N. R. F., & Solem, A. R. The contribution of a discussion leader to the quality of group thinking: The effective use of minority opinions. *Human Relations,* 1952, 5, 277–288.

29. Maier, N. R. F., & Solem, A. R. Improving solutions by turning choice situations into problems. *Personnel Psychology,* 1962, 15, 151–157.

30. Maier, N. R. F., & Zerfoss, I. F. MRP: A technique for training large groups of supervisors and its potential use in social research. *Human Relations,* 1952, 5, 177–186.

31. Moore, A. R. The nervous mechanism of coordination in the crinoid Antedon rosaceus. *Journal of Genetic Psychology,* 1924, 6, 281–288.

32. Moore, A. R., & Doudoroff, M. Injury, recovery and function in an aganglionic central nervous system. *Journal of Comparative Psychology,* 1939, 28, 313–328.

33. Osborn, A. F. *Applied imagination.* New York: Scribner's, 1953.

34. Schneirla, T. C., & Maier, N. R. F. Concerning the status of the starfish. *Journal of Comparative Psychology,* 1940, 30, 103–110.

35. Solem, A. R. Almost anything I can do, we can do better. *Personnel Administration,* 1965, 28, 6–16.

36. Thibaut, J. W., & Kelley, H. H. *The social psychology of groups.* New York: Wiley, 1961.

37. Wallach, M. A., and Kogan, N. The roles of information, discussion and concensus in group risk taking. *Journal of Experimental and Social Psychology,* 1965, 1, 1–19.

38. Wallach, M. A., Kogan, N., & Bem, D. J. Group influence on individual risk taking. *Journal of Abnormal and Social Psychology,* 1962, 65, 75–86.

39. Wertheimer, M. *Productive thinking.* New York: Harper, 1959.